The Director's Toolkit

The Director's Toolkit is a comprehensive guide to the role of the theatrical director.

Following the chronology of the directing process, the book discusses each stage in precise detail, considering the selection and analysis of the script, the audition process, casting, character development, rehearsals, how to self-evaluate a production and everything in between.

Drawing on the author's own experience in multiple production roles, the book highlights the relationship between the director, stage manager, and designer, exploring how the director should be involved in all elements of the production process. Featuring a unique exploration of directing in special circumstances, the book includes chapters on directing nonrealistic plays, musicals, alternative theatre configurations, and directing in an educational environment.

The book includes detailed illustrations, step-by-step checklists, and opportunities for further exploration, offering a well-rounded foundation for aspiring directors.

Robin J. Schraft is a Professor of Theatre at Drury University. His commercial career includes work as a director, designer, and stage manager in New York, summer stock, national tours, and Branson, Missouri. He is a member of the Stage Directors and Choreographers Society (SDC) and the United States Institute for Theatre Technology (USITT), where he served for many years as the Vice-Commissioner for Computer Applications for the Lighting Commission of the Institute. He also served on the committee that wrote the current national recommended practices for stage lighting graphics.

D1597091

The Director's Toolkit

The Directing Process from Play
Selection to Production

Robin J. Schraft

Routledge
Taylor & Francis Group
NEW YORK AND LONDON

First edition published 2018
by Routledge
711 Third Avenue, New York, NY 10017

and by Routledge
2 Park Square, Milton Park, Abingdon, Oxon, OX14 4RN

Routledge is an imprint of the Taylor & Francis Group, an informa business

British Library Cataloguing-in-Publication Data
A catalogue record for this book is available from the British Library

Library of Congress Cataloging-in-Publication Data
A catalog record for this book has been requested

ISBN: 978-1-138-09522-9 (hbk)
ISBN: 978-1-138-09523-6 (pbk)
ISBN: 978-1-315-14617-1 (ebk)

Typeset in Times New Roman and Helvetica
by Keystroke, Neville Lodge, Tettenhall, Wolverhampton

Visit the companion website: www.routledge.com/cw/schraft

Printed in Canada

To my wife, Elizabeth Schraft, my partner in life and theatre for almost my entire career and without whom neither my career nor this book would have been possible.

Contents

Illustrations

Preface

Numerous texts on directing exist, each with its own strengths and weaknesses, so why another one? Over the years I have been unable to find a text for my directing classes that follows my comprehensive agenda. What I was looking for was a book that addressed the full range of the director's functions, including working with the production staff, the rehearsal process, and the actors in the order of the production process. This book's content is based on my more than 40 years of experience as a director and designer in both commercial and academic theatre. It reflects my philosophy that a director should be conversant with all aspects of theatre and the director must be able to synthesize the work of all members of the production into the final product. To do so, the director must have an empathic understanding of each discipline.

The organization of this book follows the production process from the beginning of the director's involvement to opening night. Following the production process as an organizing element for teaching directing provides a strong organizational flow, although I do acknowledge that the needs for the course often conflict with this order. For example, typically I have my students direct several scenes prior to a final one-act play. Since these scenes do not necessarily involve the use of a production staff, I often delay the discussion of collaboration and working with designers until later in the course. To avoid inserting these topics into seemingly arbitrary locations, I maintain the organization based on the order in which the director experiences each situation. The book is organized so that chapters can be used out of sequence. In the same manner, the book may be used as a reference and, as such, not read in any specific order. Toward this end, each chapter is as self-sufficient as possible. Checklists are provided at the end of chapters where applicable.

This book is intended for students of directing as well as individuals who wish to develop skills in the subject matter. No particular expertise or prior experience with directing is necessary; however, I do assume a basic knowledge of theatre including acting, design, and play production. Over the years I have talked to my students about various texts. A common complaint is the text went into too much detail in areas the students felt were covered in other courses or by previous experience. As each reader will have a different set of strengths in theatre, all areas are covered to ensure a fundamental understanding. The book is written with the assumption that beginning directors will work on a proscenium stage. The concepts of staging are similar in all configurations but are easier to explain and understand in proscenium. These concepts can then be applied to any other configuration.

Additional topics included in this text are chapters on directing musicals, directing in nonproscenium spaces such as arena or thrust, directing nonrealistic styles, and directing in educational settings as a significant number of beginning directors will go on to work in these areas. Directing musical theatre requires extensive collaboration with music and dance professionals and adds the impact that the music itself provides to the understanding of the scenes. Directing in nonproscenium spaces requires unique approaches to stage pictures and blocking; the innate intimacy of such spaces adds complexity to the development of the characters. Directing decidedly nonrealistic styles add new demands on the director. A number of students studying directing each year have a career path that will lead toward educational theatre. While directing in this setting is essentially the same, there are considerable differences and special considerations that need to be made for those working in a school setting.

I find the process of taking a script, carefully analyzing it, developing a production concept, and working with my design team and my actors to bring this script to life, exhilarating. For me, the joy of sitting in the back of the house watching the audience experiencing my production and seeing their reactions is not found in any other aspect of theatre. Directors are by nature a strange lot. While they appear to control the production, in reality they are guiding all of the other artists toward a final product. Once the product is reached they simply fade away. Their work is only experienced by the audience through the work of others. The delicate balance between the artistic vision of the director and the implementation of this vision through the creative work of the collaborators is the essential joy of directing. Each time I return to the stage as a performer, while I am happy to be there, I find myself longing to be in the house experiencing the process from the perspective of the audience. I find no greater joy than in seeing the production concept conceived at the beginning of the process become a reality in performance. I hope you as a director can find such joy.

I wish to thank all of the individuals with whom I have worked as a director and especially my directing students for their assistance in the creation of this book. Everything you will find here is based on my experience as a director and educator and as such is a direct product of the interaction I had with those individuals. Happy directing.

Acknowledgments

I wish to thank the following people for their assistance in the creation of this book:

- All my directing students and actors in my past productions for their insights in helping me become the director and educator I am today.
- Kaley Etzkorn for the rehearsal photographs.
- Christopher DePriest, Doug Mackenzie, Chuck Rogers, and Madison Spencer for their design work.
- The following students for posing for the illustrations:

  - Joshua S. Anderson
  - Anna Mei Bromley
  - Mitch Barrett
  - Aaron Campbell
  - Sally Farrand
  - Becca Haegele
  - Payton Jackson
  - Lucas Nelson
  - Molly Powell
  - Kelsey Pressnall
  - Rachel Reese
  - William Schneider
  - Laura Spraggins
  - Micah Textor
  - Spencer Thompson
  - Deborah Tragasz
  - Teddy Trice
  - Jacob Valle
  - Meghan Wilcox
  - Kylie Wurgler

- Katherine Gibson, Greg Holtschneider, Jo Beth Nicklas, and Gretchen Teague for their contributions to the chapter on directing in an educational setting.
- Michael Engelmeyer – Great Outdoors Studios.
- Jacqueline Tygart for her assistance in finding artwork.
- A very special thank-you to my wife, Elizabeth Schraft, for her editorial work in helping to shape this book.

Introduction: What Is a Director?

BACKGROUND

In today's theatre, the role of the director is complex. It starts with the conceptualization of the playwright's script, followed by the development of production concept and style, working with the designers, the choosing and rehearsing of the actors, and finally the bringing of the script to life for an audience.

The director in theatre has a unique role. On one level the director is felt and seen everywhere in a production, but at the same time the director's work is ephemeral, not readily visible to the audience, which is contrary to the work of the playwright, the actors on the stage, and the designers. In modern theatre, the director oversees the production from conceptualization to realization, yet once the play opens the director is simply a member of the audience. This enigma defines the modern director.

While it is difficult to imagine a theatrical production without a director, the role of the director as currently understood is a relatively new idea in theatre. Traditionally, the director was merely an organizer. In classical Greek theatre the playwrights organized the production of their own plays, a concept that would continue for many centuries. During the Middle Ages, towns often hired managers or pageant masters to organize the town's cycle plays. Little is known of the manager's scope of authority or influence on the production, but, based on what we know of the period, one can assume the actors and craftsmen had great autonomy. Figure I.1, circa 1460, is a drawing of a performance of *The Martyrdom of St. Apollonia* with a man holding a large book and pointer in the upper right of center.

It is likely that he is one of these managers/pageant masters, orchestrating the process. The pageant master was often onstage during performances guiding the actors and providing them with their lines.

Figure I.1 *The Martyrdom of St. Apollonia* by Jean Fouquet

During the Renaissance, actors were hired by theatre managers. The actors' interpretations of their roles were essentially their own. While the playwright might attempt to guide or influence them, the actors were free to perform as they chose. A famous passage from *Hamlet*, in which Hamlet gives his advice to the players who will perform a play for King Claudius, is often viewed as Shakespeare's opportunity to vent his frustration with the actors who performed in his plays:

> *Speak the speech, I pray you, as I pronounced it to you, trippingly on the tongue: but if you mouth it, as many of your players do, I had as lief the town-crier spoke my lines. Nor do not saw the air too much with your hand, thus; but use all gently: for in the very torrent, tempest, and, as I may say, the whirlwind of passion, you must acquire and beget a temperance that may give it smoothness. O, it offends me to the soul, to hear a robustious periwig-pated fellow tear a passion to tatters, to very rags, to split the ears of the groundlings, who, for the most part, are capable of nothing but inexplicable dumb shows and noise: I could have such a fellow whipped for o'erdoing Termagant; it out-herods Herod: pray you, avoid it.*
>
> *Be not too tame neither, but let your own discretion be your tutor: suit the action to the word, the word to the action; with this special observance, that you o'erstep not the modesty of nature: for anything so overdone is from the purpose of playing, whose end, both at the first and now, was and is, to hold, as 'twere, the mirror up to nature; to show virtue her own feature, scorn her own image, and the very age and body of the time his form and pressure. Now, this overdone, or come tardy off, though it make the unskilful laugh, cannot but make the judicious grieve; the censure of the which one must, in your allowance, o'erweigh a whole theatre of others. O, there be players that I have seen play, and heard others praise, and that highly, not to speak it profanely, that, neither having the accent of Christians, nor the gait of Christian, pagan, nor man,*

have so strutted and bellowed that I have thought some of nature's journeymen had made men, and not made them well, they imitated humanity so abominably.

O, reform it altogether. And let those that play your clowns speak no more than is set down for them: for there be of them that will themselves laugh, to set on some quantity of barren spectators to laugh too; though in the meantime, some necessary question of the play be then to be considered: that's villainous, and shows a most pitiful ambition in the fool that uses it. Go, make you ready.[1]

In this speech Hamlet urges the players to speak clearly, control their emotions, not to make wild hand gestures, and especially not to overact. Elizabethan actors generally saw their lines as opportunities to seize the stage ("tear a passion to tatters") rather than as a means to bring subtle dialogue to life ("to hold . . . the mirror up to nature"). As popular as he was as a playwright, even Shakespeare could not contain his actors.

By the eighteenth century, acting companies typically were run by the actor-managers who were also the star performers. The audiences came to see them rather than the play. Productions were designed to feature and spotlight their performances rather than bring the words of the playwright to life. Georg II, Duke of Saxe-Meiningen, who in the 1830s established an acting ensemble dedicated to creating a more natural, by their standards, world of theatre, is generally viewed as the first "modern" director. Georg worked closely with every member of his ensemble to develop unique characters with significant depth in the overall portrayal. He designed elaborate scenery and wanted the performances to be as lifelike as possible.

A different approach to acting and theatre evolved at the end of the nineteenth century with the advent of realism and the works of playwrights such as Henrik Ibsen, August Strindberg, and Anton Chekhov. Key to this evolution was the work of the great Russian actor and director, Constantin Stanislavski. A cofounder of the Moscow Art Theatre, Stanislavski revolutionized

Figure I.2 Georg II, Duke of Saxe-Meiningen

Figure I.3 Constantin Stanislavski

actor preparation and the creation of the character by the actor. His work as an acting teacher and stage director changed the conception of the development of a play and how actors build their characters, leading to a new role for the director. From this point on, the role of the director became recognizable as we know it and has remained instrumental to the development of the play.

THE DIRECTOR IN THE PRODUCTION PROCESS

The table of organization for a theatre production today often looks something like that shown in Figure I.4.

The production is headed by the producer or artistic director who obtains the script and finds or arranges for the funding and physical needs of the production such as the theatre and rehearsal facility. Their most important selection is that of director. While it is generally held that the director is responsible for the artistic direction of the production, producers disagree on their own involvement in the artistic decisions of the production. Some producers feel the producer is first and foremost the overseer of the business aspects of the production and essentially leave all artistic decisions to the director. Other producers see themselves as intrinsically involved in the artistic development of the production, in some instances with their own artistic vision. In this case, they work closely with the director in making all key production decisions. Most producer–director relationships fall somewhere between these two extremes. Regardless of whether the producer is hands-on or laissez-faire, the producer remains the final authority on all production decisions since the producer ultimately controls the budget and hence the hiring and firing of all staff.

Depending on the nature of the producing organization and the producer, the director is either hired to direct a show and then must choose the script or the director is hired to specifically direct a prechosen script. The director may be responsible for or have some say in the hiring of the cast, the designers, and production staff or they may be selected by the producer. In either case, the artistic work of all other members of the production falls under the director. The director's key associates will be the design staff and the cast. The individuals below each designer on the chart in Figure I.4 answer directly to the designer. The purpose of the chart is to illustrate the basic organization of the production. In this model questions move in an upward direction, ultimately to the director, while solutions move in a downward direction.

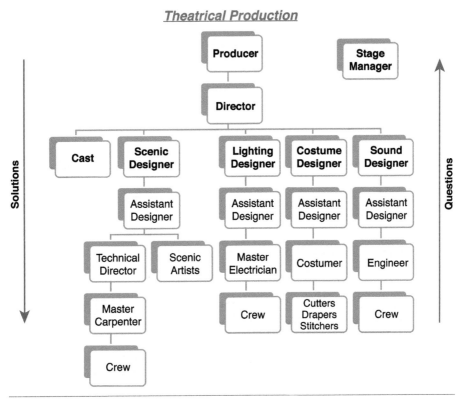

Figure I.4 Table of Theatrical Organization

The stage manager is in a box not directly in line with anyone else on the chart as the function of the stage manager changes with the progression of the production. The relationship between the director and stage manager is extremely important in any production. This relationship will be discussed in more detail in Chapter 6.

The playwright is not on this chart either as the playwright may or may not be directly involved in the production process. Except for specific rights retained in the contract with the producing organization, the playwright does not have any direct authority or influence in the production other than script changes. While the original production of a play almost always involves the playwright's presence, most revivals are done without the direct connection of the playwright to the production. These obligations and possibilities will be discussed in Chapter 1.

THE FUNCTION OF THE DIRECTOR

The director is the eyes of the audience, because without an audience theatre cannot exist. During one of my college productions the run was hit with a major snowstorm, many cast members were shuttled to the theatre on snowmobiles, and there was a real possibility that no one else would make it to the show. This prompted a philosophical discussion on what to call a performance without an audience. The best answer was hesitantly suggested: "A rehearsal?" Fortunately, an audience, albeit small, did arrive. Since the purpose of the production is to present the playwright's script to an audience, it is the prime duty of the director to represent the playwright during the rehearsal process and at the same time see the play from the audience's perspective both artistically and physically. If the meaning and intent of the production is not clear, or if the audience is not able to perceive the necessary emotions, the play will fail. The orchestration of the changes in the emotions of the audience must be carefully and consistently planned, and the director must be able to sense if the play is working for a future audience who will not have the benefit of knowing all the back stories of the script and production. The director must be able to view the work as if it is for the first time. All decisions by the director must stem from an understanding of the intended impact on the audience. As such, an understanding of the future audience is crucial.

The director's functions can best be divided into two aspects: the artistic and the managerial. The artistic functions include all interpretive aspects of bringing the script to life. This starts with determining the playwright's intent, guiding the work of the designers to create the physical world of the play from concept to reality, casting the actors, and rehearsing the actors and guiding them to the fullest creation of their characters. The director is also responsible for combining the actors' work with the designers' to produce the final product. The last step is polishing the production to present it to the audience.

The managerial functions include scheduling and time management, budget allocation decisions, and personnel management both in the initial choice of each person and later in maximizing their contribution to the production. It is in regard to these managerial functions that a stage manager becomes especially helpful in freeing the director to focus on the artistic concerns.

APPROACHES

Directors differ significantly in their approach to the art and craft of directing. The range can be defined by two polar opposite approaches. On one extreme is the laissez-faire or hands-off director. This type of director essentially sits back and allows each theatre artist total freedom while providing a loose general framework around which the production is built; the specific choices typically are left to the designers and actors with the director providing minimal correction or additional guidance. The other extreme is the director whose vision for the play is directly implemented by the designers and the actors. In this case, the creativity of the designers and actors lies in fulfilling the desires and vision of the director. This latter approach can be seen in the work of director Robert Wilson. His productions are the product of the other artists painstakingly bringing his vision to life.

There is a delicate balance between the director's conceptualization of the play and the artistic contributions of the designers and actors. The director who tightly conceives the show and expects the others to follow his or her vision ensures that the production will have complete unity and the concept will have integrity. However, this type of director may be sacrificing the creative input of others on the team, input that could improve the production. The hands-off director ensures the total artistic freedom of the designers and actors but allows for the possibility of weak integration and unity within the production. Since the designers and actors are minimally challenged by this type of director, it is possible their work will not reach full potential. Most stage directors fall somewhere between these two extremes.

The subtle balance between the vision of the director and the vision of the designers and actors is what separates directors. As directors develop as artists, they find the balance that works best for them and allows them to create theatre as they see it. In defining their approach, directors provide a set of parameters within which the play will exist, a general direction for the play, an interpretation of the playwright's work, and a production process that allows each of the designers and actors to create the world of the play and the characters based on their own interpretations. It is important that each new director takes the process of discovery seriously, for in it lies the true beauty of the collaborative nature of theatre.

DIRECTOR VS. ACTING COACH

Young theatre artists often have a skewed vision of the role of the director since it is initially based on their experience with the directors with whom they have worked. In their early experiences as an actor, designer, or technician, these young artists typically are led by a theatre educator who is on the one hand providing an artistic vision for the show and on the other hand teaching the students their craft. As students progress along their educational path, usually they begin to work with directors who provide them with increasing amounts of freedom based on the development and expansion of their skills. In contrast, the professional director is working with highly experienced and trained actors who thoroughly know their craft. In this situation, the actors do not need advice on their technique but rather guidance in the creation of the characters to fulfill the interpretation of the play. In a purely technical sense, the responsibilities of the professional director do not include developing the actors. However, almost all forms of theatre short of commercial theatre, particularly educational theatre, rely on the use of actors in various stages of development in their craft. As such, the director becomes a de facto acting coach, helping the actor to develop his or her technique while realizing the director's vision.

It is important to acknowledge these two functions and the innate relationship between them to understand the role of the director. Depending on the situation it may be essential for the director to assist in the development of the artists to achieve his vision. At the same time, it is important that the director not fall into the trap of assuming that these artists do not know their craft, as this will limit the contribution of these individuals and may stifle their creativity. While it is often necessary for the beginning director to serve as an acting coach, this is truly a separate function and not necessarily a part of their future role as a director.

QUALITIES OF A GOOD DIRECTOR

Each director has a unique set of skills and with that a different set of attributes. Successful directors will generally have a combination of the following attributes:

- **A good director has the ability to analyze.**

   The director must be able to analyze the script in order to understand the playwright's intent. It is this analysis that will guide the production and create the director's vision for the play. The analysis becomes the cornerstone of the play.

- **A good director has vision.**

   A good director must be able to visualize the play solely from the script. He or she must be able to envision the world of the play by simply reading, thereby creating a concept that will allow the designers to create the environment and the actors to populate it. It is this vision that establishes the making of the script into the play. It is this ability that will separate average directors from great directors.

- **A good director is a communicator.**

   Once the director develops his or her concept for the play, the director must be able to communicate this to the remainder of the production company. The idea is only as good as the ability of others to understand it, process it, and carry it out. If the director lacks the ability to communicate clearly and concisely, confusion and wasted time will limit the ability of the company to bring this vision to reality. Good communication becomes the foundation for creating a world for the play that exceeds the director's initial concept. This inspires the best from all involved, and provides them with a concrete direction to follow.

- **A good director is a positive leader.**

   While leadership is absolutely essential for the director, it is not enough simply to be a leader. The director must be a positive leader and role model for the production company. It is impossible for the company to be upbeat if the director is not. On the other hand, the director's enthusiasm will be infectious within the company and will increase the creativity of everyone else. The director's leadership sets the tone for the production environment.

- **A good director is a collaborator.**

   Collaboration is the heart of theatre. It is not simply a goal or tool, but rather the essence of theatre. Collaboration begins with the director. The collaborative tone the director sets at the beginning of the process creates the atmosphere within which everyone else works. While a highly collaborative director will not ensure a fully collaborative experience in the production process, a good collaborative process cannot exist without the director setting the tone.

- **A good director has people skills.**

   Directing is about working with people. A good director interacts positively. The director must relate on a personal level with each individual within the production and genuinely care about that individual's contribution. A director with good people skills finds it much easier to guide and work with these individuals throughout the process and fosters even greater creativity.

- **A good director is open to new ideas.**

A director must have a concise concept and vision for the production. However, to ensure good collaboration, the director must be willing to listen to other ideas and then genuinely consider them. Being open to the ideas of others does not necessarily mean acceptance, but it recognizes the possibility that another idea is superior. A director who is not open to ideas quickly discourages others from making contributions to the production. This limits the scope of the production to the director's initial ideas alone.

- **A good director is a good listener.**

In working with designers and actors the director must listen to their ideas and questions. At times, the solution to a situation may simply be giving them the sense they are heard. Good listeners not only hear what is being said but also process and incorporate it into their thought patterns, reflecting before making a response.

- **A good director is organized.**

To efficiently guide a production, the director must be organized. If the director does not possess this skill personally, it must come from somewhere else, usually the stage manager. While a highly organized stage manager is a major asset to any production, a good director should not have to rely on the organization of the stage manager but rather come to the process prepared.

- **A good director has good time management skills.**

To fulfill the vision the director conceives at the beginning of the production, effective time management with the production staff and cast is a necessity. If this is not done, the director may need to settle for less than was originally envisioned. Good time management involves making the best use of the overall time as well as advantageous use of every working moment within the process. In doing so, the director encourages others to be efficient with their use of the allotted time.

- **A good director is confident but flexible.**

Good directors must be confident in their vision, abilities, and decisions. They must believe in their concept, be able to passionately present their ideas and vision of the play, and have the conviction to see them through. Directors who lack confidence can easily be swayed away from their concept. At the same time, directors must be willing to modify or adapt ideas based on the input of others if these ideas prove to be a better path to follow. The balance between confidence and flexibility is a difficult balancing act for any director, but it is one all directors must be able to find.

- **A good director is enjoyable to work with.**

A good director is one with whom others want to work. A work environment that encourages the creativity of others and challenges them to produce their best work is key to a successful production. The tone of the production and rehearsal process is established by the director. If the company enjoys working within this environment and looks forward to the continuing process, it can only lead to a better production.

THE PRODUCTION PROCESS

Years ago, while conducting a survey on a topic related to the production process, my mentor advised me to ask respondents to "Describe the production process you follow." I felt this was a waste of time since I assumed all theatre professionals followed essentially the same process. Most respondents agreed with my initial assumption and chastised me for raising the question; in their opinion this was an unnecessary basic question. They sarcastically referred to textbooks and suggested I read the chapter on the production process. However, those who did describe their production process surprised me. Not one of them followed the same process. While it was safe to say the vast majority of theatre professionals followed the same basic production process, it was a mistake to assume that they all followed identical processes.

With this concept in mind, I find it more useful to think of the production process in terms of phases rather than steps. This allows the individual artist to determine the precise steps to follow to accomplish the goals of the particular phase. There are five phases to the production process:

1) ANALYTICAL PHASE

The first step for the director is to analyze the script. In this phase the director determines the needs of the play and raises questions about how the play should be produced. It is vital that the director keeps an open mind to the nature of the script and the particular challenges it presents. The mistake many beginning directors make is to try to reach quick solutions to the challenges presented by the script. The nature of theatre as typified in the United States is to find solutions as quickly as possible. It is valuable to remember that when Stanislavski approached a play it was often rehearsed and worked on for many months to allow significant time for the play to develop. Only when the play reached a stage where it was worthy of an audience did he actually go into the final rehearsal process. Time needs to be allowed to fully analyze and prepare for the production. If time is taken during the analytical phase to thoroughly question the script to determine its needs and to fully flesh out an initial understanding, allowing questions to develop and needs to be addressed, the director will be in a far better position to enter the second phase.

The analytical phase begins with numerous readings of the script. Many beginning directors ask "How many times does this mean I need to read the script?" Unfortunately, there is no simple answer to this question. An old guideline stated the director needed to read the script at least three times. The first reading was for pure enjoyment of the script, allowing the director to feel the impact of the words of the playwright while visualizing the play onstage. The second reading was for the director to start writing questions, annotating the script, and searching for the needs of the play. All subsequent readings of the script continued the process of the second reading. A good rule of thumb to determine when a script is sufficiently read is when no new questions are raised or new needs found. At this point it may be safe to move to the next phase.

Early in my career I directed a production of *Death of a Salesman*, a play I felt I knew well. After almost completing the rehearsal process I had an epiphany concerning the scene where Howard, obsessed with his new toy, the wire recorder, demonstrates it to Willy, explaining that one of its wonders is the ability to have the maid record a radio show when you are not at home.

Willy comments that he has often wondered what he is missing on the radio. Howard asks if he doesn't have a radio in his car. Embarrassed, Willy quickly answers, "Well, yeah, but whoever thinks of turning it on?" Originally, I thought Willy was not thinking through the question. I now realized that in the period in which the play is set only the wealthy had car radios. The issue was Howard's assumption of wealth versus Willy not wanting to acknowledge his lack of it. The lesson I learned was that no matter how well we think we know a script, we still need to delve deeper into it to ensure all the appropriate questions are asked.

2) RESEARCH PHASE

Once the needs and questions raised by the script are determined, it is time to enter the second phase, researching answers to these questions. An important aspect of this phase is to seek multiple solutions or answers rather than rushing to find the final solution. This allows the director to explore many possibilities while searching for the best solution to the needs and questions raised by the script. The research process will be explored in detail in Chapter 3.

3) CONCEPT PHASE

Having completed the research into the needs of the script, it is now time for the director to choose the approach and answers to begin the production process. It is important to recognize that these are not necessarily the answers or choices ultimately seen in the final production, but rather the choices that provide a place to start. The final choices are the ones onstage when the production closes. Ultimately, it is these choices that will lead the director in the development of the concept for the play. This concept will become the guiding principle around which all other production questions will be answered. It will give the play its initial direction and set the parameters within which the play will exist.

4) PRODUCTION PHASE

Having the concept firmly in mind the director can now proceed with the production phase. This phase includes the remainder of the production and rehearsal process beginning with preproduction with the designers, moving through the casting and rehearsal process to opening night. This entire phase is guided by the work during the first three phases. While new directors are often anxious to get to this phase of the process, it is vital to recognize the importance of the first three phases in order to establish a solid foundation. The quality of the production and rehearsal process, and ultimately the quality of the performances, is predicated on the caliber of the analysis, research, and conceptualization the director undertook prior to working with the remainder of the production team. Research does not necessarily end once rehearsals begin. Directors often need to go back to phases one and two to address issues not thought of in preproduction or raised during the production process.

5) EVALUATION PHASE

Once the play opens, the work of the director is essentially complete. At this point it is important for the director to take the opportunity to evaluate the work. Student directors often long for the moment they are no longer critiqued by their faculty. However, the work of directors is always critiqued, be it by the audience, critics, or their peers. To grow as a director, it is important to develop the ability, as objectively as possible, to critique. The director can then look back at the process to determine if situations were handled in the best way possible and evaluate the quality of the choices made during the process. The point is to learn in order to make better choices in the future. While the director should certainly celebrate the product, glossing over areas not handled well is foolish. Growth as a director is dependent on this skill. This process will be further explored in Chapter 18.

A FINAL THOUGHT

All directors must define their own overall style, adapting it to accommodate the specific needs of a production. It is this style or approach that separates one director from another. Many successful directors have directorial styles that others call poor; nonetheless, they produce excellent theatre and have successful careers. While their styles may not work for others, it works for them. Beginning directors must resist the urge to try to quickly define their "style." Allow time for it to develop. Experiment with different approaches. Try different techniques. Find what works in a given circumstance. I find it humorous when discussing a specific technique that does not appear to work with a beginning director and the director responds, "That is my style." The beginning director has not directed long enough to have such a style. This is a case of rationalizing behavior by calling it a "style." Give yourself time. Do not close the door to techniques or approaches but rather embrace all of them as you learn what works best for you. Remember, what works in one case may not work in another. Be open.

FURTHER EXPLORATION

1. Consider directors with whom you have worked in the past. Using the criteria in this chapter, evaluate them as directors. Would you add any additional criteria in the evaluation process?

2. Develop a checklist you can use to evaluate yourself during the directing process.

3. Considering directors with whom you have worked in the past, develop a list of items you learned from working with them. What worked for them? What didn't? What did they do that you would never do?

NOTE

1   *Hamlet*, act 3, scene 2.

PART I

The Script

Script Selection

SCRIPT SELECTION PROCESS

Working with the right script is crucial for a successful directorial experience. There are times when the director is hired or selected to direct an already chosen script. In these cases, the director can simply proceed to the script analysis. The process becomes more complicated when the director must first choose the script. Finding the ideal script places great pressure on the director, who must consider a number of criteria. Among others, the director must determine whether the script fits the mechanical needs of the intended production. These mechanical needs may include style, length, size of cast, physical needs for the setting, costume, lights, sound effects, and the nature of the performance space. In addition, the director must think about the intended audience and his own connection to the script and the message he or she wishes to communicate with the audience.

There are situations where the play chosen must fit certain stylistic criteria. Stylistic considerations can range from whether the play should be a comedy or drama, to whether it needs to be realistic, needs to be a musical, or some other stylistic concern. These choices may become more specific based on the circumstances of the intended production. Specific stylistic considerations should be identified before the search for the play begins. If the choice of style is not an issue, it can be ignored as one of the initial search criteria.

The length of the play can be an important criterion. For a given production there may be a maximum or minimum running time. The director can save time by eliminating scripts that do not fall within those parameters. The projected length of the play can be determined in many ways. One way is to count the pages and allow one minute per page for the running time. However, this method fails to consider a number of factors: how many words per page, the size of the type, the size of the page, the action implied by the script, and the tempo. A more accurate way to estimate the length of the play is to read several typical pages from the script out loud at the speed in which they would probably be delivered by the actors. The full running time can be determined by timing this reading and dividing by the pages read, then multiplying this by the total pages in the script. It is also necessary to allow for required action that may involve significant amounts of time. For example, Shakespeare described fight scenes with the simple words "They fight." Those two words could mean anything from a simple clash to a lengthy battle scene. Ultimately, the best indication of the length of the play is a reading of the full script out loud as is often done at the first rehearsal. This does not necessarily allow for the development of the tempo or comedic or dramatic pauses, but it does give a rough estimate of the probable length of the play.

> While the one page per minute rule is a working start to estimate the length of a play, a better guideline is to read several pages of the script aloud as the lines would be delivered, divide the time by the number of pages read, and then multiply by the total pages in the script.

Directors often consider cutting a script to fit time requirements. Cutting a script without the consent of the playwright has both legal and ethical concerns. Plays in the public domain, such as the works of Shakespeare, do not have legal restrictions regarding cuts to the script, but doing so still raises ethical and artistic issues. The director should be extremely careful when cutting a play to meet specific time concerns.

The size and composition of the cast is another crucial area the director must consider. The number of characters in the play and their requirements must be compared to the size of the talent pool. If the talent pool is relatively small, casting a play with a large cast can be problematic. On the other hand, if the talent pool is extremely large and it is the director's goal to maximize opportunity, a small cast show would be a poor choice. The balance between the need for men and women and their ethnic composition must also be weighed based on the talent pool. Finally, the director must think about any special considerations that must be made in the casting. For example, if two sets of identical twins are needed or if one of the roles requires a man well over 6 feet tall. Nontraditional casting is an option when considering gender, ethnic, or other requirements. These casting options will be discussed in Chapter 8. Casting for musicals increases the complexity because vocal ranges and, at times, the dancing ability of the actors must be taken into account. While not precasting the show, the director should contemplate whether the specific needs of the play can be met with the available talent that is projected to audition for the play.

The next consideration is the director's take on the physical requirements of the script. This includes the required setting or settings, necessary props, specific costume requirements as well as necessary lighting, sound, and special effects. While solutions to these requirements are not essential during the play selection process, it is important that the director be aware of them to avoid choosing a play where solutions for physical needs may not be found. For example, a director contemplating directing *A Few Good Men* must keep in mind that a large number and variety of Marine and Navy uniforms are required for the production. The ability to obtain these costumes must be assured before the play is considered. Specific requirements for the setting, such as a play with multiple locations or at least the ability to provide to the audience the idea of moving to a new location, may become a production issue later and should therefore be addressed. It is a good idea to identify "deal breaker" items. These include any physical necessity without which the play cannot be produced. By identifying these necessities before selecting the play, the director can avert future problems. When in doubt, it is best to find a solution before the play is chosen rather than having to deal with the problem afterward.

> A good rule of thumb is to identify "deal breaker" items. These include any physical necessity without which the play cannot be produced. By identifying these necessities before selecting the play, the director can avert future problems. When in doubt, it is best to find a solution before the play is chosen rather than afterward.

The director must also consider the nature of the performing space. It must be suitable for the basic nature of the play for the production to be successful. For example, a large complex musical with numerous scenic and costume requirements and a large cast will not be able to be presented to its fullest in a small intimate theatre. On the other hand, a small cast production that invites the closeness of the audience in experiencing the play will be lost in a large hall. Some plays may have particular needs that make performing in an arena or thrust extremely difficult. Other plays may be best performed in such a space. In producing a play with limited audience appeal, the play will best be served in a theatre with a smaller audience capacity. On the other hand, a popular play with the potential for a large audience will necessitate a comparably sized theatre. In productions funded through ticket sales, the size of the house becomes of particular importance to maximize the profit from the play.

While not always a key issue, the director should consider the nature of the intended audience in selecting the play. If the intended audience has no connection to the subject matter, then it will be hard to get the audience to accept and understand it. A highly conservative audience may find some subjects too difficult to handle. An older audience may have difficulty with younger issues while a younger audience may have difficulty with older issues. While the director need not pander to the audience, a wise director will consider them in making the selection.

The final criterion for play selection is more difficult to define. This criterion is based on the connection the director feels with the play. Directing a play the director feels deeply about is considerably easier and inevitably results in a better product. It is far more difficult, not to mention less fun, for a director to direct a play where there is no connection, or even worse, where the director disagrees with the message. There are no checklists for this criterion. If no connection is felt, the director probably should move on to another script. It is also important not to allow deep feelings for the play to cloud one's judgment. A director can easily be seduced into choosing a play despite the fact the play poses insurmountable mechanical problems. Also, the director should be careful in making pejorative decisions regarding play selection. If the play has an all-female cast and deals with decidedly feminine issues, does this mean the director needs to be a woman? While the easy answer is yes, it really depends on the individual. If the director feels a connection to the story and its characters, then the director probably can work with the play regardless of gender. It is important to remember that many plays about women's issues were written by men and vice versa. The same is certainly true for directors.

Choosing a play to produce can be one of the most difficult parts of the directorial process. It is essential that directors become avid readers of play scripts. It is better to have a list of possible plays in mind prior to beginning play selection than to have to start the search from scratch. Experienced directors often have a "to do" list of plays of various types and styles they would like to direct so they begin the search process with this list. Just as in the fairy tale where the princess must kiss a number of frogs before she finds her prince, the director must read many scripts before finding the one to direct.

> Just as in the fairy tale where the princess must kiss a number of frogs before she finds her prince, the director must read many scripts before finding the one to direct.

It is a good idea for the director to develop a filing system in order to recall plays previously read. This list can either be kept on index cards or in a computer database. The director should note the specific aspects of the play. Such a filing system might include the following:

- Title of the play
- Name of the playwright
- Where the play can be found
- Cast size and requirements
- Length of the play in pages and in projected running time
- Style of the play
- Major technical requirements that must be addressed for the play to be produced
- The physical action of the play (brief plot summary) (See discussion in Chapter 2.)
- The dramatic action of the play (spine) (See discussion in Chapter 2.)
- Any other notes the director feels are important

The choice of the script is extremely important for the director as it has significant implications for the success of the future production. Sufficient time must be allowed to read and research a number of plays before making a final choice. Many beginning directors fall into the trap of setting high standards for both their artistic needs and the physical needs of the production only to find such an ideal play does not exist. At some point, it may become necessary to alter standards because ultimately a play must be chosen. The dilemma this compromise creates can be avoided, or at least mitigated, if the director allows sufficient time for the search process and reads plays that meet the production's artistic and mechanical needs. Doing so significantly increases the possibility of finding a play that satisfies the director and works for the production.

> Allowing sufficient time for the play selection process and reading plays that fit the artistic and mechanical needs of the production will significantly increase the possibility of finding a play the director likes and works for the production.

SOURCES FOR PLAY SCRIPTS

To read scripts one must be able to find them. There are many sources directors can use after exhausting their personal libraries. The libraries of theatre friends and associates are another possibility. Public or academic libraries typically have script sections. For student directors, many theatre departments maintain their own script library. The next easiest source is online. Many contemporary playwrights post their scripts online making perusing them quite easy. However, a number of online script sources only make a portion of the script available without purchase. It is essential to read the full script before a final choice is made.

Scripts may also be obtained from script publishers who maintain large inventories of a variety of scripts and often act as the agents for the playwright in obtaining performance rights. Almost all of them have web pages to facilitate the search for particular categories of scripts. For example, on many sites you can search for scripts by cast size, style, length, or other requirements. The publishers generally offer a brief synopsis of the physical action of the play as well as its cast and production requirements. Typically, you need to purchase a copy. Once again, this can usually be taken care of online. A listing of many of these publishers or other script sources is included in the appendix. While this list is by no means exhaustive, it offers a good place to start.

UNDERSTANDING AND OBTAINING PERFORMANCE RIGHTS

Once the play is selected, copies of the script must be obtained and performance rights secured before beginning rehearsal. If the script was found through a script publisher, the publisher will probably serve as the agent for securing performance rights. If the play was found individually or online, the process for obtaining scripts and performance rights will be described either in the front matter of the script or online. Purchasing the script does not necessarily provide the right to present the play in public performance. Performance rights must be negotiated or arranged separately. Many beginning playwrights are willing to provide performance rights free of charge if they are notified of the production. Most plays, however, require a royalty fee.

Performance royalties vary from one agent to another. They are often based on the nature of the producing organization, whether the play is being produced for profit, and the size and location of the theatre. In many cases the performance royalties are standardized for noncommercial and educational theatre companies. On the other hand, royalties for commercial productions are based on the specifics of the production. It is important to note that performance rights must be secured and, possibly, royalty fees paid even if there is no charge for admission. It should not be assumed that because of the small scale of a production or free admission that these legal obligations do not apply.

It is often argued that small production companies and schools are simply trying to present theatre to their community and as such should not be charged. This is both a legal and ethical fallacy. The playwright is protected by law from the play's unauthorized use. This includes both the script and the performance rights. Aside from the legal concerns, there is an ethical issue. It is the playwright's livelihood to write scripts. To produce the play without payment is theft of the playwright's intellectual property. In contracting a performance arrangement, the producing organization and the playwright or playwright's agent agree to specific terms under which the play may be produced. This agreement is specified in the contract signed by both parties. In addition to stating when and where the play will be produced, this agreement typically includes other contractual obligations such as how the playwright must be acknowledged, other credits required in the program, and specific requirements or restrictions on changes in the script. This latter issue will be dealt with in more detail later in the chapter.

RELATIONSHIP WITH THE PLAYWRIGHT

In selecting a play the director creates a relationship with the playwright. This relationship may be interpersonal if the playwright is present for the production or, if not, simply through the play itself. It is both unique and special and defines the beginning of the collaborative process. The director's work stems from the creative work of the playwright and, as such, the director has certain obligations to the playwright.

The playwright creates a pretext for the play in the script. It is the director's role to interpret the script and bring the playwright's words to life on the stage. It is important to remember that the production begins with and is based on the work of the playwright. As such, it is the director's responsibility to represent the playwright's intent. If the director is working with the playwright, there is little doubt to the intent as the playwright is immediately available for explanations, to answer questions, and to express opinions during the production process. In the case of most revivals the playwright is not immediately available. In fact, the playwright may not be aware of the production other than knowing the rights were cleared. In cases where the playwright is not available, the production is based solely on the director's interpretation of the script.

How then can the director understand what the playwright means or intends? The most that can be asked of the director is that the concept for the play be based directly on what is believed to be the playwright's message. A good test for the validity of the interpretation is to test it against the entire play. If some aspect or aspects of the play do not support the interpretation, then the interpretation becomes suspect. A valid interpretation consistently works with all aspects of the play. The director cannot simply ignore or underplay parts of the play that are not consistent or supportive. If the message the director wishes to convey is not found within the play, the director cannot simply insert it. If the director still wishes to convey this message, then the director needs to find it in another play, write a play, or get the playwright's permission to modify the play. The playwright's absence from the rehearsal process does not give increased license to the director to take liberties with the play. If anything, it increases the director's responsibility since the playwright is not on hand to speak.

There is often a certain amount of friction between the director's interpretation and the playwright's intent. It is this interaction between the playwright and the director and the rest of the production team that tests, challenges, confirms, and ultimately improves the play. It is not the director's job to read the mind of the playwright in order to understand the play. A rule of thumb I use as a guideline in terms of determining my interpretation and concept for the play, assuming the playwright is not present during the process, is to ask myself whether if the playwright came to a performance unannounced would I be concerned. The playwright might not like my concept or agree with my interpretation, but assuming there is integrity in my analysis and conceptualization, I feel I have done my job. On the other hand, if I believe that to make an interpretation work I would be stretching the playwright's intent in my conceptualization, then I cannot hide behind the fact that the playwright will not see the production. In this case, I will not proceed with this interpretation.

> A general guide to help determine if the director's interpretation and concept for the play would be acceptable to the playwright is to ask the question: If the playwright came to a performance unannounced would the director be embarrassed? If there is integrity to the analysis and conceptualization the director has done his or her job.

The opportunity to work directly with the playwright is a unique one for any director. The interaction between the director and the playwright and between the playwright and the rest of the production team and cast brings a new and exciting dynamic to the production process, assuming the entire process is positive and affirmative. When the playwright does not approve of the decisions made, it is up to the director to resolve the friction and to make the decision how to proceed. There is a difference between writing a novel and writing a play. Unlike a novel, where the author controls exactly how the reader will perceive the work, in a play, the playwright's material will be interpreted by the director and the remainder of the production company; the audience will thereby perceive the play based on this interpretation. Further, each time the play is produced the interpretation will change and, therefore, no two productions will be identical. Ultimately, it is the nature of theatre that the audience sees the playwright's work through the interpretation of the director as brought to life by the designers and actors.

If there is the option to include the playwright in the production process, the director must carefully consider the responsibilities this collaboration entails. Once the decision to work with the playwright is made it cannot be undone. For better or worse the interpretive work of the director is tied to input directly from the playwright.

Whether the playwright is present or not, there is a delicate balance between the director's creativity in the interpretation of the playwright's play and in the obligation of the director to bring the playwright's message to life. It is this balance that is unique to theatre and underscores the beginning of the director's creative process.

CONTRACTUAL AND ETHICAL OBLIGATIONS

Having chosen a play and secured the rights, the director now has a set of contractual and ethical obligations to the playwright. While the director as a creative artist has the right and responsibility to interpret the play, the director also maintains an obligation to the play-wright to produce the play consistent with the playwright's message. As discussed earlier in this chapter, the playwright may not necessarily agree with the director's interpretation, but if it is internally valid the director can proceed. Different directors maintain different standards for how far their interpretation can move from the intent of the playwright. While this is an ethical question that is open to discussion, there are certain legal issues the director must acknowledge when working with the script that are not open to discussion. First, most performance agree-ments require that any changes in the script be made with the consent of the playwright or his agent. This includes adding to the script, making deletions or cuts, or rearranging the content of the script. If the playwright is working on the production, the playwright can make specific decisions regarding these changes. If the playwright is not present, getting approval for such changes is more difficult. For example, many high school one-act play competitions require the school to submit documentation showing not only that the performance rights are secured, but also that they have secured permission to shorten the play to meet the time requirements of the competition. In many cases, playwrights have refused to make such accommodations.

Directors disagree widely on the issue of making cuts or minor alterations to a script. While the legal issue is quite clear, the ethical issues are not. Many directors justify making minor cuts, particularly in changing what may be considered obscene language to locally acceptable, or at least less objectionable, language as a necessary part of making the play presentable for the local audience. While directors must decide for themselves the standard by which they make these ethical choices, they must keep in mind the legal constraints that are beyond their control and interpretation.

Plays in the public domain do not have legal restraints regarding script changes. For exam-ple, it is almost inevitable that Shakespeare's plays will be modified, edited, or changed by the director. Many directors feel that as brilliant as Shakespeare's works are, they were written for a specific time, and to make them relevant to a modern audience certain changes are neces-sitated. As a director, I sympathize with the need to make such changes, yet I also must take into consideration the apparent hubris in assuming I can improve Shakespeare's work.

The ethical and legal questions surrounding changes to dialogue do not apply to parantheti-cal notes in the play. Typically, these are notes to the actor on how to deliver the line, such as (*angrily*). This also extends to descriptions of the setting or to stage directions. In many cases these descriptions were not written by the playwright but inserted into the script upon publica-tion based on the setting and stage directions from the original production. These additions are made to clarify the action or to provide ideas to the director. Two notable contrasting examples are found in *Long Day's Journey into Night* by Eugene O'Neill and *Death of a Salesman* by Arthur Miller. At the beginning of *Long Day's Journey into Night*, O'Neill provides a descrip-tion of the setting, the living room of the Tyrone family summer cottage. He goes into specific details on decor and the location of furniture. Since this is a semiautobiographical play, O'Neill chose the setting to be that of his childhood home, and the details are based on his vivid memo-ries. This is an example of the playwright providing information as an extension of the play. On the other hand, the detailed description of the setting and the way *Death of a Salesman* should be performed was not written by Arthur Miller; it is a description of the setting as conceived and designed by Jo Mielziner in conjunction with the director, Elia Kazan. While this was a different production concept than Miller originally envisioned, he embraced this concept wholeheartedly. This production concept dominated revivals of the play until the 1999 revival on Broadway. These two examples provide insight for the director into the use of the playwright's descriptions. The director should neither automatically follow these descriptions nor dismiss them. At the least, they provide an insight into the playwright's ideas or how the play was originally staged, presumably with the involvement of the playwright. Either one helps the director in making artistic decisions. In this same way, a parenthetical direction on line delivery provides insight to the playwright's thinking but is not a mandate for how the line should be delivered.

Playwrights may provide notes for the director in the front matter of the script. These notes may include suggestions on how to handle references or how to update them to make them relevant to the audience. Suggestions from the playwright can provide valuable insight for the director if the playwright is not accessible during the production. If the playwright is present during the process and approves certain changes, this does not make them permanent changes, rather it is an acknowledgment of the immediate needs of that specific production. If a director requests changes and is denied, legally and ethically the director cannot make them.

PREPARING A PRODUCTION BOOK

After obtaining the rights to the script the director prepares a production book. While some directors prefer to work directly from the bound copy of the script, many, if not most, prefer to work from a loose-leaf notebook containing the script. The director's production book is similar to the stage manager's, but it is designed as a tool specifically for directing.

It should be noted that copyright regulations prohibit the photocopying of the script. Even though making the production book is a common practice, it is illegal to do so without the consent of the publisher. While some publishers are willing to grant permission to make the production book, others will not. Directors are advised to secure permission prior to making the production book using a copying machine.

Before copying machines the usual method of making a production book was to cut apart the bound script and paste each page on a larger piece of paper. Since the advent of these machines, it is far more common to find production book pages produced by photocopying. To avoid part of the facing page from appearing on the photocopied page, a mask created from a sheet of copier paper or heavier tag stock is placed on the machine so only the one page will be photocopied. This mask may work well for future scripts as there are a relatively small number of page sizes. The size of the mask and therefore the location of the script page on the loose-leaf paper is a matter of personal preference. The idea is to provide a significant amount of margin space for the director to place notes and blocking. Directors may also choose to slightly enlarge the type during the copying process. Figure 1.1 shows three examples of typical arrangements for a production book.

The facing page of each option provides the director with space to make diagrams or more extensive notes. To make the production book more manageable, the director can take another idea from the stage manager and divide the production book into key areas. These may include:

Figure 1.1 Production Book Script Page Layout Options

- Script—Act I
- Script—Act II
- Schedules (rehearsal and production)
- Sections for Technical Areas—Scenery, Light, Costumes, Props, Sound, etc. (These can either be individual or combined in one section.)
- Cast Information
- Analysis
- Research
- Background
- Notes
- Misc.

It is also useful to tab the pages that mark the beginnings and ends of either scenes or rehearsal units. This will make finding individual scenes easier. Directors unfamiliar with stage management can find further suggestions for the organization of the production book in any good stage management text. A final suggestion in regard to the production book is to provide some form of contact information either on the cover or on the first page so if the book is lost there is a chance it will be returned to the director. A well-organized production book is a useful tool that allows the director to keep notes and ideas together and easily retrievable, and is preferably in sight during rehearsals.

It is a good idea to provide some form of contact information either on the cover or on the first page so if the book is lost there is a chance it will be returned to the director.

PLAY SELECTION CHECKLIST

- ❏ Style or genre
- ❏ Length
- ❏ Cast size and requirements (including breakdown between male and female)
- ❏ Special casting needs (e.g., specific ethnicities)
- ❏ Technical requirements
  - Scenery
  - Costume
  - Lighting
  - Sound
  - Props
  - Effects
- ❏ "Deal Breaker" needs
- ❏ Suitability of the theatre space
- ❏ Nature of the intended audience
- ❏ Director's connection to the play

FURTHER EXPLORATION

1. Using the criteria listed in this chapter, begin a play file by preparing summaries of plays you have recently read so they can be considered for future directing projects.

2. Discuss with a playwright the relationship between the director and the playwright.

3. Discuss with a playwright their thoughts about directors making changes to their scripts in general.

4. Discuss with a playwright their feelings about directors making changes to fit the local audience or time period.

CHAPTER 2

Understanding the Play: Script Analysis

UNDERSTANDING THE PLAY

What is this play about? This is the first and perhaps most important question the director can ask. While the process of script analysis is often considered the least exciting by many beginning directors, it is, nonetheless, crucial to the ultimate success of the production and is an important part of the director's process. Young directors, especially student directors, often believe script analyses are exercises for the sake of course instruction and assessment rather than actual tools used by theatre professionals. They could not be more mistaken. In reality, all good theatre professionals complete detailed analyses prior to undertaking any role in the theatre. This includes actors, managers, designers, choreographers, and especially directors. While the script analyses of professional directors may not take the form used in a class, directors do prepare them. It is of vital importance that young directors develop the habit of carefully analyzing the play prior to commencing any work on the production.

The director begins by carefully reading the play several times. As mentioned earlier, this number varies from director to director but always involves numerous readings. At an early preproduction meeting of one of my first productions in New York, the director stated he wasn't ready to discuss this play as he only had the opportunity to read it nine times. I thought he was either making a joke or was pretentious, but now I understand that despite nine readings he still did not feel comfortable in his understanding of the play. While reading the play, the director takes notes and highlights areas of the script that need to be more carefully considered. Once reaching an initial understanding of the play the director can start the analysis.

DETERMINING AND UNDERSTANDING THE SPINE OF THE PLAY

The first step in the analysis is to determine and define the main dramatic action of the play. This typically embodies the basic conflict that creates the drama. Stanislavski described it as the "super objective" of the play. Perhaps the most commonly used term, originated by Richard Boleslavsky and popularized by director Harold Clurman, is the "spine." Clurman reasoned that by determining the spine of each character he could ascertain the spine of the entire play. In an anatomical sense, it is the spine that supports the human body. It is the backbone or spine that allows for bodily functions, movement, and defines range of motion. In the same way, the spine of the play supports the entire play, allowing all actions to be consistent and dynamic. The spine refers to the *dramatic action* of the play while the plot refers to the *physical action*. Every director develops a unique spine for the production of a particular play. What separates productions of the same play by different directors are the approaches taken to define the spine. There is no one "correct" spine. Each director seeks to determine his or her own understanding of the central conflict.

Clearly and concisely defining and expressing the spine may be the most difficult task the director undertakes in the analysis process. The spine is a concise definition of forces within the play that create the conflict and produce the resultant conclusion. All theatre is based around conflict for without conflict there is no drama. The nature of the conflict, how the characters handle the conflict, and how the conflict resolves defines the play. Early in my career I worked with a director who separated comedy and tragedy by how the conflict was handled. He said as part of the resolution of the conflict in a comedy, the protagonist got what he or she wanted while in a tragedy the protagonist did not. While this is a bit simplistic, it does serve to underscore the importance of the nature of the conflict in defining the play. Determining the spine of the play begins by first identifying the two forces in conflict. The next step is to determine the result or resolution of this conflict. This can be expressed for the play by the formula:

$$A + B \rightarrow C$$

In this formula, A and B represent the two forces creating the conflict. While they are often two characters, they may also represent other types of forces within the play. The plus sign represents the interaction of the two forces and can be replaced by any verb describing the nature of the interaction such as A combines with B, A interacts with B, A confronts B, or the like. C represents the result of the conflict that is produced by the climax of the play. In essence, two forces pitted against each other create the conflict and end in a resolution that defines the new order at the end of the play.

The key to developing an exciting and insightful production is to define as precisely as possible the nature of the elements in the spine that produce the conflict. The more specific and evocative each element, the better the production will be. To keep the spine from becoming watered down, the spine should be expressed in as few words as possible. Ideally, the formula for the spine can be expressed in three words, but adjectives in some cases may be necessary.

While being so concise greatly increases the complexity in expressing the spine, it does force the director to be completely clear.

Anton Chekhov's one-act play *The Bear* can be used as an example to develop possible spines. The physical action of the play involves a mourning widow, Elena Popova, whose seclusion is intruded upon by a landowner, Grigory Smirnov, who has come to collect a debt. When Popova refuses to pay Smirnov until the day after tomorrow, he becomes enraged and refuses to leave. Despite her protestations, he continues his boorish behavior. The argument escalates and it appears it will culminate in a duel. Popova leaves to get the pistols, and Smirnov realizes he has finally found the woman of his dreams. Upon her return, he expresses his new-found love, and despite her initial protest he gives her a prolonged kiss. When the servant, Luka, enters and sees them kissing, the play concludes with Popova indicating she has had a serious change of heart.

The conflict in this play is between Popova and Smirnov. A possible spine is as follows:

$$\text{Grief} + \text{Anger} \rightarrow \text{Love}$$

In this model, Popova's grief is in contrast to Smirnov's anger; the result of the conflict is their falling in love. While this is workable, it lacks excitement and true insight.

To refine it further, the two characters and their relationship to the conflict could be described as:

$$\text{Sorrow} + \text{Stubbornness} \rightarrow \text{Love}$$

In this case, the conflict centers around the interaction of Popova's sorrow with Smirnov's stubbornness. Strengthening the words can test the validity of the spine. While Smirnov contends he is in love, perhaps lust is a better choice. This changes the spine to:

$$\text{Sorrow} + \text{Stubbornness} \rightarrow \text{Lust}$$

In examining the play further, it becomes apparent Popova's sorrow is actually her method of demonstrating her superiority over her late husband. He was unfaithful, and Popova's extended period of sorrow is her way of showing him she is the better person. In her refusal to end her period of mourning, she mirrors Smirnov's stubbornness with her own. Likewise, both exhibit a strong passion for their beliefs and a commitment to carry them out regardless of the cost. Therefore, a better spine might be:

$$\text{Stubbornness} + \text{Passion} \rightarrow \text{Lust}$$

In this model, the conflict is not between Popova and Smirnov as individuals but rather the conflict between the stubbornness they exhibit and their resulting passion.

Developing the spine is a multistep process that continually refines and strengthens each of the elements until the strongest statement for the spine is reached. Remember, there is no single spine for a play. The various possibilities may be ranked in terms of intensity and can be tested as to whether they represent the full conflict and the resulting product of that conflict. Once the director determines the spine, this concise formula can be elaborated with a brief explanation. If the director is able, however, to fully express the spine in three to six words, this indicates a full and deep understanding of the play.

Note that a number of contemporary theatrical genres have completely different structures from the traditional model, and while they typically have a clear conflict, the result from this conflict may not be as apparent. See, for example, the plays of Samuel Beckett. While these contemporary styles may challenge traditional interpretation, almost all theatre essentially follows a similar pattern.

> The key to developing an exciting and insightful production is to define as precisely as possible the nature of the elements in the spine that produce the conflict. The more specific and evocative each element, the better the production.

IDENTIFYING THE DRAMATIC STRUCTURE OF THE PLAY

Continuing with the analysis, the director begins to break down the play into its component parts. Most plays follow a pattern of development best described by the "rising action" model. This model is based on the concept of the *well-made play*. The well-made play was codified by nineteenth-century playwright Eugène Scribe and further developed by his successor, Victorien Sardou. While the model is a workable description of theatrical structure, Scribe and Sardou were often criticized for meticulously following this model, using it slavishly as a formula for "good" plays. This led to the sarcastic term "Sardoodledom," referring to formulaic plays that rely on a close following of the pattern for success rather than creative construction. Nonetheless, the model still stands as a basic understanding of how a play is structured. The model can be illustrated as shown in Figure 2.1.

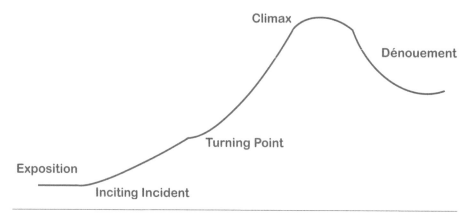

Figure 2.1 Dramatic Structure

There are five basic components to the model:

- Exposition
- Inciting Incident
- Turning Point
- Climax
- Dénouement

The *exposition* provides the audience with an explanation of the story prior to the opening act in order to understand the action to follow. This is the playwright's opportunity to provide information regarding the characters, the situation, the location, the time, or any other necessary information. The exposition is typically a relatively short portion of the opening. It may not be exciting but it is, nonetheless, necessary. Some playwrights choose to spread this information throughout the beginning of the play rather than have a single exposition. Others are successful at creatively weaving the beginning of the action with the exposition, avoiding a rather dry start for the play. A good example is Arthur Miller's *Death of a Salesman*. In the course of the opening moments all the information needed to understand the world of the play and the characters is presented, but at the same time the audience is involved in the action and drawn into the characters.

Regardless of how the exposition is handled, the action of the play is initiated by the *inciting incident*. This event, also referred to as the trigger, involves an action that starts the storyline. It is here that the playwright introduces the central conflict of the play.

The action continues and the conflict grows until the *turning point*, also referred to as "the point of no return." The central characters can no longer ignore the conflict, and the path of the play must inevitably lead toward its resolution. The turning point ensures the action and the attention of the audience. Shakespeare's *Macbeth* is a good example of an inciting incident leading to the turning point. The inciting incident occurs once Macbeth hears the prophecy from the witches. The action continues and the conflict grows as he and Lady Macbeth consider the murder of the king. The turning point is the moment Macbeth drives the knife into Duncan. Now there is no turning back. Not all turning points are necessarily as obvious as a murder, but this is an excellent example of an act that cannot be undone. After the stabbing of Duncan, Macbeth is set on a path that must, one way or the other, resolve the conflict.

Spurred on by the conflict, the action continues to develop until it reaches its ultimate resolution, the *climax*. This is often where the playwright's message is clarified for the audience. Continuing the use of *Macbeth* as an example, the climax comes during the confrontation between Macbeth and Macduff and is resolved when Macduff kills Macbeth. This act clearly ends Macbeth's reign of terror, restoring order to Scotland, and drives home Shakespeare's message regarding the abuse of power.

The action of the play essentially ends with the climax. However, there still may be issues to be resolved. The *dénouement*, from the French word for untying, settles the remaining issues and allows the audience to leave the play satisfied. In *Macbeth*, the dénouement is relatively short; Malcolm becomes king and his speech indicates the restoration of order in Scotland.

Many plays intentionally leave issues unresolved. One of the more famous examples from classical literature is from Shakespeare's *King Lear*. Midway through the play the character of the Fool disappears. There is no mention or discussion of the disappearance with the possible exception of Lear's line, "And my poor fool is hanged," but most scholars agree Lear is not referring to the Fool but rather to his daughter Cordelia. The play ends and the audience is left to wonder what happened to the Fool.

Even though this model of dramatic structure was developed during the nineteenth century, it applies equally well to plays written much earlier and with most modern dramatic literature. Certain contemporary genres, however, significantly depart from this model. In Samuel Beckett's *Waiting for Godot*, the action is circular rather than linear. Act I ends just as it began; Act II ends exactly the same way. Essentially, there is no development in the plot or resolution of the conflict, which is exactly how Beckett wished to convey his message. Most modern playwrights do not obsessively comply with the format of the rising action model, and the director should not try to arbitrarily force this model onto every play. It is intended as a useful guide to help understand the basic structure, but when it does not apply, the director needs to seek other methods.

DIVIDING THE SCRIPT INTO WORKING UNITS

Classical plays were typically divided into five acts; however, most modern plays are written in two acts with an intermission. Modern playwrights tend to structure their plays so there is a development at the end of the first act that reaches a logical pause. It is designed to leave the audience with a specific emotion to carry through intermission, and this emotion fuels the beginning of the second act. The second act then continues this development until the climax. Some modern plays have three acts. In these instances, the playwright either intends two intermissions or uses the act structure to indicate significant breaks in time and/or location.

At times these divisions may cause confusion. In contemporary theatre, a two-act play is customarily referred to as a full-length play, while one-act plays are considered to be shorter. In reality, a one-act play is simply a play with one act and it may, in fact, be longer than a two-act play. The length of the play cannot necessarily be inferred from the number of acts.

In some cases, the playwright divides each act into scenes. These scenes usually indicate breaks in the action or changes in time or location. A classical concept for scene division known as *French scenes* originated from the French neoclassic practice of structuring scenes following entrances and exits rather than dramatic needs. When working with plays with French scenes, the director needs to take this convention into account in dealing with the dramatic action of the play. For example, a lengthy scene involving a discussion between two characters that is interrupted by a minor character entering, delivering one line, and exiting is three French scenes, even though dramatically it is one continuous action.

The director should further divide the script into segments of complete units of action. These *action units* are defined by complete arcs of development in the evolution of the scene, i.e., a single action along with its reaction. The action unit is composed of a number of beats. Each beat is defined by the character's thought process. When the character begins a new thought, a new beat is created. The collection of these beats that leads to the resolution of a single action composes an action unit. These action units become valuable tools for the director both in analyzing the script and in subsequently creating workable rehearsal units. Each action unit is useful as a rehearsal unit because the actors can begin a new attack and follow it through to completion before moving on to the next unit. The director should look at the length of the action unit in considering the minimal rehearsal section it can represent. This will be discussed in more detail later both as tools for analysis and rehearsal.

> Action units provide the director with both a tool for the script analysis process and a guide to setting up rehearsals. Since they contain full units of action, they are logical places to begin and end rehearsals.

ANALYZING THE PLAY

With a basic understanding of the play, its structure in hand, and the spine determined, the director can now begin the formal analysis of the play. One of the seminal concepts for dealing with script analysis is found in *Directing: Analysis, Communication, and Style* by Francis Hodge and Michael McLain.[1] My concept of play analysis owes a debt to their work and is adapted from it. This process can be addressed by identifying each of the component parts of the analysis.

BACKGROUND

The first part of this analysis contains the same information the director determined during the initial reading of the script: the projected running time, the cast requirements, and the major physical needs. The difference is that in the script analysis all physical requirements are identified, not just those that could be problematic. This includes all specifically required scenic needs, costume requirements, and props, as well as any lighting, sound, or other technical requirements. This should then be followed by a brief overview of the plot, summarizing the physical action. The director needs to find a balance between the minute details and the summary of the physical action in order to ensure understanding of the play. The last element of these initial descriptors is the spine. The spine should be expressed both in terms of the suggested formula and by a brief explanation of what it means.

MAJOR DRAMATIC QUESTION

The major dramatic question is a standard analysis tool in which the director is asked to identify in the form of a question the major issue addressed in the play. In essence, the major dramatic question asks, "What will happen?" It takes into consideration what the play is about and gives a starting place to further analyze the play.

THE GIVEN CIRCUMSTANCES

The director needs to identify the given circumstances of the play. The given circumstances or givens is the physical information provided by the playwright to understand the play, the characters, and the action. The first of these factors establish the **location or locations**. Next the **time and/or period** of the play is identified. It is important that the director be as specific as possible based on the information provided by the playwright. This may be found in the parenthetical notes in the beginning of the play or based on information in the dialogue. The playwright might only mention the play is set in an apartment, but more specific information may be ascertained based on the conversations between the characters. The background of the playwright may also provide insight into the nature of the location even if it is not specifically mentioned. For example, most of Neil Simon's plays take place in the New York City area since he himself is a native New Yorker.

One time reference that poses unique considerations for the director is when the playwright provides the time period as "Time: the present" as opposed to a specific year. While the playwright is indicating the play be set when it was written, this does not mean it was chosen for any reason other than to keep it contemporary. For example, assuming a play set in "the present" was written in 1960, this begs the question of whether the playwright intended the play to take place in 1960 or rather when the audience experienced it. The playwright is not necessarily thinking about revivals while writing. It is the job of the director to determine the specific year based on the information within the script. It is possible that a given play necessitates being set in the year it was written due to the references or specific requirements of the script. For example, a play set in "the present" with specific references to 9/11 may necessitate being set after 2001 but not too far in the future. On the other hand, if the action of the play is not directly affected by the events of the attack, it may be possible to set the production at a later time. Moving a play to a contemporary time period may make the play more relevant to the modern audience, but it may also create conflicts with specific events that occurred at the time of writing. Good examples are found in many modern productions of Shakespeare's works. While many of his plays were set during the Renaissance, it has become popular to move them to another time to make the play more accessible for the audience. This time migration requires the director to deal with possible inconsistencies. In the case of Shakespeare, for example, modern settings often conflict with references to swords. The director needs to determine how the production will work through these issues.

To understand the play the director must have a sense of the **previous action**, the events that presumably occurred prior to the first scene. This action is rarely specified, but during the exposition the playwright often includes prior events, both short- and long-term, so the audience understands the current action and situation. In this regard one of the most interesting opening lines for a play is found in Henrik Ibsen's play *Peer Gynt*. Aase's line to Peer, "Peer, you're lying!" raises immediate questions since it is unknown what Peer said to her. Ibsen immediately grabs his audience by leaving a significant question from the previous action. Further, if there is a break in time between acts or scenes, the previous action needs to be identified so the current action is understood once the new act or scene begins.

Finally, the **significance of these facts to the total meaning of the play** needs to be discerned. For example, John Patrick Shanley setting *Doubt* in the 1960s is vital to the understanding of the play since it takes place in a Roman Catholic school and church and this was a period of significant change in Catholicism. It is the conflict between the old church represented by Sister Aloysius and the new church represented by Father Flynn that sets the stage and the parameters for the action. All given circumstances have potential importance in understanding the play as a whole. Lack of specific information provides insight into the thought process of the playwright as well. It is not enough for the director to determine that the circumstances are important but rather *why* they are important. In the same manner, the director needs to determine the significance of the information if it is not provided by the playwright.

DIALOGUE

The playwright's most crucial mode of communication with the audience is the dialogue. This is the only element of the play over which the playwright maintains total control in the production. While the interpretation and ultimate delivery of the lines are up to the actors and the director, the words themselves are the playwright's. The nature of the dialogue defines the play and the characters. As such, a careful study of the dialogue is important to understanding the play. The director should first focus on the **nature of the words** chosen by the playwright. Specific word choices have power, and by making those choices the playwright provides a direction for the character. In analyzing the word choices, the director should be looking at the types of words the playwright chooses for each of the characters. Do they differ? What can be learned from the word choices about the play and about the characters who speak them? Are the words particularly formal or informal? The nature of how a character speaks helps define the character. If the speech pattern changes in different circumstances, this can provide additional insight into the character and his or her perception of the moment. The complexity of the words the playwright chooses to utilize for a specific character provides an increased understanding of the character.

Sentence structure further defines both the play and the individual characters. The nature of how the characters speak and how they shape their thoughts provides another valuable tool for character analysis. Do the characters speak in full sentences? Do they use contractions? Are the sentences grammatically correct? Do they use colloquialisms or is their speech more formal? Do they use repetitive phrases? By a careful study of the phrasing and sentence structure the director gains valuable insight into the characters.

The **imagery suggested by the dialogue** is another tool the director can use. The playwright may create a visual image in the nature of how a character speaks. In Eugene O'Neill's *The Hairy Ape*, a play about a working-class coal stoker, Yank, on a large ocean liner, O'Neill constructs the dialogue so the rhythm of Yank's speech creates the image of the pounding steam engine of a large ship. Also, note O'Neill's use of phonetic spelling to communicate his dialogue.

> *Say, listen to me—wait a moment—I gotter talk, see. I belong and he don't. He's dead*
> *but I'm livin'. Listen to me! Sure I'm part of de engines! Why de hell not! Dey move,*
> *don't dey? Dey're speed, ain't dey? Dey smash trou, don't dey? Twenty-five knots a*

hour! Dat's goin' some! Dat's new stuff! Dat belongs! But him, he's too old. He gets dizzy. Say, listen. All dat crazy tripe about nights and days; all dat crazy tripe about stars and moons; all dat crazy tripe about suns and winds, fresh air and de rest of it – Aw hell, dat's all a dope dream! Hittin' de pipe of de past, dat's what he's doin'. He's old and don't belong no more. But me, I'm young! I'm in de pink! I move wit it! It, get me! I mean de ting dat's de guts of all dis. It ploughs trou all de tripe he's been sayin'. It blows dat up! It knocks dat dead! It slams dat off en de face of de oith! It, get me! De engines and de coal and de smoke and all de rest of it! He can't breathe and swallow coal dust, but I kin, see? Dat's fresh air for me! Dat's food for me! I'm new, get me?[2]

O'Neill's use of the repetitive D sounds coupled with the short rhythmically driving sentences creates the mechanical imagery. His choice of slang phrases and phonetic representation of words such as "Dat's" or "Dey're" further create Yank's character, defining his ethnicity, social class, and educational background. O'Neill was often criticized for his use of phonetic spelling to indicate dialect, but this spelling as well as phrasing and sentence structure are the playwright's clear choice of how he wishes to represent his characters to the director and actors. The director can choose to either verbally describe the imagery created by the dialogue or to find actual visual imagery that embodies what the dialogue is expressing. Some directors further combine these visual images into collages to represent the play as a whole.

This example also illustrates the next area of dialogue analysis, **peculiar characteristics**. One of the areas the director must look for is the playwright's use of specific characteristics within the dialogue. In the case of *The Hairy Ape*, the phonetic spelling of words, the short sentences, and the use of colloquial slang separate Yank from the other characters in the play and create a clear sense of his persona. Another example is the deliberate mispronunciation or misuse of words. This was a tool Richard Sheridan used in his eighteenth-century comedy *The Rivals*. Sheridan makes comic use of this technique by having one of his characters, Mrs. Malaprop, frequently use the wrong word in an ostentatious attempt to sound more educated. In looking at the peculiar characteristics used by the playwright in the dialogue, it is also important to note whether these characteristics are restricted to one character or setting or whether they are part of the entire structure of the play. The playwright can use this characteristic to either further create the world of the play or to separate a character within that world.

The final aspect of dialogue analysis is to look at the overall **musicality of the dialogue**. In working with the lyrics of a song from a musical, the sound is produced by the nature of the music that accompanies it. This sound creates the essence of how the playwright wishes his dialogue to be understood. In straight plays the concept of the sound of the dialogue is not as obvious. Listening to the sound of the dialogue without trying to understand the words can help the director gain another insight into the characters and the world of the play. For example, when Shakespeare uses rhyming couplets instead of blank verse for specific dialogue, the musicality enhances the meaning of how he wishes the audience to perceive the dialogue.

It is important to understand that each aspect of dialogue analysis is related to and overlaps with the other aspects. They combine to produce the overall effect the playwright wishes to convey to the audience. Changes in these aspects signal to the audience a new understanding.

The better the director understands the playwright's use of dialogue beyond the literal meaning of each word, the better the overall interpretation of the play.

DRAMATIC ACTION

In order to better work with the script the director needs to divide the play into **action units**. As noted earlier, each action unit contains one single and complete dramatic action. While length varies depending on the situation, action units are typically several minutes long. Using *The Bear* as an example, the first action unit, the exposition, could embody the exchange between Popova and Luka and end with the arrival of Smirnov, the antagonist. His arrival prevents further interaction. It is best for the director to physically divide the play into action units. Aside from convenience, it allows the director to see the length and positioning of each unit. By clearly delineating the beginning and end of each action unit, the director can later utilize them as rehearsal units.

The director should give each action unit a **title**. The title identifies what the action unit is about and the nature of the action. The more evocative the title, the more valuable it becomes. For example, the second action unit of *The Bear* could mechanically be titled "Smirnov Asks for Money." While descriptive of what physically happens in the unit, it is bland and does not evoke the drama of the scene. A better title might be "I Want My Money." The director should have fun choosing the titles. Doing so will inevitably make for better and more exciting choices.

The final step in identifying each action unit is to **summarize the action**. In physics, Sir Isaac Newton's Third Law of Motion states that "For every action, there is an equal and opposite reaction." This important scientific principle is also valuable in understanding the dramatic action within the play. Every dramatic action initiated by one character causes a reaction. This reaction is directly proportional to the initial action. The action unit consists of the initial action and the reaction it triggers. This can be expressed in the formula:

$$A \rightarrow B; B \rightarrow A$$

or

A *present tense verb* **B**; **B** *present tense verb* **A**

For example, **A** *attacks* **B**; **B** *cowers from* **A**

In the second action unit of *The Bear*, Smirnov demands payment of a debt incurred by Popova's late husband, but Popova refuses to do so as she does not have any spare cash. She tells Smirnov he will have to wait until the day after tomorrow when her steward returns from town. This can be expressed more concisely in terms of the formula: Smirnov demands from Popova; Popova refuses Smirnov.

The key to understanding the dramatic action of each unit in terms of reciprocal action is to view it in terms of cause and effect. The instigating character's action triggers a response from the other character. It is this response that leads to the next action unit or in the case of the final unit, concludes the action. If there is no reciprocity, then the unit was cut short. If there is a second action after the response, then too much was included in the unit, i.e., at least the beginning of the next action unit. The clearness of this action/response will be of particular benefit when working with the actors in rehearsing this unit.

CHARACTERS

The action of the play is driven by the characters as defined by the playwright. As part of the script analysis the director must carefully analyze each of the characters within the play. While the actors will do a similar character analysis as they begin to build their own characters, the director must also complete this analysis so each character fits into the total world of the play. This will be an invaluable aid, particularly if the director perceives the character differently than the actor. These differences will need to be resolved in order for the rehearsal process to continue. To start the character analysis the **given circumstances** for each character should be established just as was done for the play as a whole. These typically include age, physical description, background, social status, educational background, and anything else provided by the playwright about the character.

The director then needs to establish how each character's attitude changes from the beginning of the play to the end. This is referred to as "**Polar Attitudes**." It is the transition from one attitude to the other that defines the character's developmental arc throughout the play; it is not their goals or desires. How each character feels about this transition will determine the way in which it is dealt. The character may make a relatively smooth transition from one attitude to the next. However, if this arc is unusually shaped, further clarification may be necessary in the analysis. For example, if the character's attitude remains constant throughout the play and then makes a large change in the last unit, this uneven transition should be noted. In some cases, characters do not change attitude throughout the play. While this is rare, this static attitude is important in defining the character. Notably, the character of Lt. Col. Jessep in Aaron Sorkin's play *A Few Good Men* does not change his attitude from the beginning of the play to the end. Even after admitting his actions in the climactic scene he remains unrepentant and maintains he would take the same action again. This situation is unique; in most plays, it is the development of a character's attitude that is a significant part of the action of the play.

Just as the director identified the major dramatic question for the play, the director needs to identify the **major dramatic question** each character seeks to answer in the course of the play. This question can either be phrased in the first or third person, as in "Will I win the competition?" or "Will he win the competition?"

Each character has a **desire or goal**. The actions of each character are designed to achieve it. This does not mean that all characters see their goals as equally attainable. They may see it as a difficult, uphill struggle or they may assume easy victory. Their perception of how easily they can attain their goal and how much effort they are willing to put in defines their **will**. In most cases, there is an **obstacle** that stands in the way. The nature of this obstacle determines the approach or approaches the characters will use. Whether each character ultimately reaches that goal is not important. What is important is that they each have a clear goal they see as attainable, and will, to some degree, work toward it until they are either successful or defeated.

To understand the character's behavior, the **moral stance** and **behavior** of each character needs to be identified. Their moral stance expresses their ethical position. This is determined by their background and their view of life and creates the parameters for their choice of tactics in pursuing their goal. A highly ethical and moral character will choose far different tactics than one of low morals. This directly affects their decorum. Decorum defines the character's acceptance of what is considered correct or proper behavior. The nature of how the character acts is defined by their decorum.

To ultimately achieve their desire or goal, the characters must have a set of objectives. For each objective, the characters must employ tactics they feel will lead to their success. The director must create a list of **objectives** for each character and the **tactics** each character may use to attain them. If applicable, the director ties these objectives and tactics to specific action units. While actors will be much more specific in their choice of objectives and tactics to ultimately reach their goal, the director must understand the range of possible objectives and tactics as well as the parameters in order to work with the actor in developing his or her choices for the character.

Finally, the director needs to define the **initial mood intensity** of the character at the start of each action unit. By plotting this out for each action unit, a pattern is created for the changes in mood intensity of each character throughout the play.

The director's analysis of each character is not intended to replace the analysis done by the actor. It is designed to provide the director with the information needed to work effectively with the actor in defining and developing the character so that it fits seamlessly into the director's concept. Without carefully analyzing the character the director cannot comprehend the character's position in and relationship to the play. To create an overall interpretation, it is essential that the director fully understands each character.

The director needs to complete character analyses for each of the characters. In the case of minor characters, information may not be provided by the playwright given the size of the role. It is nonetheless important that even small characters be fully developed. However, if there is a group of essentially similar characters, such as a chorus of a musical, unless the director wishes to create unique identities for each one, the director can treat the group as a single character.

BASIS OF THE PLAY

To understand the idea of the play the director should begin by considering the **significance or meaning of the title**. Most playwrights believe the title of the play to be one of their most difficult and important decisions. Early in my career one of the directors I worked with who was also a playwright told me he resented the practice by many theatre practitioners of shortening play titles. He maintained that since the choice of the title required so much thought it was disrespectful not to say it in its entirety. In most cases, the title provides insight into the meaning of the play. The playwright either in the script or in some other form may have discussed the reason for that specific title. If not, the director needs to start with an exploration into the significance of the word or phrase that composes the title. On the surface, Aaron Sorkin's aforementioned play *A Few Good Men* is a reference to the Marines' former recruiting slogan: "The Marines are looking for a few good men." Since the play involves the Marine Corps, the title is immediately appropriate. Upon further exploration, the title has more social implications. The phrase "a few good men" can refer to a story about a few men who are good.

Since Sorkin chose to have only one woman in the cast, the use of the word "men" has further resonance. The director, however, needs to be careful not to read more into the title than the playwright intended. Nonetheless, the title of the play is a valuable tool in understanding the meaning of the play.

The director can also look to statements made by the playwright to help understand the message of the play. Finding **philosophical statements in lines of dialogue** allows the director to voice the message using the playwright's own words. By utilizing the words of the playwright, the director avoids reshaping the message. The famous line "To be, or not to be" from Shakespeare's *Hamlet* is a wonderful example of the playwright embodying a philosophy within a single line.

In seeking to understand the meaning of the play the director should explore **how the *physical* action of the play reinforces the spine or *dramatic* action**. The director can return to the plot summary and examine it in comparison to the spine. The question to be asked is: "How is the conflict represented in the physical action?" This is the opportunity for the director to consider the physical and dramatic action as cooperative units within the play and to explain how they reinforce each other.

MOODS

As the action progresses it is important for the director to identify the mood of each action unit. How does the unit feel? While the mood can be expressed in a detailed description, short concise descriptors, **adjectives**, are best. Words such as "calm" or "relaxed" are examples of adjectives expressing the mood of the play. By selecting the strongest adjective, the director develops a clearer and sharper sense of that mood. The mood may also be expressed by a **visual image**. This visual image may be described or an actual picture may be used. By seeking the strongest visual image, the director develops a more concise sense of the mood. Preparing an adjective and a visual image for each action unit enables the director to establish a pattern for the evolution of the play. The collection of adjectives and images combine to give an overall view of the play as well as its development.

TEMPO

It is important in the initial analysis of the script for the director to begin to see how the tempo of each action unit differs from the ones before and after. If the director does not begin the process of analysis with a basic understanding of how the tempo will vary from unit to unit, the overall feeling may become static or erratic. The director can describe the tempo of the unit in a number of ways. The tempo can be ranked on a scale, such as from one to ten, with one being the slowest and ten being the fastest; described in musical terms such as *Larghissimo* (extremely slow), *Lento* (slow), *Adagio* (slow and stately), *Andante* (walking pace), *Moderato* (moderate), *Allegretto* (moderately fast), *Allegro* (fast), *Vivace* (faster), *Allegrissimo* (very fast), or *Presto* (very fast); or by using descriptive English words, such as very slow, slow, moderate, and the like. The key is to develop a mechanism by which the director can express the general sense of the tempo of the scene in comparison to others. This does not mean

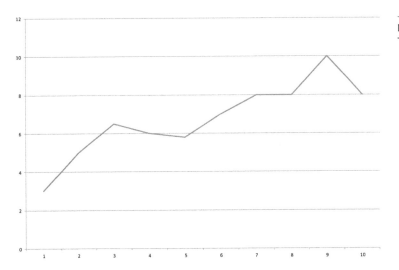

Figure 2.2
Tempo

there are no tempo variations within the unit itself. In order to compare the relative tempo of each unit a director can prepare a chart visually representing the speed of each unit. The chart provides a visual description of the flow of the changes of tempo. The chart could look something like Figure 2.2.

TONE

The director should summarize the entire analysis of the play by finding a word or short phrase. The shorter, more concise, and more evocative, the better. The director may also choose to represent the entire play through a visual image. In either case, this brief description of the tone of the play seeks to embody the play as a whole, summarizing everything that has gone before.

DETERMINING THE STYLE OF THE PLAY

The **style** in which the play is written is an extremely important as well as complex consideration. More thorough discussions of both the written style and the production implications are found in Chapter 4. The style will have significant implications in determining the production concept. The director is seeking to define how the playwright communicates the world of the play to the audience. The nature of the conventions the playwright uses will define the style.

It is best to put as much of the analysis as possible directly onto the pages of the script in the production book. While being able to refer to the analysis in its own section of the production book is valuable, it is even better if this information is immediately visible to the director while working with the cast.

SCRIPT ANALYSIS FORMAT

The script analysis format discussed earlier in this chapter is summarized in the following outline. In preparing the script analysis the director may choose to write the entire analysis in a narrative form or use an outline. If an outline is used it is important that the director provide enough information so it can be understood without referring to an external guide. It is highly recommended that as much of the analysis as possible be placed directly into the production book on the script pages. While being able to refer to the analysis in its own section of the production book is valuable, it is even better if this information is immediately visible to the director while working with the cast. As a final note, the director may or may not choose to share specific information from the analysis. The purpose of this analysis is to inform and enlighten the director's decision-making process leading to the development of the production concept for the play.[3]

OUTLINE OF SCRIPT ANALYSIS FORMAT

- ❏ Projected running time
- ❏ Cast requirements
- ❏ Physical needs
- ❏ Brief summary of the plot
- ❏ The Spine/Action/Super-objective
- ❏ Major Dramatic Question
- ❏ The given circumstances
  - Location(s)
  - Time or period
  - Any unique considerations
  - Previous action
  - Significance of these facts to the total meaning of the play
- ❏ Dialogue
  - Nature of the words
  - Sentence structure
  - Imagery suggested by the dialogue
  - Peculiar characteristics found in the dialogue
  - Musicality of the dialogue
- ❏ Dramatic action
  - Breakdown of the script into action units

- Titles of each unit
- Summarize the action (express in action/reaction)
☐ Characters (for *EACH* character in the play)
  - Given Circumstances
    - Age
    - Physical description
    - Background
    - Social status
    - Educational background
    - Other factors or descriptors
  - Polar Attitudes
  - Major Dramatic Question
  - Desire/Goal
  - Will
  - Obstacle
  - Moral stance and behavior
  - Summary list of objectives and tactics
  - Initial mood intensity of the character at the start of each action unit
☐ Basis of the Play
  - Significance or meaning of the title
  - Philosophical statements in lines of dialogue
  - How the *physical* action of the play reinforces the spine or *dramatic* action
☐ Moods (for each action unit)
  - List the mood adjectives for the scene/unit
  - Provide a visual image for the mood of the scene
☐ Tempo
☐ Tone
☐ Style

FURTHER EXPLORATION

1. Using the format discussed in this chapter, express the spine for a play you recently read. Work on refining this expression so that it is the most concise and evocative statement you can make about the play.

2. For the same play, divide the play into action units. Test these action units by expressing the reciprocal action that defines each unit.

3. For a play you recently read, identify the exposition, inciting incident, turning point, climax, and dénouement.

4. Using the outline provided, write a script analysis for a play you recently read.

NOTES

1   Francis Hodge and Michael McLain, *Play Directing: Analysis, Communication, and Style* (London: Routledge, Taylor & Francis Group, 2016).

2   *The Hairy Ape*, scene 1.

3   Francis Hodge and Michael McLain, *Play Directing: Analysis, Communication, and Style* (London: Routledge, Taylor & Francis Group, 2016).

Research Leading to a Concept

ANALYSIS TO RESEARCH

Having completed the analysis of the play, the director can now turn to research in order to develop the concept for the production. While the purpose of the analysis phase was to establish needs and/or questions based on the script, the research phase seeks to find possible solutions for them. The analysis may have also identified areas in which the director does not feel secure or areas that need to be verified before proceeding. It is vital that the director does not take anything for granted and that all aspects of the play are thoroughly covered before proceeding. There are a number of areas the director needs to research.

PRODUCTION RESEARCH

Production research refers to exploration into how the play was presented in the past. The goal of production research is not to copy or plagiarize someone else's ideas but rather to explore options previous directors used as a source of inspiration for the new production. In researching the original production or revivals in which the playwright was involved, the director has an opportunity to research solutions and approaches made by a production team in consultation with the playwright. Of course, whether the playwright agreed with those choices is unknown unless the research so indicates. As noted in Chapter 1, scenic designer Jo Mielziner and director Elia Kazan's approach to the original production of *Death of a Salesman* met with Arthur Miller's heartfelt approval even though it was decidedly different than he originally intended, and the production style remained essentially a standard for this play until the 1999 Broadway revival. A design mentor with whom I studied used to say, "There is no reason to reinvent the wheel." By this he meant that a good approach is a good approach, and while no artist should simply copy another's work, solutions to particular issues discovered by others may assist in the development of the new production. Learning how other artists addressed particular needs may help inspire the director to find an approach and gain a set of possible ideas.

Production research begins with the script itself. Either in the back or the front of many published scripts is a ground plan and often a production photo, usually from the original production. Many scripts also contain lists of the necessary items for scenery, lighting, costumes, sound, and props. While these can be a good start, be careful utilizing these lists since many of them were prepared based on the needs of the first production. The props list found at the back of the published script for Bram Stoker's *Dracula* includes six chimneys for hurricane lamps. When I prepared to direct this production, I found no mention or implied need for them in the script. Subsequent research revealed that in the original 1924 Broadway production, the howling wolf sounds made by offstage crew members could be made eerier by having the crew howl into the chimneys. Since they were used in the production, they were on the props list; however, there was no mention of how they were used. Items can also be mentioned in the parenthetical descriptions of the setting and/or costumes. They may be from the original production, not descriptions provided by the playwright.

Further research into the production of older or classic plays in general may be found in texts dealing with design, directing, or theatre history. Older plays are typically referenced in these books as examples of production values at the time. In researching the initial production of both older and newer plays, discussions of the production and often pictures can be found with the original reviews. The *New York Times* reviews and writes about all productions in New York, and back issues can be found in the *Times* online database. Other New York City publications such as the *New Yorker* also review and include articles about these productions, often with pictures. In addition to learning about the approaches for these productions, reviews also provide insight into, in at least the critics' minds, the effectiveness of the production. A comparison of reviews from different sources helps the director get a more balanced view of the play's initial reception. In looking at older reviews remember that standards have changed significantly over the years. For example, viewers of the mechanized scenery of the eighteenth century often described it as extremely realistic. While it was ingenious and beautifully done, today's audiences definitely would not apply the term realistic to the work. Styles of production prevalent when a play was written may not be the best way for the play to be produced today. However, being aware of how it was originally produced greatly assists in understanding the play. For example, Greek culture did not allow for violence being depicted onstage; it could be described but not shown. Knowing the background of the Greek theatre festivals provides insight into how and why the classic Greek playwrights structured their plays in the manner they did.

The Internet provides a quick and valuable means to conduct research into plays, particularly modern productions. Many, if not most, producers have websites for their productions as do many playwrights for their plays. The director can do a general search for productions of the play, which often include images from the productions. As in many areas, the Internet has made production research much simpler. It should be remembered, however, that there is no filtering of information placed on the Internet. Websites are not necessarily reviewed or vetted. As such, information about a given production must be verified by the director before being accepted as fact. While the same is true for information from books, newspapers, or other publications, presumably these sources were reviewed by the editors and publishers prior to publication. While verification is always an important part of research, it is especially necessary for information taken from the Internet.

> Be careful when conducting research into prior productions; they can create such an impression it can be difficult to conceive of alternate approaches. Such limitations can form significant barriers for the director in developing a concept.

Production research can have its dark side. Reading about and viewing pictures of the original production can create such an impression it is difficult to conceive of alternate approaches. Such limitations may form significant barriers for the director in developing a concept. Due to this potential limitation, many directors do not undertake production research in order to keep their minds completely clear. Other directors find production research an extremely valuable tool. The director who does not wish to pursue general production research may choose to research specific aspects of the production. Early in my directing career my initial research would explore how the original production was presented, particularly examining the original set design often illustrated in the back of the script. I soon realized I unintentionally and even unknowingly allowed this information to set parameters for my interpretation, thereby restricting my ideas. Until I had a clear sense of my concept I stopped doing this type of production research. Afterward, I used this production research to expand on my ideas. While I generally tend to avoid production research until later in my process, when I directed Aristophanes' *Lysistrata*, I pondered how I would handle the references to the erections of the male characters. Original productions of this play utilized leather strap-on phalluses. Since my production style was more modern, I did not want to utilize this classic approach. Through my research of contemporary productions, I discovered many different approaches by other directors. In this case the research opened my thought process rather than limited it.

PERIOD RESEARCH

It is important that the director understands both the period in which the play was written and the period in which it was set. The social values and standards at the time a play is written significantly affect how the playwright sees the world of the play. Research into the period may be undertaken in a number of ways. The historical context of the period can be explored through primary sources: historical documents, journals, diaries, and letters. This method is particularly valuable for older periods of history. News and magazine articles can also provide additional insight. For example, *Life* magazine (1883–2000) provides a wonderful collection of photographic documentation of all walks of life.

Secondary sources can also be valuable tools. Secondary sources involve a person's interpretation of the subject. For example, an artist's painting from the period depicts the scene as interpreted by the artist. In essence, we are seeing history as filtered by the artist. In contrast, a photograph is less filtered by the artist and therefore not as subjective. We need to take this into account since the artist's interpretation may alter the reality of the time period. We cannot simply assume the artist's interpretation is correct. For example, in the 1963 film *Cleopatra*, starring Elizabeth Taylor and Richard Burton, the costume design was often praised for its depiction of Egyptian dress; however, the design was significantly influenced by fashion of the early 1960s. As such, it is a poor idea to use the film to gain an understanding of period-correct Egyptian dress.

In preparing for my production of *Lysistrata*, it was necessary to develop a full understanding of the historical context within which Aristophanes was writing. This anti-war play expressed Aristophanes' frustration with the prolonged war between Athens and Sparta and the inability of the two sides to reach a peaceful resolution. To appreciate Aristophanes' dramatic choice of having the women force peace by withholding sex, it is important to fully understand the traditional role of women in Greek society at that time. His redefining of the role of women is important to understand since their taking control of the situation and forcing a solution was decidedly not the social norm of the day.

BACKGROUND RESEARCH

The director needs to research all relevant issues related to the play. A thorough and complete understanding of these issues provides answers to questions raised by the play and helps the director frame the context of the play within them. In John Patrick Shanley's play *Doubt*, the head of a Roman Catholic school, an older nun, accuses one of the younger parish priests of inappropriate relations with a young boy. To fully understand this play, the director must be conversant with both the structure and hierarchy of the Roman Catholic Church and the time period, the early 1960s, and especially its impact on the church. The role of the priest and the nun in the parish and the school must be fully understood. For a nun to make such an accusation against a priest during this time was simply unheard-of; if made, the protocol for doing so was strictly defined. Beyond the historical and social period in which the play is set, it is also important that the director understands the changes in the church at this time. A redefining of the church and its role in society, commonly referred to as Vatican II, placed the church in a major state of flux as the old order attempted to adjust to the new. Once this is understood, it is clear why Shanley chose to set his play, about what we do when we are not sure, in the church at this particular time.

In preparing to direct Aaron Sorkin's play *A Few Good Men*, I researched the military, particularly the Marines and the navy. Since the play involves a court-martial, military trial procedure must be understood. Knowledge of the ranks and the relationship between the branches of service is also essential. But it was most important that I develop a sense of being in the military. Following extensive research, I called on a friend, a retired Marine Lieutenant Colonel, to act as technical advisor. He offered considerable insight before I began rehearsals and worked with the cast during the rehearsal process to better enable them to understand their role and relationships. One particular event underscoring the importance of this understanding occurred during a rehearsal of a scene between the base commander, Lt. Col. Jessep, his executive officer, Capt. Markinson, and the platoon leader, 1st Lt. Kendrick. Capt. Markinson has just disagreed with Lt. Col. Jessep in front of 1st Lt. Kendrick. After dismissing Kendrick, Jessep severely reprimands Markinson. It became apparent to me that the actor playing Markinson did not fully understand the situation. I asked him to describe what he thought had just occurred. He responded that the colonel was not open to the ideas of others, and Markinson was frustrated that an idea he felt was superior was summarily rejected. Based on the understanding of the military through my research, I explained that the real issue in this scene was not acceptance of an idea but rather that an officer had openly disagreed with a superior officer in the presence of a junior officer. Military protocol necessitates that superior officers not be publicly questioned. To do so could be cataclysmic in a time of crisis. We returned to the rehearsal with this new understanding and the scene immediately improved.

With Michael Frayn's play *Copenhagen*, a hypothetical reunion between Niels Bohr and Werner Heisenberg concerning the events surrounding the creation of the atomic bomb, it was necessary for me not only to do historical research but also to research the two men, the scientific principles involved, and the other scientists discussed. I passed this information on to the actors so they could understand the context of the play. In addition, in a session I called "Quantum Mechanics for Dummies," a physicist serving as a technical advisor explained the science. While the actors could easily say the words of the script, it was essential they viscerally understood them. When a reviewer indicated she felt the actors not only understood the theories but also personally knew both the science and the other scientists mentioned, thus making their performances even more real for her, we knew we were successful.

Finding an expert in the field can be a valuable source of information into the background needed to understand the play. Extensive reading on topics related to this background can be equally valuable. Regardless of how the director gets this information, it is essential that he or she be able to process it in order to understand the context of the play and to ultimately put it all together in the production.

Early in my directing career I learned a valuable lesson on the importance of an expert when directing *The Runner Stumbles*, a play also involving the Roman Catholic Church. A local priest assisted me as a technical advisor. In this role, he answered my questions as well as those of the cast, and he also attended rehearsals to identify possible problem areas of which we were unaware. One such instance occurred during a rehearsal when the priest leaned over to me and pointed out that a word had been mispronounced. Within the play there is a reference by the monsignor to the priest that he should confine his interests to research and reflection.

The priest replies, "I am not a contemplative man." The advisor allowed that it should be pronounced con·TEM·plative rather than contem·PLA·tive. At the next rehearsal with the advisor I told him I had rechecked the pronunciation and either could be used. He smiled at me and said, "Not if you are a Roman Catholic priest." The valuable lesson I learned was to listen to my experts. I had asked the priest for his advice and counsel and then challenged it.

CHARACTER RESEARCH

Character research involves investigation into the background information that will help clarify the areas discovered during the character section of the script analysis. This may be historical research if the character is based on an actual historical figure, as was the case in *Copenhagen*. In *Copenhagen*, the character research sought not only to understand the men as public figures but also to understand them as people. For example, both Niels Bohr and Werner Heisenberg, aside from being world class physicists, were accomplished skiers and extremely competitive. When the two of them worked together they were known to take ski vacations involving highly competitive runs. The scientists were also apt to play practical jokes and silly games with each other during breaks in the lab. This type of information humanizes the characters and, while not specifically necessary to understand the play, goes a long way toward bringing the characters and their relationship to life. Even if the character is fictitious it is important for the director to understand all aspects of the character, which inevitably involves further research.

PLAYWRIGHT RESEARCH

The greater the understanding of the playwright and his or her work, the more the director can fit the play into context and better understand the playwright's message. As mentioned in Chapter 2, researching playwright Neil Simon reveals that most of his plays are set in the New York City area, and this helps us better understand his plays that are not, such as *Biloxi Blues*. This is one of Neil Simon's autobiographical plays exploring his time in basic training during World War II. By knowing that most of Neil Simon's plays are set in New York, we appreciate how much Simon's alter ego, Jerome, is out of his element. Simon's Jewish ethnicity also plays a significant role in defining the majority of his characters. This understanding leads us to conduct additional background research into the environment of the play that perhaps is overlooked. Many productions of Neil Simon's plays performed outside of New York lack thorough chemistry because the production does not fully embody the regional and ethnic implications found in most of his plays.

Arthur Miller's play *The Crucible* depicts the Salem witch trials and how quickly individuals turn on one another in order to protect themselves, and especially the evils that occur when society seeks to find its security in the condemnation of others. This play is an insightful look into a specific historical period of the American experience. While this is a powerful play in and of itself, without a thorough understanding of the background of the events that led Arthur

Miller to write this play, its full significance is lost. Miller wrote *The Crucible* in 1953 as a response to the McCarthy hearings, a U.S. Senate subcommittee chaired by Joseph McCarthy investigating the infiltration of communism in America during the 1950s. The events of *The Crucible* are based on actual history in colonial America; however, America saw history repeat itself during the McCarthy hearings. While the hearings were officially seeking to find the truth, it soon became apparent that the only way to prove innocence at the McCarthy hearings was to accuse someone else of being a communist. Many lives were destroyed by the accusations made during these hearings. Unless one was willing to name others, the likelihood was condemnation. Miller's anger as a result of this experience is clearly felt in *The Crucible*. An understanding of this context is crucial to understanding the play beyond its historical context.

The director's research seeks to place the play in the context of the playwright's body of work. Shakespeare's *The Tempest* was written at the end of his career. In *The Tempest*, Prospero, the aging Duke and magician, seeks to bring closure to the events of his life. King James, Shakespeare's patron, had an interest in the supernatural. *Macbeth*, written to win King James's favor, involves the supernatural as well. This also explains why Shakespeare, who based the plot of *Macbeth* on actual historical figures, made Banquo an early victim of Macbeth rather than a co-conspirator, since Banquo was a direct predecessor of King James. This is also alluded to by the witches when they predict Banquo will not be king but his heirs will be. Placing the play in relation to other works by the playwright helps us to better understand the play. There may be common themes present or distinct differences that make the play not fit the standard mold of the playwright's body of work.

STYLE RESEARCH

Having identified the style in which the play was written, the director then needs to conduct research into the implications of that style. (See Chapter 4 for a full discussion of style.) If the director is conversant with the particular style of the play, this research becomes less important, but if the director is not familiar with it, such research will be essential to understanding the play in the context in which it was written and how it can be presented. For example, research into Romanticism leads to an understanding of the use of conventions such as asides, where the character speaks his thoughts directly to the audience yet the other characters onstage do not hear them. While an accepted aspect of Romanticism, the use of an aside in Realism would be completely out of place. In delving into the works of Bertolt Brecht, the director needs to understand Brecht's disdain for what he referred to as "Dramatic Theatre," leading to his creation of "Epic Theatre." In *The Modern Theatre Is the Epic Theatre*, Brecht outlines the parameters for this genre, including not allowing the audience to relate to or feel sympathy for the characters, a reliance on narration over action, and the weakening, if not the destruction, of the theatrical illusion.[1] Without an understanding of this style it is extremely difficult to conceive of how to present his plays. Style is a significant issue in determining the production concept and, as such, will be discussed in Chapter 4. If the director is having difficulty categorizing the play in a particular style, research into the play may further assist in making this determination.

FINAL THOUGHTS ON RESEARCH

As noted in Chapter 2, many young directors do not always understand the full value of script analysis; the same can also be said for research. The importance of research cannot be underscored strongly enough in helping to frame a concept. In addition to all the above-mentioned areas of research, any aspect of the play with which the director is not fully conversant needs to be investigated. This may be as simple as looking up the meaning of a word or as complex as putting the play into its correct context. The real difficulty is in knowing what areas to research since the director may think these areas are already understood. The director, fully conversant with the Salem witch trials, may not see the need for extended research before preparing to direct *The Crucible*, but not knowing and fully understanding the events that led Miller to write it will significantly limit the production. An inquisitive nature is a necessity for the director. This is one of the more difficult skills the director must master.

An example from outside of theatre is the famous Beatles song *Let It Be* written by Paul McCartney late in the Beatles' career. Only recently did I learn the reference to "Mother Mary" was a direct reference by Paul to his mother, Mary, whom he lost at age 14. Suddenly, the song takes on a whole new meaning and depth in terms of the origin of the simple mantra, "Let it be." It is in understanding even the simplest references that the playwright's work is fully illuminated. We can never research enough.

> The real difficulty for the director is in knowing what areas to research since he or she may think these areas are already understood.

INTRINSIC AND EXTRINSIC INTERPRETATIONS OF THE PLAY

In considering the play and researching it, the director is examining both intrinsic and extrinsic interpretations, i.e., the internal world of the play (intrinsic) and from outside of the play looking into the world of the play (extrinsic). The director must consider both views to fully understand the play.

John Millington Synge's play *Riders to the Sea* illustrates the two approaches. The play is set in Ireland in the early 1900s. It is a tragedy about a family whose young men have almost all lost their lives at sea. Intrinsically, the play can be explored through the facts discovered in the script analysis: the harshness of the sea and the almost inevitable loss of life. Extrinsically, four factors are essential in this consideration. First, the year the play is set limits the expectations and options of the characters. Second, the play taking place in Ireland during this particular time period inevitably means the characters are devout Roman Catholics. The strength of the characters in their Catholic faith as well as understanding the relationship between Ireland and Catholicism is crucial to the interpretation of the play. Third, knowledge of the customs and folklore must also be considered. For example, the reference to seeing Michael riding on a mare after Michael's death comes from Irish folklore, which includes visions of seeing the dead on horseback. Finally, the relationship Ireland has with the sea plays an equally important role in understanding how inextricably tied the characters' lives are to it. The sea's unforgiving nature combined with the fact that the characters really do not have an alternative is equally crucial.

By looking at a play both internally and externally, significant insight is gained. Extrinsic understanding of the play allows for the realization of the parameters that govern the choices the characters can make and their range of options. It also explains the parameters that define how the play develops and the constraints the environment or other external forces play on the lives and situation of the characters. Directors cannot overlook the importance of extrinsic explorations leading to their interpretation.

HISTORICAL AND SOCIAL IMPLICATIONS IN INTERPRETATION OF THE PLAY

The historical and social implications must also be identified when preparing the production concept. Note that this may overlap with other areas of interpretation. Historical implications refer to more than understanding the period of the play; they refer to the effect on the play's meaning and development. Options or understandings available in the twenty-first century may not be valid in earlier centuries. The director must identify these factors and take them into account.

Social constraints, understandings, and norms must also be considered in the interpretation of the play. For example, the "sexual revolution" of the 1960s was not about the fact that sex and drugs were suddenly discovered, but that they were now openly acknowledged, discussed, and explored. Being able to identify the social implications in the play helps to further establish the parameters and options available to the characters.

The historical and social implications are based both on the information gleaned during the script analysis and from discoveries made during the research phase. They may also result in identifying areas for further research. The analysis, research, and interpretive phases of the director's process may become cyclical. Each time through the process may produce new questions, leading to additional research, and the further development of the production concept. For example, in the initial analysis of *A Few Good Men* the question of military ranks may be identified. Upon research the director discovers not only their meaning but also may have additional questions regarding the relationship that exists between them, leading to further research and more detail in the production concept. This research may uncover the subtle difference between the view of the hierarchy by the Marines at Guantanamo Bay as opposed to that of the navy lawyers in the Judge Advocate General's (JAG) office. This cyclical process continues until research no longer raises questions and the director feels confident to proceed.

DEVELOPING A PRODUCTION CONCEPT FOR THE PLAY

The production concept is the culmination of the director's work in the analysis, research, and interpretive exploration of the play and its world. To proceed with the development of a production concept, the director must feel confident the analysis and research is complete, all issues are thought-out, both internal and external to the play, and all considerations and dynamics in the play are taken into account. The director can now prepare the concept for the production that will be the guiding parameter for everything to follow.

If time allows it can be beneficial to the director to take some time away from the formal analysis and research to allow everything that preceded this moment to gestate, to mature and develop free from active effort. Assuming time is available, this may result in a more significant and insightful concept. However, the planned gestation must not be confused with procrastination.

The production concept is more than a simple statement. It involves the director's understanding of the play, the approach to take to bring it to life, and the parameters to be explored by the designers and the actors. The production concept should define what the production is rather than what it is not. It is acceptable, however, for the production concept to specify certain interpretations or options the director wants to avoid. The main inspiration for the production concept is the director's view of the spine. In essence, the director is creating a vocabulary for communication with the audience. This vocabulary begins with the physical world of the play as created by the designers and then continues with inhabitation by the actors. The production concept creates the context in which the designers and actors work. A sample concept statement is found at the end of the chapter.

The first part of the production concept is a brief statement discussing what the play is about and the director's vision. The statement also gives the priority of the issues the play addresses. For example, *Lysistrata* is a play about the evils of war and the necessity of peace as well as about the empowerment of women and their superiority in handling issues over men. A production concept statement regarding this play needs to address these issues and to place them in order of importance. *Doubt* is really not a play about whether Father Flynn is or is not a child molester; it is a play about how we handle ourselves when we are not sure, when we are in doubt. The play is about its title.

The second part of the production concept describes the world of the play. What type of world does the play imply? What types of images are brought to mind? For example, the world of *Lysistrata* is one dominated by men but where the superior reasoning skills of women allow the men to be easily manipulated. The men crave sex and the women use their control of it to force the men to do their bidding. The women see the futility of the conflict and force the men to find peace.

The final part of the production concept is a statement of how the play is to be produced. It is this vision that will lead the designers in setting parameters for the world they will physically create. It will guide the director's choice during casting and in working with the actors in the creation of their characters. The director may be specific or leave a wider path for the designers and actors to make their choices. Directors are not always consistent in terms of the specificity. When directing Neil LaBute's play *The Shape of Things* I was specific to my designers that the world of the play be relatively sparse, set in a void, and move easily from scene to scene. This vision also included distinct realism for the carefully selected elements of each scene. While originally conceiving the production to be performed in an intimate arena or thrust setting, I soon realized my production concept would not work within such limited space. Moving the play to a proscenium stage allowed the use of mechanical devices to quickly move between scenes. On the other hand, when I directed a collection of David Ives's plays, my production concept involved unifying the collection through some external means; however, I left the discovery of what this would be to my production staff subject to my approval. This artistic license gave the production staff the liberty to develop a very exciting premise.

The concept statement must fully address all issues of the play and serve as a clear guide in making all future decisions, setting the parameters in which the designers and actors will work. A guiding principle I learned from an early mentor in theatre was to consider the cost and effort in terms of its future impact on the audience. For example, if the question is whether it is worth securing more expensive furniture, the answer is would the audience's perception of the play be commensurately increased? If so, proceed, if not, invest the money elsewhere in the production. This maxim also applies to time and energy. Is spending the time rehearsing something worth the effort to the audience's appreciation of the play or would this time and effort be better spent in some other area? It is the production concept that will guide future decisions as to whether something fits into the world of the play or not. It is the foundation on which the production is built.

SAMPLE PRODUCTION CONCEPT FOR WIT

The plot of *Wit* follows Vivian, a distinguished professor of English Literature specializing in the Holy Sonnets of John Donne, through her final treatment for ovarian cancer in a research hospital. While the play covers Vivian's physical journey, the real journey involves her mental and emotional transitions as she comes to grace through her ultimate understanding of her life, realizing she has bypassed human compassion to intensely pursue her academic research. Vivian tells her story through scenes in real time, monologues, and flashbacks. In the process, Vivian compares Donne's search for salvation and an understanding of death with her own current experiences. Running parallel is the exploration of the dehumanizing process that comes during the treatment, compounded by having a former student as one of her physicians. Vivian's relentless search for understanding and truth is compared to that of her medical counterparts, Dr. Kelekian and his research fellow Dr. Posner, and their pursuit of a cure for cancer. Kelekian's wisdom, based on his experience, is contrasted against the brashness of Posner, his young fellow, Vivian's former student, who, like Vivian, eschews human companionship to pursue his research. Humanity is brought back to the play in the person of Vivian's nurse, Susie.

The play is the story of Vivian's journey as she confronts her impending death in a way that is completely different from her academic study of it and comes to fully see the need for human companionship. The play takes place in three realities: the episodes in the hospital, which are cold, brutal, and impersonal; Vivian's monologues directly to the audience, in which we see her true self as it evolves through the play; and Vivian's flashbacks to past key events in her life.

There is a starkness to this play that contrasts the passion of Vivian's exploration of Donne and her teaching of her students with Kelekian and Posner's similar passion for medical research. The three worlds of the play need to contrast sharply. The coldness of the hospital scenes should be amplified by the lighting and costumes. Since Susie is the eye of the storm of Vivian's experience, her costume should reflect this calmness and humanity. Lighting for the monologues should isolate Vivian and create a completely different mood from the hospital depending on the nature of the monologue. The flashback scenes should also be in contrast to the hospital while still conveying the general feeling of the scene and creating the idea that we are in Vivian's memory. The ending of the play should not come as a surprise to anyone but needs to convey her release from the illness having found peace in her life.

RESEARCH LEADING TO A CONCEPT CHECKLIST

- ❏ Areas of Research
  - Production research
  - Period research
    - When was the play written?
    - When is the play set?
  - Background research
  - Character research
  - Playwright research
  - Style research
- ❏ Interpretive Factors
  - Intrinsic factors of the play
  - Extrinsic factors of the play
- ❏ Implications
  - Historical implications of the play
  - Social implications of the play

❐ Production Concept (Expanding on the Spine)
- A description of what the play is about
- A description of the world of the play
- A statement of how the play is to be produced

FURTHER EXPLORATION

1. Using a play you have read, find sources from which you can conduct historical research
   a. to better understand the play as a whole, and
   b. to better understand how the play was previously produced.

2. Research a playwright to see what information would make you better able to direct one of his or her plays.

3. Using a play you have read, make a list of both the intrinsic and extrinsic factors that must be understood in order to interpret the play. Find sources to help you understand these factors.

4. To experiment with the impact of a production concept, explore different ways a single play could be produced.

NOTE

1   "The Modern Theatre Is the Epic Theatre." In Bertolt Brecht, *Brecht on Theatre: The Development of an Aesthetic*, 13th ed., trans. and ed. John Willett (New York: Hill and Wang, 1977), 33–42.

CHAPTER 4

Style

WHAT IS STYLE?

The term *style* is one of the most often used and least understood terms in theatre. It is further confused by the fact that it can refer to many different concepts. Style and genre are often used interchangeably. A style groups together works of art based on similar conventions. Think of style like a mailbox in a mailroom. Each mailbox is assigned to an individual based on assumed needs. When a letter arrives addressed to "John Smith," it is placed in the mailbox labeled "John Smith." When a letter arrives for "Mr. Smith," since there is only one box labeled "Smith," an assumption is made to place it in the "John Smith" mailbox. But suppose a letter arrives addressed to "Director." This letter does not clearly fit the criteria for any existing box, but since John Smith is the director, the letter is placed in his box. However, when a letter arrives for "Designer," a new mailbox must be created because it does not fit anyone who currently has a box. Over time, the "designer" box may be subdivided into "scenic designer," "lighting designer," and "costume designer." The number of mailboxes gradually increases as time goes by and different needs are identified.

The creation of labels regarding style follows a similar path. In the earliest stages of an art form there may be little reason to subdivide the discipline, but as artists take decidedly different approaches to the same art form, inevitably each approach is labeled. A style is created. The name for the style was probably not chosen by the artists but rather by external forces, most likely the critics or scholars discussing the work. These critics or scholars fit the artist's work into a style based on common characteristics. This is essentially an arbitrary labeling system with certain value judgments applied. As time progresses, the boundary line defining what fits into a particular style becomes increasingly blurred since there are differences in every work of art that seems to fit the style. The stylistic definition is based on the core values for conventions of the art form. At some point the critics and scholars subdivide the style to allow for a cleaner definition of what fits into it.

Labeling may or may not influence artists. They may follow or emulate other artists or decidedly disagree with the labeling of their work. Eugène Ionesco, considered by many to be one of the great Absurdist playwrights, despised this categorization. He preferred to think of his plays as Existential. Perhaps the only playwright who created the term for his own style, defined the style's parameters, and then wrote within this self-proclaimed style was Bertolt Brecht. Brecht referred to his style as *Epic Theatre*. He wrote a brief treatise explaining how his vision of Epic Theatre was different from what he referred to as Dramatic Theatre, and established the guidelines for the new style.

Placing a work into a given style is based on its similarities to other works. The maxim "If it walks like a duck, swims like a duck, and quacks like a duck, then it must be a duck" can be used to determine a stylistic label. If the work is decidedly different a new style will inevitably evolve through use by scholars, critics, and artists.

So what is the value of even thinking about style? Stylistic differentiation provides a vocabulary to refer to a body of work with certain similarities and an understanding of those similarities. For example, when referring to an animal as a cat there is an understanding that breeds of cats are different but all have characteristics that unite them under the term "cat." Cats and dogs are two distinct species despite their similarities. It is a common body of differences that separate them. Referring to an art form as fitting into a given style establishes certain basic elements based on knowledge of other works in the style and this establishes or invokes a shared understanding and a vocabulary that can be used. It is not identical to the other works nor should appreciation of the work be limited based on the stylistic label. Ultimately, it is the work of art that is appreciated; the style becomes far less important.

Plays can be divided into a variety of styles or genres, the parameters of which are defined by critics and scholars. This label does not necessarily define the play in its entirety or how it should be produced, but it does allow certain expectations. I recall the utter shock of a friend of mine on seeing the film musical *Evita*. He went expecting a musical but was astonished there was no dialogue, only songs. I smiled broadly at his reaction, but nonetheless it was a genuine reaction caused by his expectations based on his understanding of the style, in this case, musicals. When the musical *Hair* was written, a new stylistic term was created: "Rock Musical." In reality, *Hair* essentially followed the principles that defined musical theatre with the exception of the use of rock music. The style of music in any musical is highly influenced by and reflects the style of contemporary music of its time period. Stylistic determinations are not always logical, but understanding the qualities that divide different theatrical styles assists the director in making preliminary assumptions about a given play and presents an initial direction for its interpretation.

THE ORIGIN OF THEATRICAL STYLES

There were periods of time when style referred to a required structure within which the playwright must create the play. The French neoclassic period was characterized by a number of conventions playwrights were expected to follow. The Hellenistic Greeks created the first major style definitions as guidelines for plays to be submitted to the festivals: comedy, tragedy, and the satyr play. The satyr play passed out of existence soon after the Greek era. Each of the plays had similar conventions including the use of a chorus and the construction of the dialogue, but they were separated by expected structural differences. In the broadest sense, the terms comedy and tragedy continue to be used as the initial division of plays into styles.

The terms *presentational* and *representational* can be used as broad categories to begin defining style. A third term, *ritual*, describes the plays prior to the Greeks. Examining each of the three terms in the order they evolved helps in understanding these divisions.

Ritual Theatre describes the performances of mankind's earliest descendants. These performances are largely known through the paintings found in caves such as those in Lascaux, France. Their purpose was ceremonial; they were not for entertainment. They were aimed at ritualistically celebrating successes in hunting or battle or as an attempt to bring about fertility, good weather, good harvest, hunts, and the like. While not specifically aimed at performance, they embodied the basic elements considered in performance today: an audience, actors telling the story, and the use of music and costumes. While Ritual Theatre spawned other forms, such as the works of Antonin Artaud, it is still found in the present day, particularly in religious services and ceremonies.

Keep in mind that all stylistic determinations are essentially subjective. The director should not attempt to use them as rules but rather as guides to understanding the play.

The Greeks are credited with the first major theatrical revolution. With their introduction of *Presentationalism*, the basic structure of Ritual Theatre became more formalized with written scripts and an increased focus on the audience. In *Presentational Theatre*, the purpose of the performance is to entertain the audience while delivering a message. The use of costumes, music, scenery, and special effects are also part of this new form. Typical conventions of this style readily acknowledge the audience with techniques that include the aside, a character speaking directly to the audience yet the others onstage do not hear, and the soliloquy, the expression of inner thoughts by a character alone on the stage directly to the audience. These conventions are accepted parts of this style. The language typically found in Presentational Theatre is heightened, often more poetic, and is meant to convey emotion rather than conversation. Presentational Theatre is perhaps best exemplified by musical theatre. In this style characters bursting into song and dance are freely accepted as a convention of the genre.

The second and, to date, last theatrical revolution introduced *Representational Theatre*. This revolution occurred at the end of the nineteenth century with the advent of a new literary style for theatre, *Realism*. In this new style characters speak and behave just as they would in actual life. The audience is essentially looking in, observing behavior much like a scientist observes the behavior of animals from a blind. The term "the fourth wall" was created, referring to the removal of the theoretical fourth wall from the room separating the audience from the actors, allowing for the audience's observation of the play. The main thrust of this style is to create realistic behavior and situations so the audience can analyze and react to the choices made by the characters. Representational Theatre remains very much a part of theatre to the present day.

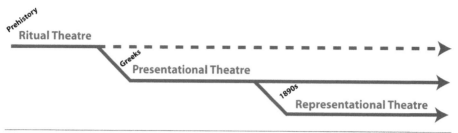

Figure 4.1 Theatrical Stylistic Revolutions

The three revolutions are illustrated by the chart in Figure 4.1. Note that after each revolution the remaining style or styles continue through to the present day; however, Ritual Theatre has a limited existence following the presentational revolution. Both presentational and representational forms of theatre continue to the present day with each producing new styles within their parameters.

MODERN THEATRICAL STYLES

The evolution of theatrical styles grew out of the presentational revolution; the Greeks created the first style categories of comedy and tragedy. Beginning in the eighteenth century, the early style prevalent in Presentationalism was *Romanticism*. This style was characterized by ornate language and more sweeping plot lines. The acting style emphasized grand gesture and great oratory.

Representationalism, commencing in the late 1890s with the advent of a new literary style, *Realism*, and epitomized in theatre by the works of Anton Chekhov, August Strindberg, and Henrik Ibsen, strove to depict life faithfully. *Realism* focused on the choices made by the characters as a result of their actions. The dialogue was lifelike with believable situations. As Realism continued to develop, *Naturalism* came into being. Like Realism, Naturalism used real-life dialogue and attempted to portray life realistically, but it was further characterized by the extension of reality and the focus on the impact of the environment in limiting the choices open to the characters. This was in contrast to the free will typically explored in Realism. In production, Naturalism often created a hyper-Realism on the stage.

An artistic reaction to the real-life depictions in Realism created a new set of genres and a return to a presentational format. These styles rebelled against Realism, feeling that Realism limited the creative expression of the artist by simply trying to re-create life. These anti-realistic styles are often referred to as *Isms*, denoting the last three letters in their names. The first of these is *Expressionism*. In Expressionism, reality was distorted to emphasize that the truth lies within man. This style was influenced by mechanization in the early to mid-part of the twentieth century, and industrial themes are often found within Expressionism. Following the destruction from the world wars and the unthinkable power of the atomic age, a new style evolved, *Absurdism*. Absurdism explored the breakdown in communication mankind was experiencing and mankind's attempt to rationalize its existence in a world seemingly gone mad while at the same time trying to find, unsuccessfully, meaning in life and the ability to express it. Closely related to this is *Existentialism*, which grew out of a philosophical movement of the same name. Existentialists emphasized the existence of the free individual determining his or her own destiny. Many of the great existential philosophers were also noted existential playwrights such as Jean-Paul Sartre and Samuel Beckett. Existentialism and Absurdism are closely related and significantly overlap in many definitions. Also developing as a style during the early to mid-1900s was the aforementioned *Epic Theatre* of Bertolt Brecht. This style seeks to both separate the audience from the performance, reminding them that they are observing a play and are not allowed to develop sympathies for the characters, and to motivate the audience to take action against the injustices depicted in the play.

Perhaps the most significant development within Presentationalism was that of musical theatre, which evolved from its European operatic roots. Just as in opera, musical theatre is highly presentational, relying on new versions of conventions such as soliloquies and asides and turning them into songs. The sweeping tales in the musical are told not only through dialogue but also song and dance. Musical theatre remains a major component of theatre and, perhaps, the greatest contemporary example of Presentational Theatre.

Artists from other disciplines such as fine art and music will quickly notice the similarity theatrical styles have with their own. In fact, the evolution of theatrical styles, with the possible exception of Epic Theatre, follows that of styles across the art world. Presentational styles such as Existentialism and Absurdism reflect even more fully their philosophical counterparts.

DETERMINING THE STYLE OF THE PLAY

As previously noted, the director needs to determine the style of the play as part of the script analysis. This task can be accomplished through research and by an analysis of the play's structure. It is possible the director can identify the style of a well-known play by researching critics' writings. While this may be helpful, the real purpose in determining the style is to understand the implications suggested by that categorization. For this reason, it is well worth the director's time to see not only how conventional wisdom categorizes the style of the play but also to personally determine what elements indicate this style. It is of no use for the director to identify a play as being in a certain style if there is no understanding of the implications of that determination.

Beyond looking into what others have written, the director can determine the play's style by analyzing its structure as well as the conventions used to communicate its message. The first step is to analyze the dialogue to determine if it is realistic. Is it written in the vernacular? Is the plot line lifelike? If the answers are yes, then the play probably fits into Realism. On the other hand, if the dialogue is not in the vernacular, the situations are overextended, and the play makes use of conventions not seen in life (for example, an aside), then the play fits more into the world of Presentationalism.

To make finer distinctions in the style, the director can attempt to ascertain if the play fits that of known styles and the implications of that style in terms of the production. Certain production styles are frequently associated with a literary style. The more experience the director has in theatre criticism and theory, the better able the director is to make these determinations. The director's most important decision is to decide how the world of the play can be perceived and subsequently communicated. The director starts with determining whether the play is presentational or representational and then looks for similarities that characterize the given style. For directors not fully conversant with theatrical styles, the definition initially can be limited to presentational or representational and further clarified with descriptions of the elements of the play.

> It is far more important to determine the elements of a play that provide insight to its style than simply to label it.

STYLE VS. MODE

Having identified the literary style of the play, the director now establishes the production style. The process is complicated by yet another use of the word "style." To clarify this process, I prefer to use *style* to refer to how the play is written and *mode* to refer to the style of the production, i.e., how the play is presented, and will continue this usage throughout.

The obvious assumption is that for each literary style there is a corresponding theatrical mode, and to some degree this is true. For example, when presenting a play in the style of Epic Theatre, there are certain performance mode traditions that apply. The director should be familiar with the standard aspects of the performance mode often associated with the style. However, the director should keep in mind that there are no rules to presenting a play. The selection of the mode as part of the production concept is based on how the director wishes to communicate the play.

The following example can be used to clarify mode. A person traveling abroad does not speak the country's language, needs directions, and stops a local person on the street for help. If the two cannot communicate in the country's native tongue, they may see if they have a common second language. Once a means of communication is established, the process of asking questions can begin. The selection of a language to communicate is the same process as determining the mode. Until the audience understands the method of communication, the message cannot be expressed. The audience enters the theatre with certain expectations of communication. An example in simple theatrical parlance is, once the houselights dim, the audience expects the show to begin. If the show begins beforehand, the audience will, at least initially, be confused as their expectations are not being met. The more conversant the audience is with the nature of the play, the more they will expect certain performance conventions to be present. The mode chosen must keep the expectations of the audience in mind whether the director intends to follow them or not. The man shocked by the lack of dialogue in *Evita* was expecting the standard conventions of musical theatre to apply, in this case, dialogue. When he did not experience it, he was distanced from the production. This does not mean the director has to give the audience what they envisage. Rather, it means the director needs to understand their expectations and help them make the transition to the method of communication used.

As a young college student, I had the opportunity to attend a performance of the Liquid Theatre in New York City. My exposure to theatre was previously limited to fairly traditional productions, and I was totally unprepared for the experience I was about to have. The performance was in the Guggenheim Museum rather than in a theatre. The play began with the audience meeting in one of the galleries where the cast, dressed in essentially the same type of clothing as the audience, started to play theatre games. It was impossible to separate the audience from the performers. I was so startled and intimidated by the bold performance style I nervously found an exit. Not until several years later did I understand the experimental qualities of the Liquid Theatre and realize the opportunity I missed. Using my reaction as an example, the production did not reach an understanding with me as to how to comprehend the conventions of the performance. If this was the standard reaction of the audience one would say the fault lies with the production, but since it was not, the fault was mine. The director can either fulfill the audience's expectations or move away from them depending on the reaction sought. Breaking the audience's expectations must be carefully considered by the director.

DETERMINING THE MODE FOR THE PRODUCTION

The director needs to determine how to frame the production concept while keeping in mind the expectations of the audience and utilizing these expectations to help communicate the play. While it may be consistent to employ a production mode that directly matches the literary style, it is not necessarily the best option. A contrasting mode might emphasize the play better than a matching mode.

In their 1986 production of *Rhinoceros* by Eugène Ionesco, directed by Kazimierz Braun, the Guthrie Theater chose a unique mode to convey what is generally considered an Absurdist play. Ionesco explores the subject of conformity, a standard theme of Absurdism, emphasizing the banality of a situation and particularly the inability to effectively communicate. In this play, a small French town is suddenly overrun by rhinoceroses. Massive destruction and loss of life ensues; however, the townspeople are more concerned with issues such as whether the rhinoceroses are Asian or African rather than whether this is possible or why this is happening. Typically, when this play is produced, the mode seeks to reflect the "absurdity" of the play. The rhinoceroses are usually highly stylized, often portrayed by actors wearing headdresses. For the Guthrie production, the decision was made to accent the key issue of the characters' acceptance of the existence of the rhinoceroses by contrasting the absurdity of the play with a realistic production mode. The designers carefully studied rhinoceroses and produced lifelike models of rhinoceroses that would then be automated to run across the stage or smash the walls. The idea was to place the audience in the same world of the characters rather than as observers. This is an example of using a decidedly contrasting mode in order to best communicate the style of the play.

Disney's first two Broadway productions further exemplify the use of mode. In its first Broadway play, *Beauty and the Beast*, the director, Robert Jess Roth, chose a mode that sought to duplicate the imagery of the animated film on the stage. While specifics of the costumes and scenery changed, the look was essentially the same.

In contrast, for *The Lion King*, their second production, the director, Julie Taymor, took a completely different approach. Taymor chose to abandon the look of the animated film and to create an altogether different mode. This decision took into account that almost the entire cast is made up of animals. Taymor chose to utilize masks and puppets inspired by African tribal themes. She further stylized the movement of these masks and puppets into the choreography and staging. The decision to have the actors' faces clearly shown below the mask but having the actors play to the mask created a unique world that blended fantasy and reality.

While both of these Disney stage productions were inspired by Disney animated films, in each case the director chose a completely different mode to bring the story to life on the stage. In the same way, having interpreted a script, the director can choose from several possible modes to present the play. The obvious mode is not necessarily the best choice.

In looking for a mode, the director needs to take into consideration not only the essence of the story and the message of the play but also how the audience will experience and relate to them. The mode must work for both the nature of the dialogue and the action. Considerations may include:

- How the set and costumes are structured
- How the lighting appears compared to nature
- How the characters interact as compared to lifelike situations
- Whether acting conventions are employed (e.g., asides or soliloquies)
- Whether the actors acknowledge the presence of the audience.

Once the mode is chosen it will determine the parameters for the creation of the production. The mode determines the conventions that will be used and must be consistently maintained. For example, if the director chooses a realistic mode, such as naturalistic dialogue without acknowledging the presence of the audience, all elements of the production must follow suit. If later in the play a nonrealistic convention is inserted, such as a character speaking directly to the audience, the audience will be pulled from the otherwise realistic mode and have to process this decidedly presentational technique. On the other hand, the director may choose to use this contrasting convention to deliberately dissociate the moment from the remainder of the play. In this case, the director chooses a risky option, since in selecting a disparate moment there is a risk of losing the audience's understanding and focus. Another example is to break "the fourth wall" and have actors move into the audience's space. While this can be a very dynamic element of staging, it must be consistent with the overall mode of the production and not arbitrarily inserted for effect or convenience. All elements of the production need to fit within the framework of the mode. Decisions to deviate from the mode must be carefully and consciously thought through.

The mode not only applies to the environment created by the designers but also to the style with which the actors create their characters. If the actors create their characters through contrasting conventions that do not fit into the same mode, the audience will have difficulty understanding the play. The director must ensure that every element of the production is consistent with the mode. The world of the production is its "universe." There can be only one universe for the play. If elements of the play, including the approaches of the actors, are inconsistent with that universe they will appear incorrect.

It is the mode that establishes a vocabulary with the audience. The audience becomes accepting of this world as the production progresses. To understand each new element or theatrical convention, the audience uses the vocabulary of the production as a tool to process this element. For example, if two people are having a conversation in English and one arbitrarily inserts French words, the other one will be momentarily separated from the conversation or perhaps completely confused. It is consistency that provides the means to communicate new concepts to the audience. Japanese Kabuki theatre has a tradition of having individuals dressed in black move scenic elements. It is understood by the audience that their black attire indicates they are not part of the scene; while they are fully lit and in plain view, the audience ignores their presence. Westerners in their initial exposure to Kabuki often find this to be distracting. However, as the production progresses Westerners grow to understand and accept it.

The director must critically evaluate every choice in the production to ensure it is consistent with the mode. The mode is a tool for communicating the director's concept to the designers and actors as well as a tool to evaluate the specific choices made.

> The world of the production is its "universe." All elements including design choices and actor approaches must fit into this universe in order to allow the audience to fully understand and appreciate the play.

FURTHER EXPLORATION

1. Choose a play for which you have a solid understanding and identify as precisely as possible the literary style based on its content. Research may help ascertain how most critics identified this style.

2. Once you have chosen the style of the play in Activity 1, identify possible modes with which this play could be produced. Having selected a number of possible modes, decide which mode provides the best method to communicate the play as you understand it.

3. After viewing a play:
   a. determine the style of the play and the mode with which it was produced.
   b. critique how well the mode fits your perception of the style. How effective was the mode in communicating the style to the audience?
   c. consider how consistently the mode was implemented.

PART II

The Production Staff

C H A P T E R   5

Working with the Production Staff

THE ROLE OF THE DESIGNERS

Having completed the analysis phase with a solid understanding of the script and a planned mode to communicate the play to the audience consistent with the director's understanding of the spine, the director is now ready to enter the preproduction phase. As such, it is vital for the director to understand fully the individual and combined contributions of the designers. It is in this phase that the director begins working with the designers on the planning of the production. The designers are crucial since they create the world of the play. It is vital for the director to understand fully the individual and combined contributions of the designers. The director needs to see the concept of the design as a single contribution even though it is created by a number of individuals.

Robert Edmond Jones, a famous American designer from the early part of the twentieth century, referred to the designer's contribution as the creation of the "envelope." This idea is perhaps the best place to begin to understand the designer's contribution. Most mail is contained in an envelope, an everyday item that is usually overlooked and yet serves several significant purposes. An envelope provides an important physical function; it contains and protects the contents. When looking at the envelope certain assumptions are made. If it is a formal business envelope with a typed address, the assumption is its contents are business related. If the envelope looks personal and has a handwritten address, the assumption is quite different. The return address provides additional information to be used in making assumptions about

Figure 5.1
Robert Edmond Jones

the contents. The size and shape of the envelope creates parameters as to the contents, with physical, intellectual, and emotional expectations. The initial expectations about the contents of the letter are made before opening the envelope; however, once the envelope is open these expectations are replaced with the reality of the actual contents. The envelope no longer has significance. In most cases, the expectations based on the envelope are met. Where the expectations are not met, the surprise will either be welcome or not depending on the perception of the recipient. For example, if the expectation is a personal letter and there is only a bill, the recipient is not happy. The envelope can have such a strong impact that it may never be opened due to the assumption of its contents based on the envelope alone.

The production's design serves essentially the same functions as the envelope. The design is the audience's first contact with the play, and their initial opinions about the production will be based on what they see just as the initial opinion about the contents of the letter was framed by the envelope. The design provides the physical environment for the production. This environment establishes the parameters in which the action takes place. For example, a small setting limits the space available for the action and creates tight parameters for staging. The time period of the costumes is one of the strongest indicators to the audience of when the action takes place. Light on only a portion of the stage limits the action to this area and focuses the audience's attention on it. The expectations established by the design lead the audience into the world of the play. If the play subsequently does not meet these expectations, much like a disappointed reaction to the contents of the envelope, the audience may be disenchanted or perhaps confused. While the design is an important part of theatre it is not why the audience comes. Ultimately, it is the message of the play that matters and determines how the audience reacts to the production. No matter how significant the contribution of the design environment is to the production, without the portrayal of the characters telling the story, the play cannot exist. On the other hand, without the contribution of the design, the play may be lackluster and harder to understand. While the individual designers in each area create smaller portions of the overall environment, collectively they create the entire environment. For this reason, the director must ensure that all aspects of the design work cohesively in the creation of the total world of the play.

The designers create an important premise for the play. Their work will set opportunities and necessary limitations for the staging, and therefore it is imperative that the director maximizes their contributions to set the stage for the rest of the production. While changes in the designs can be made after working with the actors, these changes are at best difficult and costly, and more often not possible. For this reason, it is important that the vision of the director be clearly communicated to the designers, and the director must make certain before proceeding with the production that the designs do, in fact, fully meet his or her concept as well as the needs of the play.

THE DIRECTOR'S RELATIONSHIP WITH THE DESIGNERS

Aside from the director's possible work with the playwright, the work with the designers is the earliest part of the collaborative process in the production. The director will work with the designers sooner and far longer than with the actors. Many beginning directors find their relationship with designers to be far more awkward than their relationship with the actors. This is most likely because a majority of beginning directors have a greater understanding of acting than they have of design. The director should not feel this way. The director's work with and responsibility to the designers as well as the director's dependence on them is exactly the same as with the actors. The difference is the nature of the work. The ideal structure of this relationship is perhaps best exemplified by the "Dream Team" created in the 1970s. The Dream Team referred to the working relationship of director Michael Bennett, scenic designer Robin Wagner, costume designer Theoni V. Aldredge, and lighting designer Tharon Musser who began their collaborative work on Michael Bennett's *A Chorus Line*. Following *A Chorus Line*, the production team continued to work together, actually securing common studio space so they could continue the production planning process and have immediate contact with one another. From a director's perspective, such a close working relationship allows the director to be part of the evolution of the designs from initial creation through to final product. While this close and special relationship is not necessarily typical of all director/designer relationships, it does illustrate the ideal and underscores the importance and benefits of having a close working relationship. Many directors develop relationships with a design team and whenever possible work with them.

Before discussing how the director can best work with the design team, an understanding of the basic contributions of each designer as well as their collective contribution to the production needs to be established.

CONTRIBUTIONS OF THE DESIGNERS

The scenic designer is responsible for the creation of the overall physical environment. This environment provides the audience with the necessary information needed to understand the play. This may include the location, the time period, the environment, and the socioeconomic status of the inhabitants. The scenic designer creates both the floor plan and the visual look of the setting. Typically, the setting conveys both the style and the mood of the play, establishing the context for the other designs. While it has the most dominant impact on style and mood, it is also the least changeable during the performance. Therefore, it is important that the setting encompasses the full range of the mood. It is not enough to have different looks; *how* the setting changes from one look to another is just as important. The director needs to work with the scenic designer in planning these transitions *before* the design is complete since the nature of these transitions will impact not only the cost and complexity of the setting but potentially the overall look. The setting may need to be modified to accommodate the ability to shift the scenery between scenes. The time it takes for the transitions to occur and the impact on the audience are a significant factor in the overall movement and flow of the action of the production. A production's otherwise good tempo can be ruined by slow scene shifts, particularly if there are numerous changes. As noted in Chapter 3, despite my initial intent for a small intimate production, I chose to move my production of *The Shape of Things* to a proscenium theatre to facilitate the numerous shifts. The resulting design incorporated a revolving stage that allowed each scene to rotate into view quickly either carrying the actors into their location or allowing them to walk into it.

Equally important, the setting creates the floor plan that will determine the nature of the stage pictures and the blocking. Once the floor plan is created the parameters for the blocking are also established. The director's relationship to the floor plans will be further discussed in Chapter 10. The floor plan not only provides the opportunity for the staging, it also defines its limitations. This mechanical concern of how the setting provides for the action is one of the most crucial preproduction decisions. While subtle changes may be made in the floor plan during rehearsals, it is quite possible that major changes will not be workable. As such, the importance of the decisions regarding the setting cannot be overstated. The designer communicates the scenic design to the director through a combination of views that generally include a rendering or scenic model as well as a floor plan or plans showing the overhead view of the setting and the location and dimensions of its elements (see Figures 5.2, 5.3, and 5.4). It is imperative that the director carefully review these plans and the rendering to be sure of the overall look as well as the floor plan.

Notice how the overall look of the setting in *Richard III* (Figure 5.5) captures the whimsical spirit of Shakespeare's play while transporting the play to a post-apocalyptic future. The setting also accommodates numerous playing areas as well as a great deal of open space for

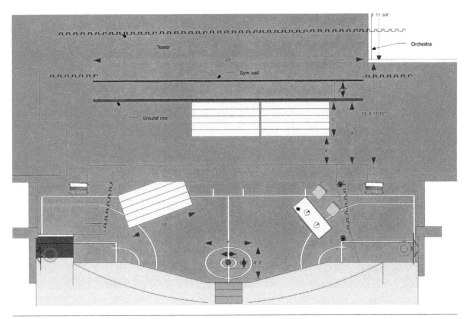

Figure 5.2 Floor Plan for *The 25ᵗʰ Annual Putnam County Spelling Bee*
Scenic Design by Doug Mackenzie. Courtesy of Doug Mackenzie

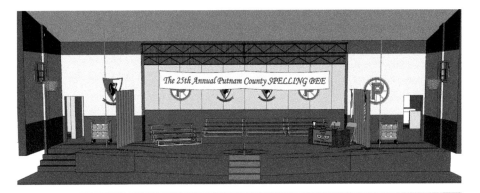

Figure 5.3 Rendering for *The 25ᵗʰ Annual Putnam County Spelling Bee*
Scenic Design by Doug Mackenzie. Courtesy of Doug Mackenzie

staging. In this way the setting becomes somewhat of a "play scape" for the actors under the guidance of the director.

If the work of the scenic designer is best at showing the overall play, the work of the costume designer is best at showing the nature of the individual characters. Through the costume design each character is set in time and space. It also helps establish the age, social status or position, and the personality of each character. Since costumes can be readily changed, they

Figure 5.4 *The 25ᵗʰ Annual Putnam County Spelling Bee*
Scenic Design by Doug Mackenzie. Courtesy of Drury University

Figure 5.5 Scenic Design for *Richard III*
Scenic Design by Chuck Rogers. Courtesy of Drury University

reflect changes within the character either by full costume changes or by simple modifications. For example, the evolution of a character within the scene can be accented by the actor removing his jacket, loosening his tie, and rolling up his sleeves. In addition to being able to capture the individuality of each character, the costume design as a whole also helps create the time period, location, overall mood, and style of the show. It is important that the director communicate with the costume designer both the intended physical needs of the costume, such as pockets, and the nature of the action of the actor wearing the costume. It is critical that the needs be met in the costume design rather than having to either modify the costumes or change the staging at a later date. Since the designs are usually completed prior to casting, the costume design provides the initial embodiment of the characters as conceived by the director. While the director may keep the costume designs in mind during casting, it is possible the costume designs may need to be modified after the cast is selected. The costume designer communicates the design through renderings. These will also serve as inspiration for the actors. While it does not always occur, it is also possible that the costume designs will be modified based on the actors' creation of their characters. Figure 5.6 shows the designer's intent for three of the costumes for a production of *Doubt*.

In the photograph in Figure 5.7 of a production of *She Stoops to Conquer*, the overall style of the production is clearly embodied in the costumes. In this case, the director wished to stage Oliver Goldsmith's comedy from the late eighteenth century in a fusion of style combining the original period with the 1980s. Mrs. Hardcastle's dress couples the period style of the eighteenth century in overall line by utilizing, for example, panniers, while at the same time utilizing the length and interior lines of the 1980s.

The major function of the lighting designer is to provide visibility for the production. Without the lighting designer's work the show would be in the dark. But more important, the lighting designer provides selective visibility. The lighting designer focuses the attention of the audience where the director wants it to be while reducing attention on the other areas. The best illustration of this is a single spotlight on an actor. Since all else is dark, the audience naturally looks at the actor. This same principle can be applied by making one actor brighter on a fully lit stage. The audience's attention is naturally drawn to the brightest location. The use of follow spots in musical theatre is a good example of this principle. The lighting also has one of the most profound impacts on the perception of the mood of the scene. Throughout our lives the nature of light affects our mood. When thinking of a romantic setting, we think of soft lighting reminiscent of a candle. If the same scene were placed in a brightly lit setting more reminiscent of fluorescent lighting, the mood would be much harder to create. Since lighting can be changed simply and quickly during a show, it is ideal to be able to sculpt the mood of each scene by either subtly or not so subtly changing the lighting. Changes in focus can be rapidly accomplished in the same way. Lighting also provides necessary information for the scene. In the case of an exterior setting, the approximate time of day can be told by the nature of the lighting. Once again, since the lighting is easily changeable, the transition in time can be perceived. The basic nature of the lighting also helps explain the location based on an assumption of qualities of light that typically exist in different settings. For example, the light in a living room is different from the light in an office. Lighting also allows us to see the

Figure 5.6 Costume Renderings for *Doubt*

Costume Design and Renderings by Madison Spencer. Courtesy of Madison Spencer

Figure 5.7 Costume Design for *She Stoops to Conquer*

Costume Design by Madison Spencer. Courtesy of Drury University

three-dimensional quality of the actors, the setting, and the costumes by creating highlights and shadows. This effect will be highly dependent on the lighting designer's use of angle and focus to reveal the texture and shape of people and objects. Since the lighting is highly dependent on the setting and the costumes, it is often completed after the other areas. Unfortunately, this often means that the lighting designer is not brought in until the setting and costumes are finalized. This prevents the lighting designer from having creative input during the initial development of design ideas. For this reason, the director should be sure to include the lighting designer in all preliminary discussions. One of the greatest challenges the lighting designer has is communicating the design to the director and the other designers. While drawings are possible, the difficulty in capturing the highlight and shadow within each scene often makes this a less viable tool. Modern computer applications provide the possibility of computer visualization of the lighting, but this also has some limitations. The actual lighting design is conveyed through a drafted plan (see Figure 5.8).

It is important that the director be absolutely clear with the lighting designer in terms of what is wanted or needed to be sure these can be accommodated once the lights are hung and colored since the lighting designer's actual creation of the looks for each scene must be made quickly during the technical rehearsals just prior to opening. A director waiting until technical

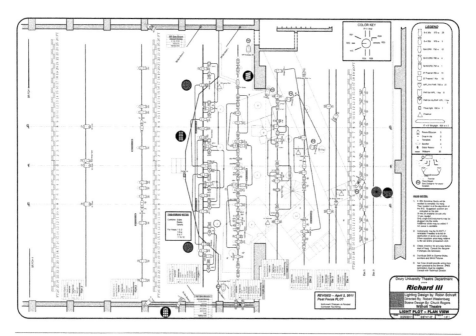

Figure 5.8 Light Plot for *Richard III*

Lighting Design by Robin Schraft

rehearsals to ask the lighting designer for a specific look, such as a blue wash, runs the risk that the designer is unable to accommodate the request since the light hang will not provide for it. Had the director made this need known during preproduction, the lighting designer could have provided for the specific request in the light hang. By the end of the production process the director often forms a unique relationship with the lighting designer due to their extremely close work during the technical rehearsals.

Figure 5.9 is a photograph from a production of *Richard III*. The lighting, coupled with smoke and haze, assists in creating the energy and frenetic feeling of the climactic battle sequence leading to the defeat of Richard. Note how Richard, wearing a long black coat, is visually accented in whiter light compared to the remaining troops.

The newest of the design fields is sound. Even though the use of sound is one of the oldest technical considerations in theatre dating back to the Greeks, the practice of having a separate sound designer is far more recent. Unlike the other designers, the sound designer works with a medium that cannot be visually represented. Since the entire design is heard rather than seen, the sound designer's collaboration with the director is different from that of the other designers. The sound designer typically contributes three areas: mechanical support so the actors can be heard through the use of microphones on the stage and/or on the actors; music that underscores scenes or facilitates transitions; and the sound effects either directly called for in the script or others that enhance the mood. While it is easy to think of sound designers as providing purely functional support, the director needs to think of the sound designer's contribution as

Figure 5.9 Lighting Design for *Richard III*

Lighting Design by Robin Schraft. Courtesy of Drury University

equal to those of the other designers. The choice of music creates specific feelings that can greatly enhance the perception of the scene by the audience. Even in the choice of mechanical sounds, such as doorbells, the sound designer reinforces the mood of the show. In this way, the contributions of the sound designer directly impact the overall perception of the show far beyond the mechanical information.

While each area of design provides for different needs, the designs combine to produce the overall look of the production. The combined impact of all the design areas reinforces the style and mood of the play and provides the necessary information the audience needs to understand it. It is important for the director to be aware of the impact the designers have in creating this environment as a whole as well as the individual aspects that each designer contributes.

COLLABORATION

Theatre is a collaborative art. No single artist can produce a theatrical production. A number of years ago I attended a meeting in the studio of a friend of mine who is both a production manager and lighting designer. On his desk was a photograph of a group of people surrounding Patrick Stewart. When I asked about the photograph he told me it was the production staff for Patrick Stewart's "one-man" show, *A Christmas Carol*. The "one-man" referred to Patrick Stewart playing all the roles not that the entire production was mounted by one person, as seen by the number of people in the photograph. All theatre artists acknowledge their work is intertwined and interdependent with the work of the other artists on the production.

Unfortunately, collaboration is too often seen as a necessary evil in which one must participate to produce theatre. I remember a director sarcastically saying the role of the director was to finely analyze and conceive a show leading to a carefully crafted production concept only to watch others mess it up. While attending a theatre conference some time ago it seemed no matter the topic of the session, somehow the discussion swung to collaboration and the problems of having to work with people who did not share your vision. Finally, an older man pointed out that this discussion of collaboration reminded him of the way collaboration was defined during World War II. During the war, a collaborator was a person who "aided and abetted the enemy." It was interesting to think that at this conference, collaboration was in fact being considered as working with the enemy. These two stories do not represent what collaboration should be. However, in too many cases there is a failure to establish a productive collaborative process. This poorly formed environment results in one of three forms of collaboration: *Defensive collaborators* are those who collaborate with their colleagues to protect their area of the production. Their interest in the work of others is solely to protect the quality of their own work. *Offensive or need-based collaborators* are those who collaborate for the opposite reason. They are collaborating to get what they need in the production. They acknowledge that their art is dependent on the work of others and must collaborate to get their work done. *Puppeteer collaborators* are those who see collaboration solely as the execution of their vision. They see the other artists on the production team simply in terms of being able to carry out their vision.

Theatre is not just collaborative because it has to be; collaboration defines theatre as an art form. It is this reliance on collaboration that makes theatre a unique art form. Directors need to embrace collaboration to achieve a final product even greater than they originally envisioned.

While all too often collaboration degenerates into one of these categories, the director should always strive for pure collaboration. In a pure collaborative process the final product is greater than the sum of its parts. The work of each artist is enhanced by working with the other artists. Theatre should be viewed as a collaborative art not because it must be but because it should be, and the director needs to partake of all the benefits that pure collaboration provides. How does one know if such a process is in practice? My definition of pure collaboration is when the team looks at the final product and it is impossible to identify individual contributions. Each idea may have started with one artist, but by the time it reached fruition several artists helped reshape and direct the development.

How then do we ensure a good collaborative process? The spirit of the collaborative process is established by the director who begins the production process with a clear production concept resulting from a solid understanding of the script and its dramatic action, thus providing the limits and the direction for the production staff to follow. Each of the designers is then free to develop an individual concept within this framework. By establishing this open collaborative spirit the designers are encouraged to interact with one another. Much of the director's leadership after the establishment of the production concept can be framed in the form of questions to the production staff. These questions will seek to challenge the designers to create even stronger work. The director can often achieve far more by getting the designers to be reflective rather than simply assigning them tasks. Pure collaboration requires the commitment of all the individual artists to seek the best collaborative solution resulting in the final product. Although there is innate friction among the artists, each striving for the best work in their area while at the same time being open to the ideas and contributions of others, in a good collaborative process this friction leads to better art.

Good collaboration begins with the director. The director must establish an environment that is conducive to collaboration at the start of the production process.

DIRECTING THE DESIGN AREAS

While few directors have difficulty in directing the actors, many directors have some difficulty directing their designers. The reality may be that when directors know little about the artistic field of the designers, they may feel unqualified or at least hesitant working with them. This sometimes results in directors being either too autocratic or too vague and accepting. Directors need to see their work with the designers in the same way they see their work with the actors. Just as the director would not tell an actor how to act, the director should not tell the designers how to design. In the same way that the director serves as the eye of the audience when working with the actor to make sure the spine of the play is being communicated in each moment, the director needs to take the same role with the designers. The director should begin the relationship with each designer by clearly communicating a vision for the production. At the same time, the director should invite the designers to provide feedback. This opens up a two-way path for communication. It also may enhance the original vision. It is helpful for the director to prepare lists of the needed elements as provided by the script or as envisioned for each design department. This ensures that as the designers develop their designs they are also fulfilling the needs as seen by the director. Areas or elements the director does not wish to be incorporated in the designs can also be expressed at this juncture.

One of the beauties of collaboration is the necessity to explain to others what you are seeing and in the ensuing dialogue giving the rationale for these decisions. This forces the director to think clearly about his or her vision and to be able to clarify it in discussion with others. As a director who is also a designer, I do not particularly enjoy designing shows I direct. Aside from the split in focus, it means that as a director I lose the collaboration with that designer. Early in my career I often served as director and designer for my productions. I jokingly said the designer knew intuitively exactly what the director wanted, and when the designer made changes the director knew instinctively that they were done. On the surface this may seem ideal, but in reality it is not collaboration, it is only one person's vision. Without the collaboration with other artists my work was never challenged, my vision never needed explanation. In essence, no one disagreed with me as director or designer. Neither I nor the production benefitted from the collaborative nature of theatre.

> The director should clearly present his or her concept and needs to the designers to limit the necessity for changes. Be careful of making assumptions.

In communicating a vision to the designers, the director needs to make sure the message is not only clearly sent but also understood. As a director, I worry less about whether others understand if they ask questions. If they just nod and say yes, then I worry because I am not sure of their understanding. Perhaps they do understand, but on the other hand, they may only think so. The lack of exchange is not reassuring. After providing a vision to the designers, the director needs to be open to new ideas or possibilities. This openness to the ideas of others also establishes an environment that values the contribution of each person and thus enhances the collaborative spirit. If the director has specific desires, these need to be communicated up front. It is frustrating for a designer to have idea after idea turned down only to learn that the director already had a specific vision in mind, and until the designer presented that vision it was simply not going to be accepted. A good deal of time and energy could have been saved, not to mention frustration avoided, if the director had made this need known from the start. The director also needs to allow sufficient room for the designers to be creative. If the production concept is so narrow that the designers' only option is to execute the director's vision, then their creative expression cannot be called into use. As a director, it is important to encourage designers to voice their views even if it is not in full keeping with the director's concept. At the same time, it is important that the designers realize that ultimately it is the director's concept that must be realized, and if they cannot persuade the director to alter this concept, they must follow it.

In engaging with the work presented by the designers, the director should respond just as when working with the actors. Hopefully, the director does not shut down an actor's interpretation because it is ineffective, but rather works through questions and has a discussion with the actor to find a stronger interpretation. The director needs to respond to the designers in the same way. It is of no help to the designers to be told something does not work or is wrong. They need to know what it is that the director does not like and engage in a dialogue as to how to better express this element. The underlying key here is that the director needs to respect the work of the designers. If the director is intimidated by the designer's work, the director will be afraid to engage in discussing it. If the director does not respect the designer's work, the director will simply see the designer as a functionary to carry out the director's ideas. The director who appreciates, respects, and understands the work of the designers is in the best position to work with them. As such, it is wise for a director to develop a working knowledge of each of the design areas in order to be conversant with and have empathy for their work. The more the director understands the design fields, the better the director will be at communicating with these artists and the less dependent on them as the sole source of information with regard to the design area.

To avoid problems during the polishing and technical rehearsals, the director must ensure good communication throughout the rehearsal process so all departments are aware of any changes to the needs as they were originally specified and any additional needs that grow out of the rehearsal process.

PRODUCTION MEETINGS

It is important for the director and the designers to have regular meetings not only before rehearsals begin but also during the rehearsal process leading up to the technical rehearsals. In many production environments production meetings are scheduled and led by the production manager. If not, the director may need to organize them. In either event, the director needs to be prepared at each of these meetings to keep the designers updated on the rehearsal process as it impacts the design areas. For example, letting the scenic designer know that all drawers in a cabinet need to work and not have false fronts or making sure the costume designer knows the right jacket pocket needs to be functional. It is also important to ensure that all the production areas are communicating with one another. I was involved in a show where a prop needed to fit into a pocket only to find out at the dress rehearsal that the pocket was not large enough to accommodate the prop. The props coordinator knew the prop was needed, the costume designer knew the prop should fit in a pocket, but neither was aware of the necessity to communicate about the size. The production meetings also provide an opportunity for furthering collaboration between the production departments. The director needs to be clear about the needs of the show and to be careful not to assume that something will be provided. Simple reports without discussion should be avoided.

A FINAL THOUGHT

Collectively, the designers create the environment for the play. They provide the opportunities as well as the necessary restrictions and obstacles. By embracing the work of the designers and bringing them fully into the collaborative process, the director significantly enhances the quality of this environment and provides a better "play scape" for the play. The key is clear communication, good collaboration, and solid respect all around.

FURTHER EXPLORATION

1. Discuss with a group of designers what they would like to know from a director before beginning the production.
2. Talk to the designers about methods and areas they would prefer directors did not use or include.

3. Sit in on a production meeting and observe how well the communication and collaborative process is occurring. How effective was it? What were its major strengths? How could it have been improved?

4. Based on a script analysis and production concept you have previously prepared, compile the information you would share with your designers so they may begin the design process.

5. Choose a design area where your knowledge is limited and talk to a designer in that area to find out more about what you need to know as a director.

6. Role play an initial production meeting with different individuals playing the roles of director, stage manager, and designers. What did you discover?

Working with the Stage Manager

THE STAGE MANAGER'S ROLE IN THE PRODUCTION

The stage manager is theatre's greatest gift to the director. A director who works with a good stage manager never wishes to work without one again. A good stage manager significantly increases the director's ability to be creative by freeing him or her to focus solely on those aspects of the production. Ironically, many directors do not know how to make the best use of their stage manager and, thus, lose many of the benefits. To fully realize what the stage manager can contribute to the director's work, it is necessary to understand the stage manager's functions.

THE STAGE MANAGER'S FUNCTIONS

The purpose of the stage manager and his or her staff is to maximize the efficiency and creativity in each rehearsal and to ensure the best possible performance. Borrowing a term from Gene Roddenberry's *Star Trek*, this is the **Prime Directive** of the stage manager. If a function falls within this directive, then it is most likely the stage manager's responsibility. The stage manager's functions can be divided into categories depending on the phase of the production.

PREPRODUCTION

During preproduction, the stage manager's function is to get ready for the production, primarily by preparing the production book and becoming familiar with the show. As part of this process the stage manager prepares *plots*. These plots are lists of needs from the script based on the information provided by the playwright either as a statement or in the dialogue. The stage manager carefully works through the script making separate plots for scenery, costumes, lighting, sound, and any other necessary areas such as special effects. A good stage manager does not allow artistic interpretation to affect information on the plots. For example, on the plot for the lighting needs the stage manager notes if the script calls for a light to be turned on at a specific point. The stage manager does not note that the lighting should change because of the mood shift unless noted by the playwright. The stage manager also indicates if an item crosses between two or more technical areas to ensure proper communication occurs during the production. For example, if the script calls for lightning, the stage manager cross-references the note on the plots for both Lighting and Sound so the nature of the effect can be coordinated. In addition, the stage manager prepares a pronunciation and definition plot in which names, terms, and words that may not be known to the members of the production can be identified, defined or explained, and pronounced correctly. The props plot is one of the most valuable lists for the stage manager. Until the properties manager creates a list, the stage manager's plot is the working props list. The director may choose to take advantage of any of these plots either to replace his or her own listed needs or to double-check to see if anything is missed, keeping in mind that the stage manager's lists do not include interpreted needs that may be on the director's lists such as the desire to utilize a prop that is not mentioned in the script. Figure 6.1 is a sample props plot created by the stage manager for my production of *Doubt*. Note that the stage manager has cross-referenced a number of elements that apply to either the set or costume departments. She has also indicated the location of the tea cups with a question mark since the tea cups are assumed but not specified in the script. Act and scene designations are not used since the playwright has not made these designations.

The stage manager establishes the lines of communication among the members of the production team including organizing the preproduction meetings. During these meetings, the stage manager takes notes that will be published for the production team. It is vital that the stage manager be involved in the process from the beginning in order to be familiar with all discussions and decisions made regarding the production. Having this knowledge greatly assists the stage manager in resolving any issues that arise in the future. For example, a decision may be reached at an early production meeting regarding the handling of a particular technical issue. If later in the production process one department implements a different approach resulting in difficulties for another, having the original planned solution in the report will benefit the stage manager in remedying the situation.

It is always a good idea for the director to meet with the stage manager prior to the start of the production to establish expectations and answer any of the stage manager's questions. Doing so will help ensure the start of a good working relationship.

DOUBT
Props Plot

Page	Item	Character/Location	Notes	Cross
14	Desk	set		set
14	Chair	set		set
14	Ledger	on desk		
14	fountain pen	on desk		
14	Handkerchief	James		
14	Bonnet	Aloysius	Black	costume
14	glasses	Aloysius	rimless	costume
21	Whistle	Flynn		
21	Basketball	Flynn		
22	Bench	set		set
22	Bush	set		set
22	Burlap	set		set
22	mulch?	set		set
22	shawl	Aloysius	black	costume
27	phone	on desk		
27	chairs	set	number?	set
27	tea pot	Aloysius		
29	sugar bowl	in desk		
29	tongs	in desk		
27	2 tea cups	?		
28	watch	Aloysius		costume
30	notebook	Flynn	small, black	
30	ball point pen	Flynn		
35	notebook	on/in desk	Aloysius looks up phone number	
39	prayer book	Flynn		
40	earplug	Aloysius		
40	transistor radio	behind desk?		
40	purse?	Mrs. Muller		costume

Figure 6.1 Sample Props Plot

AUDITIONS

The main function of the stage manager during the auditions is to allow the director to totally focus on the casting decisions by relieving him or her of all administrative and managerial responsibilities. The stage manager sets up and organizes the audition space as the director wishes. As the auditionees arrive the stage manager provides them with instructions and answers their questions. The stage manager is also responsible for controlling the audition materials and keeping order during the auditions to eliminate or reduce distractions. Ultimately, the primary job of the stage manager is to enable the director to make better casting decisions. Some directors will even seek the stage manager's opinion regarding specific actors if the stage manager has had previous experience with them or for insight into the actors' behavior outside of the audition room.

REHEARSALS

Once the production enters the rehearsal phase, the stage manager assumes the duty of providing for the mechanical needs of the rehearsals. A good stage manager is the first to arrive at the rehearsal space and the last to leave. The stage manager prepares the rehearsal space so it is properly set up prior to the arrival of the actors and director, including arranging the rehearsal set and furniture and making sure rehearsal props are ready. As the actors arrive, the stage manager checks them in to be sure all needed actors are present and calls any missing actors. The stage manager notes in the production book all blocking and information provided to the actors by the director to avoid confusion in the future. As the cast moves off book, the stage manager prompts as the director wishes. During the rehearsal, the stage manager handles any issues that might otherwise distract the director. The stage manager answers cast questions whenever possible to avoid interrupting the director, and assists in maintaining the rehearsal schedule established by the director, tracking the time between breaks and the length of each break, reminding the actors of future scheduling and, if the schedule is drawn up daily, making sure it is delivered. Following each rehearsal, the stage manager writes a rehearsal report with what was accomplished, and provides any necessary information to the production staff. This latter information typically pertains to questions or changes in the technical needs.

Many directors also find other assignments for their stage managers. In a union setting, the types of tasks the stage manager may or may not do are specified in the Actors' Equity contract; in a nonunion setting, this is worked out between the director and the stage manager. For example, some directors have their stage managers hold line rehearsals. This allows the director to work on other aspects of the production. The director sometimes has the stage manager or the assistant stage manager take notes during the rehearsal. This may be a very practical use of the stage manager or assistant's time, but the director needs to be sure this does not interfere with the myriad of other tasks the stage manager must complete during the rehearsal. The stage manager may also be responsible for all scene changes that occur during the rehearsal, may stand in for missing actors, and may call or simulate any technical issues that affect action. For example, if a telephone is supposed to ring interrupting the action of the scene, the stage manager can either ring a rehearsal bell or simply call "phone." This assists the actors by providing the motivation for their response to the cue, and it makes the subsequent integration of technical aspects far easier since the actors are already accustomed to responding. This becomes especially important in shows where the actors have to hold and then break out of the hold, such as at the end of almost all musical numbers. There is usually a musical punch, or button, on which the performers freeze, hold for applause, and then break, returning to the action. A decision must be made as to what will trigger that release. My personal preference is that the action holds until the lights change. This becomes the cue for all the actors to break and move on. By having the stage manager call "lights" during rehearsal, the actors become accustomed to waiting for the cue. It is amazing how difficult it is to get the actors to wait for the lights if they have grown accustomed to breaking whenever they feel like it.

TECHNICAL REHEARSALS

As the rehearsals enter the technical rehearsal phase, the stage manager takes on additional responsibilities. The stage manager establishes lines of communication with all participants at the technical rehearsal, organizes the technical rehearsal schedule and, within the parameters established by the director, maintains that schedule. The stage manager also assists the designers as much as possible. The stage manager's knowledge of the staging is particularly valuable in assisting the designers, especially with regard to last-minute changes. The stage manager records all the technical cues in the production book, establishing with the designers and the director exactly when these cues should occur. The stage manager may also be responsible for the organization of the stage crews and overseeing their work. During this time, the stage manager organizes the backstage space to facilitate the execution of all technical requirements and attempts to ensure all members of the production company are kept safe. This may include clearing crossover paths and actor entrances, ensuring there is adequate light backstage to allow for safe movement, and marking any potential hazards. Finally, during the technical run-throughs, the stage manager calls all the cues, refining this process into the dress rehearsals.

DRESS REHEARSALS

Typically, the dress rehearsals are run by the stage manager in the same manner as performances. The stage manager is responsible for preshow, intermission, and postshow checklists, ensuring that everything that needs to be done, set, or prepared is completed. A cast and crew sign-in sheet is posted so the stage manager can easily tell if everyone is present and can call any missing individuals. The stage manager anticipates potential problems and prepares for them in advance. Ultimately, it is up to the stage manager to solve any problems or situations that develop during the dress rehearsals and subsequent performances. The stage manager's production book now contains all information related to the show and is the ultimate resource to resolve any issues that arise.

PERFORMANCES

Since the director's role in the production is essentially complete after the final rehearsal and typically he or she is no longer present, the stage manager takes over full responsibility for maintaining the production. This is especially important in commercial theatre where productions have extended runs without the presence of the director. While the production is a living entity and will continue to grow, the job of the stage manager is to preserve the vision of the director and the designers, ensuring that all technical elements are upheld so that the production continues to look as it did at the first performance. This includes providing feedback to actors who are changing interpretations or modifying the original intent of the production.

Given that the stage manager is present from the beginning of the process and is therefore aware of all issues that affect the production, during the final rehearsals and subsequent performances the stage manager can utilize this information to prevent unwanted situations from occurring, for example, changes in character interpretation or an approach that moves away from the original production concept. The stage manager is also able to resolve any other issues or problems that develop. In commercial theatre, it is also standard practice for stage managers to rehearse understudies and, unless the director wishes to do so, actors' replacements.

> The stage manager has many diverse tasks and, as such, it is nearly impossible to generate a complete list. The best practice is to use the "prime directive" of the stage manager, described at the start of the chapter. If the task fits this guide, it is a valuable use of the stage manager. If not, it should be someone else's task.

THE CARE AND FEEDING OF YOUR STAGE MANAGER

The director must strive to nurture a working relationship with the stage manager to ensure the best environment in which the stage manager can effectively function. This directly benefits both the director and the production. The expectations of the director need to be clearly expressed to the stage manager. As a director, I prefer to meet with my stage manager as soon as he or she is brought on board to talk about my expectations and to allow the stage manager to ask any questions. One of the questions stage managers frequently ask directors at an initial meeting is: "What do you expect of me?" All too often the director's response is: "The standard stage management duties." Unfortunately, this response assumes everyone understands and agrees on this list of duties. The stage manager's question is better answered by the director providing as much specific information as possible. This includes particular tasks the director wishes the stage manager to do or not do as well as any activities that may annoy or be bothersome. For example, some directors want to have the final word at the end of every rehearsal. Any announcements by the stage manager need to be made prior to the director's closing comments. Many directors prefer to meet with the stage manager following each rehearsal to review that rehearsal, identify needs to be addressed in future, and, more specifically, to plan the next rehearsal. Minimally, this gives the director the opportunity to inform the stage manager of the particular needs for the next rehearsal.

Prompting the actors during the rehearsal is an important but often challenging part of the stage manager's responsibilities. The director needs to specify how closely he or she wants the stage manager to hold the cast to the script at each given point in the rehearsal process as well as the guidelines for the procedure for cutting of the rehearsal when the line is missed or mistakenly delivered. The director further needs to support the stage manager by sharing this information with the cast. In this way, when a stage manager, following the director's instructions, cuts the action and corrects a small error in the line delivery, the actor knows it is not the stage manager's decision to be this precise but the director's. While the director needs to clarify exactly how rehearsals are to be run in general, it is particularly important that the director clarify the procedure for technical and dress rehearsals. This includes how and when required cuts in the action are to be called. It is recommended that the director and designers indicate their need to the stage manager who will then call the cut. By doing so, only one voice is heard by the cast and confusion is avoided. The director's parameters should also include whether time will be allowed to go back to correct problems. While many beginning directors think they understand the function of a technical or dress rehearsal, there can be a great variation in their understanding. Good stage managers do not assume practices followed in the past are the ones to follow now, but rather seek clarification from the director. For example, in a prior production, the stage manager may have timed breaks during rehearsals and called for the company to return; in the current production, the director may only want the stage manager to indicate to him or her that the break is over and not call the cast back until instructed.

It is important for the director to reinforce to the cast the stage manager's position as an authority figure. Seasoned actors positively respond to the stage manager as they are aware of how much the stage manager can help them. Less experienced actors may not have this innate respect. The director can further establish the stage manager's relationship with the cast by not making the stage manager the "bad guy." It can be tempting for the director to have the stage manager handle all the negative aspects of the production. The problem is that the cast associates all this negativity with the stage manager, causing a serious impediment in their relationship. It is also suggested that the director refrain from publicly correcting or repri-manding the stage manager. The director should feel free to make the stage manager aware of anything with which he or she is not happy or wants handled differently, but this should be done privately. The relationship between the stage manager and the director is unique. Once a director finds a stage manager with whom he or she enjoys working, the director will often seek to work with that stage manager again. For this reason, it is not uncommon to see a director/ stage manager collaboration occur over numerous productions.

The director must take good care of the stage manager. It is important for the director to recognize the difficulty of the stage manager's task. The stage manager's job was once defined as "being responsible for the entire production in the dark, from the back of the theatre, with one ear covered, behind glass."

WHAT THE STAGE MANAGER IS NOT

As important as it is for the director to understand what the stage manager is there to do, it is equally important that the director understand that the stage manager should not be asked to do anything that interferes with his or her principal responsibilities unless that responsibility takes precedence. Having the stage manager perform tasks outside his or her responsibilities may impede the stage manager from doing far more necessary tasks. For example, it is not a good idea to send the stage manager out on errands during rehearsal. While the stage manager may appear to be the ideal person for such a task, being away from the rehearsal process means not only is he or she not assisting the director in the production, but also, perhaps even more importantly, the stage manager is missing what goes on during the time away, which may have serious implications later. Furthermore, the stage manager is not a whipping boy. While the stage manager may be an easy target for the director to vent his or her frustrations upon, it is simply unfair to make the stage manager bear this burden.

As noted at the beginning of this chapter, the stage manager is a gift to the director and the director should make good use of the gift.

FURTHER EXPLORATION

1. Talk to a stage manager and find out what he or she prefers to know from the director before starting to work together for the first time.
2. Talk to a stage manager and find out what actions or practices by a director really are bothersome and how as a director you can avoid this.
3. Talk with both experienced stage managers and directors about their working relationship. How did their relationship evolve?
4. Observe an experienced stage manager interacting with the director.

PART III

Auditions and Casting

Auditions

PURPOSE OF AUDITIONS

The audition process should be considered differently from the actual selection of the actors. The director and the actors do not see the auditions from the same perspective. For the director, the purpose of the audition is to view each actor in the talent pool to determine who is most suitable for each role; it is the start of the director's interaction with the actors. For the actors, it is an opportunity to demonstrate to the director why they are the best choice for the play. These two groups have decidedly different objectives. From the actors' perspective, the sole purpose is to be cast. For the director, auditions are critical. It has been said that 90 percent of good directing is completed in the auditions. While this percentage may not be accurate, choosing the right cast sets the tone for the rehearsal process and significantly increases the likelihood of an excellent production. Conversely, the wrong choice may limit the possibility for excellence and certainly make the rehearsal period more difficult.

The director must enter the audition process thoroughly prepared with clear and concise initial ideas about each character but still have an open mind; it is possible that an auditionee may present a possibility for the role the director had not foreseen and who may prove to be a superior choice. The audition process can be stressful for the director as there may be a large number of actors to audition before narrowing down to the final cast.

Most actors feel nervous at auditions as there is significant tension created by the competition for roles. The auditioning process can be equally stressful for the director since the quality of the production will rest heavily on finding the right cast.

TYPES OF AUDITIONS

There are different types of auditions from which the director can choose to get the greatest sense of how the talent pool fits the needs of the play.

The first distinction is between the initial or general audition and the callback audition. The general audition allows the director to prepare a short list of actors for each role and then to consider these actors more carefully in the callback auditions. This short list should contain at least one choice, but preferably more, for each role. The dynamics of one actor playing off another may change the director's opinion of that actor, which may mean that a seemingly ideal choice for a role in the general audition is ultimately not the best. The more choices the director has in the callback auditions, the more options for making the final choice; however, the greater the number of choices on the short list, the longer and more complex the callback process. The director needs to find a balance between having enough options and having a workable callback list. If the talent pool is relatively small, the general audition may serve less to cut down the number and more to provide the director with the opportunity to plan more specific approaches for the callback auditions. If the talent pool is large, it is essential that the audition list be pared down to a number the director can reasonably and completely audition in the time and number of callbacks provided. In this case, there may be a series of callback auditions. At each of these callbacks the director will further refine and shorten the list until ultimately arriving at a final choice for the cast. Multiple callback auditions are common in commercial theatre since they provide the director with the best process of working through the auditionees. However, that may be time prohibitive, especially in noncommercial theatre, and, therefore, the director often casts the play based on one or two callbacks.

Standard procedure for general auditions is for actors to prepare either one or two monologues of specified length that provide the director with insight to their ability and how well they will fit into this specific play. Sometimes the general audition includes a number of directors casting separate plays. In such instances, the actors' monologue choices become a bit more generic since they cannot necessarily gear them for a particular play. The director needs to take this into account in preparation for the auditions as well as in the selection of the short list. In the case of a musical, in addition to a monologue, the actors generally prepare a short musical selection and possibly a brief dance audition. While specialty needs such as stage combat are occasionally part of the general audition, these are usually saved for the callbacks. If callback auditions are not possible, then the director must make choices based solely on observations during the general audition.

Typically, the procedure for the callback auditions is to have the actors read selected scenes from the play in pairs. This gives the director the opportunity to see the actors in the context of the roles and evaluate their interaction. Ideally, the director will have each actor read with all of the other actors being considered for the opposite role. Unfortunately, this may necessitate a larger number of readings than time allows. Given that there are probably additional roles to cast, this may be impossible unless additional callback auditions can be planned.

It is also possible for the director to totally bypass auditions. Actors may be selected based on the director's personal experience with them or the director's perception of the actors from their previous work. This is often the case in commercial theatre when casting lead roles; the director and/or producers may have an actor in mind and will contact him or her directly to see if there is interest. In this situation, the actor does not audition. There are also times when the nature of the production makes auditions either impossible or at least impractical, leaving this method of selection the only option for the director. For example, scene work in a directing class. The director must make choices based on prior knowledge and does not have the opportunity for the actors to demonstrate their ability. As such, the choices can be somewhat uninformed. Although auditions are always a better idea, there are times when they simply are not possible.

A second distinction in types of auditions is if they are categorized as *open* or *closed*. Generally, an open audition refers to auditions in which all auditionees are in the room, while in closed auditions the actor auditions privately for the director and possibly other members of the staff. There are advantages to both scenarios. Since all actors are present for open auditions, the advantage is they can quickly be called up. Also, in an educational setting, the actors may benefit from seeing the other auditions. The major advantage to closed auditions is the actor auditioning is not distracted by the other auditionees; it is also easier to maintain order. Customarily, general auditions are closed while many callback auditions are open. Note that in a commercial theatre in a union setting, open auditions refer to auditions open to both union and nonunion members; closed auditions are open to union members only.

PROCEDURES FOR AUDITIONS

Most general auditions follow a similar procedure although the director will need to specify the exact process. The auditionees may either sign up for a particular time slot or wait to be called to present their audition material. Having a sign-up sheet before the audition provides benefits to both the director and the auditionees. For the director, it means a smaller number of people will be at the audition at any given time period; for the auditionees, it means they know exactly when they need to be ready to present their audition, saving them significant time. The difficulty for the director, however, is projecting in advance the amount of time allotted for each audition. If more time is needed than planned, the auditions will gradually fall further behind schedule. If less time is needed, the director will waste time waiting for the next auditionee. In determining the amount of time for each audition, the director must consider the length of time for the monologue or monologues to be presented; for interviews, if they will be held; and for actors to enter and exit the audition space. It is also a good idea for directors to place short breaks for themselves in the schedule. Standard practice is to require auditionees be ready several minutes prior to their audition so if the audition is running ahead of schedule, they are prepared. In some large auditions the auditionees are often brought into the audition room in small groups to save time with the transition between each auditionee. This information is often included in an audition procedures announcement, a sample of which can be found at the end of this chapter.

Each actor is expected to bring a one-page résumé to the audition. Typically, the résumé includes a head shot. A photograph is particularly valuable at sizable auditions as it helps the director remember the actor's face. Some companies may also have their own audition form for the auditionee if they need specific information not found on most résumés. A sample form can be found at the end of this chapter. Minimally, the director needs contact information, but it is also helpful to have information regarding the actor's past experience. The résumé or audition form is usually given to the stage manager who brings it to the director, or, in some cases, the actors bring it to the audition room and give it to the director themselves. While general auditions may be held in a theatre, they are often held in studios or smaller rooms. A clear space for the actors to perform their monologues is set up facing a table long enough for the director, any assistants, and any staff members to be comfortably seated. A chair for the actor to use if desired is customarily provided. Many times there is a taped X on the floor to indicate where the actors should begin. If the director then wishes the actor to read a scene, the stage manager reads with the actor.

Many directors prefer to begin an audition with a brief interview. This is especially beneficial when the director does not know the actor. It gives the director an opportunity to become acquainted and to see how the actor speaks and behaves when not in character. This is also an opportunity for the director to ask any pertinent questions that may affect casting. A brief interview helps to start the audition less formally and thereby reduces tension. Following the interview, the director will then ask the actor to begin the audition monologue. Upon completion, the actor leaves and the next actor comes in.

Once all the actors have presented their audition monologues, the director deliberates and prepares either the callback list or the cast list if casting is decided solely in the general audition. The setup for callback auditions is similar to the general audition except additional performing space will be needed to accommodate the actors as well as chairs for the actors who are waiting to audition. The director then calls up actors to read preselected sections from the script. Each actor is kept as long as the director needs to have him or her read and is then dismissed. After hearing all actors read in the combinations desired, the director then prepares the cast list or the new callback list if there will be another callback audition.

> The stage manager can serve as an invaluable asset to the director during the audition process by taking care of the mechanical issues of setting up the audition space and taking care of administrative procedures, thereby freeing the director to focus on the casting process.

The cast list announcement not only contains the names of the actors and their roles but also any initial announcements, such as location and time of the first rehearsal, where the actors pick up their scripts, and/or any other instructions the director wishes the actors to know prior to the first meeting. If the play is being produced commercially, contracts with the actors need to be signed to finalize the legal agreements.

Generally, if the play has particular needs such as music, dance, stage combat, or other special skills these will be addressed during the callback auditions. If the specialty areas are handled by someone other than the director, a separate space may be provided so they can be done in conjunction with the acting audition. The director and the other staff members will then compare notes at the end of the audition to prepare the cast list or subsequent callback list.

PLANNING FOR THE AUDITION

Given the importance of the audition it is imperative that the director be prepared. As discussed in Chapter 2, as part of the script analysis and production concept the director carefully analyzes each role with a projected characterization. Going into auditions, the narrowness with which the director conceives of the characters is predicated on the projected size and diversity of the talent pool. Assuming a large and diverse talent pool, the director can narrowly conceive each role with the assuredness that there will be actors who meet these conceptions. One of the more famous casting stories is from the 1939 film *Gone with the Wind*. Producer David O. Selznick and George Cukor, the original director, auditioned more than 1300 actresses for the lead role of Scarlett O'Hara before casting Vivien Leigh. On the other hand, if the anticipated talent pool is much smaller, unlike that of Selznick and Cukor's, and the casting decision must be made at the end of the auditions, the director will be well served to enter the auditions open-minded. Regardless, the director needs to have a firm understanding of each character and the physical requirements desired as well as those that are absolutely necessary. Having a clear plan will simplify the preparation of a callback list and ultimately the cast list. If a physical attribute for a given role is essential, it is unnecessary to consider those actors who do not possess it. However, while that attribute may be an ideal, if it can be worked around, the role may be easier to cast.

The audition announcement provides all of the particulars regarding the audition process. This includes the name of the play and its playwright, the time and location of the audition, and the procedure auditionees are expected to follow. If there is a sign-up for specific time slots prior to the auditions, the announcement should specify when and where actors can make these arrangements. The announcement should also include information regarding how the audition process will proceed, especially how the general audition will be conducted and if callbacks will be held. If there are callbacks, the announcement should include a description of how the callback auditions will be conducted as well as when, where, and how the callbacks and subsequent cast list will be posted.

Guidelines to assist the actors in their choice of audition monologues should also be provided in the announcement. If the director has particular requirements, these need to be specified. The director may have prepared a brief description of each character and what is being looked for in that character. This is also an opportunity, more commonly found in non-commercial theatre, for the director to indicate if a given role includes areas some of the talent pool may find difficult or objectionable, such as strong language, overt sexual situations, or the like. To keep the auditions on schedule, the announcement should also indicate the maximum time the monologue or monologues may take.

In addition, the audition announcement should include any particular expectations of the cast, such as availability for rehearsals, the starting date and projected time for rehearsals, and the performance dates. It should be posted in such a way that a projected talent pool will have access to it. Many theatres maintain web pages with specific audition pages and/or use social media to provide this information.

The director needs to prepare audition materials. Assuming the general audition uses monologues prepared by the actors, no additional material is needed. The callback auditions normally utilize readings from the script. A sufficient number of scripts need to be available for the actors. If the director wishes the actors to briefly prepare prior to the reading, an even greater number of scripts will be necessary. This can be problematic in a small cast show where there are a limited number of scripts. The use of the actual rehearsal scripts also creates a security issue since they are necessary for the rehearsals.

Another means of providing readings for larger numbers than the available scripts and reducing security issues involves the use of *sides*. A side is a short section of the script containing only the necessary material. These are also used in some larger productions for actors who are onstage for a limited time. The preparation of sides for auditions allows the director to choose readings for each set of characters. These readings should call for the full emotional and dynamic range of each character. Readings with two characters help the director focus on the two actors and allow both parts to be equally dynamic, a factor not always the case in scenes with three or more. It is helpful to have several scenes for each set of characters so the director can see the full range of each actor as he or she fits the character. The director may also choose particularly problematic scenes to see how the actor handles them. The stage manager is responsible for these audition sides, which are typically destroyed immediately following the audition. It is necessary to check with the play's publisher for permission to prepare sides.

The final steps in organizing the auditions involve ensuring the audition space is set and any necessary information is ready. As previously stated, a good stage manager will be invaluable to the director both in the preparation and the management of the auditions.

THE USE OF CALLBACK AUDITIONS

During the general audition, the director looks to reduce the overall number of auditionees to a more manageable number by eliminating actors who are wrong for a given role, do not demonstrate sufficient acting technique, or have deficiencies within their performance, such as insufficient projection or diction. The director further notes any insufficiencies not great enough to exclude the actor but that will need to be worked on during the rehearsal process to secure a solid performance. The director can decide during the callback auditions if these impediments are sufficient reason not to cast the actor. It is inevitable that early in the director's career or if working in an educational setting the director will be working with actors who need further development. The director needs to decide how these issues factor into the casting process. As the director's career continues and increasingly experienced actors audition, this issue diminishes sharply.

Aside from the actor's technique demonstrated in the general audition, the director is looking to determine how well an actor fits a given role. This is an intangible aspect. The director's concept for the character involves physical as well as emotional characteristics. While it is not crucial that the actor physically have these characteristics, the actor must be believable in the role and bring the emotional characteristics to bear in performance. Depending on the nature of the audition monologue the director may have to "read between the lines." For example, if the director is auditioning actors for a farce and an actor auditions with a comedic but somewhat serious monologue, the director needs to project how well the actor fits the farcical environment to determine whether to call the actor back. Actors do themselves a great service by carefully selecting audition monologues. However, not all monologues can meet the needs of a particular play if the general audition is for multiple plays. The director may err on the side of having too many names for callbacks to ensure a range of choices during the callback auditions. Ideally, the callback list should contain only those actors the director would consider casting. However, especially in educational theatre, directors may have a "courtesy callback" as a reward for a superlative audition or for some other reason. Some directors prefer to list just the actors on the callback list; others list the actors and the roles for which they are being considered. Listing just the actors gives the director total flexibility in the callbacks, which is especially valuable with a small talent pool. However, it does not provide the director with a preliminary guide for pairing the actors nor does it help the actors focus their preparation for the callbacks. On the other hand, listing the roles for which actors are being considered enables the actors to better prepare for the callbacks and provides the starting division of the actors, but it may limit the director's options or make additional readings necessary. Whichever method is chosen, the director can make changes to help facilitate the audition process. Prior to the callbacks the director should provide some guidance to the actors concerning interpretation of the characters. It is assumed the actors will be familiar with the play prior to the callbacks unless the script is not publicly available or the producer does not wish to make it available outside of the production process. In this case, the director will need to provide detailed information for the actors in order to facilitate the audition process.

Whether or not the director specifies actors for particular roles on the callback list, the director needs to have such a list to work from. The director may also consider initial pairings to save time during the callback process. Doing so can help clarify the director's intent. Unprepared readings are commonly referred to as *cold readings*. Cold readings give the director a different insight to the actor. In the general audition the director saw how the actor handled a carefully prepared monologue. In the cold readings the director has the opportunity to see how the actor handles new material. Good actors will familiarize themselves with the script to aid them in this process. The director can further mitigate the cold readings by providing the actor with the sides to briefly read through and prepare the scene either before or during the callbacks. The director should be open during the callback process to pairings or possibilities not necessarily seen in the initial audition. As a director, I am often surprised at callbacks by how poorly an actor fits a role given the general audition, but I am even more surprised when I discover actors as possibilities for roles I had not considered them for based on the general audition. These pleasant surprises can be quite helpful for the director.

The director can use techniques other than cold readings as part of the callback audition process. Having an actor improvise scenes may provide the director with insight into how well the actor thinks on his or her feet. The director needs to determine how important this skill is to the role since an actor who is not good at improvisation may still be perfect for the role assuming improvisation is not a consideration. Movement exercises are another technique that may be utilized if the roles call for unique or stylized movement. Directors often ask actors to try a scene again, providing them with a different direction. This may be done simply to determine how well they take direction. Some directors even go so far as to ask actors to play the roles in what would seem to be an inappropriate manner just to see how well they take direction. Whether this is done specifically as a test, providing suggestions to an actor during the callbacks can be beneficial, particularly if the actor is going in a direction that does not fit the director's concept. Rather than eliminating that actor it may be valuable to see how the actor handles the part with additional guidance.

When time allows at the end of the callback auditions I often ask actors if there are any parts or scenes for which they were not asked to read but would like to. While this is primarily a courtesy, it occasionally may reveal an insight I had not seen previously. If nothing else, this courtesy ends the audition on a positive note.

HOW TO IMPROVE THE QUALITY OF THE AUDITIONS

Assuming the director's goal is to select the strongest cast possible, it is in the director's best interest that the audition process allows the actors to do their best work. The overall tone of the audition should work toward relieving the tension and anxiety that often accompanies the audition process. Even though it is stressful for the director, given the gravity of the decisions to be made in a relatively short time, it is important that the director project an atmosphere of calm. Just asking the actor at the end of the interview "What are you going to share with us today?" eases the actor into the monologue. A sincere "thank-you" from the director ends the audition process in a positive manner.

The question of the degree of formality for the audition is often raised. On the one hand, the audition needs to be a formal process, but on the other, excessive formality defeats the purpose of the openness necessary in an audition. Every director defines their own level of formality. The nature of this formality can be established when the actor enters the audition room. The courtesy of the director goes a long way to encourage the strongest audition possible from the actor. The coldness of auditions often seen in films is generally not a reality. A good guide for directors is to treat the process as they would want to be treated if they were the actors.

An area of difficulty for a director during the auditions is often where to focus. While obviously listening intently to the actor's audition, the director also needs to take notes and may not always appear attentive. The reality is unavoidable if the director is to have notes to refer to later. Experienced actors know they should not focus their audition directly at the director since doing so may intrude on the director's space. The director should, however, refrain from unnecessary distractions during the audition, such as conversations with colleagues. This is a matter of courtesy for the auditionee. Even if the director is bored with the actor's audition it is best not to show it.

During callbacks it is equally important that the director create an atmosphere that provides the actors with the most favorable opportunity to perform, thus increasing their chances of being cast. Providing guidance or directions during the callbacks helps the auditionees understand what the director is looking for and enables them to better fit their audition to meet those needs. Unless the director's goal is to see how well an actor handles new material, providing the actor with an opportunity to at least briefly prepare cold readings during the callback process will inevitably produce better work.

The image the director conveys to the actors should be carefully thought out, including manner and behavior. Actors understand the importance of dressing appropriately for auditions, avoiding being too formal or too casual. The same is true for the director. The director needs to be mindful that the future cast will come from this pool of auditionees.

METHODS FOR KEEPING NOTES ON THE ACTORS

The number of actors at a general audition may range from a small group to more than several hundred, and the audition may last several days depending on the situation. If the audition pool is small and/or the director is familiar with the actors' work, it is easier for the director to remember them. However, if the opposite is true, the director needs to develop techniques to remember each actor in order to make the strongest casting decisions. While extensive notations may be valuable afterward, taking these notes during the audition forces the director to shift attention away from the actors for considerable amounts of time. Noting each actor's audition monologue choices often helps refresh the director's mind to the specific audition. These notes may be on a separate pad or written directly on the actor's résumé or audition form. Some directors find it useful to work with laptops or tablets to record their notes. I also find it useful to have a worksheet listing all the roles by gender. A sample worksheet is included at the end of the chapter. When I see an actor with potential for a specific role I list him or her under the character name along with an indicator of the strength of potential. A rating scale of one to ten or the use of asterisks works nicely. In addition, I note any issues to examine during callbacks. Perhaps the audition monologue did not necessarily show their full range or there is a mechanical issue such as projection. Likewise, I find it helpful to highlight areas on their résumé or audition form to explore further during the callbacks. If a photograph is provided, I note if it accurately reflects the actor. On occasion, actors may look quite different from their head shot. Having such a note is helpful if I cannot place their face based on the photograph.

After the general audition is completed and a callback list prepared, I prefer to set up a callback worksheet based on the chart created for the general audition. It is on this much more organized worksheet that each actor is ranked and any particular issues to look for during the callbacks are noted. This worksheet serves as a principal tool to keep track of which actors read for specific roles and my thoughts regarding their strength. During the callbacks it is useful to take occasional breaks to allow the actors an opportunity to collect their thoughts and for the director to reflect on the auditions and to plan the next stage. As possibilities become clearer I make special notes on the callback worksheet. The goal at the end of the auditions is to have all the information needed to make casting decisions.

It is in the director's best interest to create an audition environment that will allow the actors to show their best work. A good guide for directors is to treat the process as they would want to be treated if they were the actors.

DIRECTOR'S DECORUM

Actors occasionally complain about the behavior of the directors during auditions. A friend of mine recalls stepping onto the stage at a large regional audition only to see a number of directors leave for lunch. Another actor grievance is watching directors on their cell phones during the audition. These are obviously egregious examples, but the directors' decorum says a great deal about the process they are starting. In considering their decorum for auditions, directors would be wise to consider the following:

- Treat the actors as they expect the actors to treat them.
- Understand that they set the tone of the audition and should not be surprised when the actors follow their lead.
- Think about how they wish to be perceived.
- A disarming tone can do wonders to relieve audition tensions and lead to better auditions.
- Be attentive. The actor has worked hard to prepare for the audition; the least the director can do is listen carefully.

AUDITION CHECKLIST

❐ Be sure the script analysis and production concept are complete and concise and there is a clear concept for each character.

❐ Plan the number of and format for the auditions. Determine if there will be callbacks.

❐ Determine the date for the audition and arrange for a location.

❐ Prepare and post the audition announcement. Be sure to include:

- the name of the play and its playwright
- the time and location of the audition
- the procedures and format for the audition
- the guidelines and expectations for the audition material
- the maximum length of the audition material
- whether there will be callbacks
- any other information the actors need to know.

❏ Set up the audition location. Be sure to provide a table for yourself and the staff as well as a chair for the actor to use in the auditions if needed.

❏ Prepare a plan for taking notes during the audition.

❏ Following the general audition, prepare and post the callback list.

❏ Conduct the callback audition. Be sure to acquire all information needed to make the casting decision.

❏ Considering the auditions, make a cast determination.

❏ Post the cast list with any initial announcements.

SAMPLE AUDITION PROCEDURES

By Neil Simon

AUDITION PROCEDURES

Auditions for *Rumors* will be held on Monday, January 24, beginning at 6:00 p.m. in the Studio Theatre in Springfield Hall (room 210).

You must sign up for an audition slot on the Theatre Call Board in Springfield Hall opposite room 108. The auditions will be closed auditions, meaning only the director will be in the room during your audition. Please plan to arrive at your audition <u>at least 20 minutes prior to your appointment</u>. If you fail to make an appointment, you may come to the auditions after 6 p.m. and you will be taken in the first available opening.

If your schedule prevents you from being able to audition at that time, please contact the director prior to the audition.

For the auditions, you must prepare ONE short monologue from a contemporary comedy. Neil Simon comedies, except for *Rumors* and *The Star-Spangled Girl*, are totally acceptable.

The monologue should be 35–90 seconds.

Please see the director if you have any questions.

Please note the following:

- The auditions will consist of **TWO** parts:

1) An **INITIAL AUDITION** on Monday of the prepared audition selection.

2) A **CALLBACK AUDITION** (2nd readings) to be held on Tuesday, January 25, at 7:00 p.m. in Wilhoit Theatre.

   A list of those requested to come to the Callbacks will be posted on the Theatre Call Board in Springfield Hall on Monday night after the initial auditions.

- The cast list will be posted on Tuesday evening, January 25, on the Theatre Call Board in Springfield Hall.

Suggestion for the auditions:

- You should familiarize yourself with the play prior to the auditions. *Rumors* is on reserve in the library. Callbacks will consist of cold readings taken from the play. A knowledge of the play will definitely assist you during all parts of the audition process.

Notes about the production:

- *Rumors* **will start rehearsal immediately, beginning on Wednesday, January 26, at 7:00 p.m.**
  The production dates are March 2–5 with both matinee and evening performances on Saturday, March 5.

SAMPLE AUDITION FORM

Audition Form

Name _____ Male _____ Female _____

Local Address _____

Box No. _____ Phone _____E-mail _____

Major(s)/Minor(s) _____

Circle one: Freshman Sophomore Junior Senior Fifth Year Graduate Other

Age _____   Height _____

List your last five (5) roles:

Character	Play	Producing Organization	Year
1			
2			
3			
4			
5			

List any roles you are especially interested in:

Indicate the roles, if any, you will NOT accept:

Are you interested in being an Assistant Stage Manager if not cast?   ☐ Yes   ☐ No

☐ **Callbacks will be held on Tuesday, January 25, at 7:00 p.m. If you will <u>NOT</u> be available at that time please check the box.**

---------------- Please do not write below this line ----------------

SAMPLE AUDITION WORKSHEET

Rumors

Audition Worksheet

Women:	*Men:*
Chris Gorman	*Ken Gorman*
	Lenny Ganz
Claire Ganz	*Ernie Cusack*
	Glenn Cooper
Cookie Cusack	*Officer Welch*
Cassie Cooper	*Officer Pudney*

FURTHER EXPLORATION

1. Prepare an audition announcement for a hypothetical play.

2. For the hypothetical play chosen in Activity 1, prepare a description of each character to be provided to the actors prior to auditions.

3. For the hypothetical play chosen in Activity 1, choose readings from the script that can be used for the callback auditions.

4. Sit in on auditions with an experienced director and observe how he or she interacts with the auditionees.

CHAPTER 8

Casting

THE IMPORTANCE OF CASTING DECISIONS

All directors understand that casting is one of the most important and difficult decisions they will make regarding the production. The greater the competition for each role, the more difficult the director's decision. Casting decisions are extremely subjective. While some actors may simply be "wrong" for a given role, many actors are viable possibilities. In the end, the director must make essentially cold decisions in choosing a cast. In making these decisions, the director acknowledges that in casting a given actor, the possibilities other actors may have brought to the role are eliminated.

In some cases, actors are "precast," that is, selected without auditions, when there is a desire to have a name performer in the role or a guest artist has been hired. It is my experience in academic theatre that many students feel most roles are precast, making the auditions mere formalities. As a director with many years of experience in both academic and commercial theatre, I can vouch that despite the prevalence of this belief, overall it is a myth. While I am sure precasting does occasionally occur, the majority of the time it is purely the perception of the students. This myth may be supported by the fact that the best actors are cast more often, leading to the belief that casting was made prior to the audition.

I cannot say strongly enough that a good director should base casting decisions on the qualities the actor demonstrates during the auditions. Casting for any other reason is not a service to the production or the actors. However, there is a difference between the practice of precasting and the practice of having potential actors in mind when selecting a play. For the director working with a relatively limited talent pool, it is important to consider whether each role can be well cast before choosing the play. The director should be able to think of at least one actor, if not more, in the talent pool who could potentially play each role. The purpose of this is to give the director confidence that a good cast can be had. The director should then use the audition process to make the selections.

While it is occasionally necessary to precast a role, the director must enter the audition process with an open mind and make his or her casting decisions based on the auditions.

CRITERIA FOR CAST SELECTION

While some directors make their casting decisions purely on instinct or "gut feelings," it is advisable for the director to consciously think about several factors. The order will change depending on the needs of the play and of each particular role, but, in some way, they must all be kept in mind. A casting worksheet summarizing these criteria can be found at the end of this chapter. The director needs to consider how the actor fits the given role. Regardless of how good actors are, if the audience does not accept them in the role they will not succeed. An example of the importance of audience acceptance can be seen in the 1968 film *Once Upon a Time in the West*. In this film, director Sergio Leone cast the talented and popular actor Henry Fonda as the villain. This was decidedly against type for Fonda, who always played the likable hero. While the film was a box office success in Europe and is generally regarded as a critical success, it was a box office failure in the United States. The consensus was that the financial failure of the film in the United States was largely due to the audience not accepting Henry Fonda as a villain. While there are many examples where the opposite is true, it is important for the director to think about how well the audience will accept the actor in the role. The audience's perception of the actor is just one factor. For example, if one character is supposed to be intimidated by another, the audience must be able to believe the intimidated character feels threatened. This does not mean the audience accepts only obvious choices but rather the choice must be believable.

The director's perception of the role defines the beginning parameters for the character. The casting decision should be for an actor who embodies the director's vision. This decision should go beyond a consideration of the audience's acceptance. Fitting the role includes both physical and emotional aspects. Ideally, the actor should physically fit the director's vision. In some cases this is more important than others. In the original casting of the role of Jonathan Brewster in Joseph Kesselring's classic comedy *Arsenic and Old Lace*, there was an important physical consideration since a line in the script states that the character "looks like Boris Karloff." The reference was made by the playwright as homage to Boris Karloff's portrayal of the monster in *Frankenstein*. While it was not the playwright's initial intent, the director of the Broadway production, Bretaigne Windust, convinced Karloff to undertake the stage role. Ironically, when a film version was produced it was decided to keep Karloff on Broadway, and film director Frank Capra cast Raymond Massey in the role. Windust's clever idea to actually use Karloff was an ingenious solution for the casting necessity; however, directors of revivals have had to find other ways to deal with casting this role in a believable fashion.

The actor must also fit the role emotionally. The actor's basic persona must be consistent with that of the character and, in addition, the actor must be able to convey the character's emotional range. In most cases, fitting a role emotionally and having the correct persona is more important than the physical look of the actor. If the audience is able to relate to the character through the actor's emotional embodiment, it is more willing to accept the physical appearance than the other way around. Using the example from *Arsenic and Old Lace*, while the physical resemblance to Karloff as Frankenstein is important, it is far more important that the actor emotionally embody the character.

The director must further consider the actor's range. Some actors can play a broad range of roles while others are more limited. This does not mean the latter group of actors is less talented, but rather they fit a narrower range of characters. The director's concern is if the role in question falls within the actor's range. This includes the aforementioned believability but more important, it includes both the emotional and acting range. The actor must be able to perform and be believable in the entire range of the role. It is for this reason that directors have actors read from a number of scenes for each character during the auditions so they can see the actor in each stage of the character's development. The actor must also be able to believably handle the transitions in this development. In casting the role of Adam in Neil LaBute's *The Shape of Things*, the director must choose an actor who can portray the introverted, shy, and self-conscious Adam prior to his remaking by Evelyn. Evelyn gradually transforms Adam physically, emotionally, and socially into a much more "desirable" person. The same actor must embody this physical and emotional transformation not only by the end of the play but also during the course of the play. The audience must be able to believe each phase of this development.

An important consideration is the actor's ability to interact with a partner. This refers to both the actor's technical partnering skills as an actor in general and how well the relationship with the other character in the scene is embodied and conveyed. Partnering, especially sharing, is an important skill the actor needs to demonstrate during the audition. Just as important, if not more so, is how well a given actor relates to a given partner. Even though an actor may be individually the best choice for the role, another actor may be a better choice overall because of the relationship conveyed with the partner. This aspect is often referred to as "chemistry." This is not something that can be taught, it simply exists. Hopefully, this chemistry is seen during the callback auditions. While it is possible this relationship will develop during the rehearsals, if the two actors lack initial chemistry the likelihood is significantly lower. Pairs and groups of actors are frequently seen working together in plays and films due to the chemistry they project. Actors who have had a prior working relationship have a greater chance of chemistry. However, actors who have never met before may naturally and quickly form such a relationship.

The actors' skill levels are another consideration. This refers to the acting skills the actors possess and how well they apply their technique to their roles. Some actors innately possess the skills while others may work extremely hard for many years and never reach the same level. The director's principal concern needs to be with the actor's skill at the time of the auditions and the likelihood of its growth during the rehearsal period. It is important that the actor be mechanically able to perform the role. This includes the technical skills of analyzing the character and bringing it to life as well as the actor's ability to move well onstage, have clear diction and enunciation, and project well enough for the size of the theatre. In addition, the actor must also possess or have the capacity to learn any specialty skills necessitated by the role. If the character must engage in stage combat, for example, and it is not possible to select an actor with training in this field, it is minimally essential that the actor have the capacity to attain the necessary skills. It is important for the director to learn to distinguish between the actor with genuine technique versus the actor with the ability to put together a well-constructed audition. Early in my career, I was directing a university production in which a fairly weak student actor gave a strong initial audition. Based on this audition, and partly as a reward for such good work, I gave the actor a callback. The actor continued to impress me and was cast in one of the supporting roles. To my dismay, the actor grew very little. This experience taught me the difference between a single good audition and the genuine ability to play a role. The director needs to be careful not to overestimate his or her ability to help the actor overcome deficiencies in the limited time of the rehearsal. While the actor may grow during this time, the director needs to consider how much growth can occur.

> The director needs to be careful not to overestimate the growth an actor can make during the rehearsal process. Significantly improving in weaker areas or completely learning a new skill is often unlikely in the relatively short rehearsal process.

The director needs to take into account several other factors including the actor's overall experience as well as the type of role being cast. An actor with experience is generally a more predictable choice. A great deal can be said for experience; however, an actor with little or no experience is not necessarily wrong for the part. Past experience, particularly if it is similar to the role in question, provides the actor with a base in the current production. There is an assumption that if the actor did well in the past, the actor can do so in the future. It helps if the director has knowledge of, or can verify, previous work, although this, too, can backfire. I once directed a stage musical in which my music director convinced me to precast an actor in the lead role based on his recent work with him in an opera. After meeting the actor I agreed that he seemed perfect for the role so I went with the recommendation. This actor was brilliant in early rehearsals, demonstrating a natural understanding of the role and possessing incredible vocal talent. This all fell apart as we moved off book. To my horror, I realized the actor could not learn lines. In fact, the harder I worked with him, the less he remembered. I had to make significant compromises to finish the production. The fact that the actor had little prior experience onstage aside from concertizing could have been a warning of potential future problems. Experience can also help an actor in dealing with the pressures of a role. In a production of *Death of a Salesman* I directed, two women were in final consideration for the lead role of Willy's wife, Linda. One of the women was an experienced veteran performer; the other was a relative newcomer. Both of these women embodied the role and demonstrated equal abilities in portraying the character. While it was a close decision I chose the newcomer based on an undefinable quality she possessed. The role of Willy was played by an experienced and powerful actor who unfortunately intimidated the woman. In this case, her inexperience did not give her a base to handle the situation. While I was able to resolve the situation and secure a strong performance, in retrospect I would have been better off casting the more experienced performer. The value of experience also extends to the style of the play. Actors who have worked with a particular style on previous occasions have an advantage over the less experienced. This is especially true in performing the works of Shakespeare. While experience should not be the ultimate deciding factor in determining the cast, the director needs to take it into consideration.

The actor's ability to work well in the production environment and, especially, to take direction is equally important. Actors who take direction well are easier to work with and their work generally results in a superior production. This aspect also relates to the personality of the actor. Some actors are simply more desirable to work with than others. This is true both for the rest of the cast and the director. While it is not the most important criteria in the casting decision, it is one the director needs to acknowledge. Given the choice between two actors equally right for the role, I will easily choose the one with whom it is more pleasant to work. The experience will be more pleasurable for all concerned. A difficult actor makes the production less enjoyable and more arduous for everyone. On the other hand, the actor may be so right for the role and so strong an actor it may be worth the effort despite the issues. The balance is determined by weighing how much of an asset the actor will be to the production versus how much of a problem it is going to be to work with him or her. Is the actor worth it? Behavior during the audition often helps the director get a read on the actor if he or she has not worked with the actor previously. It is logical for the director to assume the actor's behavior will not improve once cast. One technique used by many directors is to talk with the stage manager regarding an actor's behavior while waiting to audition. The stage manager can often provide insight into the actor's professionalism and personality. The director may also talk to other directors regarding experiences working with a given actor. The director, however, needs to be careful since other directors' experiences do not necessarily predict the experience he or she will have with the actor.

One of the biggest issues directors face is balancing the actor's physical type with the acting quality brought to the role. How well an actor physically fits a role is a key consideration for the director. At the same time, the actor's abilities are also important. To put it simply, should the director cast for the look or for the ability? Every director needs to find the answer to this question. *Typecasting* can refer to the practice of casting an actor based on persona, physical appearance, or having already performed in a similar role. While an actor may physically fit the type it does not necessarily mean he or she is best for the role. In general, the director and the production are better served with the more experienced actor than the one who primarily has the "look." Too many directors find when they allow physical type to be the main criterion that the character the actor develops is shallow and lacks the potential for growth. Although from the actor's perspective typecasting may prove to be an asset in securing some roles, it can limit their range and casting possibilities. However, directors often find it a major advantage to cast an actor the audience easily sees fitting a given role.

Directors must be careful when considering a weaker or less experienced actor simply because he or she physically fits the part. While there are times when this may be necessary, it is generally a less desirable casting option.

Another issue each director must consider in the casting decision is prior knowledge of the performer. How the director processes previous experiences with the actor is a decision each director must make for him- or herself. For example, if an audition is not particularly strong, the director may take into account a previous experience with the actor and determine that the audition was not fully indicative of the actor's potential. While directors need to utilize every tool at their disposal in making casting decisions, it is important that they not stray into precasting the role. While a previous experience can, and to some degree should, affect a director's decision, it is important for the director to keep an open mind during both the audition and subsequent casting process. Directors working in an educational environment have other issues to think about. An early directing mentor of mine wrote an article for a theatre journal discussing criteria for directors. One of his points was that directors needed to avoid taking any action just because "it is for the good of the actor." His position was it was not a responsibility or right of the director. While this position is essentially true in commercial theatre, it is highly questionable in non-commercial theatre, especially in educational theatre. In the educational setting, the director has to think about the development of the actor. The value of the opportunity for the actor is a factor in the casting decision. This, of course, may be in direct opposition to the discussion in this chapter. Following this logic the director will make the casting decision based on factors not related to the quality of the audition or the actor's ability to fit the role. The discussion of this topic is an ongoing one in educational and noncommercial theatre. It is a topic that will be explored in more detail in Chapter 22, "Directing in an Educational Environment."

The director needs to process all of these factors when making casting decisions. It is impossible to establish a single order of priority that applies to all casting situations. For each production the director must decide what is the most important aspect or aspects with regard to a given role. In making this decision priorities are established based on an interpretation of the characters and how the director wishes to present them to the audience. Beginning directors can gain valuable insight into this process by evaluating their casting choices after the production to determine whether they feel they prioritized correctly or at least if they maximized the possibilities. However, they will never know if a different casting choice would have been better since they can only evaluate the choices that were made.

> The director has to take all the criteria into account in making casting decisions; however, the importance of each criteria will change from production to production.

THE PROCESS OF MAKING CASTING DECISIONS

The specific process the director takes to reach a cast list varies from director to director and from production to production. In many cases, directors begin with the principal roles, move on to supporting roles, and end with the lesser roles. Other directors may choose to make casting decisions by pairs of actors as they appear in scenes in the play. Still others may start with the most difficult role to cast and move on to the easier. My preference is to begin with the roles I am most certain about and then progress to the roles for which I am less certain.

Experience and ability are almost always a better reason for casting an actor than the physical look of the actor.

A good starting point for the director is to eliminate actors from the callback list who are no longer under consideration. The director should then group the remaining actors by role and begin deliberations. This becomes far more complicated if actors are being considered for a number of roles. If this is the case, the director can begin by listing the principal choices for each role and comparing these options with the casting options for roles that are partnered with the first role. It is possible that in looking at the potential pairs of actors a single pair will quickly rise to the top of the list making further deliberation unnecessary. In looking at the possibilities the director needs to keep in mind the strengths and weaknesses of each actor. After a preliminary cast list is developed, the director should review it to ensure the actors best fit their roles, and the choice of each actor complements the choices made for the other roles. Once this is completed to the director's satisfaction, it is advisable to take one final look at the other actors under consideration to ensure an actor was not overlooked.

It is a good idea for the director to carefully review the final cast list before posting it to ensure that an actor was not overlooked and there are no mistakes. Correcting errors on the cast list after it is posted can be difficult if not impossible and at the very least embarrassing for the director.

NONTRADITIONAL CASTING

One of the more interesting considerations in establishing parameters for casting is based on the concept of nontraditional casting. This is the practice in which the director breaks from the expected norm in casting a given role. The two best examples of this are cross-gender and cross-racial or ethnic casting. In cross-gender casting the director casts a person of the opposite gender. In cross-racial or ethnic casting, the director casts an actor whose race or ethnicity is not normally associated with the role or perhaps in direct opposition to the role as described in the script. Nontraditional casting opens new possibilities for the director in both casting and interpreting the play. One reason for pursuing nontraditional casting may be for the notoriety. Unusual casting choices create an external interest in the production. Choosing to cast along these guidelines is essentially "being unique for the sake of being unique." If the director does not have an aesthetic reason for these casting options, the play is not truly enhanced. A far better reason to utilize nontraditional casting is to bring a new and hopefully more vibrant approach to the play. A production of Shakespeare's *Othello* in 1997 by Washington, D.C.'s Shakespeare Theatre made a unique use of nontraditional casting. For this production, film and television actor Patrick Stewart was cast in the role of Othello opposite a cast of

African-American actors. The production did a complete race reversal. It was often referred to as a "photo negative" approach. The role reversal allowed for a unique exploration of the play. The decision not to make any changes to the lines allowed the flipped racial separation to speak for itself. The race and ethnicity of the roles in this play are vital to its message. The nontraditional approach mirrored the intended race but explored the same values. In other cases, the director may choose to cast a single role in a race, ethnicity, or gender not normally associated with it. The 1996 Broadway revival of *A Funny Thing Happened on the Way to the Forum* starred Nathan Lane in the lead role of Pseudolus. When Lane left the show in 1997, he was replaced by Whoopi Goldberg. Since the play draws much of its farcical comedy from sexual innuendo, derived directly from Roman plays, having a woman play the role distinctly changed the interpretation of the role and the play. While it can be argued that this was largely a publicity ploy, the unique interpretation provided the basis for an entirely new take on the musical. In an interview, Whoopi Goldberg emphasized the fact that this play is fundamentally about the desire to be free. In her opinion, her African-American legacy provided a special insight into this role. As such, the gender reversal was actually less important to the play than the racial change.

Another strong example of both cross-racial and cross-gender casting is found in the Broadway production of the musical *Hamilton*. In this play about Hamilton's rise from obscurity to his role as a founding father to his death following a duel with Aaron Burr, all the principal roles other than King George are cast from actors of color. The concept emphasizes that America is a nation founded by immigrants, dramatizing the difference between the king and the colonists. In addition, the chorus of soldiers included women as well as men to break down gender roles. The casting decisions also made no attempt to resemble the actual historical figures. The audience response to this concept was overwhelmingly positive.

Nontraditional casting may be an intentional decision on the part of the director to refocus on the meaning of the play or it may be a tool the director uses to cast an otherwise ideal person into a role. When I directed Shakespeare's *The Tempest*, I was not happy with the choice of actors for the role of Gonzalo. Gonzalo is the advisor to the king and is the main voice of reason in the play. He provides a stabilizing influence through his use of logic. While I did not have a male actor I liked for the part, there was a female actor who was ideal. The use of a woman in this part not only served the purpose of putting a stronger actor into the role, it also allowed me to use her gender as a counterpoint to the male presence in the play. Apart from the female ingénue role of Miranda, all the other characters in *The Tempest* are men. By casting Gonzalo as a woman, I could explore the aspect of the woman as the voice of reason in a world of scheming or inept men. I was pleased with the result and believe it significantly strengthened my overall interpretation beyond solving a mechanical casting situation.

There are times when race, ethnicity, and/or gender are too important to the plot or the message of the play. In this situation, nontraditional casting may work against the play and undermine the meaning or make it so difficult for the audience to accept the premise that the play is significantly weakened. Nontraditional casting can, however, open up new possibilities for the director and should be considered.

It is essential that the director keep firmly in mind that each individual actor brings all of his or her physicality to the role. This includes gender, race, and other physical aspects. This is part of how the actor makes his or her portrayal unique. Nontraditional casting does not ignore this but rather avoids traditional considerations in the decision-making process.

UNDERSTUDIES

Should understudies be cast as possible replacements for the main cast? In commercial theatre, the use of understudies is a necessity since the play will hopefully have an extended run and there is the possibility an actor may be unable to perform. Given the commercial reliance on the performance for revenue, having understudies in place who can assume the role until the original actor returns protects the production. In productions with shorter runs, commercial or noncommercial, the answer is more difficult. Even in a short run it is possible one of the actors may be unable to perform. In this situation an understudy would save the performance. On the other hand, one must think about the time required to rehearse the understudies. This becomes an issue both in terms of rehearsal time and consideration for the understudies. The director and the other actors may be willing to take the time to rehearse the understudies, but in a production with a short run the highly unlikely event that an understudy will be needed makes the choice far less desirable. A great deal of energy may have been expended on both sides with nothing in return. In commercial theatre, understudies are compensated even if they do not perform. In noncommercial theatre, the only reward for the understudies' efforts is the opportunity to perform. The director and the producer need to decide if having understudies is worthwhile to the production.

CHANGING YOUR MIND

Another issue directors must consider is the nature of their commitment to their actors. Can a director change his or her mind after posting the cast list and replace one or more of the actors during the rehearsal period? While the replacement of actors does occur, it is an action the director must take advisedly. In selecting the cast the director creates an understanding with these actors. This understanding expresses confidence in the actors and is a commitment by the director to work with them through to the performance. The actors' side of this understanding is that they will carry out their responsibility to the best of their ability and perform the roles as best they can. This two-way agreement creates a bond between the director and the actors. If the director breaks this bond, it raises the issue of whether other actors may also leave the production if they are not content. The director would certainly be dismayed if after the rehearsal period started an actor decided to leave the cast. Should actors feel any differently if they are told to leave the cast by the director once the rehearsal process has begun? Sooner or later all directors regret making a specific casting decision. While the production might be better served by the replacement of the actor, the implications of the action must be considered. Does the director give implicit permission for actors to leave the production if they are unhappy? If the director desires and expects the loyalty and hard work of the cast, does the director not owe the same loyalty and hard work to them?

This principle is not necessarily absolute. If the issue is mechanical, such as attendance and punctuality, the director has every right to remove the actor since the actor has broken his or her agreement to be in the cast. The issue is a bit murkier if a director feels the actor is not trying hard enough, is wrong for the part, or is not reaching the director's standard, because the agreement really has not been broken. On the other hand, the director has a responsibility to produce the best production possible. It can be argued that it is not only the director's right but also duty to replace the actor. As a director, I do not expect more from my actors than I do from myself. As such, my ethos as the director is once I have placed actors in the cast I will not remove them as long as they are living up to their obligations.

When working in commercial theatre with paid actors, the dismissal of an actor is a different issue, essentially a business transaction. The terms of the actor's contract specifies the parameters for the termination as well as the compensation due. But even in commercial theatre the practice has serious risks. If actors feel they may be replaced if the director is unhappy with their work, even if specified under their contract, they may be inhibited from taking chances in the development of their characters and may not develop them as fully as they could if they felt safe in their environment. In this regard, commercial and noncommercial theatres have a similar issue. Directors have varying opinions on whether to replace actors. This is one of those areas where directors must make their own decision. It is a matter that must be taken seriously and carefully considered.

Replacing an actor once rehearsals have begun must be carefully considered. The director needs to take the overall good of the production into account and keep in mind that once a cast member has been dismissed there may be a feeling that actors can leave the cast if they are not happy. Further, if the actors feel vulnerable, they may be afraid to experiment with their characters and fail to develop them fully.

CASTING WITH OTHER DIRECTORS

A final issue in the casting process involves casting a play from a talent pool from which other directors will also be casting. This situation arises when a theatre holds a common audition for either all or a portion of the season rather than by individual play. The advantages to this practice are the actors only need to audition once, and the directors have equal access to all the actors so the director of the last play does not have to settle for whoever is still available. This situation is also seen in group auditions where a number of production companies take part. It is a common practice in summer theatre for companies to participate in regional auditions to cast their shows. The advantage for the actors is they are auditioning for a number of companies; the advantage for the theatre companies is a larger talent pool. In both of these cases the casting decisions have additional considerations for the director. In lone auditions, the premise is when the director posts the cast list the actor will accept the role and be available for the production. Where many directors are casting from the same talent pool, the directors are potentially competing for specific actors. In some cases, the directors will meet after the auditions to discuss their needs and mutually decide how to share the actors if there is overlap in their initial casting decisions. In a commercial group audition, it is more likely the directors will not have such a discussion but rather will approach each actor they wish to cast in the hope that the nature of the role or the nature of the compensation the actor will receive, either monetary or otherwise, will entice the actor to accept their role rather than one with another company.

Given the possibility that actors may not accept roles or directors will need to negotiate with other directors for the actors, it is important for the directors to have options in their casting so if their first choice is unavailable they have an alternative. This obviously creates significant problems in casting pairs of actors based on the nature of their relationship with the other actor in the scene. Directors will sometimes cast actors in groups so that in order to cast any of the actors they must be able to cast all of them. This can be a frustrating experience for the director, but it is not an uncommon situation. Even in major commercial theatre, a director casting a principal role must assume the actor is also auditioning for other productions and, as such, may turn down the offer. This is simply another reality that directors must accept.

CASTING WORKSHEET

Name _____ Role _____

Believability in Role	1	5	10
Physical Fit for Role	1	5	10
Emotional Fit for Role	1	5	10
Actor's Range for Role	1	5	10
Interaction with Scene Partners	1	5	10
Acting Skill			
Analysis/Portrayal of Character	1	5	10
Movement	1	5	10
Diction & Enunciation	1	5	10
Projection	1	5	10
Specialty Skills (if needed)	1	5	10
Previous Experience	1	5	10
Ability to Take Direction	1	5	10
Personality of Actor	1	5	10
Acting Quality for Role	1	5	10
Previous Knowledge of Actor	1	5	10
Other	1	5	10

FURTHER EXPLORATION

1. Talk to an experienced director to see how he or she approaches casting decisions.

2. Poll as many directors as you can to see how they feel about replacing actors. Compare their positions with how you feel on the issue.

3. For a play with which you are familiar, determine the traits necessary to consider in casting each role. Which of these roles is strongly paired with another?

Scheduling for the Production

PLANNING

Once the director has finalized the cast list it is time to begin the actual rehearsal process. Before the start of rehearsals, the director develops plans for the rehearsal process, which is actually a subset of the overall production calendar. This production calendar may or may not be developed by the director. If the company has a production manager, he or she is generally responsible for the production calendar, in which case the director provides insight as to when production elements will be needed in the rehearsal process. If the production calendar is not planned by a member of the production team, then it is up to the director to do so.

THE PRODUCTION CALENDAR

The production calendar provides a schedule for all elements within the production. Of particular importance to this schedule are the various due dates for each element. While the production calendar may contain specific dates, in many cases it only contains the major ones that affect more than one element. For example, for the scenic department, the production calendar might include the due date for the preliminary design plans, the due date for the final design plans, the start of construction, expected completion date for major scenic elements, the load-in of the set onto the stage, the first rehearsal onstage with the set, and the completion deadlines for the set. The production calendar will also include the dates for preliminary production and design meetings as well as the regular production meetings, actor rehearsals onstage, the technical rehearsals, the dress rehearsals, and the opening of the show.

One of the key functions of the production calendar is to establish communication among the departments to accommodate interdepartmental needs. For example, the lighting designer's light plot cannot be completed until the ground plan is finalized. As such, it is important for the lighting designer to know when the ground plan will be completed. Certain elements of the production might conflict with one another. For example, scenery and lighting may not be able to work onstage at the same time. In this case, the production calendar will specify each department's time onstage. The completion deadlines for sub-elements of each design department allow each department to plan for areas that overlap with the other departments. The production calendar is also an opportunity to ensure that sufficient time is allowed for the completion of each element. Finally, the production calendar provides the framework to determine if individual elements or the overall production are on or behind schedule.

A director may be dependent on a technical element to rehearse scenes of the play. The production calendar gives the completion date of the technical elements so the director can plan the rehearsal schedule accordingly. The Neil Simon farce *Rumors* that I directed involved a great deal of action with a grand staircase and numerous doors. I arranged with both the scenic designer and technical director to have the functional set completed quite early in the process. By doing so, we were able to rehearse the timing of these actions on the set almost from the beginning of the rehearsal period. In another instance, I was directing a farce for a summer theatre that required all rehearsals to be in a rehearsal space until days before opening. The set would be built and assembled in the scene shop and then loaded onto the stage after the closing of the preceding show. I was able to work with the technical director to facilitate a series of rehearsals on the set in the scene shop midway through the rehearsal process to ensure that the timing would work. This planning on the production calendar enabled me to schedule these rehearsals without interfering with construction. Some productions maintain a master calendar that includes all the elements of the production calendar plus the rehearsal calendar and the individual schedules for each department. Even if only the essential elements are listed, the production calendar is a valuable guide for planning the production. Figure 9.1 is an example of a production calendar.

It is imperative that all members of the production team be consulted regarding dates on the production calendar. It is pointless to arbitrarily set a date that is impossible to meet.

THE REHEARSAL CALENDAR – PREPLANNING VS. DAILY SCHEDULES

While the production calendar is important to the director, the director's major concern is the rehearsal calendar. There are essentially two approaches to the development of the rehearsal calendar. The first option is to plan rehearsals with the specifics for each rehearsal to be determined daily or in short groups of time. The major benefit to this approach is that immediate rehearsal needs can be scheduled, but the exact time for each section of the rehearsal is not required. For example, it may be difficult for the director to predict how long it will take to block Act I. The disadvantage is the director can lose track of time spent on each section of the rehearsal and run out of time by the end of the rehearsal period. As an actor, I performed in a show in New York where the director did not want to begin rehearsing Act II until Act I was firmly in hand. As a result, over three quarters of the rehearsal time was spent on Act I, leaving Act II seriously under-rehearsed.

The second option calls for the director to fully plan the rehearsal process including what will be undertaken at each rehearsal. The major advantage is that the time allocated for each element of the play can be carefully planned. The disadvantage is that these projections of time may be inaccurate and force ongoing schedule changes. This can be mitigated by planning only the first part of the rehearsal period. Once the director sees how the needs are developing, the final part of the rehearsal can be planned.

These approaches have implications for the actors as well as the director. In the first approach, actors must assume they are required for all rehearsals unless notified. In the latter approach, actors can plan around rehearsal dates and gear their preparation to the specific scenes they will be rehearsing. In commercial theatre, where actors are paid to be available for rehearsals, this is a minor issue; however, in noncommercial theatre, allowing the actors to make better use of the time they are not needed is a courtesy. Whether I am working in commercial or noncommercial theatre, I expect full preparation and focus from my actors, and therefore I try to maximize each actor's time at rehearsal not only as a courtesy but also to underscore this expectation. In planning rehearsals, I try to group rehearsal units with the same actors. This is only possible when I am working intensely on individual scenes and will not be the case for either act run-throughs or full run-throughs. Despite this, I fully acknowledge there may be times that due to production necessities an individual actor's time may not be fully maximized.

Regardless of the approach taken, the director can utilize the action units identified during the script analysis as rehearsal units, allowing the focus to be placed more intensely on scene work. Using these action units enables the director to focus on smaller parts of the play while ensuring that the actors can begin and end each rehearsal unit with arcs of development. Further, the director needs to be sure to preplan specific goals for each rehearsal in order to maximize the time available. While the director may choose not to share these goals directly with the cast, it is important for the director to have them firmly in mind.

PLANNING THE AMOUNT OF TIME NEEDED

While directors would love to have the luxury of an infinite amount of time for rehearsal, this is almost never the case. Generally, the time available for rehearsal is preset by the production company. In commercial theatre, it is often dictated by the money budgeted to actors' salaries. In noncommercial theatre, it is usually set by the availability of the actors and rehearsal space. What will be different is the time spent each week for rehearsal. If the time allocated for rehearsal is not predetermined by the production company, it is up to the director to allot time for the rehearsal process.

The Runner Stumbles – Production Calendar

as of 8/23/2015

NOVEMBER–DECEMBER 2015

SUNDAY	MONDAY	TUESDAY	WEDNESDAY	THURSDAY	FRIDAY	SATURDAY
1 November	2	3	4	5	6	7
8	9	10	11	12	13	14
15	16	17	18	19 **Production Meeting** 11:00 – room 108	20	21
22	23	24	25	26	27	28
29	30	1 December	2	3 **Production Meeting** 4:30 – room 108	4	5
6	7	8	9	10	11	12

Thanksgiving Break

Scenery and Costumes resolved prior to break

Christmas Break — December 13–January 18

JANUARY–FEBRUARY 2016

SUNDAY	MONDAY	TUESDAY	WEDNESDAY	THURSDAY	FRIDAY	SATURDAY
17 JANUARY	18 All Technical Plans Complete Supplies ordered	19 Shops Open Construction Starts	20	21	22 Seating Chart Complete	23
24	25 Set up for Auditions AUDITIONS	26 Set up for Callbacks Cast List Posted AUDITIONS	27 Rehearsals Start (Designers to present designs at Table Read)	28	29 Deadline for all cast measurements	30
31 Set with seating taped out in Studio 1st Blocking Rehearsal	1 FEBRUARY Light Plot Complete	2 Start light hang	3 Rehearsal Props Complete Rehearsal Costumes Complete	4	5	6
7	8	9	10 CAST OFF BOOK	11	12 Set Complete for Load-in	13 Last day to hang lights without set
14 SET LOAD-IN	15 Rehearsal Sound Complete Makeup Finalized	16	17	18	19 Full set with seating and backstage masking complete	20 Focus Call??
21	22 Show Props Complete	23	24 All Sound and Music Approved	25	26 ALL Tech Complete	27 DRY TECH (Light and Sound Cues)
28 ACTOR TECH (w/Costumes)	29 Resolve any final technical issues DRESS REHEARSAL I	1 MARCH DRESS REHEARSAL II	2 PERFORMANCES	3 PERFORMANCES	4 PERFORMANCES	5 PERFORMANCES
6 STRIKE	7 Return all borrowed items	Black – General Burgundy – Director/Cast Blue – Set Red – Costumes Green – Lights Magenta – Sound Orange – Props Brown – Makeup Cyan – Management				

Figure 9.1 Production Calendar

Just as there is an old standard of one minute per page in judging a play's running time, there is a similar standard for judging the length of rehearsal time, one hour of rehearsal for each page of dialogue. The goal of the director is to find the ideal amount of rehearsal time that ensures quality work without the play becoming over-rehearsed. An over-rehearsed show is tired and lacks vibrancy and energy. To find the ideal amount of time, the director must take a number of issues into consideration.

It is generally better to plan for more rehearsals than you project are needed. These additional rehearsals can be canceled, and the cast will appreciate the time off.

The length of the play is the first consideration. Assuming a three-hour rehearsal period, a three-hour play could be run through once while a one-and-a-half-hour play could be run through twice. A longer play will either have more scenes or longer ones than the shorter play, necessitating additional time to work on the smaller units within the play.

The next issue is the complexity of the play. This can affect the amount of rehearsal time required even more than the length. The complexity of the play may include the nature of the language used by the playwright, for example the works of Shakespeare. It is harder for the cast to develop their characters in one of his plays than in a contemporary play unless they have had significant Shakespearean acting experience. Special needs such as choreography and music is another complexity that may affect rehearsal time. Fortunately for the director, the book portions within a musical are typically shorter and may necessitate less time. Stage combat is another good example of special needs. To make stage combat both believable and safe, the director must ensure adequate time is dedicated to the combat. A play involving stylized movement would also require additional rehearsal time.

Experience is another factor in determining rehearsal time. Casting experienced actors make rehearsals more efficient and productive, thus making better use of the time allotted. Experienced actors do their homework, allowing rehearsals to be even more productive. If the director is working in an environment of relatively new and unskilled actors, time will be needed during the rehearsals to assist them in developing their characters far more than when working with skilled actors. The same is true for dance; rehearsals for dance with trained dancers is far more time efficient than having the choreographer teach basic technique to those who are not.

The director also must consider how much, if any, rehearsal time will be lost as the actors move off book. For many actors, the natural progression of developing their characters and smoothly moving off book does not have any effect on the progress of the rehearsals. In cases where the director is working with less-experienced actors, the likelihood increases that the progression of the rehearsals may be significantly set back once the actors put down their scripts. The director must have an understanding of the actors to predict how much of an impact this will have on rehearsal time.

In addition to more intense work on rehearsal units, the director also has to allow time for periodic run-throughs of the play to make sure that continuity and an understanding of the overall arc of the play are being developed. These run-throughs are even more essential if the director consistently rehearses individual units out of their natural order. The rehearsal schedule also has to allow rehearsal time for the technical elements of the play. A play with complex scene changes integrated into the action requires extensive rehearsal time with both the crew and the actors. Similarly, a production with many complex light cues necessitates additional rehearsal time. For most productions, the director needs to assume that the technical rehearsals are to be used solely for the technical elements and not for actor development. As such, it is best that the director plans for the play to be essentially prepared as it moves into the technical and dress rehearsals.

Beginning directors should be careful to allow enough time for the rehearsal process when directing their first scenes or short play. Even though the rehearsal time needed is far less than for a full-length play, it is generally a good idea, if possible, to plan for extra rehearsal time. It may be difficult to find time in the future, and it is easily cancelable if deemed unnecessary.

PHASES

While not all rehearsal plans follow the same schedule, most rehearsals include the following phases:

- Read-through or Table Read
- Blocking
- Character Development
- Polishing
- Technical Rehearsals
- Dress Rehearsals.

READ-THROUGH OR TABLE READ

Most directors begin the rehearsal process with a cast meeting and read-through. It is at this meeting that the director has the opportunity to discuss with the actors the nature of the production and elaborate on the concept. The discussion usually starts with an introduction of the production staff and the cast members and their respective roles. This is especially important if the actors do not know one another. The director can then take care of all functional necessities, such as ascertaining that contact information is correct; going over initial cast duties, such as costume measurements; and discussing the expectations of and procedures for the rest of the rehearsal process. As a director, I like to take this opportunity to distribute a company policy sheet summarizing the policies and expectations for rehearsals. These policies include both the general policies I have for all my productions and any specific policies related to this production and the production company. While most, if not all, of these policies are generally understood by the actors, following an idea from stage management, the production is well served by specifying these policies up front to avoid confusion or negative feelings later. It is also a good idea to provide a brief explanation for what can appear to be arbitrary policies.

The 25th Annual Putnam County Spelling Bee
COMPANY POLICIES

The following policies are designed to help avoid misunderstandings and ensure as smooth a rehearsal process as possible. All company members should read and observe them at all times. If you have any questions – ASK!!!

1. Be aware of the rehearsal schedule. Know when and where you are expected to be at rehearsals.

2. Be on time to all calls. Be ready to start working at the call time. Allow yourself enough time to arrive and warm up for the rehearsal. To expedite the rehearsal, all actors should engage in warm-ups **prior** to the start of the rehearsal. We will warm up vocally as a group.

3. If you are **unavoidably** delayed, please be sure to call or at least send a message to the stage manager.

4. Conflicts with the rehearsal schedule should not occur; however, if you foresee one, please see the director immediately.

5. Check the Call Board **daily** for changes in the schedule or other announcements Announcements will also be posted via email. Last-minute changes will be sent by text.

6. Please silence all cell phones during rehearsal. Do not answer the phone as doing so will interfere with the rehearsal process. If you are waiting for a crucial message, you may leave your phone with the stage manager.

7. All cast members should wear appropriate rehearsal attire as soon as possible. This should include footwear and clothing suitable for your character in the given scene. Be sure you are aware of costume changes and accessories that might affect the rehearsal process. See the director and/or costume designers for information regarding your costume(s).

8. The script is rented and must be returned following the final performance. **Place all marks in the script in pencil only. Do not use pens, markers, or highlighters. All marks must be erased before you turn in your script.** Please be careful not to lose it since not only will it be difficult to replace and you will have lost all your accumulated notes and blocking, but you will be financially responsible for paying the replacement fee.

9. All cast members should develop a character profile and analysis. This should include all the information stated as well as implied in the script in addition to any information you must create to complete the profile. The completed profiles can then be discussed with the director.

10. Lines MUST be learned as quickly as possible. (Note the absolute deadline on the rehearsal calendar.) Being off book earlier will be a major asset to the development of your character, your fellow actors, and the production. This is especially true for musical numbers. The final deadline for being off book is October 24.

11. Please do not make any major physical changes in your appearance without consulting with the director. **This especially includes haircuts.** All cast members will need to have haircuts/hairstyles consistent with their character(s). Please check with the director to be sure you understand what is needed.

12. Be responsible for all outside preparation, rehearsing, and/or materials needed from you. Make specific note of any words or concepts that you do not understand.

13. Please do not leave the rehearsal area for any reason without letting the stage manager know where you are going.

14. **Smoking is prohibited anywhere on campus.**

15. Be very careful with food in the theatre. Be sure to clean up after yourself. To avoid accidents, water and other drinks must be in a sealed "sipper-type" container. **Eating and/or drinking anything other than water is prohibited whenever in costume or in the dressing room.**

16. Visitors will be allowed to most rehearsals at the discretion of the director as long as it does not conflict with the rehearsal process.

17. It is each actor's responsibility to know where we are in a scene. Be ready for your entrances!

18. All cast members should have a small notebook (a steno pad or electronic means) to keep production notes and director's notes following run-throughs. iPads, smartphones, or tablets work equally well.

19. Please assist your fellow performers by remaining quiet during rehearsals and not causing any distractions in the wings or the rehearsal room.

20. Actors must return props to their proper location. Be aware: actors are responsible for checking all their props before each rehearsal and performance. Prop locations for both rehearsals and performances will be designated by the stage manager.

21. As a courtesy, all actors should assist the stage manager in cleaning up after each rehearsal.

22. Please do not cross in front of the director during rehearsals. If you need to get to the other side of the theatre, cross behind the director.

23. All company members will be given two (2) complimentary tickets for the production. You must pick up your vouchers from the department secretary. Reservations are to be made at the box office.

24. Although highly unlikely, in the case of inclement weather the director will decide whether to cancel rehearsal. In any event, individuals should always use good judgment regarding travel for rehearsals. Cast members should make every effort to avoid being in any location that may make travel to rehearsal more difficult or dangerous.

25. Actors are responsible for hanging up all costumes or rehearsal costumes after each rehearsal and performance.

26. When in doubt, ask!!!

Important Phone Numbers:

Director	–	Office – XXX-XXXX
		Home – XXX-XXXX
		Cell – XXX-XXXX
Stage Manager	–	XXX-XXXX
Box Office	–	XXX-XXXX
Theatre (Backstage)	–	XXX-XXXX
Scene Shop	–	XXX-XXXX
Costume Shop	–	XXX-XXXX

Figure 9.2 Company Policy Sheet

For example, if you are rehearsing in a studio with a dance floor, one of the policies might specify that actors must wear approved rehearsal shoes, and street shoes are not permitted. Explaining that this policy is designed to protect the floor from dirt and abrasive materials provides a rationale for the policy. In a commercial setting, these policies may already be part of the actors' contracts. Figure 9.2 is an example of a company policy sheet.

> To ensure sufficient time during the technical rehearsals, the director should not plan on working with the actors. Doing so takes the focus away from where it should be and generally is counterproductive for the actors. As such, the director needs to have the actors fully prepared prior to the technical rehearsals.

The director's interpretation of the play and the production concept are the next topics of discussion, followed by a presentation from each of the designers. A costume designer with whom I worked early in my career typically handed each actor a copy of the rendering for their costume at this first meeting. The actors liked this so much I now ask all my costume designers to do so, if possible. Background information the cast will need to begin rehearsals is then provided by the director or dramaturg. This information may include a brief biography of the playwright or information about the location, parameters, or period of the play. If I have technical advisors in particular areas, I then ask them to briefly set the stage for their work with the actors in creating the world of the play. This also gives them the opportunity to discuss ideas for both the play and the individual characters the actors must start to embody.

Following the presentations and discussions, in most instances the remainder of the rehearsal involves a reading of the script. This process, often called a read-through or a table read, allows the actors to hear the play as voiced by each of the actors. It also provides the director with an opportunity to explain any concepts, define any words, or clarify any issues in the play. The director may do this during the read-through or wait until afterward. In some cases it is valuable to follow the reading with an open discussion of the play. If the read-through is not interrupted, it can also provide insight into the play's projected running time. It is also desirable to allow time for the actors to express their opinions or ask questions.

Given the length of the script and the presentations and discussions, it may take more than one rehearsal to accommodate all the above. The director needs to consider how much time in the rehearsal process can be dedicated to these discussions and the read-through. If the show is complex, the director may have more than one read-through. While some directors feel having actors sit and read is a waste of rehearsal time, others believe that until the cast fully understands the script they should not get away from the table. This is an issue each director has to decide for him- or herself. At least as a beginning practice, a single read-through and discussion is a valuable start to the rehearsal process. I often follow the read-through by having the actors read the script again on their feet on the rehearsal set. I do not provide any blocking or other directions but allow the actors to explore the play on their own. This rehearsal expands on what was discovered in the read-through and also allows me to see the instinctive nature of the actors' movements. I can use these movements as a basis for my future staging of the play.

BLOCKING

The director provides the basic structural framework for the play by creating both stage pictures and the movement between them, commonly referred to as blocking. Assuming the director will provide preplanned blocking, time must be provided for this process. If the cast will improvise the blocking, commonly referred to as organic blocking, the process may be included in the subsequent rehearsal phase. Typically, the director will provide at least a minimal structure for the staging that is conducted during this phase. If so, this is a fairly mechanical phase, but the nature of the blocking and the stage pictures are the initial foundation for the relationship between the characters and for individual character development. The blocking will then be refined, altered, or perhaps completely changed depending on the development of the play during later rehearsals.

The time required by this phase depends on the complexity of the blocking and how much of it the director will prescribe. Relatively simple blocking for a full-length play may be completed in one or two rehearsals. A safer time allotment is to plan three to four days for a full-length play. The director does not usually include choreographed movement, stylized staging, or stage combat at this time. It is an excellent idea to allow the actors to repeat the blocking. This serves as an opportunity for the actors to be sure they understand it and for the director to see the movement in its totality. The decision over whether to have this repetition depends on the total time allocated to this phase. Blocking can be as precise as specific movements or as generic as simple entrances and exits. If the director is not formally blocking the play, it is time to progress directly into the next phase.

CHARACTER DEVELOPMENT AND SCENE DEVELOPMENT

Character development and scene development occupy the bulk of the rehearsal process. The director should dedicate as much time as possible to this phase. It is here that the director and actors will work through the individual action units, developing the characters and building the play. In this phase, the director must allow sufficient time for the actors to freely experiment with their characters as they explore tactics to achieve their goals. For the most part, the actors will make good use of their time for this exploration. It is important for the director to keep in mind not only the analysis of the individual characters but also the objectives of each action unit in the context of the entire play. During the course of this phase, the director refines the development of the plot to express the dramatic action. It is here that having as much of the analysis as possible directly on the pages of the script to serve as reminders and for quick reference will be of real benefit to the director. Rehearsals may be in the chronological order of the units within the play or the director may choose to rehearse them out of sequence either to work with similar units in closer proximity to each other or to maximize the actors' time at rehearsals. Rehearsing units in chronological order maintains continuity, but it places equal emphasis on each unit. By rehearsing out of order, the director can focus on each individual unit and allow connections between units that would otherwise be separated. This will be discussed further in Chapter 14. This phase should include periodic run-throughs to ensure the smooth development of the overall arc of the play. This is especially important if the play is rehearsed out of order. As a general guideline, it is best not to allow more than three rehearsals before returning to the same material. Allowing more than that risks the loss of the details and discoveries made in the rehearsals. It is generally more productive to rehearse a unit more often than to dedicate a single lengthy amount of time. This is particularly an issue for musicals where significant time may be dedicated to the choreography and music. If the blocking is not routinely repeated, the progress is quickly lost. It is also a good idea to schedule regular full run-throughs so the actors can see their characters' development in its continuous arc and so the director can see how the play is developing. Designers, especially the lighting designer, will also want to see early run-throughs to facilitate their planning.

POLISHING

The final phase of the rehearsal process, prior to the addition of the technical elements, is referred to as the polishing phase. During this phase, the director focuses on ensuring that the play as a whole is evolving along its natural arc, its meaning is being clearly developed and conveyed, and the overall rhythm, tempo, and pacing are appropriately progressing. Throughout the life of the production, the play will continue to grow and mature. However, it is during the polishing phase that the ultimate parameters for the world of the play are refined. By doing so, the director makes sure the play will not wander off course as the performances progress. During the later polishing rehearsals, the director may wish to incorporate some of the mechanical elements of the production, such as costumes or shifting scenery, if they directly affect the play's flow and development. The director then avoids forcing all of these elements into the technical and dress rehearsals and allows time, if necessary, to rework the blocking to accommodate them. At this point, the cast should be utilizing all props and, as much as possible, all physical elements of the setting.

The polishing phase also provides time for the cast to focus on their final choices. This should not be misunderstood to say that the play should become static. I once worked with a director who told an actor early in the rehearsal process to "dip it in plastic," i.e., to lock in his performance and repeat it from that point forward. Such a comment shows a significant lack of understanding of the organic quality of the play.

Ideally, between three and six rehearsals should be planned as full run-throughs to work on polishing. The director will need to determine whether it is better for the production to spend additional time in more intense scene work or in polishing. If the director was successful in conducting the development work in the preceding phase, there should be sufficient time left for the polishing rehearsals. If the actors are ready to add the technical elements, the production will continue to develop through to opening. If, on the other hand, there are still significant issues, such as unresolved character choices or tactics or the general rhythm and development of the show is not consistent, the addition of these technical elements may further complicate

> The end of the polishing phase is an excellent time to have planned one or two extra rehearsals as a cushion; these may be canceled if, in the director's opinion, the play is ready to go into the technical phase.

the process by creating additional obstacles to overcome prior to opening. For this reason, the goal of the director is to have the play appropriately developed by the final run-through prior to the start of the technical rehearsals.

TECHNICAL REHEARSALS

All the technical elements are added to the production during the technical rehearsals. These rehearsals are purely for the technical elements. Their interactions with one another and with the actors are rehearsed and polished. So as not to impede the process, the director should refrain from working with the actors other than to integrate them with these elements. The time committed to the technical rehearsals is planned during the preproduction meetings based on the complexity of the technical elements. In a play with no scene changes and few light changes, this can be accomplished in a single rehearsal. A play with a large number of technical elements may require several rehearsals. While the director and the actors have had weeks to prepare for this moment, the designers must implement all of their work in the limited time of the technical rehearsals. This is particularly true for the lighting designer, who typically writes all the light cues and works on their integration into the play during this time. The stage crew who will carry out the technical aspects during the production must also learn, master, and refine their work during technical and dress rehearsals. The technical rehearsals are often considerably longer than the standard acting rehearsals because of the intense amount of work that must be accomplished. Even if acting rehearsals were between three and five hours long, it is probably wise to allow up to eight to ten hours for the technical rehearsals. Union productions limit standard rehearsals to eight hours but provide for a limited number of ten-hour rehearsals for technical rehearsals.

The technical rehearsals are often divided into two parts. One part would involve only the technical personnel and the designers; the other part adds the actors. A technical rehearsal where the actors are not present is often referred to as a *dry tech*. It is during this time that individual cues for both lighting and sound are written, and the crews rehearse the execution of all technical requirements. A variation on this is referred to as a *paper tech*. The paper tech is a technical rehearsal away from the theatre where the director, designers, stage manager, and related personnel plan on paper how to accomplish the technical aspects. In extremely complex shows the paper tech saves stage time. However, by not actually having the technical elements in operation, the paper tech may not take all the complexities into account. While a paper tech can be valuable, it is important to remember that it is not a replacement for the onstage rehearsal time necessary to physically implement these aspects. The designers cannot write their actual cues prior to their arrival in the theatre nor can scene shifts be worked out without using actual stage time. This is not to say they cannot be significantly preplanned, but they do necessitate stage time. If time is limited or the production is extremely complex, the designers may write cues in blind, that is, they may write theoretical cues to use as a base once they are in the theatre. While this may be helpful, it can also be less productive for the designers than the time it takes to write them. The decision to incorporate this process must be carefully considered with the designers.

While some directors choose not to be present during technical rehearsals where actors are not present, this practice should be discouraged. Although not absolutely necessary, it is more helpful to the designers and saves considerable time if the director comments, shares concerns, or can answer questions during the dry tech process, rather than waiting until the aspect is fully implemented to request changes. The dry tech process can be long and tedious especially for the director, with lengthy periods of sitting and waiting for the next element to be completed. Nevertheless, the director's presence is extremely valuable. At the end of the dry tech process the cues are written, rehearsed, and entered in the stage manager's production book, enabling the stage manager to call the cues going forward.

> The dry tech process can be long and tedious especially for the director, with lengthy periods of sitting and waiting for the next element to be completed. Nevertheless, the director's presence is extremely valuable.

The second part of the technical rehearsals is the *actor tech*. During this rehearsal, the play is run in its entirety, integrating the technical aspects with the work of the actors. Generally, this rehearsal involves a large number of stops or cuts to resolve issues, fix cues, address safety concerns, or adjust staging to meet the technical needs. These cuts can prove frustrating for the actors since they are now used to uninterrupted run-throughs. Their work typically suffers during these rehearsals due to the cuts, but it is important that the actors maintain the tempo of the play since this will have an impact on the timing of cues. Unless this adversely affects the play, the director should be open to resolving these issues by implementing minor adjustments in the staging or the actors' work. In a production with simple technical aspects, the actor tech is essentially a run-through. Most of the time, however, the actor tech is almost totally for the integration and implementation of the technical elements.

If sufficient time is not planned for the technical rehearsals, the ensuing dress rehearsals will not run smoothly, and it is possible that the opening performance will suffer. The director needs to understand and make sure the actors understand the necessity to the production for these elements to be fully worked out. In a technically complex play, it may be necessary to plan multiple days for both dry techs and actor techs.

> Safety is paramount for the cast and crew during the technical rehearsals. Be sure the actors and crew understand that anyone can call a cut if a danger is perceived. This will allow the issue to be safely addressed.

A modified technical rehearsal plan, a *cue-to-cue* rehearsal, may be implemented if there are significant gaps in time between technical elements. For example, if all the technical elements occur at the beginning and ends of the acts, the rehearsal will run until there is a break between cues of at least several pages, stop, and then jump ahead to shortly before the next cue and continue until the rehearsal is completed. Since the major objective of the technical rehearsal is the integration of the technical elements, significant time can be saved by skipping those sections of the script without them. Taking cuts for shorter intervals is generally coun-terproductive since the time it takes to stop, find a starting place, and begin again often uses as much time as actually running the segment. While a cue-to-cue rehearsal can be a major time-saver, it does have shortcomings. First, by jumping ahead, neither the actors nor the crew knows how much time there is between the series of technical elements. For example, if the crew has to prepare for the next shift during the scene, they do not know how much time they have since the scene was not run in its entirety. Second, it is also possible that there may be technical problems in the skipped portions of the scene. For example, an actor may walk into a portion of the stage that is not lit. This situation will not be noticed until the play is running in its entirety during the next rehearsal, now requiring a fix.

DRESS REHEARSALS

Dress rehearsals are the final rehearsals prior to opening. The term dress rehearsal is often thought to indicate the cast is now in costume. This is not necessarily the case; the cast may have begun rehearsing with costumes much earlier. This is a reference to a rehearsal where all elements of the production are present and run as if it were a performance. The number of dress rehearsals is dependent on the time that can be committed after the technical rehearsals and prior to opening. If there is more than one dress rehearsal, earlier dress rehearsals may be stopped if major complications arise. At least one dress rehearsal should be run exactly as if an audience were present, without stopping to resolve any problems. Assuming the dress rehearsal runs just like a performance, the time needed for the rehearsal is equal to the length of the run of the play plus whatever time is necessary to get ready and for notes following the rehearsal.

It is important for the director to establish with the production staff exactly how the dress rehearsals will be handled. For example, the first dress rehearsal following the actor tech may be designated as a dress/tech. In this case, the production will run as a performance but will be stopped to resolve major technical issues. The advantage to such a rehearsal is that technical issues can be immediately resolved, but the disadvantage is that the actors are not given a full and uninterrupted run-through. The director needs to make it clear that while actor issues were not addressed during technical rehearsals, technical issues cannot interrupt dress rehearsals unless specifically allowed. The director's attention during the dress rehearsals should be on the play as a whole to ensure that all of the elements are working together. This is also the opportunity for the director to give the cast final polishing notes. It is often the practice for the director to meet with the production staff following the dress rehearsals to discuss technical issues that arose during that rehearsal.

Many directors find it useful in planning the rehearsal schedule to start with the opening performance and work backward to auditions.

ESTABLISHING GOALS FOR EACH REHEARSAL

While understanding the different emphases of each of these phases provides the director with a structure to initially divide the rehearsal process, it is important for the director to further subdivide the rehearsals in terms of more specific goals for each rehearsal. While having a goal of "work on characters" is a start, the director needs to be more definitive, for example, "work on tactics in Unit 1." More specific goals give the director a clearer sense of what to work on in the scene and allow a more concrete understanding of the status of the rehearsal process. It is difficult for the director to know whether the production is behind schedule if the goals are vaguely stated.

One goal the director needs to specify at the beginning of the rehearsal process is when the actors should know their lines without using the script, commonly referred to as being *off book*. Directors have differing opinions on how quickly actors should be off book. It is generally agreed that the actors cannot fully engage one another, and certainly will have difficulty handling props, until they can put down their scripts. To free the actor to fully engage both his or her partner and the props, some directors feel the actor should be off book as early as possible, potentially even before the rehearsals begin. On the other hand, as the actors learn their lines they also begin an unconscious process of learning the delivery and approach to the lines. Actors who are off book prior to the start of rehearsals often unconsciously embed the delivery of the lines into the learning of them. As such, they essentially have to relearn the lines during the rehearsal process. Actors who learn their lines during the rehearsal process gradually memorize the words and embody the delivery they have been utilizing. Following this logic, some directors feel it is better for the actor to be off book later in the rehearsal process. This does not mean the actors should learn their lines solely in rehearsal. It is the actors' job to learn their lines and to work on their characters outside of the rehearsal environment. Assuming the director wishes the actors to be off book at some point during the rehearsal process and not before, it is important to allow adequate rehearsal time for the actors once they are off book to fully realize their characters and interact with their partners. Directors who allow actors to use their scripts until they are closer to the end of the rehearsal process limit the development of the actors. This development does not fully take place until they put down their scripts. It is generally recommended that actors be cleanly off book for at least one third of the rehearsal process. My personal preference is to encourage actors to move off book as quickly as possible, including doing some scenes with their script and some scenes without. I tell the actors that when they wish to be prompted to set their scripts down. The stage manager will note that this is an indication they wish to be prompted. I do not, however, allow the actors to lower their scripts and try to be off book. I want them to either have the confidence to set the script down and be prompted or use the script to read the lines. This option is, of course, only applicable up to the off-book deadline. I have found that by implementing this lines policy I can significantly avoid the problem of losing rehearsal focus to line prompting once reaching the lines due date.

PRESENTING THE PRODUCTION AND REHEARSAL SCHEDULES

After preparing the production and rehearsal schedules, the director presents them to the production staff and the actors. There are essentially two ways they can be presented. The first is to put all the information on a calendar. The advantage is that it is easier to visualize how each of the elements fits into the time period and see the relationship between the various dates. The difficulty is that the calendar limits the amount of information for each entry. The second is a chart format that allows the director to include as much information as necessary. In comparing the rehearsal schedules as shown in Figures 9.3 and 9.4, both schedules have many rehearsals that include sections broken down by rehearsal units. The rehearsal schedule for *The 25th Annual Putnam County Spelling Bee* in Figure 9.3 has fewer divisions within each rehearsal and fits nicely in a calendar format. The rehearsals for *A Few Good Men* in Figure 9.4 are given in a chart format as there are too many time divisions during each rehearsal to clearly indicate on a calendar. The specific goals for each rehearsal are not indicated on either of these forms. I prefer to keep this information in my production book.

The 25th Annual Putnam County Spelling Bee
Rehearsal Calendar
(as of 9/25/2016)
October 2016

SUNDAY	MONDAY	TUESDAY	WEDNESDAY	THURSDAY	FRIDAY	SATURDAY
						1
2 Work Scenes Full Cast 7:00	3 Work Scenes Full Cast 7:00	4 Work Scenes Full Cast 7:00 (No Matt till 8)	5 Work Scenes 7:00 TBA 8:00 Full Cast (No Chloé, Asher, Troy till 8)	6 Work Scenes Full Cast 7:00	7	8
9 Work Thru Full Cast 7:00	10 Work Thru Full Cast 7:00 CAST OFF BOOK	11 Choreography Full Cast 7:00 (No Matt till 8)	12 Choreography 7:00 TBA 8:00 Full Cast (No Chloé, Asher, Troy till 8)	13 Choreography Full Cast 7:00	14	15
16 Work Thru Full Cast 7:00	17 Work Thru Full Cast 7:00	18 Work Thru Full Cast 7:00 (No Matt till 8)	19	20 No Rehearsal	21	22
23 Fall Break No Rehearsal	24 Work Thru Full Cast 7:00	25 Work Thru Full Cast 7:00 (No Matt till 8)	26 Work Thru Calls TBA (No Chloé, Asher, Troy till 8)	27 Work Thru Full Cast 7:00	28	29
30 Work Thru Full Cast 7:00	31 Work Thru Full Cast 7:00					

Given the ensemble nature of this production, all cast members will normally be called for each rehearsal. You will be released once your scenes are finished. We will let you know each night whether you are needed at the start of the next rehearsal and, if not, give you a new call time. **Assume you are called to all rehearsals unless you have a class or work conflict that the director knows about and is indicated on the calendar.**

Figure 9.3 Rehearsal Schedule (Calendar Format)

A FEW GOOD MEN
Rehearsal Schedule

Week 1:

Wed	Aug 30	7:00	Full Cast Read Through
Thurs	Aug 31	7:00	Block
Fri	Sept 1	3:00	Character work

Week 2:

Sun	Sept 3		NO REHEARSAL
Mon	Sept 4	7:00	Full Cast – Finish Blocking; I-23; II-11
Tues	Sept 5	7:00	ALL Marines – Military Training
		7:20	ALL Navy – Military Training
		7:40	1-15; 1-17; 1-2; 1-7; 1-11; 1-12; 1-20; II-1; II-6; II-10; II-12 – Sam, Jo, Kaffee, Howard
Wed	Sept 6	7:00	I-23; II-11; II-14 – Kaffee, Jo, Sam, Ross, Randolph, Dawson, Downey *(MPs, Sgt-at-Arms)*
		7:20	II-5, II-7 – add Stone
		7:40	II-9b – add Kendrick
		8:00	II-9a – add Howard
		8:30	II-13 – add Jessep

> Please check with the director if you are present in any of these scenes but do not have lines to see if you need to attend.

Thur	Sept 7	7:00	I-1 – Dawson, Downey
		7:20	I-6 – add Jo
		7:30	I-9, I-19 – add Sam, Kaffee
		7:45	I-19i – add Kendrick
			I-22, II-4
		8:00	I-16, I-18 – add Jessep, Markinson
		8:30	I-3, I-4 – add Whitaker, Lyle, Dave
		9:00	I-10, I-21 – add Ross
Fri	Sept 8	4:00	I-4i, I-16i – Santiago
		4:20	I-14 – add Dawson, Downey
		4:30	I-3i – add Markinson
		4:45	I-13 – Kendrick, Dawson, Hammaker, Thomas
		5:00	I-5, I-8 – Jessep, Markinson, Kendrick, Tom
		5:15	II-2 – add Stone
		5:30	II-3, II-8 – add Orderly

Week 3:

Sun	Sept 10	7:00	Work Act I – FULL CAST (except Stone) Randolph Call at 8:20
Mon	Sept 11	7:00	Work Act II – FULL CAST (except Santiago and Whitaker)
Tues	Sept 12	7:00	1-15; 1-17; 1-2; 1-7; 1-11; 1-12; 1-20; II-1; II-6; II-10; II-12 – Sam, Jo, Kaffee, Howard
		9:20	1-10 – add Ross

Figure 9.4 Rehearsal Schedule (Chart Format)

Calendar format schedules are generally easier to read and result in less confusion than charts. As such, it may be preferable to use calendars unless there is simply too much information to be included.

FINAL THOUGHTS

Regardless of the philosophy with which the director prepares the rehearsal schedule, it is important to take into consideration all the needs of the play. It is better to overestimate than underestimate the time required for rehearsals since it is easy to cancel rehearsals, but it is difficult to find time for additional ones. The director should also keep in mind potential external factors such as weather or illness that may cause a loss of rehearsal time. In any event, the director must make it clear that the schedule may have to be modified to fit the needs of the production as they develop.

SCHEDULING CHECKLIST

PRODUCTION SCHEDULE

- ❏ Prepare a list of all production components to be included in the calendar
- ❏ Schedule production meetings
- ❏ Plan due dates for each component including, but not limited to:
  - Technical plans complete
  - Begin construction of set and costumes
  - Auditions
  - Start of rehearsals
  - Departmental deadlines
  - Stage management deadlines
  - Load-in
  - Rehearsal versions of designs (e.g., rehearsal sounds)
  - Final completion date
  - Technical rehearsals
  - Dress rehearsals
  - Strike
  - Postproduction deadlines
  - Other
- ❏ Adjust schedule to accommodate components that need other areas to be complete before they can be addressed
- ❏ Create calendar

REHEARSAL SCHEDULE

❏ Determine date of opening performance

❏ Determine dates for auditions and/or start of rehearsals

❏ Determine the time needed for each phase of the rehearsal process

- Table Read
- Blocking
- Character and scene development
- Polishing
- Technical rehearsals
- Dress rehearsals

❏ Divide the time between Auditions/start of rehearsals and the first performance between the phases listed above, adjusting the allotted times as needed

❏ Check the schedule to determine if:

- Sufficient time is allotted to each phase
- The same section of the script is revisited at least every three to four days
- Sufficient run-throughs are provided to ensure continuity

❏ Adjust the schedule as needed

❏ Create a presentation model for the schedule

FURTHER EXPLORATION

1. Choose a play and make a list of all technical elements that need to be completed during the rehearsal process to facilitate the rehearsals.

2. Based on the list prepared in Activity 1, make a list of all the technical deadlines for the production and prepare a production calendar.

3. Talk to various designers regarding their needs during the technical and dress rehearsals.

4. Prepare a rehearsal schedule for a hypothetical production. Include the necessary components and then develop specific goals for each rehearsal.

5. Prepare a rehearsal schedule for a scene or play you are directing complete with specific goals for each rehearsal. After each rehearsal, note if and how well each goal was met.

PART IV

Floor Plans, Stage Pictures, and Blocking

Developing the Floor Plan

THE DIRECTOR'S RELATIONSHIP TO THE FLOOR PLAN

The process for developing movement onstage incorporates three elements: (1) the floor plan (the physical layout for the use of the stage), (2) stage pictures (static images creating compositions with the actors for key moments in each unit onstage), and (3) blocking (the movement of the actors from one stage picture to another). Each of these elements will be explored in the following three chapters.

The development of the floor plan creates the possibilities for the stage pictures and blocking. The floor plan not only provides the possibility for the director to create these images, but it also supplies the parameters that constrain the movement to certain areas of the stage. A well-developed floor plan allows for the easy creation of the stage pictures and blocking; a poorly developed floor plan is problematic. Normally, the floor plan comes from the work of the scenic designer; nevertheless, it is vital that the director has the skills to create a well-constructed floor plan in order to understand and evaluate the one developed by the scenic designer.

In a full production, the director collaborates with the scenic designer in both the development of the floor plan and the overall look of the setting. It is important for the director to be certain the designer's floor plan offers the best potential for the staging the director wishes to incorporate. The inability to effectively collaborate can lead to subsequent staging issues. While some directors give the scenic designer a sample floor plan, this is not a recommended practice. Rather, as a guide, the director conveys to the designer ideas and needs of the production in terms of possibilities and desired limitations. If there is not a scenic designer, as is frequently the case in early work by a director, it is the job of the director to develop the floor plan. While this places the full burden of responsibility on the director, it also gives the director the opportunity to learn the necessary skills for creating a floor plan that can be applied when working with scenic designers in the future.

While the floor plan is generally part of the scenic designer's work, it is crucial for the director to develop the skills of creating and evaluating floor plans to ensure they will meet the staging needs of the play. If the director simply accepts the floor plan as given, there is a risk the production concept will not be brought to full fruition.

UNDERSTANDING THEATRE ARCHITECTURE AND ITS IMPLICATIONS FOR THE PRODUCTION

Different forms of theatre architecture have an impact on the floor plan as well as the production as a whole. In most cases, the location for the play is predetermined, but occasionally the director chooses the theatre space. If the location is predetermined, the director needs to understand how to maximize the strengths of this configuration while minimizing or working around its limitations. If the director has the option of choosing the space, then understanding the implications of each configuration is critical.

The **proscenium theatre** is often considered the "standard" configuration for contemporary theatre. Almost all Broadway theatres have proscenium configurations. Developed during the Renaissance, the proscenium theatre is the most recent of the configurations and is characterized by the proscenium arch, from which it derives its name. The arch serves as a portal for the audience to observe the play, framing the stage in the same manner as a picture frame. The audience is typically seated parallel to the proscenium arch. Figure 10.1 is a plan or overhead view and Figure 10.2 is a section or side view of a proscenium theatre.

An imaginary line may be drawn along the proscenium arch (represented in Figure 10.1 by the dashed line or *plaster line* extending across the upstage line of the proscenium arch) separating the theatre into two houses, the stage house, where the play is performed (on the top in Figure 10.1), and the audience house (on the bottom). A grand curtain is often used to close the proscenium opening both before and after the play. In many proscenium theatres there is also an *apron*, an extension of the stage from the proscenium arch toward the audience. The apron lets the action onstage break through the proscenium arch and enter the environment of the audience. While this allows for more intimacy with the audience, it also increases the distance to any action framed by the arch upstage of the plaster line. The areas to the left and right of the stage behind the proscenium arch are the *wings*, which provide for hidden entrances of actors as well as possible locations from which to move scenery. Many proscenium theatres also have a fly system or *flies*, a large airspace above the stage where both flat scenery, called *drops*, and three-dimensional scenery can be raised and lowered to the stage, facilitating rapid scene shifting.

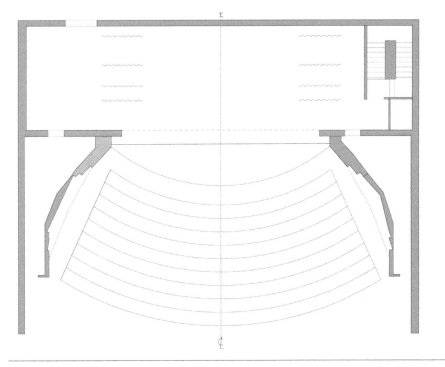

Figure 10.1 Proscenium Theatre (Plan View)

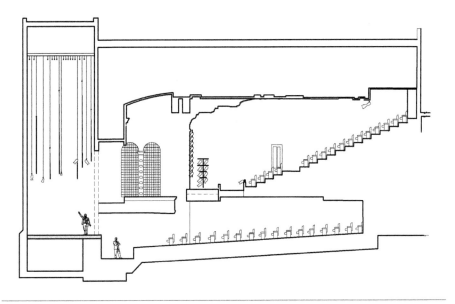

Figure 10.2 Proscenium Theatre (Section View)

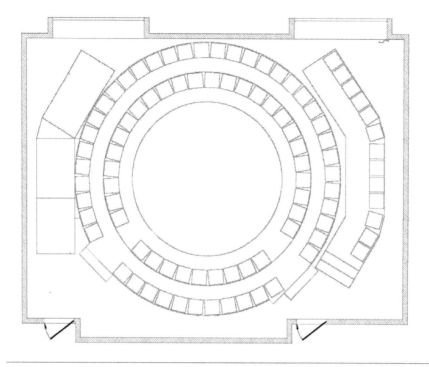

Figure 10.3 Arena Theatre

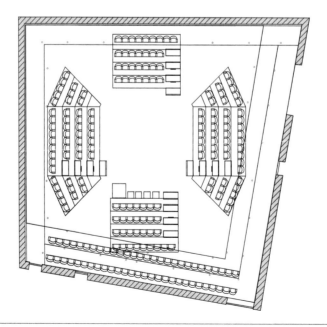

Figure 10.4 Arena Theatre

The space in the wings and flies is one of the major advantages of the proscenium theatre as it facilitates changing scenery. Since the audience faces the stage from one side, it is possible to use tall scenery and high elevations such as platforms and stairs. These advantages completely separate the proscenium stage from the other configurations. In addition, proscenium stages often have an *orchestra pit*, a lowered space directly downstage of the proscenium arch. Having an orchestra pit for the musicians reduces or eliminates the sight line problems for the audience and acoustically assists the music.

The proscenium stage also establishes a distinct separation between the world of the play and the world of the audience. In a pure proscenium stage with no apron, there is a clear separation between the actors and the audience, an invisible *fourth wall* that psychologically divides the two worlds. The use of an apron mitigates this by creating a more intimate relationship with the audience.

Given these characteristics, the proscenium stage is often the best mechanical choice for plays that necessitate sizable casts, large-scale scenic needs, especially heights, and rapid scene shifts. Beyond these mechanical needs, the proscenium stage creates the most formal relationship between the worlds of the play and the audience. It also provides the most uniform view of the stage for the audience since the entire audience is looking at the play from one side.

Perhaps the oldest form of theatrical configuration is the **arena theatre**, dating back to theatre's prehistoric roots. In this configuration, the audience sits completely around the acting area, which can be circular or square. This configuration is also known as *theatre-in-the-round*. The actors and the audience share the same physical environment and airspace. Figures 10.3 and 10.4 illustrate typical arena configurations.

Given that the audience observes the play from all sides, there are scenic and staging restrictions to the use of arena theatre. Scenic elements are low since any elements with height would create visual obstructions for part of the audience. No matter where the actors stand, their backs will be to some part of the audience, and unless they are dead center, they will be closer to one part and farther from others. Entrances for the actors are from the aisles. Since doorways and stairs create visual obstructions, for the most part they are not used.

Staging a play in an arena configuration generally allows for a greater intimacy between the play and the audience. The audience's proximity to the actors is significantly closer than in a proscenium theatre, dividing the maximum distance by about one-fourth. There is no psychological separation between the two worlds. Since the actors are so close to the audience, in some cases inches, they can relate to the audience even to the point of directly engaging them.

Thrust theatre dates back to the ancient Greeks and is characterized by the audience sitting on three sides of the acting area. Thrust can be considered to be a compromise between arena and proscenium. While it provides the intimacy of arena theatre, it also allows for a wall farthest from the audience for taller scenic objects, giving all members of the audience a similar viewing angle of this wall.

Entrances can be either from the aisles, as in arena theatre, or from the wings along the upstage wall, as in the proscenium theatre. In fact, some thrust stages have a proscenium arch framing the upstage area farthest from the audience. Since the thrust stage has wing space some

Figure 10.5 Arena Theatre

Courtesy of Drury University

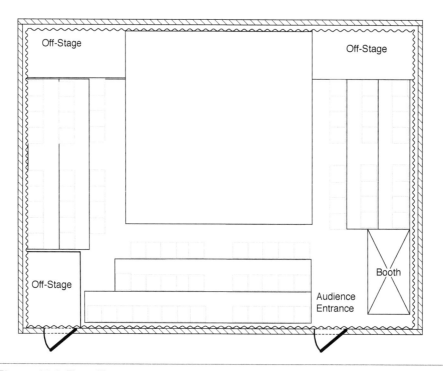

Off-Stage

Off-Stage

Off-Stage

Booth

Audience
Entrance

Figure 10.6 Thrust Theatre

scenery can be shifted to and from there. Using a thrust theatre provides similar intimacy to an arena theatre while incorporating some of the mechanical advantages of the proscenium theatre.

The final architectural configuration is a flexible space commonly called a **black box theatre**. The black box theatre draws its name from the fact that it is usually a rectangular or square space painted black that can be configured into any desired theatrical configuration through the arrangement of the seating platforms and other masking. A black box theatre allows the production to make the choice of theatre configuration specifically for each production. Figure 10.7 shows a typical black box theatre without any configuration. Figure 10.8 shows the same space configured in what is commonly referred to as "Alley Theatre." In this configuration, the audience is seated on two sides of the performing space.

Once the director and scenic designer know the theatre configuration for the production, they can turn their attention to the creation of the floor plan.

A theatre space, in most cases, is provided by the producer, leaving the director to put the configuration to its best use. When the director is able to choose the theatre space, the strengths and challenges of each available space must be carefully thought through. Key issues to consider include the desired intimacy of the performance, the size of the audience, the mechanical needs of the production, and the nature of the desired staging.

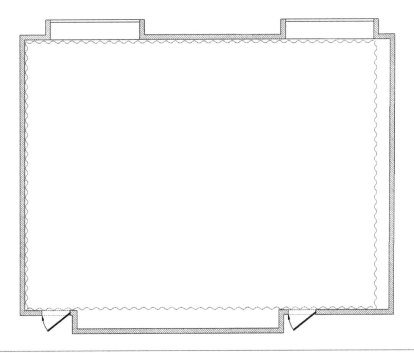

Figure 10.7 Black Box

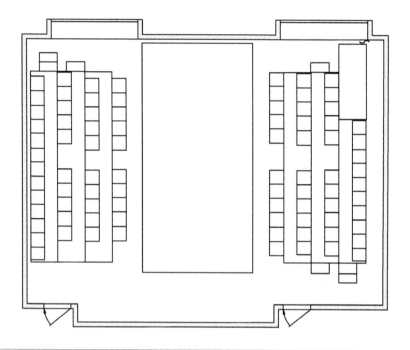

Figure 10.8 Black Box in Alley Seating Configuration

WORKING WITH THE SCENIC DESIGNER ON DEVELOPING THE FLOOR PLAN

It was established earlier that prior to starting the rehearsal process the director needs to make sure the scenic designer's floor plan meets the needs for the production. Although minor changes are possible throughout the production, major changes may be impossible once the floor plan is set. Perhaps the most important aspect of the floor plan is to provide for the basic nature of the action. Figures 10.9 and 10.10 show two floor plans consisting of a series of platforms, each with a six-inch difference to the next.

The major difference between the two settings is in the lines that define the platforms and levels. The floor plan in Figure 10.9 is composed of rectilinear lines, while the floor plan in Figure 10.10 comprises mainly curvilinear lines. The harshness of the lines of the first compared to the softness of the second creates different ambiences for the play. The natural action on each setting will tend to follow the lines of each floor plan. The rectilinear style of Figure 10.9 naturally inspires movement in straight lines and sharp angles, while the curvilinear lines of Figure 10.10 tend to result in movements in gentle arcs with softer turns. Due to the relative sense of harshness in Figure 10.9, this type of floor plan tends to work better with dramas and tragedies; the sense of softness in Figure 10.10 generally works better with comedies. While this may be somewhat of an overgeneralization, it underscores the importance of the floor plan matching the nature of the play with the actions the play implies.

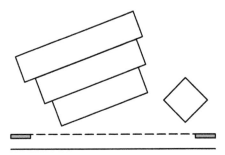

Figure 10.9 Rectilinear Design

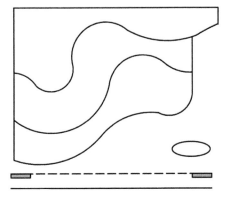

Figure 10.10 Curvilinear Design

A floor plan significantly cluttered with obstacles causes the blocking to involve short lines rather than long sweeping ones. This is neither inherently good nor bad; it simply depends on the reason for the desired action. Obstacles force the actors to find ways around them, while open spaces permit unimpeded action. The ability to make direct crosses allows the actor to embody the strength of the action, while making changes in direction softens or mitigates it. The amount of space available for the actors determines the amount of movement. While an open stage provides no impediments to the staging, the lack of constraints may prove problematic later on. For example, a play necessitating a more claustrophobic feeling will not work well in a large open space.

In communicating with the scenic designer, the director needs to articulate any specific needs as well as the nature of the movement the floor plan must support. The scenic designer and director should also discuss any areas the director particularly wishes to avoid. The first consideration is the type of floor plan that will work best for the play.

TYPES OF FLOOR PLANS (PATTERNS OF SCENERY)

There are a number of basic types or patterns of scenery used in theatre. The **box setting** is probably the most common form of scenery for interior plays. This setting is a series of walls that essentially form a box. The audience watches the play through the wall that is not there. These sets are usually realistic and attempt to create the full sense of an interior on the stage. Figure 10.11 illustrates an example of the typical box set.

Box sets not only include the walls with doors and windows but also the furniture appropriate for the room. Some box sets even have ceilings for added realism; however, the ceiling can create numerous problems for the lighting. Box sets work best on proscenium stages, especially when contained inside the proscenium arch.

One of the oldest forms of scenery, dating back to the Renaissance, is the **wing and drop** setting. From that time until the modern theatre, almost all scenery, both interior and exterior, was done with wing and drop settings. In the modern theatre, wing and drop settings are customarily only for exteriors or for more stylized productions. The wing and drop setting consists of a drop covering the entire upstage painted to depict the scene. The sides of the stage are masked by a series of panels or curtains parallel to the proscenium arch that also may be painted. Connecting the two panels across the top is a header that provides top masking. By flying in a new drop and either sliding or flying the wing panels in and out it is possible to quickly change the scenery. Entrances and exits are facilitated in the space between each of the wing panels. Wing and drop settings can also be used to describe a setting that features an empty stage masked by black drapes on the sides and back.

By the beginning of the twentieth century, stage scenery began to include three-dimensional elements. **Three-dimensional settings** are fully dimensional scenic units with platforms and

Figure 10.11 Box Set, *The Misanthrope*
Scenic Design by Robin Schraft. Courtesy of Drury University

Figure 10.12 Three-Dimensional Setting, *Traveler in the Dark*
Scenic Design by Christopher DePriest. Courtesy of Drury University

levels for staging. They allow the actors to physically interact with and on the set. Any setting with full dimensionality or levels fits into this category. Figure 10.12 shows an example of a three-dimensional setting.

One subcategory of three-dimensional settings is the **unit setting** (see Figure 10.13). A unit set is a permanent set of units utilized in all of the settings. Changes are accomplished by the addition or subtraction of scenic elements to and from the basic unit. These may include insets in the stock unit and/or furniture and other smaller units. Notice in Figure 10.13 the basic unit is changed by adding wall/door units on each wing, flying in different scenery, and the addition of furniture. Lighting is also utilized to differentiate the scenes.

Another variation of three-dimensional settings is the **space stage**. The space stage is a minimalist approach to scenery where the entire setting is depicted solely by a series of platforms, stairs, and/or ramps. Locations are changed by moving to a different area of the stage, supported by the use of lighting. Few, if any, changes are made to the actual setting during these transitions. The space stage in Figure 10.14 also makes use of rotation to further differentiate the scenes.

Realistic interior settings can be stylized through the use of a **fragmentary setting**, sometimes referred to as **selective realism**. In a fragmentary setting, selected elements are removed with only the essential elements remaining. Figure 10.15 is an example of a fragmentary setting. Note the lack of walls above the wainscot leaving only the window, door, chimney, and roof line.

Figure 10.13 Unit Set, *Merry Wives of Windsor*

Scenic Design by Robin Schraft. Courtesy of Drury University

Figure 10.14 Space Stage, *Candide*

Scenic Design by Robin Schraft. Courtesy of Drury University

Figure 10.15 Fragmentary
Setting (Selective Realism),
Boat Without a Fisherman

Scenic Design by Robin Schraft.
Courtesy of Drury University

Fragmentary settings are particularly helpful in reducing the sense of realism, facilitating rapid shifting between different sets, and reducing the cost of construction. Aside from the elements removed, the fragmentary setting is essentially the same as a box setting.

A type of design that not only does not cover or hide the methodology of its construction but rather incorporates these elements into the design is a **constructivist setting**. Constructivist settings work especially well with the expressionistic plays of the early and mid-twentieth century. These settings celebrated the mechanical sense gained from showing the bracing and mechanical support of the structures. Typically, these settings are fairly minimal. Figure 10.16 illustrates a constructivist setting.

Figure 10.16 Constructivist Setting, *Company*

Courtesy of Drury University

Figure 10.17 Simultaneous Staging, *Doubt*

Scenic Design by Madison Spencer. Courtesy of Drury University

Simultaneous staging is a pattern of scenery that originated during the Middle Ages with medieval cycle plays. Each play was performed on a stage called a pageant wagon. At the end of each play the audience moved on to the next wagon. In the same way each individual play in the cycle was performed on a separate wagon, modern applications use a variety of levels or areas of the stage to represent different locations as well as lighting to help focus the attention of the audience (see Figure 10.17). Simultaneous staging provides an approach to plays that require more detailed settings for each location but allows the action to move quickly from one area to another or even exist in multiple places at the same time. Simultaneous staging is a particularly useful option if the action returns to the same place a number of times. It is similar to a space stage except the locations are more realistically defined rather than simply suggested.

MEETING THE NEEDS OF THE SCRIPT

The director must take into consideration a number of factors from the script so the necessary elements are incorporated into the floor plan.

PROVIDING FOR PATTERNS OF MOVEMENT

The director should think about the patterns of movement, i.e., how the director envisions the actors traversing the stage, to be incorporated into the staging. These patterns of movement are determined by the overall style and mood of the play as well as how the director wishes to convey the relationship between the characters. The projected patterns of movement will affect the basic lines of the floor plan as well as the amount of open space or lack thereof. The amount of open space versus elements that inhibit large movements will determine the nature of the action.

PHYSICAL NEEDS

The physical needs of the play need to be identified by the director, who compiles a list of the items that must be incorporated into the setting. These are specified by the playwright in descriptions or parenthetical notes or implied in the dialogue. For example, if the scene calls for a character to write a letter at his desk, the setting must incorporate a desk. If the character enters the room and takes off her coat, then the setting must have a place for her to put it. The director must also keep in mind items that are not necessarily specified. For example, in a scene that takes place in a park, adding a bench will provide a focal point as well as an opportunity for the characters to sit even though the script did not directly call for a bench.

Another consideration for the director are the elements that may not be used but become important because by not using them the characters are conveying the choice not to do so. The underlying sense of a scene in which two characters are having a conversation that starts with one seated and inviting the other to sit down may be furthered by having more than two chairs. By having choices of where to sit, the second character can convey his or her feelings toward the first. The director should also note exceptional uses for items in the setting. The setting may call for a table, but if the director intends one of the characters to stand on it, the table must be able to bear the actor's weight.

ENTRANCES AND EXITS

The director must identify the number of entrances and exits and the relationship between them as the setting also provides for their limitations. For example, if one character must be trapped onstage with another, the setting needs to prohibit the first character from leaving. Or, if one character needs to exit without seeing another character enter, then the entrance and exit must be positioned accordingly. The relationships of the entrances and exits also need to make logical sense to the audience. For example, in an interior setting on the fourth floor of a building, the upstage wall can contain a window, but it logically cannot also have a door. While there might be a plausible explanation, the audience will be unnecessarily distracted.

The director also should contemplate the value the location of each entrance and exit has for the characters. Figure 10.18 shows a floor plan of a box set with four doors. Each door provides the actors with a different value as an entrance and exit. Actors making an entrance through upstage center door A have a strong entry since the entrance faces downstage and they make their entrance directly toward the audience. On the other hand, to exit through door A, the actors must turn their backs to the audience and cross upstage to the door. This action creates a much weaker exit. Side entrances reduce the impact of an upstage entrance or exit by neutralizing the action.

An entrance through door D has the same value as the exit. By moving the door either upstage or downstage on the side wall, variations in the value can be achieved. An entrance through door B is stronger than one through door D because the entrance is farther upstage from the audience generally allowing for a downward cross rather than a lateral one, but slightly weaker as an exit. Door C provides an entrance or exit closest to the audience; however, an entrance through door C inevitably leads to an upstage, and hence weaker, cross. Conversely, an exit through door C is stronger than one through door B since it involves movement downstage.

The direction of the door swing also affects the blocking. Figure 10.19 illustrates six possible door swing directions. Doors that swing onto the stage, as illustrated in doors B, C, and E, will have the effect of having the door enter before the actor. This is particularly strong in doors B and C. Doors with offstage swings, doors A, D, and F, generally allow the focus to be on the actor. Side doors with the hinge on the upstage side, as in door F, provide a more natural

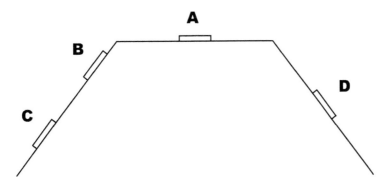

Figure 10.18 Box Setting Entrances and Exits

Figure 10.19 Door Swing
Direction

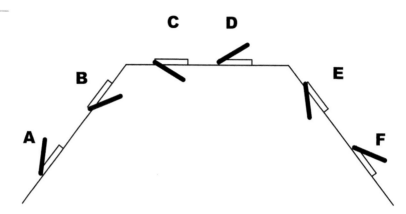

Figure 10.19 Door Swing
Direction

masking of the offstage area. Of the six examples, D and F provide the best direction for the door swing. Despite this, the direction of the door swing should be consistent with architectural conventions. Residential exterior doors typically open into the building while those of commercial buildings open out.

The type of entrance or exit can be further affected by scenic elements. Placing furniture near the door, for example, requires the actors to move around it as they enter or exit. Entrances and exits from wing and drop settings follow similar guidelines.

SPATIAL NEEDS

Spatial needs refer to the amount of space needed for the setting and the action it contains. The nature of the setting of the scene has direct implications to the amount of space required onstage. If the scene takes place in a bedroom, a stage setting 60 feet wide will appear ludicrous. Although some theatrical license can be applied in determining the floor plan based on the needs of the play, the amount of space utilized by the setting must be believable to the audience, at least within the world of the play. The amount of space for the action must allow for creative blocking while still giving the audience clear sight lines to the actors. In general, wider, shallower spaces have better audience sight lines than narrower, deeper spaces. The maximum amount of space that can be dedicated to the setting is determined by the size of the stage. However, the director should refrain from feeling it is necessary to use it in its entirety. The amount of space can be cut down by a combination of bringing the masking farther onstage and lighting only the portion of the stage utilized. I remember adjudicating a regional high school play competition where the stage was considerably larger than those of many of the competing schools. One director, feeling the entire stage had to be utilized, expanded the setting to accommodate the much wider space. Unfortunately, the setting was a kitchen, and by expanding the width there was now more than 25 feet between the kitchen table and the counter. Not only did this look odd, but the staging was also significantly stressed. At one point, the actor playing the mother had to give a lengthy speech while crossing repeatedly back and forth from the counter to the table. While this probably worked on her high school's stage, the extra width required her to trot back and forth while delivering her lines.

In general, the setting should always be centered on the stage. The exception may be the utilization of one side of the stage while the other is being set for the next scene. A play with a single setting that is not centered appears off-balance to the audience and creates a greater distance to the audience on the far side of the stage.

SIZE OF THE CAST

The size of the cast, or at least the maximum number of actors onstage at any one time, determines the minimum amount of space needed in the setting. Sufficient space to move freely must be considered. The 60-foot-wide bedroom mentioned in the last criterion may have to accommodate a large chorus performing a choreographed musical number. It may be necessary to adjust or compromise in other areas to fit the entire unit onstage and still maintain adequate sight lines for the audience, particularly if using a space stage or simultaneous staging. As with spatial needs, increasing the amount of space by increasing the depth of the area may provide additional space, but it may also create a sight line problem to see the upstage actors. On the other hand, wider but shallower settings limit the blocking to mainly one side or the other.

TYPE OF ACTION

The action implied and necessitated by the scene must be taken into account. A scene with two people sitting at a table does not require much space. On the other hand, a two-person scene involving physical combat needs significantly more space not only to accommodate the action but also to ensure the safety of the actors. A setting with numerous obstructions can be either helpful or detrimental depending on whether they provide motivation or simply get in the way. Both the information from the script regarding the staging and the director's vision for staging need to be considered. A setting that incorporates a series of progressively increasing levels heading upstage can improve sight lines to upstage actors. The same setting, however, may produce serious impediments to movements that now involve ascending or descending the levels. The style of the play is another consideration. For example, comedic movement is different from dramatic movement.

CHANGES IN SETTING

In plays containing more than one setting, attention must be paid not only to the development of each individual setting but also to how the settings shift. While this is really an issue addressed by the scenic designer, the nature of the transition from one setting to the other involves the director since it affects the pacing. The flow of a play with numerous short scenes can be seriously interrupted if at the end of each scene the action must be halted for the setting to be changed. The individual settings may be ideal in and of themselves, but the loss of energy during the shifts is detrimental. Working out how to handle these changes must be done prior to the start of rehearsals. Too many directors make the mistake of waiting until technical rehearsals to address scene changes. An alternative to changing the setting for each scene might be to use simultaneous staging. Since each scene is set on a different part of the stage with the actors moving between them, lights can be used to shift the focus of attention. Of course, this only works if all the necessary settings can be onstage while still providing a workable space with good sight lines for the audience. In any event, the issue of changing scenery must be taken into account during preproduction. To plan for the changes both the number of settings and the necessities involved in performing the shifts must be evaluated. This is particularly true when working with contemporary scripts, which are often written with a more cinematographic approach involving short scenes in different locations.

It is crucial for the director to foresee potential issues inherent in the floor plan so opportunities for staging can be maximized. The floor plan should be tweaked to make it as valuable a staging tool as possible.

USING THE FLOOR PLAN TO FOCUS THE AUDIENCE'S ATTENTION

Aside from action, the attention of the audience is typically attracted to the most interesting point on the stage. To ensure the floor plan allows for the creation of intriguing stage pictures, it is important to understand the visual tools that help focus the audience's attention.

CONTRAST

The first tool is contrast. The audience generally places its attention on the element, person, or group that is different from the others. If everyone is standing, the audience's attention will be drawn to the person who is seated. If everyone is facing to the right, the audience's attention will be drawn to the person facing a different direction. A leading character associated with a group may wear essentially the same costume, but it is distinguished from the others by a contrasting color. The floor plan needs to provide the possibility to direct focus through the use of contrast.

MOVEMENT

The attention of the audience is naturally drawn to the person who is moving, assuming everyone else onstage is standing still. This includes physically crossing to another part of the stage as well as movement of the body. The setting must support this concept, and the floor plan must facilitate the necessities of the scene without requiring movement other than what is used to focus attention. The floor plan also needs to allow for crosses to change the focus of the audience's attention.

HEIGHT

Assuming all other factors are equal, the audience's attention is drawn to the actor at the highest elevation. The floor plan can significantly help with this by providing different levels for the actors. The difference in levels does not need to be substantial. Slight increases of 4 to 6 inches can produce significant changes in the focus of the audience.

ANGLE

Angles can also be used as a tool in focusing attention. By changing the angle of an object, and hence the way an actor uses it, the visual interest and focus are also altered. Visual interest can be increased by rotating an object slightly to avoid it being parallel to the audience. The amount of this rotation depends on how the actor should relate to the audience as well as to the other actors onstage. This rotation is often referred to as *raking*. Since raking has a number of applications it will be discussed in more detail later in this chapter.

SCENIC POINTING

Scenic pointing refers to the creation of the elements of the setting that naturally lead the audience's attention to an intended point. This may be done through a number of visual techniques, the most common of which is the use of converging lines on the setting. Progressive changes in a series of objects will have a similar effect. However, scenic pointing can work against the director if the director wishes to stage a key moment away from an intended point.

STAGE AREA

The location of a scene can be significant to the audience's perception. An individual who steps onto a stage to address the audience typically stays as close to the audience as possible and moves to the center of the stage. Location is a natural principle that is utilized without any particular forethought. This principle can be applied to the relative importance of each

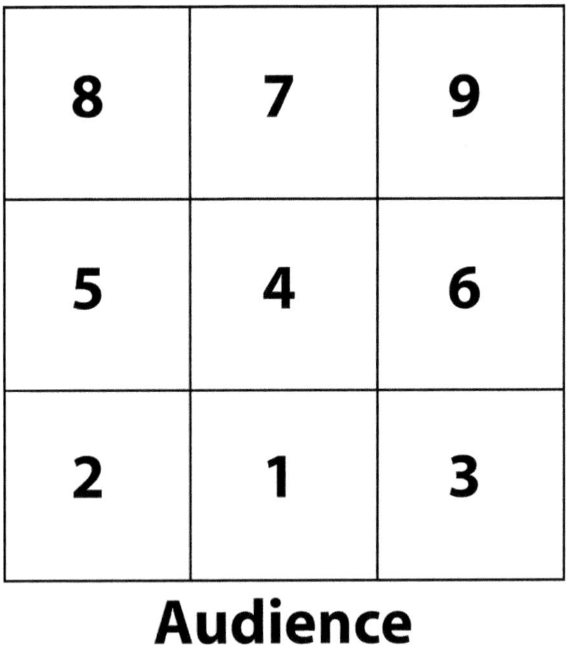

8	7	9
5	4	6
2	1	3

Audience

Figure 10.20 Acting Areas in Order of Importance

area of the stage. Figure 10.20 is a chart indicating the relative importance of each area of the proscenium stage as generally perceived by the audience with one indicating the most important and nine the least important. The increased significance to the stage right side can be attributed to the fact that when reading one looks at the page beginning on the left side and moving to the right. This should not be intended as an absolute maxim for the use of the stage but rather as a guide for focusing the attention of the audience. To keep the audience's attention and provide variety, the director needs to be careful not to rely on this principle too completely and stage all scenes down center.

SPEECH

The audience's attention is naturally drawn to the person who is speaking. While this is really not an issue for the floor plan, the floor plan does need to have the physical space to allow the director to use speech as a tool to focus attention.

LIGHTING

Lighting can also be used as an aid to the other tools to focus the attention of the audience. For example, within an otherwise evenly lit scene, the audience's attention will be drawn to the more brightly lit actor. While lighting is not a factor of staging or in the creation of the floor plan, the director should consider the possibilities for which it can be used to alter the audience's attention. Although the director can work with the lighting designer on using lighting to help focus attention, if the scene is badly staged, lighting will not be able to save it.

MARK ANTONY'S FUNERAL SPEECH

A good example of how all these tools can be combined is to look at the possibilities in creating the stage picture for Mark Antony's funeral speech in act 3, scene 2 of *Julius Caesar*. In this scene a large group of Roman citizens are being addressed by Mark Antony following the assassination of Caesar. Since all the actors are wearing similar costumes, the audience's attention can be drawn to Mark Antony by adding some contrasting elements to his costume, separating him from the others. The fact that he is the character who is speaking will innately draw the audience to him. In all probability, Mark Antony will remain stationary during his speech; therefore, other action that creates competing visual interest should be avoided. Attention to Mark Antony can be significantly increased by placing him on a higher level than the crowd and by the angle that Mark Antony faces them. Patterns in setting and the arrangement of the crowd of Romans can also direct the audience's attention to him. Finally, his visual interest can be further increased by making him slightly brighter than everyone else. The use of stage area in this case is a bit more intriguing. While down center is the most interesting area, using it would make relating Mark Antony to the crowd more difficult. The stage area rankings could be used to determine that Mark Antony be placed on stage right rather than left. Figure 10.21 is a painting showing one possible stage picture for this scene.

Figure 10.21 *Julius Caesar*, act 3, scene 2, by G. E. Robertson

CREATING VISUAL INTEREST USING THE SCENIC AXIS

Once all the needs of the script are identified and consideration is made for focusing the audience's attention, the floor plan can be created. The initial tendency is to try to re-create the same floor plan as is seen in life. This concept is best understood by applying it on a proscenium stage. Figure 10.22 is a basic floor plan of an actual room with the furniture against the walls and a large open space in the center. The removal of the downstage wall allows the audience to look into the room. While this arrangement works for an actual room, it presents a number of problems as a theatrical floor plan. All the elements of the setting are either parallel or perpendicular to the axis of the theatre created by the intersection of the centerline with the plaster line (the line of the proscenium arch) as indicated by the blue lines in Figure 10.23 and limit visual interest and staging possibilities.

It also creates significant sight line problems for the audience. In most theatres the audience seating is wider than the proscenium arch, and this floor plan limits visibility for the audience from the sides (see Figure 10.24).

An improved floor plan is shown in Figure 10.25. The side walls are angled, or raked, to give improved sight lines as well as a more interesting set axis that does not follow the theatre axis. While doing this deviates from reality, it actually creates a view of a room similar to an actual room.

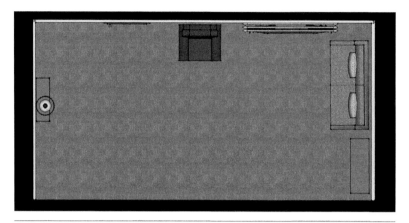

Figure 10.22 Room Floor Plan

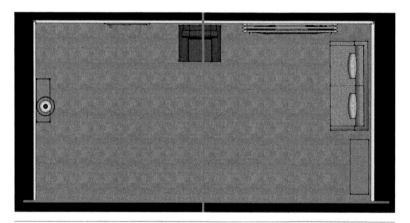

Figure 10.23 Axis of the Theatre

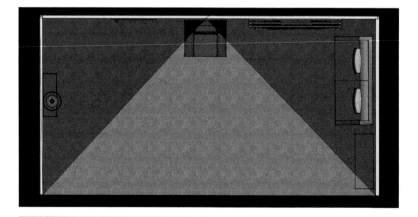

Figure 10.24 Obstruction of Sight Lines

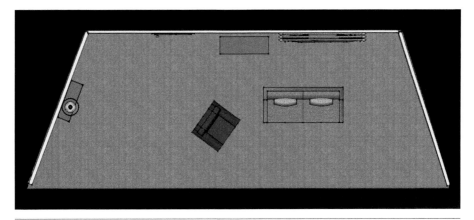

Figure 10.25 Reconfigured Floor Plan

Most people are familiar with the train track example of the effect that distance plays on perception. This is referred to as *perspective*. When looking down a set of straight train tracks the tracks appear to converge until they meet at the horizon (see Figure 10.26). This same principle is at work when viewing a rectangular room.

When standing at the center of a wall in an actual room and looking straight across, the distant wall appears narrower and the side walls seem to angle out (see Figure 10.27). Placing the same room onstage and viewing it from the audience gives a completely different view (see Figure 10.28).

Figure 10.26 Perspective

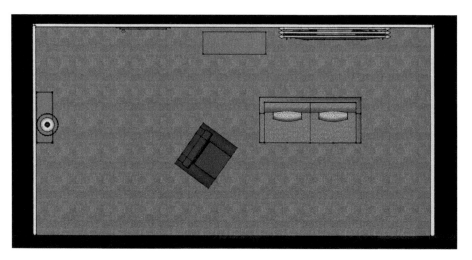

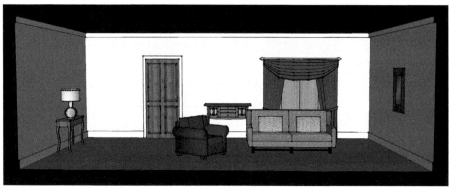

Figure 10.27 Setting of a Square Set in Plan View and as Seen From the Plaster Line

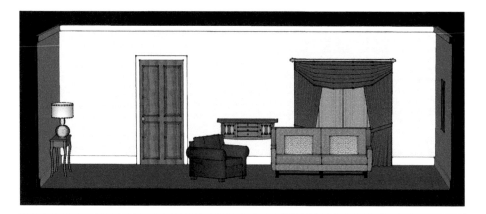

Figure 10.28 The Same Setting as Seen by the Audience

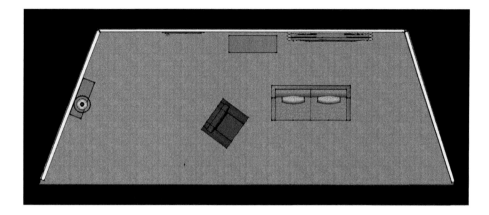

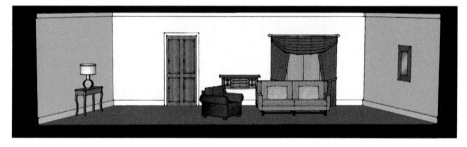

Figure 10.29 The Same Setting as Seen by the Audience After Perspective Alteration

Raking the walls of the set not only improves the sight lines but also provides a view that is consistent with the audience's expectation. Scenic designers refer to this as *perspective alteration* (see Figure 10.29).

Rearranging the furniture will lead to improved conversational groups. Moving the sofa and chair brings the action closer to the audience while allowing staging to occur both above and below the sofa group. The side chair creates alternative seating and conversation options. Other scenic elements placed along the walls provide further motivation for actors to cross to them.

Rotating the axis of the set as created by the dominant features so it is not parallel to the theatre axis will give a more dynamic visual image. The sight lines for the audience must always be considered in the floor plan or portions of the audience will have an obstructed view. Allowing the actors to move around furniture or other scenic elements also improves the staging. Finally, the floor plan should always have alternatives for staging and reasons for the actors to move to different parts of the stage. If a large open space is required for the action of the scene, the floor plan must give a reason for the characters to move into this area. Placing a scenic element there can fulfill this function. Exterior settings or those on a more open stage should follow similar guidelines. Unless it is absolutely impossible, or directly works against the script, seating possibilities should be provided in any setting. Likewise, it is also beneficial to have elevations, particularly upstage, to facilitate more dynamic stage pictures. The most difficult space for a director to stage is one that is completely open since there is no rationale for movement.

BALANCE

Balance is a significant factor in determining visual interest as it relates to both the overall look of the setting and the floor plan. Balance refers to the visual sense that neither side of the stage appears "heavier" than the other. The actual weight is obviously not an issue; it is the visual weight of the object that affects the perception of balance. Having both sides of the stage mirror each other guarantees balance; however, unless this symmetry is particularly desirable for the scene, this form of balance works against dynamic visual interest. This type of balance is referred to as *symmetrical balance*. It is sometimes assumed that to have balance the setting must be symmetrical. In reality, balance can be achieved through asymmetry as well, referred to as *asymmetrical balance*. Asymmetrical balance is achieved by creating the perception of an equal but not identical distribution of weight on both sides of the centerline. A more massive object on stage right can be balanced by placing a number of smaller objects on stage left or

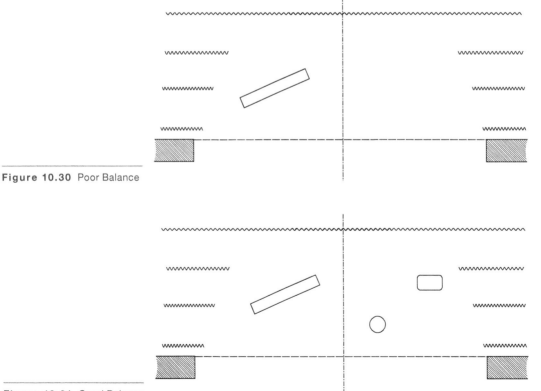

Figure 10.30 Poor Balance

Figure 10.31 Good Balance

by placing a single small object farther from center. If one thinks of the stage as sitting on a balance beam with the fulcrum on the centerline, objects are placed to either side of center to maintain the visual balance. In general, asymmetrical balance creates a more pleasing look than symmetrical balance. However, balance of some form is essential to create a pleasing picture. The actors need to be considered in determining this balance as well. If a large group of people are onstage during an entire scene, then this mass of people must be considered as part of the balance along with the scenic elements. Figures 10.30 and 10.31 illustrate how balance can be achieved asymmetrically on an open stage.

SUGGESTIONS FOR IMPROVING THE FLOOR PLAN

As floor plans are developed and reviewed, the director can use the following suggestions as guides to improving it.

RAKE THE SETTING

Try to avoid having the set axis parallel to the theatre axis whenever possible. Many static floor plans may be improved by rotating the set slightly relative to the theatre (see Figure 10.32). The angle should be significant enough to look intentional.

LEVELS

Levels are a director's friend. Changing the heights of characters is a valuable tool in shifting the focus of the audience. Levels on the upstage portions of the stage improve visibility of those actors, giving the director more freedom to use the entire stage when creating stage pictures.

DOORWAYS

When placing doorways in the setting consider the value of their location in terms of entrances and exits. A weak exit may be acceptable if it results in a stronger entrance and that entrance is more important to the scene. If doable, have doors open offstage and upstage to allow the actor to be the focus of the entrance or exit.

TABLES

Round tables are generally less challenging to stage around than rectangular or square ones. The circular footprint makes it easier to move around the table and to stage at any location at the table. If a round table is not an option, a square table set so it is not parallel to the centerline is the next best choice. If several people must be seated at the table, audience sight lines will be improved if the downstage portion of the table is left unused, although it is inevitable that at least some of them will have their backs to the audience. Judiciously choosing which characters sit in each location will enable more important characters to face toward the audience. The angle at which the table is placed can further assist in improving sight lines.

Figure 10.32 (Top) Before
Raking Set Axis; (Bottom)
After Raking Set Axis

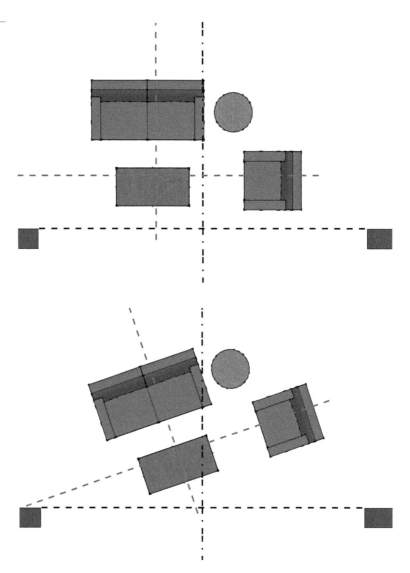

Figure 10.32 (Top) Before Raking Set Axis; (Bottom) After Raking Set Axis

BEDS

Beds can be as problematic as tables. It is best to keep the angle of the bed so it is not parallel to the centerline. If the scene calls for more than one person to lie on the bed, find a position for the bed that provides the most desirable sight lines for the scene. This may be the exception to raking, placing the bed so the actors' feet are toward the audience. It will be helpful to either tilt the head of the bed slightly or place additional pillows on the bed to raise the heads of the actors. While it is preferable to have furniture away from walls, doing so with the bed does not generally provide a pleasing look. Having actors cross upstage of the bed is often a weak action.

Figure 10.33 The Effect of the
Size of a Sofa

CHAIRS

In choosing chairs for the setting, be conscious of the implications the type of chair has on its use by the actors. A stool may be sat on from any angle. Chairs with arms limit how far the actor can turn to either side when seated. On the other hand, if the arms will support weight, the actor can also sit on them. High-back chairs have a unique look but also create obstructions for the actors standing behind them, particularly if the actors are short. It is important to think about how far the actor will sink into the padding of a chair as it is more difficult for an actor to get out of an overstuffed chair. Finally, take into consideration the amount of floor space used. A large overstuffed chair may be good for the scene, but the amount of floor space may be a problem.

SOFA SIZE

The same considerations noted for chairs should be applied in choosing a sofa (see Figure 10.33). Another factor to keep in mind is the length of the sofa, which is dictated by the maximum number of people the director desires to sit on it. If only two people sit on the sofa, the length becomes less of an issue but may still be important in terms of providing additional options for the actors. For example, if a male character needs to sit down next to his female partner and the sofa is just long enough for the two of them, he cannot use how he chooses to sit on the sofa to communicate how he feels about his partner. On the other hand, if the sofa is long enough to accommodate more than two people, where he sits on the sofa relative to his female counterpart can quickly convey his intent. If he sits as close to her as possible this tactic becomes readily apparent.

The director needs to consider how the audience will perceive the physical choices made by each character in the scene. The floor plan should be evaluated in light of these choices. This often means having items in the plan that are never used but would offer options to the characters.

USING KEY SCENES TO DEVELOP OR EVALUATE THE FLOOR PLAN

The director can use key scenes as a guide to develop or evaluate the floor plan. In considering these key scenes, the director determines the physical relationships that need to be conveyed in the resulting stage picture. The director then develops or evaluates the floor plan using this stage picture to determine the location of the elements of the setting or evaluate the existing floor plan to see if it is feasible. While it is important for the floor plan to work for the rest of the scene as well as the play, if it is not maximizing the stage picture for the key moment, it is not as beneficial as it could be. It is sometimes useful for the director to draw a stage picture and provide it to the scenic designer as a guide for preparing the floor plan. On one occasion my scenic designer and I met in the theatre and had a particularly exciting preproduction conference. We decided on a space stage approach to the play. I discussed with the designer exactly how I wanted to arrange each scene, and the nature of the location and height of platforms evolved during this discussion. By the end of our conference we had developed a rough floor plan that the scenic designer could then refine.

Failing to make certain the floor plan initially provides for both general blocking and key stage pictures may require the director to make significant compromises in the staging later in the rehearsal process. The director should always consult with the scenic designer before moving any furniture or objects in the setting to ensure that the overall look is not compromised.

DRAWING THE FLOOR PLAN

The scenic designer usually communicates the floor plan through carefully drafted drawings such as those in Figures 10.34 and 10.35. Formal floor plans are important in the planning and construction of the setting but may be too detailed for the director. This is particularly the case if the director is developing the floor plan. The floor plan for the director should look more like Figure 10.36. This drawing provides the director with sufficient detail to block the show. A planning trick utilized by some directors is to use a penny to represent each actor on the

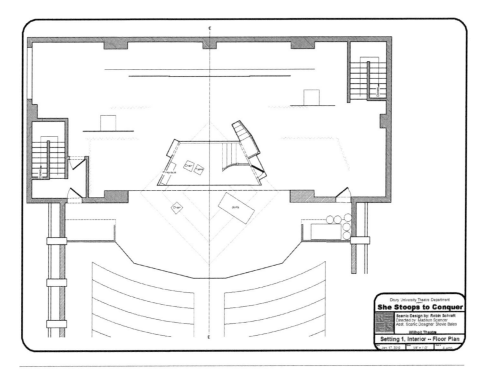

Figure 10.34 General Floor Plan

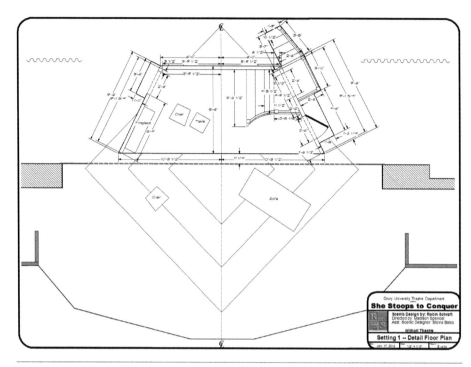

Figure 10.35 Detailed Floor Plan

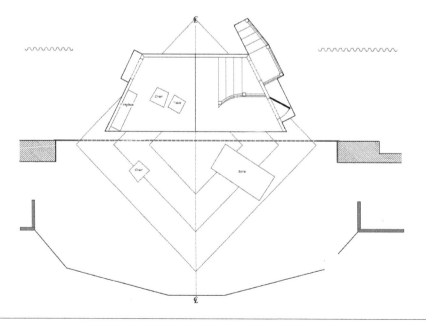

Figure 10.36 Director's Floor Plan

floor plan, assuming the plan is drawn in 2" = 1' scale. The diameter of a penny represents the amount of space occupied by the typical actor. The coin can then be used to determine whether characters will fit between scenic elements as well as how many actors can comfortably stand together in a given space. While the floor plan drawn by the director can represent the setting less formally, it is important that it be drawn to scale. If an exact scale is not used, each element of the setting must be proportionally correct to the other elements. For example, if the sofa is 2 inches long, the end table cannot also be 2 inches, but rather about three quarters of an inch. If all of the elements of the setting are not proportionally drawn, the floor plan will be useless for staging and will not be representative of the setting that ultimately appears on the stage. Some directors prefer to draw floor plans on graph paper to help maintain the scale; others find the graph paper distracting. An architect rule, a ruler in various scales, is particularly helpful for the director in drawing a floor plan. Directors who are not familiar with drawing to scale should consult a good scenic design or stagecraft text.

Once the plan is finalized, it is time to tape out the basic outline of the setting, including stage elements such as the proscenium arch, on the floor of the rehearsal space. The rehearsal furniture should be similar in both size and nature to the furniture to be used in the production. If the performance chair will have arms, the rehearsal chair should also have arms. The location of the furniture should be spiked with tape on the floor as well. The transition of the play to the set will be much easier for the actors if the tape outline closely approximates the actual setting.

Carefully planning and/or reviewing the floor plan during preproduction will not only make the subsequent staging easier and facilitate the creation of stronger stage pictures and blocking, but it may also prevent the need for changes at a later date that may be costly and problematic or even impossible.

FLOOR PLAN DEVELOPMENT CHECKLIST

PRELIMINARY CONCERNS

❑ Actor–Audience Interface

- Intimate
- Formal

❑ Necessary Mechanical Needs to Change Scenery

❑ Size of the Acting Area

❑ Special Needs

THEATRE ARCHITECTURE
- ❏ Proscenium
- ❏ Arena
- ❏ Thrust
- ❏ Alley
- ❏ Black Box

PATTERN OF SCENERY
- ❏ Box Setting
- ❏ Wing and Drop Setting
- ❏ Three-Dimensional Setting
  - Unit Setting
  - Space Stage
- ❏ Fragmentary Setting (Selective Realism)
- ❏ Constructivist Setting
- ❏ Simultaneous Staging

MEETING THE NEEDS OF THE SCRIPT
- ❏ Patterns of Movement
- ❏ Physical Needs
- ❏ Entrances and Exits
- ❏ Spatial Needs
- ❏ Size of the Cast
- ❏ Type of Action
- ❏ Changes in Setting

FOCUSING THE AUDIENCE'S ATTENTION
- ❏ Contrast
- ❏ Movement
- ❏ Height
- ❏ Angle
- ❏ Scenic Pointing
- ❏ Stage Area
- ❏ Speech
- ❏ Lighting

CREATING VISUAL INTEREST

❑ Rake the Scenic Axis

❑ Perspective Alteration

❑ Balance

USE KEY SCENES

FURTHER EXPLORATION

1. For one of the plays with which you have been working, develop a list of the physical needs the setting will require.

2. Based on the list developed in Activity 1, draw a floor plan of the setting utilizing a theatre space with which you are familiar. Critically evaluate the setting to determine how it can be improved using the guidelines in this chapter.

3. Read Eugene O'Neill's play *Ile*. This play is set on a whaling ship in 1895. One of the key elements of the play is the organ that belongs to the captain's wife. While it is not used until the end, it is part of a crucial aspect of the play. Develop several floor plans, each utilizing a different position for the organ. Test each plan using a key scene early in the play and in the final moments. How does each position of the organ affect both the earlier scene and the later one?

Creating Stage Pictures

WHAT IS A STAGE PICTURE?

The development of stage pictures and the floor plan go hand in hand. The floor plan determines the configuration of the stage pictures; conversely, the stage pictures determine the floor plan. It raises the age-old question: "Which came first, the chicken or the egg?" Stage pictures are static images that create the look that carries the feeling of the scene and promotes its understanding. A stage picture can be thought of in terms of a *photo call*. While many shows are photographed during a rehearsal, it can be difficult for the photographer to capture the best looks. The photo call provides the director with the opportunity to document the show with specific poses that most fully express the play. Strong stage pictures provide anchor points within the production and are an excellent starting point toward good blocking.

The ideal way to identify key moments for stage pictures is to look at each action unit. For each unit there will be one or possibly more key moments in the relationship of the characters. For example, Mark Antony's funeral speech in *Julius Caesar* (see Chapter 10, Figure 10.21), where Antony is standing before a crowd of Roman citizens is a key moment.

While these key moments will apply to stage pictures in any theatre configuration, they are more complicated in nonproscenium settings since the viewing angle of the audience depends on which side of the stage they are seated. The remainder of this chapter will assume a proscenium configuration to provide a consistent audience viewing point. Stage pictures in other configurations will be discussed in Chapter 21.

Strong stage pictures provide the director with a powerful tool to communicate his or her concept to the audience. The director needs to be sure the floor plan will support these pictures.

THE PROCESS OF DEVELOPING STAGE PICTURES

Having identified the key moments for stage pictures, the next step is to develop the staging for them. How does the director feel about each moment? How does the director want the audience to feel? Act 1, scene 3 of *Macbeth* can be used to illustrate the development of a stage picture. In this scene, Macbeth and Banquo encounter the witches and receive the prophecies that lay the foundation for the rest of the plot. The nature of the encounter is not only crucial for this scene but also for the entire play.

Using his or her analysis, the director now begins to think about how to convey the essence of the scene to the audience by identifying where to have the audience focus its attention. Is the scene about Macbeth, Macbeth and Banquo, or about the witches? For the purpose of this example, assume the focus of the scene is Macbeth, specifically how Macbeth receives the prophecies, underscoring the importance of the witches. In this interpretation, the attention should be on Macbeth even when Banquo is addressing the witches. Further, the witches need to be seen as a collective group rather than three individuals. Figure 11.1 graphically represents a starting point for this image.

Notice there are two distinct groupings. Upon closer examination of the scene it is the first witch who begins and ends the encounter with Macbeth, and it is Banquo who first responds

Figure 11.1 Initial Grouping

Figure 11.2 Developed Grouping

to their initial greeting. Based on this information, the arrangement is reconfigured (see Figure 11.2).

By moving Macbeth slightly downstage of the witches and Banquo, Macbeth's presence is increased with the audience, but by turning his profile toward the witches he shares the focus with them. By having the first witch in the center, a balance is created since she both begins and ends the encounter. Banquo, however, is placed in a slightly diminished position by being farther upstage, but since he faces downstage his position is slightly strengthened. This creates a primary focus on the witches, whose more interesting positions will further secure attention, with a secondary focus on Macbeth and just beyond him, Banquo.

The previous look can now be enhanced with the use of levels. Figure 11.3 shows the addition of three levels with a 6-inch rise. Macbeth's presence is established by having him in the farthest downstage position, but at the same time his slightly upstage angle deflects some of the attention toward the witches who, with the highest position onstage, get increased focus.

The elevation of the first witch over the other two provides an additional focus, allowing her to be slightly behind the other two witches and yet above them. This setting creates the first look that will lead to the second.

After the witches' greeting in which they tell Macbeth he will be king, the picture changes as Macbeth reflects on this startling news, and Banquo questions the witches concerning his fate.

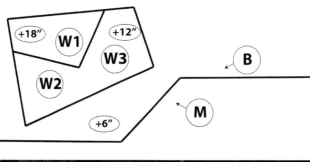

Figure 11.3 Addition of Levels

This second picture (Figure 11.4) opens Macbeth to the audience for his reflection and allows Banquo to directly question the witches. The focus is pulled to Macbeth with his cross downstage. Banquo then reestablishes himself when he speaks to the witches. After the witches exit, Banquo will cross down to question Macbeth, creating the final picture.

A good stage picture is the product of effectively staging the actors so the audience perceives their relationship, and the audience's attention is focused where the director wishes it to be.

The composition of the scene from *Macbeth* can be examined using many of the tools discussed in Chapter 10. It relies on the use of contrast with the five people onstage. This contrast is seen in the grouping of the witches and in their posture, and by the fact that Macbeth's angle is decidedly different from any of the other characters. Smaller changes in focus within the picture will be made as each character speaks since the audience's attention will be momentarily drawn to the character speaking. Rather than statically posing, the witches will continue to undulate, making them a more interesting part of the composition. Macbeth's turn and cross from the first picture to the second will likewise pull the attention to him for that moment. The

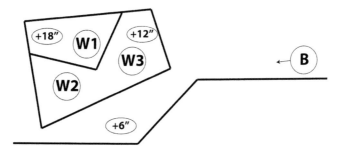

Figure 11.4 Second Picture

use of elevation for Banquo, and especially the witches, further contributes to the composition. Their raised elevation allows them to remain a meaningful part of the composition despite the fact that Macbeth is farther downstage and closer to the audience. In addition, the witches' position to the audience's left provides a slightly greater significance for them. Overall, the picture includes variety, which keeps it visually interesting.

Effectively staging the actors so the audience perceives their relationship and captures the audience's attention produces a good stage picture. A film director can use close-ups to focus the audience's attention. The stage director must rely on staging to serve this function.

DEVELOPING A STAGE PICTURE FOR *ILE*

The creation of possible floor plans for Eugene O'Neill's play *Ile* was the subject of Activity 3 at the end of Chapter 10. The last moments of the play are one aspect of this floor plan that can be utilized to explore how stage pictures can change depending on the interpretation. *Ile* takes place aboard a whaling ship in 1895. The crew has been searching for whales for nearly a year without success and the ship is now blocked by ice to the north. To compound matters, Captain Keeney's wife, Annie, is aboard. Mrs. Keeney underestimated the impact of being at sea for this long and has become despondent. Despite pleas from the crew and even a threat of mutiny the captain refuses to turn back. Finally, the captain acquiesces to his wife's pleas and agrees to return home. No sooner has he made the decision than the mate informs him the ice is breaking up and they have spotted whales. The captain changes his mind and orders the ship to pursue the whales.

> *[KEENEY reenters from the doorway to the deck and stands looking at her angrily. He comes over and grabs her roughly by the shoulder.]*
>
> KEENEY: Woman, what foolish mockin' is this? (She laughs wildly, and he starts back from her in alarm.) Annie! What is it? (She doesn't answer him. KEENEY'S voice trembles.) Don't you know me, Annie?
>
> *[He puts both hands on her shoulders and turns her around so that he can look into her eyes. She stares up at him with a stupid expression, a vague smile on her lips. He stumbles away from her, and she commences softly to play the organ again.]*
>
> KEENEY: (swallowing hard – in a hoarse whisper, as if he had difficulty in speaking) You said – you was agoin' mad – God!
>
> *[A long wail is heard from the deck above: "Ah bloooow!" A moment later the MATE'S face appears through the skylight. He cannot see MRS. KEENEY.]*
>
> MATE: (in great excitement) Whales, sir – a whole school of 'em – off the starb'd quarter 'bout five mile away – big ones!
>
> KEENEY: (galvanized into action) Are you lowerin' the boats?
>
> MATE: Yes, sir.
>
> KEENEY: (with grim decision) I'm acomin' with ye.
>
> MATE: Aye, aye, sir. (Jubilantly) You'll git the ile now right enough, sir.
>
> *[His head is withdrawn and he can be heard shouting orders.]*
>
> KEENEY: (turning to his wife) Annie! Did you hear him? I'll git the ile. (She doesn't answer or seem to know he is there. He gives a hard laugh, which is almost a groan.) I know you're foolin' me, Annie. You ain't out of your mind – (anxiously) be you? I'll git the ile now right enough – jest a little while longer, Annie – then we'll turn hom'ard.

I can't turn back now, you see that, don't ye? I've got to git the ile. (In sudden terror) Answer me! You ain't mad, be you?

[She keeps on playing the organ, but makes no reply. The MATE'S face appears again through the skylight.]

MATE: All ready, sir.

[KEENEY turns his back on his wife and strides to the doorway, where he stands for a moment and looks back at her in anguish, fighting to control his feelings.]

MATE: Comin', sir?

KEENEY: *(his face suddenly grown hard with determination)* Aye.

[He turns abruptly and goes out. MRS. KEENEY does not appear to notice his departure. Her whole attention seems centred in the organ. She sits with half-closed eyes, her body swaying a little from side to side to the rhythm of the hymn. Her fingers move faster and faster and she is playing wildly and discordantly as the Curtain falls.][1]

Following are five possibilities for staging the final moments of the play using three basic walls to form a box set. No scenic needs are considered in this exercise other than the position of the organ and the doorway and the implications they have for the positions of the captain and Mrs. Keeney. The organ poses a unique staging problem, making it difficult to see Mrs. Keeney's face and hands. For the purpose of this example, the organ will have a low enough profile that Mrs. Keeney's face can be seen when seated behind the organ.

In Version 1 (Figure 11.5), the organ is positioned along the plaster line so Mrs. Keeney (labeled MK) faces the audience as she plays. The doorway is positioned diagonally opposite. The audience sees Mrs. Keeney's face clearly but not her hands as she plays the organ; the captain (labeled C) is in quarter profile.

Version 2 (Figure 11.6) mirrors the previous arrangement. The organ faces upstage with the door on the diagonally opposite wall but now downstage. Only Mrs. Keeney's back and hands are seen clearly as she plays the organ. The captain is in three-quarter profile looking away from the audience.

Version 3 (Figure 11.7) keeps the door and the captain in a similar position as Version 2 but now the organ is placed midway against the opposite wall. The organ and Mrs. Keeney are in profile and the captain is in three-quarter profile.

In Version 4 (Figure 11.8), the organ is positioned along the plaster line so Mrs. Keeney faces the audience as in Version 1, but now the organ is in line with the door, which remains in the same position as in Version 2 and Version 3. This keeps the captain and Mrs. Keeney in the same plane.

Version 5 (Figure 11.9) modifies Version 2 by turning the organ so it faces downstage. Mrs. Keeney now faces the audience with the captain in three-quarter profile.

While every director will undoubtedly have an opinion regarding the strength of each of these versions, they all provide viable options for the conclusion of the play. The difference

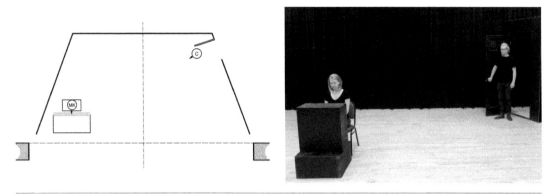

Figure 11.5 *Ile* Final Picture Version 1

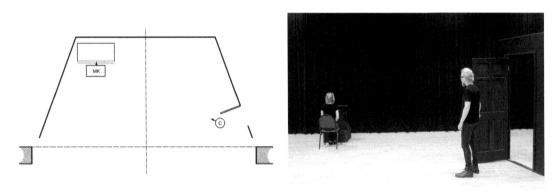

Figure 11.6 *Ile* Final Picture Version 2

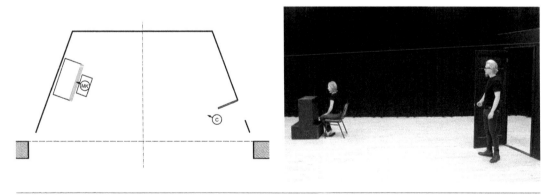

Figure 11.7 *Ile* Final Picture Version 3

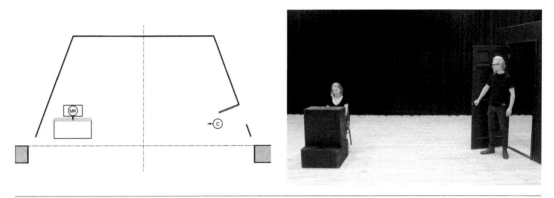

Figure 11.8 *Ile* Final Picture Version 4

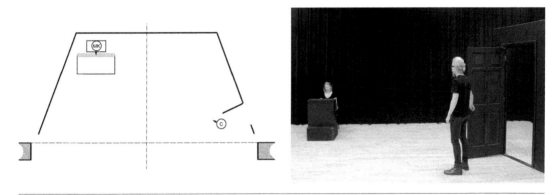

Figure 11.9 *Ile* Final Picture Version 5

among them is in how the director wishes the audience to understand the end of the play. Versions 1, 4, and 5 place a distinct emphasis on Mrs. Keeney's face; however, they all have limited visibility of her body movements. Version 2 allows the audience to see Mrs. Keeney's body movements but sacrifices the connection to her face. Version 3 shows Mrs. Keeney's face and body movements in profile.

Note the captain's position relative to the audience. When it is somewhat closed to the audience, that is, he is facing upstage more than downstage, the audience will tend to look where he is looking rather than at him. On the other hand, when his position is somewhat open, that is, he is facing downstage more than upstage, his expression becomes a more significant part of the scene. In Version 4, the captain is in profile, an angle that embodies more neutrality on his position.

Combining both the organ and exit positions in different ways creates subtle nuances in the understanding of the scene. In Version 1, the audience's attention is strongly placed on Mrs. Keeney as she frantically plays the organ. When the captain turns back at the door to look at his wife, the action grabs the audience's attention and both the captain's and Mrs. Keeney's faces are seen. This picture emphasizes both her madness and the impact it has on him. In Version 2, Mrs. Keeney is in the upstage right corner of the setting. More of the physicality of her madness is evident but none of her facial expressions. The captain's cross through the door for his exit brings him toward the audience; his turn then redirects the audience's attention back upstage toward Mrs. Keeney's isolation, returning the final attention to her. Her upstage position emphasizes her isolation. Version 3 is similar to the view of the captain as in Version 2, but since Mrs. Keeney is in profile, both her face and body are partially seen. The audience has the benefit of seeing her full expression as well as the ability to focus on the captain's reaction. Version 4 is essentially the same as Version 1, but since the captain is closer, his importance is greater, although the full effect of his reaction is slightly mitigated by being in profile, placing more focus on Mrs. Keeney. Version 5 allows the focus to be on Mrs. Keeney's face while having the benefit of keeping the captain in a more open position as he turns from the door. Adding levels is another possibility for staging the final moments of the play. By placing the exit up a flight of stairs onto a small platform, the relative importance of the captain is changed. The addition of these stairs and level will also need to be considered as the timing of the entrances and exits will change.

Any number of other pictures can be used for this moment. These five illustrate some of the different messages that can be conveyed by simply changing the position of the actors in the picture. The key factor in deciding which picture best expresses the play is where the director wishes to place the understanding. Is it a play about Mrs. Keeney's madness brought on by her husband's stubbornness? Is it a play about a man obsessed with his mission whose wife pays the ultimate price? Or is the ultimate meaning somewhere between the two? The director's decision will be a direct product of the script analysis and, more important, the spine guiding the play's interpretation.

In this examination of the stage picture for the final moments of the play, the needs of the other scenes were ignored. The director's actual choice for the position of the door and organ will be heavily dependent on the final moments but must work for the rest of the play as well. Versions 1 and 4 pose particular problems for the earlier scenes because the organ occupies or obscures a significant portion of the setting. Even if any one of these versions is the ideal choice for the final moments, the director may have to compromise his or her interpretation to meet the needs of the rest of the play. The final decision regarding the floor plan must be based on a consideration of *all* the moments in the play. Compromises can favor certain moments while hindering others as long as the hindrance does not damage the overall quality and understanding of the play.

> The choice of stage pictures determines where the director wants to place the audience's focus. The final floor plan will be based on providing the physical environment for all the moments. While the floor plan can favor certain moments, it is important to ensure that the overall quality and understanding of the play is preserved.

SUMMARY

As evidenced by the examples from *Macbeth* and *Ile*, there are a series of concepts or tools that can help the director make artistic choices in the creation of stage pictures to better convey the meaning of the play and focus the audience's attention. The most important of these are as follows:

PROXIMITY TO THE AUDIENCE

The closer the actors are to the audience, the greater the audience's perception of their importance. As actors move toward the audience, they gain strength; as they move away, they relinquish it. Actors upstage of other actors may be completely or partially blocked from the audience's view and have diminished significance. On the other hand, if an actor is extremely close to the audience, as is possible in arena or thrust staging, the proximity may be intimidating to the audience.

THE ANGLE OF THE ACTOR RELATIVE TO THE AUDIENCE

The strength of the angle of the actor relative to the audience has an immediate impact on the audience. An actor facing the audience has the strongest position, while an actor facing upstage has the weakest. Positions to either side are generally neutral. This is not meant to imply that one angle is superior to another, rather the relationship becomes a tool controlling the audience's perception of the character at any given moment.

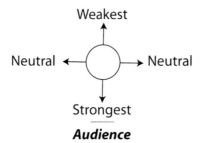

Figure 11.10 Strength of Angle Relative to the Audience

THE ANGLE OF THE ACTOR RELATIVE TO HIS OR HER PARTNER (OPEN OR CLOSED POSITIONS)

The angle of the actor relative to the audience is directly related to the angle relative to his or her partner. If Actor B is downstage of Actor A, Actor B is closed off to some degree from the audience. Conversely, if Actor B is upstage of Actor A, Actor B forces Actor A to be closed off from the audience. The greater the angle, the more open or closed the actor becomes. In this way, an actor can give focus to another actor by moving to a position downstage or take it away by moving to a position upstage.

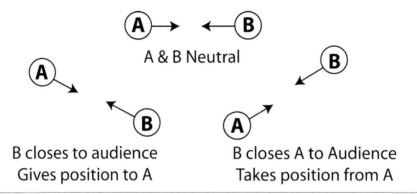

Figure 11.11 Strength of Angle Relative to Partner

THE IMPACT THE POSITION HAS ON THE STRENGTH OF THE CROSS INTO AND OUT OF THE PICTURE

The director cannot consider a stage picture in the abstract without giving some thought to the crosses both into and out of the picture. A good stage picture allows for a well-intended cross for all the actors, especially the actor who should have the principal focus. The pictures should be considered not only for the expression of the moment but also for the potential for solid blocking.

THE IMPACT OF USING ELEVATION

The inclusion of different elevations allows for better stage pictures and should be used whenever possible. Placing actors on different levels enables the director to create more dynamic stage pictures as well as increases the freedom to use all parts of the stage.

CONTRAST

Stage pictures can be enhanced when the elements within the picture are separated by contrast. This contrast can be through any of the tools used to create the composition such as elevation, position onstage, angle, proximity, movement, or other factors such as costume and lighting.

MOVEMENT

Movement is one of the most powerful tools for focusing the audience's attention. The audience's attention will naturally be drawn to movement onstage whether intended or not. Unintentional movement must be avoided; intentional movement can be used to point the audience's attention where the director wishes it.

LOCATION ONSTAGE

The actors' location onstage has an impact on the audience's perception. This involves not only their proximity to the audience but also their position to the right or left of center as well as their position relative to their partner.

CREATION OF GROUPINGS

If there are more than two people onstage they typically form into groups. These groups must be consciously identified, developed, and distinguished by the director. It should be clear when looking at the people onstage who is part of each group and who is not, as well as how the groups relate to each other. A group's size can be made to appear larger by spacing and staggering, especially if small level changes can also be employed for upstage actors. Generally, the appearance of groups can be improved by the use of triangles rather than lines in the staging.

FINAL THOUGHTS

The creation of the floor plan and stage pictures can occur simultaneously. If the floor plan is developed first, then the creation of stage pictures for key moments can be used to test the workability of the floor plan. If stage pictures initially evolve as a guide to the creation of the floor plan, they can be polished once the floor plan is complete. The stage pictures will be further refined as the blocking (movement) is developed. The director should be open to the discovery of new and improved stage pictures as a result of the blocking process with the cast.

STAGE PICTURE CHECKLIST

❏ Proximity to the audience

❏ The angle of the actor relative to the audience

❏ The angle of the actor relative to his or her partner (open or closed positions)

❏ The impact the position has on the strength of the cross into and out of the picture

❏ The impact of using elevation

❏ Contrast

❏ Movement

❏ Location onstage

❏ Creation of groupings

FURTHER EXPLORATION

1. Develop stage pictures for key moments for any of the plays with which you have been working.

2. For a given moment in a play, develop a series of alternative stage pictures and explore which of these best expresses what you are trying to convey to the audience at that moment.

3. Work in small groups to compare and critique your work in Activities 1 and 2.

4. Read Wendy Wasserstein's play *Tender Offer*. Using the beginning of the play as an example, create a series of stage pictures based on different interpretations of the relationship between the father and daughter.

NOTE

1   *Ile* by Eugene O'Neill.

Blocking

PREPLANNED VS. ORGANIC BLOCKING

Having completed the floor plan and the principal stage pictures for each action unit, the director's attention turns to the blocking of the show. In many cases, the director follows the initial read-through of the script with one or more rehearsals dedicated to the mechanical blocking, providing the actors with specific actions. This is often referred to as **preplanned blocking** because the director prepares the blocking prior to the rehearsal to establish a foundation for the physical structure of the play. Other directors prefer not to preplan blocking but to allow the actors to spontaneously decide the actions they feel are most appropriate for the character in the moment. This approach is referred to as **organic blocking**. But which option should the director choose? When is one better than the other? There are strengths and weaknesses to both approaches.

The major advantage to preplanned blocking is that it provides the director with almost total control of the physical action in the play and enables the director to fully utilize the initial stage pictures as the basis for the movement into and out of each picture. By controlling the action, the director can carefully consider the nature of each actor's movement, provide each actor with an initial sense of the character in the scene, and give significant guidance to the type of approach to be taken in the moment without having to overtly specify it. Preplanned blocking also allows the director to maintain control of the quality of the pictures created onstage through the action and to determine how effectively the actions work from the audience's perspective.

There are two major weaknesses to preplanned blocking. First, the actors are not contributing to the show through their own choices. Their insight might have provided a better approach to the scene both in terms of character development and staging, but they did not have the opportunity to explore it. Second, preplanned blocking runs the risk of appearing unmotivated in its application. Blocking always needs to appear directly connected to the actors and internally motivated by the moment. When the director provides the actor with the blocking, it is possible the actor is simply following the blocking mechanically. For preplanned blocking to be effective, the director must fully understand the dynamic connection between emotion and action. Without this understanding, the blocking will lack an authentic presence.

The principal advantage to organic blocking is that it is always internally motivated by the actor. In other words, the action is a direct outgrowth of the actor's expression of his or her character at the moment. The actor is free to explore the character through movement and how he or she engages his or her partner. Line delivery is codeveloped with movement allowing each to fully enhance the other. The actor instinctively will do only those actions that feel relevant. On the other hand, while the actor may feel the action is completely consistent, it may not appear so to the audience. Since the actor's viewpoint is from his or her character's, the actor is not in the position to tell if the action works for the audience. This problem extends to the mechanical viability of the action in terms of its implications on the sight lines and the creation of stage pictures as well as to whether the action fully expresses the character's intent to the audience. More experienced actors tend to work extremely well with organic blocking; less experienced actors need the structure of preplanned blocking.

Both preplanned and organic blocking have their advantages and disadvantages. The director needs to determine which approach works best in each circumstance. Inevitably, the choice is a mix of the two. The balance will be determined by the needs of the script, the time available for rehearsal, the experience of the actors, and the vision of the director.

It is recommended that beginning directors start their process with preplanned blocking. This ensures they are in control of the blocking, not relying on their actors to produce it. Preplanned blocking forces the director to be proactive, thinking through the nature of the actions rather than reacting to the blocking provided by the actors. Once the actors have the initial framework, the director can always provide the actors with the liberty to modify it organically. The director can then combine the preplanned work with the actors' work to create the final blocking. This also allows the beginning director to develop a more fundamental understanding of how blocking affects the presentation of the script and will enable them to work better organically with their actors.

Experienced directors tend to use a combination of preplanned and organic blocking in staging the play. They combine the benefits of both approaches while minimizing the drawbacks. The decision as to how much blocking should be preplanned versus organic depends on several criteria. The experience and skill of the actors in spontaneously creating viable blocking must be considered. Experienced actors often have an instinctive understanding of what good blocking should be, while less experienced actors may not. The director will probably get a fairly good sense of their skill level during the auditions. The complexity of the scene and its implied staging are another factor. Scenes involving intricate physical interaction or with numerous characters generally do not stage well organically since the actors are unable to judge if the blocking is working from the audience's perspective. On the other hand, scenes between two actors involving close interaction are often better staged organically. The director needs to be equally prepared in using either form of blocking and should create a contextual framework for the staging before allowing the actors to move organically. This framework needs to include the parameters of the setting as well as where the key elements, particularly entrances and exits, are located. Regardless of the approach taken, the appearance of the blocking and its use as a tool for furthering the scene and focusing the audience's attention is solely the director's responsibility. Even in a largely organically blocked show, the director must correct and adjust the blocking to make sure it works for the audience by having a visual sense of how the message and energy of the scene will be fulfilled in movement. The director can then work with the actors to develop the movement in the same way as when working with the actors on character development, not by instruction, but rather by questions, suggestions, encouragement, or any other means of communication that works in the instance. One possibility that may steer the director toward utilizing organic blocking is the mistaken idea that the director does not need to spend time to prepare it. This decision is pure laziness on the part of the director and is not a valid reason to choose this approach.

> It is solely the director's responsibility to ensure the blocking works to further the scene and to focus the audience's attention.

The principles involved in blocking need to be purposefully incorporated into the staging either by the director's preplanning or by adjustment of the organic movement of the actors.

PURPOSE FOR BLOCKING

Blocking serves many purposes, and having a good grasp of its individual purposes leads to a more comprehensive understanding. Listed below are the purposes served by blocking.

BLOCKING HELPS CREATE THE OVERALL SENSE OF THE SCENE

The audience's overall understanding of the scene is enhanced by the nature of the movement and the resulting pictures. The amount of movement or lack thereof furthers this sense by instilling the same feelings in the audience as if the audience were actually in the environment. Compare the sensations experienced watching people in the middle of a bustling train station or busy street with the graceful interaction of two ballet dancers. As an observer, the movement does not have a mechanical effect, but it has tremendous impact on your perception of the moment. The overall rhythm and perception of the scene is a product of the combined movements of all the actors.

BLOCKING HELPS CREATE THE INDIVIDUAL NATURE OF THE CHARACTERS

While the overall blocking leads to a sense of the scene, individual blocking helps establish the nature of each character. Every person moves differently. It is the nature of the movement that contributes to their overall ambience as well as the audience's perception. Different movements customized for each character further develop the character. Consider the nature of the movement of a variety of animals who feel threatened by those who invade their environment. Compare your perception of the threat posed by each of the following: a large lumbering bear with a lack of grace and steady speed; a cougar racing full speed over a great distance; a large slithering snake. In each case, the threat is genuine, but your perception of it will differ based on the nature of the movement. It is why hikers often run when confronted by a large bear given its size and lumbering gait, even though the bear can easily outrun them. Each character should have a different quality to their movement.

BLOCKING HELPS PROVIDE FOCUS

It is important to establish where the audience should look at each moment in the scene. In film, the director accomplishes this by working with the Director of Photography and then the editor to choose the specific camera angles for individual moments. They mechanically determine where the audience should look as well as how narrow their focus should be. The stage director does not have these options. The stage director accomplishes this through the movement of the actors and the resulting stage pictures. It is one of the strongest forces for attracting the audience's attention. This becomes especially important during the staging of a scene involving three or more people.

When an actor moves, this naturally draws the audience's attention. If the director desires the audience's attention to be on someone other than the moving actor, something must be done to make that person more interesting to watch. In extremely large theatres where seating is a sizable distance from the stage, the audience may have difficulty identifying who is speaking, particularly if microphones are used, placing all sound from the speakers. In this case, it is a common practice for an actor to make a gesture before speaking to attract the audience's attention. However, extraneous or unnecessary movement can also distract the audience. The director must ensure other actors are not moving unless the attention should be drawn to them.

BLOCKING HELPS BUILD ENERGY

If the stage picture remains static for too long, the energy is easily lost. Scenes involving seated characters talking to one another can be particularly challenging. The director needs to find opportunities to ensure the energy is not lost, either through the introduction of movement and/or through the energy created by the tension of the scene. While constant movement is distracting and can be overpowering, it is important to find occasional opportunities for movement. For example, farces often derive their high energy from the frenetic use of the space.

BLOCKING HELPS MAINTAIN INTEREST THROUGH CHANGES IN STAGE PICTURES

To avoid losing visual interest, the director varies the stage picture by having the actors move. This helps maintain the interest of the audience. It is important that the picture not be changed for the sake of change; the new picture must provide the audience with a new sense of the scene.

BLOCKING HELPS REINFORCE THE MESSAGE FOR THE AUDIENCE

The physical relationship between the characters is further established by the nature of the blocking and stage pictures. The director uses blocking to underscore what is happening in the play, clarifying the message for the audience and reinforcing the dramatic action.

PRINCIPLES OF BLOCKING

Good blocking meets the physical needs of the scene and helps to express the scene's dramatic action while creating visually pleasing images focusing the audience's attention. To create good blocking, the director must understand its basic principles.

CROSS

The most basic element of blocking is the cross. Crossing refers to all movements by an actor moving across the stage. Crosses may be to another actor, a scenic element, or an open space. The value of the cross depends on its speed and angle relative to the audience. The cross can be further differentiated by its speed and length as well as by whether it is straight or curved.

TURN

A turn refers to the actor changing direction. Turns may occur at the beginning or end of a cross or without any cross. The strength of the turn depends on the change in direction of the actor relative to the audience.

CHANGES IN ELEVATION

Changes in elevation can occur through different blocking movements. The actor can ascend or descend to a platform, ramp, or set of stairs, resulting in raising or lowering the actor relative to the stage. The actor may also change elevation by sitting down or getting up from a chair. This simple act can change the elevation of the actor's head by several feet. Sitting in a chair changes the dynamic of the character relative to a standing actor. The actor may also sit on the stage floor. This action lowers the actor's head significantly and changes the dynamic of the character in the scene.

Figure 12.1
Use of Elevation With Chair

Figure 12.2
Use of Elevation With
Platform

COUNTER CROSS

The counter cross refers to an actor crossing in the opposite direction of another actor's cross. It must be motivated by the initial cross. The result of the counter cross may be the exchange of positions by the two actors. A counter cross may also move the second actor to a new location motivated by the first actor's initial cross. To be used effectively, the second actor should not begin the counter cross until after the first actor has begun to cross.

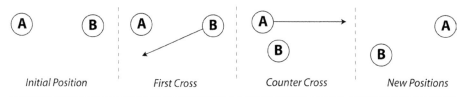

Initial Position   First Cross   Counter Cross   New Positions

Figure 12.3 Steps for a Counter Cross

DISTANCE BETWEEN ACTORS

When one actor crosses toward another, the actor will stop at an appropriate distance from the other actor. What constitutes appropriate distance is based on a collective cultural sense of

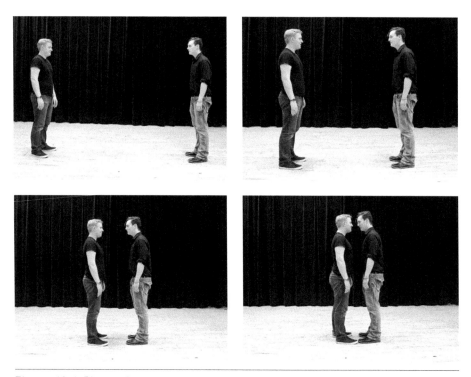

Figure 12.4 Distance Between Actors

personal space as well as a perception of the relationship between the characters. In real life, if a person comes into our personal space we feel uncomfortable, but if this person stops too far away we feel disengaged. The director can make use of the concept of personal space to define the relationship between two characters by controlling the distance between them, keeping in mind how the distance is perceived from the audience rather than the actual physical distance. Four examples of this distance are found in Figure 12.4. While none of them are generically incorrect, each creates a different relationship between the individuals.

MICROBLOCKING

Microblocking is the staging of small movements. Most of the time, the director is only concerned with the overall movements of the actors and leaves the smaller movements, sometimes called stage business, to the individual actor's discretion. However, there are times when the actors will not have any large movement for a period of time or large movement is not possible. The director can utilize smaller movements to microblock the scene to ensure sufficient variety for visual interest or to open up the action for the audience. Microblocking may also refer to small changes in the angle of an actor seated in a chair or in the direction of the actor's head.

ADJUSTMENT

Adjustment refers to smaller crosses that an actor makes in response to the cross of another actor. If, for example, the initial cross of the second actor blocks the sight lines of the audience to the first actor, an adjustment is needed. While such a situation is often avoidable, there are times when it is not. For example, an actor is standing upstage of a small table with a telephone on it. The second actor crosses to the table to answer the telephone, requiring the first actor to make a small movement either left or right to stay open to the audience. Most experienced actors make these adjustments automatically, but the director needs to be aware of the need to maintain good sight lines for the audience.

CHEATING

Making a slight adjustment in angle to maintain an open position to the audience is known as cheating. Normally, cheating is only necessary on a proscenium stage, but it may have applications for arena or thrust in special circumstances. Experienced actors carry out this action on their own much as they do adjustments. There are times, however, when the director needs to instruct an actor to cheat out to open up an action to the audience or cheat in to deliberately conceal it (see Figure 12.5).

A variation on cheating is the *proscenium cheat*. In this case, two actors in conversation will turn at slight angles to each other to open up the conversation to the audience (see Figure 12.6). While this is often a necessary practice on the proscenium stage, the director must be careful not to allow it to become exaggerated or overused. Doing so may force the play to become far too stylized.

Basic cheating is accepted by the audience in the same manner as architectural adjustments in the setting. However, if cheating makes the relationship lose its organic sense of reality, then cheating works against the play and the audience will not accept it.

Figure 12.5 (Left) Stage Position Without Cheating; (Right) Stage Position With Cheating

Figure 12.6 (Left) Stage Position Without Proscenium Cheat; (Right) Stage Position With Proscenium Cheat

USING BLOCKING MORE EFFECTIVELY

To create more effective blocking, the director needs to make appropriate use of the elements of blocking to best embody the intention of the character in the scene. The director can make use of the following concepts to do so:

STRENGTH OF THE CROSS

The director can control the strength of the cross by manipulating its implementation. The speed with which the actor crosses is a powerful tool. An actor rushing or slowly walking toward another actor conveys different emotions. Generally, the more urgent the need for the cross, the more rapid it will be. Along with the speed of the cross, the angle relative to the audience also affects its strength. Figure 12.7 illustrates the range of strength crosses have based on the relative angle to the audience. Crosses directly downstage toward the audience are the strongest; conversely, crosses directly upstage from the audience are the weakest. Crosses perpendicular to the centerline are neutral. Angles between these four directions fall between weakest and strongest depending on how close they are to direct downstage or direct upstage crosses. The director must set up the potential for the angle of the cross in the preceding picture to facilitate it.

> The director needs to be careful an actor is not trapped, requiring a weak cross to get out of the position. It is better to avoid the situation than find a solution once it occurs.

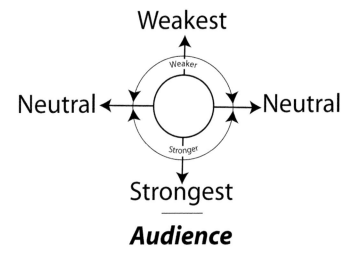

Figure 12.7 Strength of the Direction of the Cross

LINEAR VS. CURVED CROSSES

Most crosses are linear in nature. In life, the natural tendency is to take the shortest path, i.e., the path of least resistance. Stage crosses, unless intentionally highly stylized, should follow natural actions, which are essentially dictated by the physical environment. Walls create the most distinct guides to movement. It was previously established that a box set can be improved through perspective alteration, angling side walls to improve sight lines. This action also affects the nature of the crosses. If the side wall is perpendicular to the audience, crosses that naturally follow this wall would be straight upstage or downstage. Angling the wall influences the crosses by making them more diagonal relative to the audience. Curved surfaces or obstructions encourage curvilinear movement. If the director wishes to have a softer movement implied through the use of curves, this action must be predicated on the inclusion of curvilinear surfaces to inspire the actions. An arcing cross without some physical entity providing the inspiration or path will appear unnatural.

LENGTH OF THE CROSS

A cross covering a great distance magnifies all the other factors. While longer crosses allow more time to deliver lines, shorter crosses may be equally powerful. Short staccato movements versus longer more flowing movements create different emotions. The floor plan determines the length of the crosses. Large open areas allow for longer crosses; floor plans that include elements scattered throughout force the crosses to be shorter with numerous changes in direction. If the director wishes to incorporate long crosses into the staging, these crosses must be accommodated by the floor plan before staging commences.

USE OF TRIANGLES

If two actors are present in a scene, the blocking creates a line between the two. However, if three actors are present, the result is a triangular relationship. Triangles are automatically formed by the three actors; the key for the director is to deliberately use the nature of these triangles. Figure 12.8 illustrates three possible triangles.

In Examples A and C, the distance between the three actors is fairly even, preventing the formation of groups. In Example B, Actors 1 and 2 are closer together than they are to Actor 3, creating an apparent grouping. In comparing Example A with Example C, the focus is determined by where the actors are looking. If Actors 1 and 3 in Example A are looking at Actor 2, this will force the actors to close themselves off from the audience more significantly than in Example C, placing even greater emphasis on Actor 2. There is nothing inherently better or worse about any of the examples. The key in choosing between them lies in understanding the relationship between the three characters in the scene. In all three examples the audience's attention is directed to the actor speaking or in the direction the majority is looking. By manipulating the distance between each corner of the triangle, the director can control the relationship between the characters and the audience's perception of the scene.

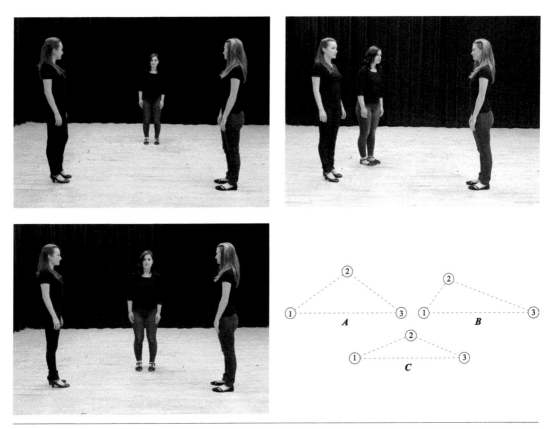

Figure 12.8 Comparison of Triangles

USE OF LEVELS

The use of levels in blocking is essentially the same as with stage pictures except that in blocking, the nature of the change in level also has implications for movement. They provide the director with the ability to significantly alter the focus of the audience by adding vertical movement to the blocking. For example, consider an actor ascending a staircase. The average step has a rise of 6 to 8 inches. The action with a 6-inch rise is decidedly different from that of a 12-inch rise. A rise greater or less than this range results in an action that feels unnatural to the actor and appears awkward to the audience. While an actor may climb steps with a 12-inch rise without great difficulty, the actor will have a major challenge descending the same steps. The nature of the action of an actor going up a ramp is decidedly smoother than going up a staircase. Ramps may allow for a gentle transition between levels; however, the director needs to realize the implications for the pitch of the ramp. I have seen instances where actors had to get a running start to make it up a ramp due to its pitch. The texture of the ramp and the actor's shoes are another consideration. How an actor transitions between levels is a factor determined by the floor plan and must be carefully considered in preproduction. Large differences in height are needed only if the setting or script calls for it.

GIVING AND TAKING FOCUS

As previously mentioned, as an actor crosses downstage the strength of the cross increases relative to the audience; the actor's final location relative to the other actors also has an impact on the audience's perception and focus. Example A in Figure 12.9 shows two actors facing each other in a neutral position relative to the audience. The new relative positions in Example B are created by either Actor 1 moving upstage or Actor 2 moving downstage. If Actor 1 moves upstage (a weaker cross) and then turns to face Actor 2, Actor 1 opens up slightly to the audience forcing Actor 2 to turn upstage, closing Actor 2 and taking away the focus. Alternatively, if Actor 2 moves downstage (a stronger cross) but then turns upstage closing slightly, this allows Actor 1 to turn downstage giving Actor 1 the focus. Such action is either called giving or taking focus. This type of movement can be used to shift the focus from one actor to another depending on where the director wants the audience's attention at that moment.

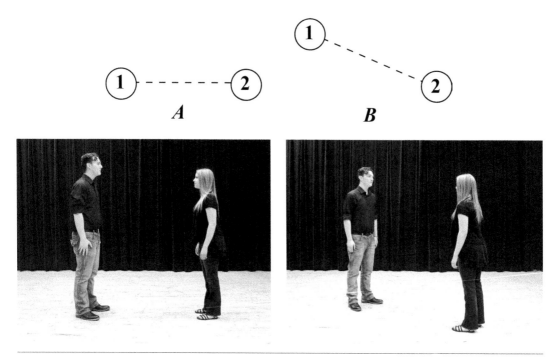

Figure 12.9 Giving and Taking by Changes in Stage Position

CONTRAST

Contrast refers to one element being different from the others. Simply crossing provides sufficient contrast to draw attention; however, if multiple actors are moving, contrasting the movement of one actor to the others will keep the focus on this actor. After the movement is complete, it is important that the audience still maintains the visual focus necessary for the scene. Providing contrast in the new picture is a major tool in ensuring that this occurs.

In comparing the set of pictures in Figure 12.10, the evenness in the arrangement of the actors in the top left picture makes finding the focus difficult. The top right and the bottom row of pictures shows various ways in which contrast can be applied to create visual focus. If one character should always maintain focus, one of the best tools for this is costuming.

Figure 12.10 Contrast – Top Left Photo With No Contrast; Top Right Photo and Bottom Row With Variations in Contrast

CROSSING AND/OR FACING UPSTAGE

The practice of having an actor face upstage is often misunderstood. Young actors are often told never to turn their backs to the audience. Many directors, too, are leery of having actors cross straight upstage and remain with their backs to the audience. While upstage crosses are technically the weakest stage direction, and facing upstage completely closes the actor to the audience, crossing and/or facing upstage can be an extremely strong and bold choice in the right circumstances. The sharp contrast of an actor facing upstage may create a unique focal point. The director may build intrigue by having the actor turn upstage, thus closing the actor completely. The action may also be a strong method of giving the stage to someone else. While having the actor's back to the audience is not standard blocking, it does provide a potentially strong option in the director's blocking arsenal.

KEEPING THE BLOCKING MOTIVATED

For blocking to remain vital and connected to the characters it must look like a direct extension of the characters' tactics rather than a strategically planned movement serving a mechanical need. To ensure this occurs, the blocking must be internally motivated by the actors. The key to blocking is making it seem organically part of the character's thought process, not something the actor was told to do by the director. The director must make sure the actor understands the reason for the action. On the whole, the blocking is designed to reinforce the dramatic action of the scene and, as such, the motivation should be readily apparent. If the actor does not understand the rationale for the action or does not agree with it, the likelihood is the action will appear unmotivated. In this case, the director needs to discuss with the actor the goal of the blocking. If the actor disagrees with this goal, the director and actor must come to an understanding regarding the interpretation of the moment. Ultimately, should the actor continue to disagree and is unable to make the action appear motivated, the director must change the blocking to maintain the integrity of the scene. Most actors make every effort to incorporate the director's blocking once they understand how it integrates with their characters.

There are times when an action is necessary for a purely mechanical reason, such as moving the action to one side of the stage for a scene shift to occur on the other. An internal reason for the action must be developed by the actor for it to appear motivated. As long as the actor finds a valid internal reason for the action, and continually plays this rationale, the action will seem organically part of the scene. In any event, regardless of how or why the blocking evolved, it is vital that it always looks like an integral part of the action of the scene rather than a mechanical tool.

Keeping the blocking motivated is one of the most important considerations in staging.

BLOCKING PITFALLS TO AVOID

In addition to ensuring the blocking appears internally motivated, there are other potential pitfalls the director needs to avoid. Pitfalls create images onstage that may not please or may distract the audience. Some of the major pitfalls include:

SIMULTANEOUS MOVEMENT

Simultaneous movement refers to multiple characters moving at the same time. While this may not necessarily be a problem, there are several possible pitfalls. If all the crosses have equal value, the focus will be momentarily confused. The extent of this problem depends on what else is happening in the scene. One type of simultaneous movement that is almost always problematic is when two actors cross in parallel lines at the same time and speed. This can be avoided by either having one actor delay the start of the cross or by having the actors move at different speeds.

FORMING STRAIGHT LINES

Actors moving together to a new location often regroup in a straight line. Unless the line is absolutely necessary for the scene, it will look awkward. The solution is to have some of the actors move either slightly upstage or downstage of the line. Experienced actors generally adjust themselves to avoid this situation, but less experienced actors may need to be told.

Figure 12.11
(Top) Straight Line; (Bottom) Staggered Group

TWO-DIMENSIONAL BLOCKING

Blocking that is limited to one lateral plane of motion, most often movement back and forth across the stage, is referred to as two-dimensional blocking. This can be avoided through the proper floor plan. A floor plan that utilizes elements distributed in three dimensions naturally leads to better blocking because the elements provide reasons for the actors to move in all directions. Two-dimensional blocking is easily seen when the crosses become repetitive, but fortunately fixing the situation is not complicated.

STAYING SEATED TOO LONG

Having an actor sit may be either a tool to change the dynamic relationship between standing and seated actors or a necessary part of the scene as described in the script. When an actor is seated, it is easier for the energy of the scene to weaken. This may be because the audience perceives the expenditure of less energy by the seated actor and transfers it to the scene, or the seated actor is more comfortable and may settle in, thus losing energy. This becomes an issue especially when using comfortable, heavily padded furniture. The more comfortable the actor, the more likely the loss of energy. This energy loss may continue as long as the actor remains seated. If at all possible, the director needs to find reasons for the actor to rise and move. This does not mean the actor should move around the set continually; however, maintaining the same stage picture for too long will work against its energy. In cases where getting up is impossible, such as two people seated in a restaurant, the director needs to find other means to maintain the energy. This can be done through microblocking as well as ensuring that the vocal energy can carry the scene.

> The question should not be at what point is the motivation found for the seated actor to rise, but, rather, at what point is the motivation needed for the actor to stay seated.

ONE STEP MOVEMENT

A cross should always move the actor fully from one location onstage to another. As a guide, all crosses should require at least two steps. The obvious exceptions are small adjustments to accommodate sight lines or for mechanical reasons within the scene. Short crosses will appear ineffective and should be avoided.

NOT PLANNING FOR CROSSOVERS

When planning the blocking the director needs to consider whether an actor who exits on one side of the stage needs to enter on the other. If the director fails to plan for necessary crossovers, major complications can arise once the play moves to the actual setting. Most settings and theatres provide for crossovers upstage of the setting or the upstage drop or with stairs on both sides of the stage for crossovers beneath it. Regardless of how they are accomplished, time is a factor. This crossover time may be further complicated by a costume change or some other adjustment. Run-throughs should be held periodically if rehearsing with rehearsal units as the problem may not become apparent until the scenes are run contiguously.

OVERRELIANCE ON CHEATING

While it is important to make adjustments onstage to ensure the audience has a clear view of the action, the director needs to be careful not to rely too heavily on cheating out to the audience. This is particularly true if proscenium cheating is constantly and mechanically used. If the actors cheat too far to the audience, they will lose connection with one another and the play may become too presentational. The director needs to find a balance between genuine character interaction and the blocking that allows the audience to have clear sight lines.

Figure 12.12 (Left) Appropriate Cheating; (Right) Too Much Cheating

EXTRANEOUS MOVEMENT

It is important that the director makes sure any additional or unnecessary movement by the actors does not distract or pull the focus of the audience.

USING PROPS

Part of the blocking inevitably utilizes props. Props, or properties, are any objects the actor uses, refers to, or physically interacts with. Props can be divided into three categories: floor props, hand props, and decorative props. Floor props are any props that occupy floor space and that the actor may sit on, stand on, or interact with in some way, such as chairs, tables, and beds. Hand props are those the actor physically uses in a scene. These may be objects mandated by the script or selected to enhance the character. The final category, decorative props, are those items onstage purely for decoration rather than practical purposes. These may include articles on the setting or the costumes.

It is important for the director to incorporate floor props and hand props into the blocking. This ensures there is a plan for the actor to obtain the prop and then to get rid of it once it is no longer needed. Floor props should be utilized from the beginning of rehearsals. If the performance furniture is distinctly different from the rehearsal items, significant rehearsal time with the performance furniture should be planned. Hand props should be integrated into the rehearsal process as quickly as possible. They can be beneficial in the development

Figure 12.13 The Author Explaining a Prop to an Actor During a Rehearsal of *Wit*

Photograph by Kaley Etzkorn, Courtesy of Drury University

of the character and possibly provide reasons for staging beyond their mechanical use. Many directors prefer not to use hand props until the actors are off book since holding the script and props can complicate the rehearsal process. Miming of the prop should be avoided because it forces the actor to focus on the creation of the "object" rather than its use. For example, an actor miming holding a glass may neglect to mime picking it up and putting it down. Rehearsal hand props may be used to keep the performance props from breaking during rehearsal. As with floor props, the amount of time actors need to rehearse with the performance hand props depends on how closely the rehearsal props resemble them. Aside from meeting the mechanical needs of the script, hand props may be a useful tool in both envisioning the characters and the overall sense of the play. A well-chosen prop can provide the actor with the opportunity to further explore his or her character as well as provide an added visual element to the scene. The director needs to be careful that hand props do not become a crutch for the actors to externally convey, rather than truly embody, the character.

The blocking also has to consider the placement of the props. If a prop will be used again, the director must plan where to position it so it is accessible when needed.

PLANNING, RECORDING, AND COMMUNICATING THE BLOCKING

The director should work from the floor plan to create the blocking for each of the previously developed stage pictures. While some directors plan the blocking in their heads, many directors prefer to work with some physical representation of the actors on the floor plan. The diameter of a penny placed onto a ½"-scale floor plan occupies about 18 scale inches, the approximate diameter of the typical actor. One technique is to place labels with the names of the characters on the pennies and to use them to plan the staging. This method prevents the director from placing more actors into a space than will comfortably fit. Leaving the coin representing the actor by the exit that was just used reminds the director that a crossover for that actor may be needed. This method is also beneficial in planning the physical relationships involved in the staging. The physicality of each actor must be accounted for by the director since the height of the actors impacts the blocking. If an initial run-through with the actors on their feet is scheduled immediately after the table read, the director can gain valuable insight from the organic blocking of the actors. The director can then use this insight when refining the blocking to ensure it will be motivated. As the director plans the action it should be recorded in the script or diagrammed on copies of the floor plan. A helpful method for recording and communicating the blocking involves stage directions. While the vast majority of beginning directors are familiar with the concept of stage directions, many are not conversant with the more subtly refined descriptions for the relative locations onstage. Figure 12.14 shows the standard definition of these areas.

Up Stage Right (USR)	Up Stage Right of Center (USRC)	Up Center (UC)	Up Stage Left of Center (USLC)	Up Stage Left (USL)
Stage Right (SR)	Stage Right of Center (SRC)	Center (C)	Stage Left of Center (SLC)	Stage Left (SL)
Down Stage Right (DSR)	Down Stage Right of Center (DSRC)	Down Center (DC)	Down Stage Left of Center (DSLC)	Down Stage Left (DSL)

Figure 12.14 Stage Areas

The use of stage areas is particularly helpful when blocking on an open stage. When blocking on a setting with scenic elements the director can note locations by references to the elements such as "downstage right of the sofa." To simplify this notation the director can utilize standard abbreviations employed by most stage managers in recording the blocking during the rehearsals. While every stage manager and director uses a slightly different set of symbols, the following list is an excellent starting point:

X	Cross
SR, SL, US, etc.	Stage Directions
→	to
↑	Rise
↓	Sit
⊓	Table (Furniture symbol)
Һ	Chair (Furniture symbol)
Ent	Enter
Ex	Exit
^	Place where an action starts

These symbols can be combined to record the following actions:

Bruce crosses to Cynthia.

B X → C

Cynthia crosses to the table, picks up a book, and crosses to the downstage right chair and sits.

C X → ⊓ (picks up book)

X → DRh↓

Cynthia rises and exits through the downstage right door.

C↑ Ex DR door

Bruce crosses to downstage of the down left table during Cynthia's line.

B X → DS of DL ⊓ (Note that in this case the B indicates the cross by Bruce even though Cynthia is speaking.)

Note that the characters were referenced using their first initial. If more than one character begins with the same letter, the first two letters can be used, for example, Cy for Cynthia. When dealing with a large group of unnamed characters, such as a chorus, the director can either use numbers or refer to each character by the actor's name. Arrows are used to indicate direction, and diagrams of the furniture can be used as shorthand. To indicate where the action takes place in the script, the director can place a caret (^) in the location where the action begins. The key is for the director to keep the shorthand as simple as possible so the script is uncluttered and still easily understood.

Finally, the director needs to communicate the blocking to the actors. The blocking rehearsal or rehearsals are a fairly mechanical process in which the director provides the staging to the actors. While this can be done seated at a table, doing so relies too heavily on theoretical action, and the director does not have the opportunity to make adjustments until seeing the actors onstage. It is better for the director, designer, or stage manager to start by explaining the taped outline of the setting on the rehearsal floor and then giving the actors their initial locations. The actors can then begin their lines with the director interrupting to provide the next set of actions. To save time, the director can provide small groups of blocking to the actors. In communicating the blocking the director may also include the thought process behind the action. For example, rather than simply indicating one actor should cross to the other, the director could phrase it: "Cross angrily to the other actor in a threatening manner." It is important that the actors write the blocking down in their scripts rather than memorize it. The stage manager will also be noting the blocking in his or her production book. The stage manager's blocking notes will become especially important as the blocking continues to evolve since it will probably change from what was written in the director's script, making the stage manager's notations the most current and reliable. If at all possible, it is best to allow the actors to repeat the play once they have all the blocking to ensure they have it correctly and the director is happy with the results. This should not be taken to imply that blocking does not change; blocking matures as the play develops.

BLOCKING CHECKLIST

❏ Does the blocking help create the overall sense of the scene?

❏ Does the blocking help create the individual nature of the characters?

❏ Does the blocking help focus the audience's attention?

❏ Does the blocking help build energy?

❏ Does the blocking help maintain interest through changes in stage pictures?

❏ Does the blocking help reinforce the message for the audience?

❏ Are the following principles fully applied?

- Cross
- Turn
- Changes in elevation
- Counter cross
- Distance between actors
- Microblocking
- Adjustment
- Cheating

❏ Is the blocking used as effectively as possible?

- Are the crosses appropriately strong?
- Is the nature of the cross (linear or curved) used appropriately?
- Does the length of the cross fit the action?
- Are triangles effectively used?
- Are levels used effectively?
- Is the focus appropriately maintained by giving and taking the focus?
- Is contrast effectively employed to provide visual interest and focus?
- Are upstage crosses effectively utilized?

❏ Is the blocking consistently motivated?

❏ Are the major blocking pitfalls avoided?

❏ Are props used effectively?

FURTHER EXPLORATION

1. Choose an action unit from a play you analyzed and develop possible blocking for it.

2. Work with another director who developed blocking for the same action unit you did in Activity 1 and compare it to your blocking. Try to determine how the blocking underscores your different interpretations of the play.

3. Utilizing a short scene, develop several variations on the blocking. How does each one change the dynamics of the scene? How can you utilize the blocking to best support and differentiate each character?

4. Utilizing the stage pictures created for *Tender Offer* in the Further Exploration section of Chapter 11, craft the blocking that evolves from these pictures to further develop the different interpretations of the relationship between the father and his daughter.

PART V

The Rehearsal Process

CHAPTER 13

Working with the Actors

DEVELOPING A RELATIONSHIP WITH YOUR ACTORS

Perhaps the closest relationship the director has with any part of the production is with the cast. This relationship can range from friendly to far more formal. Regardless, the director must always remain as the head of the production, maintaining the respect of the actors. Many beginning directors suffer feelings of inadequacy. These feelings are frequently compounded when working with actors whom they feel are more experienced and talented. This sentiment is based on the assumption that to be a good director, one has to be a good actor. Although many good actors do become directors, this is not a prerequisite. An analogy can be applied from the world of professional sports. While many successful coaches began as athletes, typically they coach those who are far better athletes than they were. Just as an effective coach does not have to personally outplay the members of his or her team, the director does not need to be a better actor than his or her cast. Keep in mind there is a difference between director and acting coach. An acting coach's role is to develop the actor's technique; the director's role is to conceive and guide the production, working with the actors to achieve his or her vision. It is often incumbent upon a director to double as an acting coach when working with inexperienced actors, but it is not perforce part of the job description. Some beginning directors even go so far as to cast weaker and less experienced actors to avoid the feeling of inferiority. Doing so is totally unnecessary; there is no reason to limit the production in this manner.

Directors have different approaches for securing the best performance from their cast. These techniques extend from quietly discussing to cajoling to screaming to even threatening. Unfortunately, too many directors take their cue from a model often considered the standard of basketball coaching. In this model, the coach attempts to get the best work from his or her players by yelling, stamping, shoving, or belittling them. While many successful coaches employ these techniques, such actions are inappropriate for directors. Directors need to maintain control of their emotions and strive to find ways to help their actors discover the best path to the final product. That is not to say the director's purpose may never be better served by the occasional and well-placed use of emotion, but this needs to be the exception, something the director chooses to do. Every director needs to establish the line that will not be crossed when working with the cast. There are numerous stories of major-name directors using underhanded tactics or even lying to their actors to obtain the best performance. In many cases, they were quite successful. Nonetheless, this should not be taken as the standard. Every director needs to make the decision for him- or herself. There is simply no "right" way.

TYPES AND FUNCTIONS OF CHARACTERS

To help the actors develop their characters, the director must determine the type of character each actor is portraying and determine their function and purpose within the play. There are a number of standard characters found in most plays. These include:

THE PROTAGONIST

The protagonist is generally considered to be the major character in the play. It is this character around whom the playwright has centered the plot. The protagonist's actions create the dramatic and physical action as the protagonist attempts to reach his or her goal.

THE ANTAGONIST

The antagonist is the character who works in opposition to the protagonist, seeking to prevent the protagonist from reaching his or her goal and is often the villain in the story. The protagonist's success depends upon defeating the antagonist.

THE FOIL

The foil is the character who serves as a contrast to another character, usually the protagonist. The foil serves as a vehicle for the playwright to amplify the traits of the other character.

THE FRIEND OR CONFIDANT(E)

The confidant(e) is a friend of one of the characters. The playwright uses the character as a vehicle for the principal character to be able to discuss his or her true feelings.

THE FUNCTIONAL CHARACTER

The functional character appears in the play for a specific purpose. This character is a tool the playwright uses to make something happen. Once this function is served, this character is no longer needed in the play.

THE STOCK CHARACTER

The stock character refers to a character type who is easily recognized by the audience. These characters are not fully developed and are frequently somewhat stereotypical. Examples of stock characters can best be seen in the commedia dell'arte, but stock characters continue to exist in contemporary drama.

THE MINOR CHARACTER

Minor characters are utilized by the playwright to round out the cast and are not essential to the plot. They are often similar to the functional character. The difference is that the minor character may have more than one function in the play.

THE VOICE OF REASON OR *RAISONNEUR*

The *raisonneur* serves as the voice of reason in the play. Representing the viewpoint of the author, the *raisonneur* is the calming voice in the midst of chaos or the character who provides insight that helps the other characters, usually the protagonist.

UNDERSTANDING THE ACTOR'S PROCESS

While not needing to be a skilled actor, the director must fully understand the process through which the actor builds the character and approaches the play. Actors use many different techniques in developing their characters. Perhaps the most famous of these was the technique taught by the Russian acting teacher Constantin Stanislavski. Many modern approaches to acting were inspired by his work. Some techniques, such as Stanislavski's, involve internally motivating the character through tapping emotions; others utilize more external approaches. The approach of the actor to the role is really not a concern of the director, who seeks only to help the actor reach the fullest sense of the character consistent with the production concept.

Every character is a product of the elements that define it. The director must have a clear sense of each of these elements and work with the actor toward a consistent sense of the character. Some of these elements are included in the director's analysis; others are defined during the rehearsal process. The purpose of every character is to reach a **goal**. The overall goal is the total of the minor goals found in each action unit and represents the character's objective. The character's path to this goal is blocked by an **obstacle**. The obstacle is what creates the conflict. The character may have an overall obstacle toward their overall goal as well as obstacles within each action unit toward attaining their minor goals. In working toward their goal the character interacts with their **other**. The other refers to the character or characters who either must be overcome or who will help them reach their goal. Typically, the other is the actor's scene partner. To overcome the obstacle, working with or against the other to realize their goal, the character will utilize **tactics**. Tactics refer to the actions or approaches the character takes to achieve their goal. These will change if the initial tactics are not successful. These concepts often do not apply in decidedly nonrealistic plays. In these cases, the director needs to develop an appropriate vocabulary to work with the actors.

It is important for the director to understand that each actor may approach their role with a different methodology. This is not the director's concern. Rather, the director must challenge the actor to find the strongest interpretation of the role, making the boldest choices consistent with the production concept.

The director's function is to challenge the actor to use the most dynamic tactics consistent with the character. The more dynamic these tactics and the higher the stakes, the greater the tension and the more involved the audience. A tightrope walker walks across a single rope stretched between two towers. The skill of the tightrope walker is in maintaining balance. This skill is the same whether the rope is 6 inches off the ground, 30 feet off the ground, or stretched between two skyscrapers. Disallowing environmental factors such as wind, the tightrope walker uses the exact same skill set in all cases. The difference is the price of failure and the reward of success. While the skills may be the same, the increased danger of the tightrope walker at greater heights mesmerizes the audience. The tightrope walker, too, has a greater sense of urgency with the increase in danger. This tension of the performer combined with the transferred tension to the audience intensifies the performance. By ensuring the actors choose tactics and situations with both the greatest reward for success and greatest cost of failure, the director heightens the audience's enjoyment of the play.

The director's work with the actors should begin with both the director's and the actor's character analyses. The character analysis is the foundation for the development of the character. The play provides several insights to each character: the character's self-perception; the perception of the character by the other characters, which may corroborate, enhance, or conflict with the character's self-perception; and given circumstances that offer further insight to each character. The director now compares the analysis of each character with the actor's interpretation. By combining these resources, the director develops and communicates a picture establishing the parameters within which the actor builds the character. The director cannot assume the sources within the script are necessarily correct. For example, the description given of a character by another character may not be true, but rather how that character sees him or her. The director must work through the combination of the insights into the character to develop a complete understanding. It is essential for the director and the actor to agree on the general nature and purpose of the character so the director can work with the actor to define the function and purpose of the character in each scene as well as the entire play. The character's purpose needs to be considered in light of both individual unit goals and the overall goal. Assigning a verb to each of the character's lines is a useful technique for the director and the actor to provide the character with an initial attack. The verb is a one-word description summarizing succinctly and insightfully the nature of the action expressed when delivering the line. This may also be thought of as the subtext for the line. Examples might include: cajole, confront, comfort, attack, and listen.

The director needs to promote appropriate physical contact between the characters whenever possible. Contact provides a strong emotional connection for the audience and a clear stimulation for the actor. These sensations often lead to a greater connection with the acting

Figure 13.1 The Author Working With Actors

Photograph by Michael Engelmeyer – Great Outdoors Studios. Courtesy of Drury University

partner. Experienced actors understand the value of physical contact; less experienced actors may have to be encouraged to find the opportunities. Inexperienced actors may even shy away from physical contact. Generally, experienced actors' sense of personal space is such that they feel comfortable when others touch them just as they feel comfortable in touching others. The director needs to assess where each of the actors are in this regard and ensure that the necessary physical contact is being made. This should be introduced early in the rehearsal process. Scenes involving characters where contact is out of place provide the opportunity to utilize the desire for contact coupled with the restriction it cannot occur. It is important for the director to make sure this tension comes across to the audience to prevent these scenes from becoming sterile. Contact of an intimate or intrusive nature must be separately addressed to ensure the actors feel safe.

> Physical contact is essential for actors to develop strong connections with their partner and through this, the audience. A good director will encourage this contact.

Not all characters are aware of what is and is not true. Each character bases their understanding of truth on their perception of what occurs in the scene. One of the great dualisms in theatre is that all the actors know the truth even though their characters do not. In some cases, it is valuable as a character development tool for actors not to share their internal process or their perception of the truth or reality. This may allow for more genuine interaction between the characters. For the most part, the director should be fully aware of the realities within the play. Although it is not essential to know each detail of the internal process for the actor, it is important for the director to know the truth in the play.

I faced an interesting situation when directing a production of *Doubt*. The play centers on the issue of what to do when we are not certain, in other words, have doubt. The head of a Catholic school, an older nun, believes a young priest is having inappropriate relations with one of the young male students. The playwright, John Patrick Shanley, never supplies conclusive evidence one way or the other. He deliberately and carefully crafts the play so the opinion of the audience is based purely on their perception and understanding of the circumstances provided. Even Sister Aloysius, the older nun, only has circumstantial evidence as a basis for her accusation. The sole character in the play who knows for certain if the priest is a pedophile is the priest. The premise of the play is not to determine whether the priest is guilty but to explore our behavior when certainty is not possible. The dramatic action of the play works equally well with either interpretation. I decided to take a directorial gamble in my production concept and did not make the decision. Instead, I left it to the actor playing the priest to decide for himself. I instructed him not only to withhold his decision from the other actors but also from me. For the first time as a director I was directing an actor whose character I did not fully understand. I made this determination to maintain the eye of the audience. Since doubt is the essential element of the production concept, I did not want to feel in observing the actor's work that the actor was portraying the priest as clearly guilty or innocent. I worked with him to avoid this clarity. The gamble worked and I was able to maintain the aura of doubt throughout the play. While I do not recommend this practice as the norm, there are times ambiguity in the production concept helps the production.

COMMUNICATING WITH YOUR ACTORS

One of the most important skills a director must develop is good communication. The way the director communicates is a reflection of his or her relationship with the cast. Directors who take a more authoritarian or controlling approach are apt to use direct statements and give instructions. Directors with a more collaborative approach tend to discuss and question. The latter approach is generally more productive since it fully engages the actors in the rehearsal process and allows their insight into the characters to become part of the evolution of the play.

By opening with a discussion during the table read, the director begins the rehearsal process with the premise that interaction will be a key part of developing the play. The director is empowering the actors to express their views of their characters and the play, set within the parameters of the director's production concept. At the same time, the director may gain insight from the actors' perspective and a better understanding of the beginning of the actors' processes. In doing so, the director is making full use of the collaborative concept. The director can use this discussion throughout the process as key moments in the play are approached and to confront developmental impasses during scene work.

In addition to discussion, one of the director's best tools is questions. Questions instead of statements further emphasize the importance of the actors' ideas in the development of the scene. This is often a better technique for helping an actor conceptualize the scene and their role since it does not have the appearance of imposing ideas. The rehearsal process is well served if the director regularly asks "How does that feel?" Aside from allowing the actor to express feelings about the direction the scene is taking, it defuses the potential for a situation in which the actor does not fully agree with their character's path. Rather than waiting until the effect is seen in ongoing rehearsals, the director can deal with the actor's concern immediately. This question can be applied to any rehearsal situation from blocking to character interaction. It is particularly valuable after the initial work with the scene as well as subsequent changes in approach, either physically or emotionally. The director may ask this question when observing that an actor is not comfortable with a scene. In this case, the question becomes a diagnostic tool to aid in the scene's development.

An extension of the use of questions as a directorial tool is what I call "Multiple-Choice Directing." This technique involves using two or three different approaches to the scene from the blocking to the interaction of the characters. After setting up the approaches, I ask the actors to fully commit to each one in working the scene. Afterward, I ask the actors which one felt better. Many times, this is the option selected. Although I do not always use this technique, it is a tool that proves beneficial in the right circumstances.

While it is important to listen to the actors, this does not mean the director must always agree with them. If the director has created an atmosphere of genuine give-and-take, the actors will understand if the director does not always go along with their ideas. Simply asking the actors "How does that feel?" can go a long way to ensure their engagement.

One of the downsides to questions and discussion as a directorial tool is the chance that the actors will develop a direction or interpretation with which the director disagrees. For this tool to be effective, it is imperative that the actors' choices are genuine, and the director is open to the possibility of accepting them. Once the door is open to input from the actors, the director must be careful if the actors disagree. If the director simply dismisses their opinions, the actors will inevitably cease expressing them. On the other hand, it is essential for the director to maintain his or her directorial vision and not allow the actors to pursue their individual interpretations at the expense of the spine of the play. A balance must be found between the two. Actors can be steered by a skilled director into a thought process consistent with the director's vision by carefully worded questions. A good guideline is to ask questions only in areas where insight is wanted, and to provide direction where it is essential to maintain the production concept. This minimizes the number of times the director does not accept the actors' ideas. Assuming the director is open to actors' ideas and the cast genuinely believes this, they are generally quite willing to accept when the director disagrees and they need to pursue the director's interpretation. As in the case with designers, if there is an idea the director wants pursued, it is better to state it rather than ask a series of questions until the actors finally arrive at the desired answer. If the director is honest with the cast, the cast will reciprocate. In this way, the director still maintains control of the production while allowing a fair amount of freedom for the actors to pursue their ideas.

A good communicator is also a good listener. One of the skills the director needs to develop is how to respond to questions from the actors. During the course of the rehearsal process the actors will have many questions. The less experienced director will quickly answer each of them; the more experienced director will look for the underlying question. For example, when an actor asks, "How should I cross?" what the actor really may be questioning is how their character feels in the situation. I was once approached midway through the rehearsal process by a student actor who told me he had purchased tickets to a major concert prior to being cast and just realized he had a conflict with the actor technical rehearsal. The question he asked was "Can I miss the rehearsal?" The simple, obvious answer was "No." However, I knew the actor was asking a deeper question. He wanted me to make the decision for him. In lieu of answering the question directly, I turned the question back to him. I reaffirmed how essential his presence was at the rehearsal and how his absence would adversely affect it. I pointed out I could not physically stop him from going, and, obviously, I was not going to replace him if he chose to go, but the final decision was his. His next question, "So I can't go?" reaffirmed my assumption he was trying to shift responsibility to me. I answered, "The choice is yours. You know what is at stake." The actor ultimately chose to be at the rehearsal, the only correct choice, but, more important, the actor made the decision on his own.

Often the best response to an actor's question is "What do you think?" By turning the question back to the actor, the director avoids a simple answer and instead helps the actor think through the situation and answer their own question. If the director disagrees with the actor's response, the director can then open a new avenue of exploration by offering an opinion as a possible option to explore. Actors tend to look to directors for quick answers to what are actually more complex questions. A simple answer may be more expeditious, but it limits further exploration by the actors. It is usually more beneficial to guide the actors through self-discovery than provide the answer. The director can facilitate this by discussing the situation with the actor either alone or with the scene partner. Asking insightful questions can help the actor rethink the situation. The director should also not be afraid to say, "I don't know" or "I would rather not say." While there are aspects of the production for which the director must provide further guidance, it is equally important the director insist on the actors finding the rest on their own. If the director simply provides all aspects of the production to the actors, the resulting show will inevitably be less developed.

As a director, do not ask questions if you are not prepared to deal with all possible answers.

Since one of the director's major functions is to view the rehearsals from the eye of the audience, the director can utilize this in communicating with the actors. Instead of stating, "Cut back on the anger," the director can say, "From out here, I perceive a great deal of anger. Is this what you intend?" If the answer is no, the actor will make the appropriate adjustment;

if the answer is yes, then the director can ask questions regarding the reasons and may offer an alternative approach. By framing the question in this way, the director helps maintain the actor's importance in the developmental process of the scene and will probably get a better result. The director needs to remember the actors cannot see from the audience's perspective and they must rely on the director. What can a director do if the actor disagrees with the director's interpretation and no amount of discussion or guidance will change it? One of the great ironies in directing is that directors rarely win arguments with actors. While the general assumption is since the "power" rests with the directors they will ultimately get their way, the reality is most often the opposite. An actor can be told to follow the director's guidelines and interpretation, but if the director is unable to change the actor's opinion, the actor will continue to at least subliminally use it to develop the character. If the production has a long run it is almost inevitable that the actor will slowly move back to their own interpretation. Therefore, it is in the best interest of the production to find a compromise. The results will be far better than having the actor begrudgingly following the director's instructions.

One of the director's key responsibilities during the rehearsal process is working with the actors to develop what is commonly referred to as the "arc," the developmental trajectory for the play. The term implies a smooth curve, but the arc may actually follow an irregular path. The arc describes the process of the evolution of the play from inciting incident to climax. The director needs to determine the arc of each individual action unit and how it contributes to the development of the overall arc to ensure a smooth evolution. Each unit's arc becomes a building block of the overall arc for the play. The ultimate development of the overall arc is finalized during the polishing rehearsals in much the same way a carpenter sands each component individually but finish sands the entire project once it is assembled. Each character will also have an arc representing their transition from one polar attitude to another. The arc of the character must naturally fit into both the arc of the scene and the overall arc of the play. The final development of the arc, the polishing phases, will be discussed in more detail in Chapter 17.

> Directors rarely win arguments with actors.

WORKING WITH ACTORISMS

In working with the actor, it is crucial for the director to identify and correct inconsistent or distracting mannerisms. I refer to these actor mannerisms as *actorisms*. While every character is developed through the actor, including their individual mannerisms, these mannerisms are only relevant when intentionally used to further the character. A positive use of an actorism can be found in the television series *The West Wing*, a series about the president and his staff in the West Wing of the White House, developed by Aaron Sorkin and starring Martin Sheen as President Bartlet. Due to Sheen's limited use of his left hand, he had a unique way of putting on his jacket by flipping it over his head. This mannerism was incorporated into the series to become a facet of the president's character. However, when actorisms distract the audience from the character, reminding them they are watching an actor instead of the character, they must be eliminated from the actor's portrayal. The director needs to take the actor and his or her experience into account when addressing actorisms. There are many examples of these mannerisms. Listed below are actorisms actors frequently use, especially beginning actors.

LEG AT ANGLE

Standing with more weight on one leg than the other is one of the most typical actorisms. People who are uncomfortable standing straight often develop this habit. It is not uncommon for it to be transferred to the stage. Unless used intentionally, this mannerism projects indifference and generally weakens the actor's presence onstage.

T-REX ARMS

T-rex arms refer to the unusual mannerism whereby actors keep their elbows near their sides and gesture solely by moving their forearms. This is not only visually annoying, but it also limits the expression of the actors by constraining their gestures and restricting the amount of apparent energy in each gesture. Actors should always be encouraged to make full gestures.

Figure 13.2 Leg at an Angle   **Figure 13.3** T-rex Arms

Figure 13.4 Cheating Out – (Left) None; (Center) Correct; (Right) Extreme

CHEATING OUT

The process of cheating out should not distract from the internal interaction in the scene. Some actors instinctively cheat out more fully than necessary, making the action appear artificial. I have even seen actors who were primarily trained on a proscenium stage try to cheat in arena theatre. Although by definition it is impossible to do so, the actors are creating a de facto downstage and, as such, the mannerism must be eliminated.

ARMS BEHIND BACK

Actors, especially beginning actors, often feel uncertain about what to do with their arms. One of the most difficult challenges can be standing still and staying neutral onstage. A resulting actorism is for the actor to place their arms behind their back. While this can be a valuable tool in developing the character, generically it is a weak position that may cause the audience to speculate about what is behind the actor's back. The actor is using the position as a crutch to feel physically comfortable onstage.

HANDS IN POCKETS

An actor placing their hands in a jacket or pants pockets is simply a variation on placing their arms behind their back and has similar implications for the audience.

CROSSED ARMS

Another variation to placing their arms behind their back or their hands in their pockets is to stand with arms crossed over the chest. Once again, this position can be useful in character development if it is employed appropriately and sparingly. The problem lies in extended or

Figure 13.5 Arms Behind Back

Figure 13.6 Hands in Pockets

Figure 13.7 Crossed Arms

Figure 13.8 Fidgeting with the Costume

Figure 13.9 Touching Hair

repetitious use since the act tends to emotionally cut the actor off from the audience. It also limits the ability to appropriately use the hands.

INSERTING "HUHS" OR OTHER EXTRANEOUS SOUNDS

On occasion, actors will insert unnecessary sounds between words in the dialogue. This can include the addition of actual words or sounds, including gentle hmms. A particularly bad habit involves the expulsion of air creating a quiet "huh" sound. Inserting unnecessary sounds drains energy from the scene by releasing the energy of the character.

FIDGETING WITH THE COSTUME

Some actors fidget with their costume once they start wearing it. This is particularly true if the costume has elements that are foreign to the actor. Since they feel unnatural, the actor is unintentionally drawn to them. Fidgeting with the costume may also be a physical release of nervousness. In any event, it inappropriately draws the attention of the audience away from where it should be and weakens the character.

TOUCHING HAIR

Similar to fidgeting with the costume, actors may release tension by playing with or brushing their hair with their hands. As in the last example, this mannerism is distracting for the audience.

SHUFFLING OR MOVING FEET

Small movements of the feet that result in shuffling or adding minor adjustments to their position is another variation on a mannerism caused by the difficulty of standing still. This extraneous movement is both distracting for the audience and significantly weakens the character and therefore must be eliminated.

* * *

Since by definition these actorisms are unintentional mannerisms that find their way into the actor's portrayal, the director needs to follow a process to eliminate them. The first step is to make the actor aware of the mannerism. While it is possible the actor may eliminate it based on a note following the rehearsal, the second step is for the director to point out the mannerism each time it occurs so the actor can correct it. The director can simply call out a single word, such as "Hands," to indicate the inappropriate mannerism. The third step in the process is when the actor recognizes the mannerism and corrects it without the director pointing it out. The final step is when the actor eliminates the mannerism from the character. This process takes time so it is important to start working on removing unwanted actorisms at the beginning of the rehearsal process. Beginning directors often make the mistake of waiting to address these issues only to find they do not have enough time to reduce or eliminate them.

Directors need to be aware that their communication techniques may have to be modified to meet the individual needs of each actor. This is true whether dealing with experienced or beginning actors. Techniques appropriate to one group may be inappropriate to another. If the cast has mixed abilities, the director will need to address the actors in groups based on the level of their abilities.

FURTHER EXPLORATION

1. Observe actors either in a rehearsal or in acting exercises to try to identify actorisms that are not appropriate for the character. Think about how you would work with the actor to remove these mannerisms.

2. Talk to actors regarding how they like directors to communicate with them. It may also be beneficial to ask the actors for directorial communication techniques they do not like.

3. Develop a list of communication techniques that you prefer directors use with you and those you do not.

Rehearsal Techniques

PLANNING FOR THE REHEARSALS

The planning, organization, and running of rehearsals are the responsibility of the director. Since directors rarely have more time than they need, it is essential to maximize every minute. Assuming a rehearsal period of five weeks with six rehearsals per week, if even two minutes are lost at each rehearsal, one hour total will be lost by the end of the process. Keeping in mind how easy it is to lose two minutes, it is crucial to be aware of time during the rehearsal process. Even if time is not an issue, making the best use of it is only fair to the actors. The different approaches to a rehearsal schedule were initially discussed in Chapter 9. The approach chosen serves as the basis for planning each rehearsal. The stage manager can help with staying on schedule. At the end of each rehearsal the director needs to assess the progress to determine if modifications are necessary. While it is counterproductive to move on to the next phase of rehearsal if the actors are not ready, it is more harmful if the production becomes bogged down in an early phase, limiting the time for the later ones. A careful balance between the two must be maintained.

ORGANIZATION OF THE REHEARSALS

While each director follows a slightly different pattern for organizing rehearsals, most directors have a basic format. A standard format for most of the rehearsals provides continuity for the actors. The suggested format involves the following:

PREREHEARSAL

Before the scheduled start of the rehearsal, the stage manager makes certain the rehearsal space has all furniture and props correctly positioned, adequate lighting and ventilation or heating, and a work space for the director. The director can then use the moments before the rehearsal to talk informally with the actors. It is important for the rehearsal to begin at the stated time. Waiting for actors gives the impression it is acceptable to be late. Even if production business is handled at the start of the rehearsal, actors may perceive the rehearsal is late since they did not begin actual scene work. To avoid this, it is best to formally start the rehearsal on time or at least to state what is being done if scene work does not start immediately.

INITIAL ANNOUNCEMENTS

Some directors choose to start each rehearsal with a brief set of announcements; others prefer to wait until the end of the rehearsal since the actors have the greatest energy at the beginning. I prefer to use the opening announcements to set the stage for the upcoming rehearsal. It is a good idea to begin each rehearsal with a clear set of goals so the actors can anticipate the process the rehearsal will follow. If, for example, I plan to run an act without interruption, I want the actors to know they can count on not stopping and repeating areas and concentrate on the specific objectives I provide. It is important for the director to start the rehearsal on a positive note; it is suggested any information the cast may perceive as negative be saved for the end of the rehearsal if at all possible.

WARM-UP EXERCISES

Many directors disagree on the merits of beginning each rehearsal with warm-up exercises. Almost all acting coaches feel actors cannot perform to their fullest potential until they are warmed up physically, emotionally, and vocally. The issue each director must address is whether rehearsal time should be used for warm-ups or if it can be assumed the actors will warm up prior to the rehearsal. In physically or vocally demanding plays, the warm-up is as much of a necessity to prevent injury as it is a means to a better performance. In less physically and vocally demanding plays, the issue is more of a question. The advantage to having actors warm up individually is that each actor may have different needs. The advantage to group warm-ups, in addition to the warm-up itself, is that it can become a bonding exercise for the cast. The director can consult most acting texts for a variety of warm-up exercises. Warm-ups are especially important if the director notices problems. Upon starting run-throughs for *Noises Off*, a particularly physical farce, I noticed the cast lacked energy. As a warm-up, I had them run several laps around the set, which included a staircase and large platform. This successfully invigorated the cast and was used at the start of every subsequent rehearsal and the performances. The cast also began to warm up in character, allowing them to prepare both mentally and physically. In some cases, it is necessary for the warm-ups to focus on relaxation to remove tension and external anxieties. In others, the warm-ups need to focus the energy of the actors. During the final run-throughs of *The Shape of Things*, I noticed the first scene always lacked energy and focus even though the actors were fine for the rest of the show. When the first scene was re-run at the end of the rehearsal this was not a problem. The solution was to use the first scene as a warm-up prior to rehearsal. The cast continued to do this through the run of the production.

SCENE WORK

The actual rehearsal of the play, scene, or action unit is now conducted. It is important for the director to have a clear sense of what is to be accomplished and manage the time accordingly.

PLANNED BREAKS

Unless the total rehearsal period is relatively short, less than 90 minutes, the director should plan breaks for the cast to relax, get a drink, or use the restroom. The standard for breaks per Actors' Equity Association, the actors' union covering both actors and stage managers, is either a short break every hour or a longer break every 90 minutes. This is generally a good guideline for all rehearsals. The director, too, may choose to take a break. I have worked with directors who planned lengthy rehearsals but minimized the time each group of actors rehearsed without a break. The directors then continued rehearsing with a different group of actors. Directors need to consider the possible impact on others in making this decision. For example, the stage manager, like the actors, needs a break periodically but does not wish to leave the director during the rehearsal. Breaks should be for a specific amount of time and not allowed to exceed it. The timing of breaks is usually the responsibility of the stage manager. Individual casts may prefer fewer breaks to finish earlier, and it may be a good idea if it does not adversely affect rehearsal.

WRAPPING UP

The director should find an opportune moment to wrap up each rehearsal as time is ending. Simply cutting off the scene may leave the cast feeling unfulfilled. I typically have an agreement with my casts not to start a new scene ten minutes prior to the announced end of rehearsal, but I do permit a scene to run up to ten minutes past the announced ending time to finish the unit.

ANNOUNCEMENTS

There should be time for announcements at the end of each rehearsal. These may include publicity calls, costume fittings, reminders of the next rehearsal and/or observations by the director. Incorporating time for these announcements is both considerate of the cast and helps ensure they remain focused. Functional announcements are usually made by the stage manager. Major announcements may need to be made at other times if the full cast is not present.

It is important for all members of the cast and staff to realize that missing or being late to rehearsals or performances has serious ramifications. Therefore, they need to do everything possible to avoid it.

KEEPING REHEARSALS ON TASK

To keep on task, the director must have a clear sense of the intended goals for each part of the rehearsal. Rehearsal goals should be as precise as possible and be able to be completed within the allotted time. It is foolish to allow only 30 minutes of rehearsal to choreograph a complex musical number or to assume a character will be completely developed in one rehearsal. Having clear-cut goals enables the director to focus on these tasks and to better assess whether they were achieved. Generic goals such as "work on characterization" do not provide specific enough guidelines and, as a result, it is impossible to assess if sufficient progress was made by the end of the rehearsal. A better goal could be "Strengthen the immediate goals of each character in the scene" or "Develop the relationship of the two characters by further expanding their backstory based on the scene in rehearsal." Since rehearsal time is limited, having a specific plan for each rehearsal provides sufficient time during the overall rehearsal schedule to accomplish the necessary goals without running out of time to meet them. A mistake many directors make is to try to accomplish too much, too quickly. The director needs to use the entire rehearsal process to fully meet the needs of the play and to avoid overwhelming the actors at any given time. It is better to have the actors focus on the immediate goal and then move on to the next one.

Although it is necessary for the director to stay on schedule, it is also important to be flexible and consider the overall needs of the production. For example, an actor may have greater difficulty in mastering a scene than the director projected. There are times, however, when the director needs to follow the schedule mechanically. When I was directing *West Side Story*, the production had so many facets, including complex music and choreography, my production staff and I agreed to divide early rehearsals with simpler goals into 30-minute units and rotate on schedule. Longer periods of rehearsal were provided for more complex goals such as initial staging and choreography. Goals not met during the allotted time were accommodated in a different time slot or by scheduling an additional rehearsal. The stage manager was tasked with maintaining the schedule. This was an unusual situation since typically I prefer greater flexibility within the process. This flexibility was maximized when I directed *Copenhagen*, a small cast production in which all actors were present in every scene. Each rehearsal began where the previous rehearsal ended. This provided great flexibility, but it necessitated keeping the progression of goals in mind to ensure the overall rehearsal process stayed on track. Having specific goals for each rehearsal also lets the director know if the production is ahead of schedule. This allows the director to adjust the process to avoid over-rehearsal and peak the show prior to opening.

Restraint and patience are important virtues for the director when planning the goals for each rehearsal.

GIVING THE ACTORS NOTES

The way the director interacts with the actors during the rehearsal process varies from director to director. Some directors prefer smaller rehearsal units, pausing at regular intervals to work with the actors; others prefer to run larger rehearsal units without stopping. There are strengths and weaknesses to both approaches. Having actors rehearse complete arcs, typically action units, without interruption lets them build and complete the arc. Many actors prefer this method; however, since the action unit is usually several pages long, if the director waits until the end, the notes for the actors can become disjointed. On the other hand, the director who stops the action at opportune points and works on the individual beat can provide immediate feedback to the actors. This tends to work better in early rehearsals. In early rehearsals, the director is normally working with the actors on small developmental elements and it is beneficial to stop more frequently. Later rehearsals, focusing on polishing and the development of tempo, will suffer if the actors are interrupted. The director needs to be aware of the impact of the cut. When the director stops the action, each actor's thought process in the development of the arc of the scene is interrupted. If the scene is building in a weak or improper direction, it is generally beneficial for the director to stop it immediately to set it on a better path. However, it might also be beneficial to see where the actors take their characters. Whether the notes are given immediately or at the end of the rehearsal unit, it is important to confine the notes to the intended goal of that rehearsal. Notes outside of the immediate goal can confuse the situation and undermine the task at hand.

The director must also take into consideration the needs of the individual actors. Some actors respond better if allowed to complete the arc; others benefit from periodic corrections and guidance during the build. It is possible that the needs of the actors will differ, and the experienced director will develop a different approach with each actor. When giving the notes at the end of the unit, the director can keep the context of the notes clear by referencing both the actor and the specific line. Many directors find it difficult to keep notes organized mentally and prefer written ones unless stopping immediately. The director needs to make sure the written note is complete enough to remember what to share with the actor. One of the major disadvantages to waiting until the end of the unit is the actor may not remember the action. If so, the director's note may not have any value. Occasionally, I have given actors a note about a moment I really liked at a point in the scene, only to have them tell me they do not remember what they did. Being as specific as possible in the note helps to prevent this situation.

Using questions as a communication tool with the actor should not be interpreted to mean the director cannot or should not provide direct instructions to the actors. The director needs to determine the most effective communication tool in each instance. One communication technique discouraged for directors, however, is providing the actor with an example of how a line should be read or acting out the action, often called a line reading. This can be interpreted by the actor as the single correct manner and thus should be imitated. Unfortunately, this not only takes the actor out of the creative process, reducing the actor's contribution, but it also limits the creative process for the entire scene. When a director provides line readings and acts out actions it is usually out of frustration that the given moment is not working. It is far better if the director retains confidence in the cast and guides them to find the answer. Another issue often raised regarding communication is whether the director should even be onstage. While some purists believe a director coming onstage is "invading" the world of the actor, this is not the majority opinion of most directors. While agreeing the director should not go onstage to demonstrate what is wanted from the actors, they do feel the director coming onstage allows for a closer proximity to talk with the actors than from the audience.

Once run-throughs begin, the director's main communication tool with the actors is through notes at the end of the run-through. These notes need to continue in the same style used by the director earlier in the rehearsal process. For example, if the director's style was to ask the actors questions to let them find the solution on their own, now is not the time to start dictating how they should act. These notes will typically fall into the following categories:

- Reinforcement of earlier ideas regarding the character's development

- Reminders of areas discussed but that the actor tends to forget

- New areas of concern. These should be carefully handled so as to remain supportive.

- General notes to the entire cast, such as pace or energy issues

- Procedural notes regarding the evolution of the rehearsal process

I prefer to start the note session with questions for the cast such as, "How did you feel it went?" or "Did you experience any problems?" In giving notes, it is important that the director be supportive and respectful of the actor's work, just as in earlier rehearsals. The director should try to balance the notes to each member of cast and avoid singling out one or two actors either positively or negatively. If this is necessary, the director should speak to these individuals privately. Also, the director should not underestimate the power of informal discussions with the actors after rehearsal. The same principles may be applied to notes for the designers or stage managers.

Some directors prefer to email notes to the actors after the run-through. The advantage is it saves considerable time; the disadvantage is the removal of personal interaction, eliminating the opportunity for the director to expand or clarify the note if the actor does not understand. When giving notes to my cast at the end of a run-through I always make certain I have eye contact. I can tell from the actor's response if the note is understood or if the actor disagrees. Actors should be encouraged to have a pad, tablet, or smartphone to write down the notes so they will remember them and work on them in their own time.

> Whenever the director gives an actor a note, it is crucial for the director to make sure the actor fully comprehends it. Eye contact helps ensure this understanding.

KEEPING MUSCLE MEMORY IN MIND

The director must not underestimate the power of muscle memory in the process of building a production. Just as laboratory mice quickly learn patterns through conditioning, actors quickly develop an understanding of the scene based on repetition in rehearsal. This idea of condition-ing was applied to acting by Stanislavski later in his career. It was based on the concept that actors become both physically and emotionally conditioned to the scene through the repetition of the events they rehearse. To this end, it is important for the director to allow the actors to build emotional and physical memories during the rehearsal process that trigger the appropriate emotions. At the same time, the director needs to eliminate incorrect or unsuitable emotions or actions as they will inevitably become part of the conditioning of the actors. Physical effects such as actorisms or mispronounced words will be increasingly difficult to correct as the rehearsal process continues. For example, if the director makes a pronunciation change late in the rehearsal process, on occasion the actors may revert to the original pronunciation. Never underestimate the power of muscle memory.

Each element added to the rehearsal process, such as costumes, props, or makeup, contrib-utes to the development of the play and its characters, and functions as a building block toward the final product. Once introduced, it becomes part of the muscle memory and should not be removed. The perfect illustration of the consequences of removing an element can be seen in the difficulty of having a quality brush-up rehearsal following a hiatus. While it is obviously dangerous to let the show go dormant for five to ten days between performances, minus the element of the audience, the cast feels the play is flat, and the caliber of the rehearsal is limited.

> Whenever possible, the director should turn challenges in the rehearsal process into oppor-tunities for furthering the development of the play.

REHEARSING SCENES INVOLVING VIOLENCE

Violence onstage needs to be addressed in a completely different manner from any other part of the development of the play. Stage violence can range from simple slaps or pushes to full stage combat. The planning of major acts of violence needs to begin during preproduction. Since the basic approach to all stage violence is to have the victim control the action rather than the aggressor, these actions cannot evolve from the motivation provided by the scene. It is absolutely essential for the director to secure a qualified fight choreographer. Ideally, the fight choreographer is involved from the beginning to make certain the setting provides a safe environment for the actors. I know of a commercial production where the lead actor was sidelined with a detached retina following a staged fight in a performance. All acts of violence must be carefully staged for the safety of all participants, and rehearsed separately and meticulously over a long period of time so the actions become mechanical and, once inserted in the scene, remain controlled. In addition, the director needs to have contingency plans in the event the unexpected happens. Swords break, actors slip, and many unforeseen events can happen that affect staging of the combat. The cast needs to be prepared for these possibilities. All fight sequences should be run through prior to every rehearsal and performance to make sure the actors fully remember the steps. It is also important that safety breaks be provided for all acts of violence in case an actor is inadvertently injured during the scene. Once the scene is fully integrated it may be difficult to distinguish actual pain from the appearance of it, even for the actors involved in the scene. By providing these breaks, the actor can ascertain if his or her partner is really hurt and have a planned method to complete the scene without the rest of the combat. In addition, both the safety of the audience, especially in an intimate setting such as arena staging, and the audience's response to the act of violence must be considered. The scene may appear so real and graphic that the audience is emotionally taken out of the scene and stops caring about the character and begins worrying about the actor. On the other hand, this visceral response may be the director's intent.

> The staging of any scene with violence must place the greatest emphasis on the safety of the actors and audience. While it is important for the scene to look good and evoke the necessary response from the audience, this cannot replace the safety of all concerned.

ACTING EXERCISES TO ADDRESS PARTICULAR NEEDS

While acting exercises are generally considered a tool for actor development, they can also be used for both character and scene development during the rehearsal process. Below are six examples of exercises that address particular needs or situations in the rehearsal process. Directors should be on the lookout for additional exercises that can be utilized in other situations.

PUSH–PULL

The "Push–Pull" exercise, based on the work of Augusto Boal, is particularly useful in developing the interaction between actors in scenes involving intense attempts to control the situation. In this exercise, the two actors ignore the stage blocking and face each other with palms held up (see Figure 14.1). The actors then imagine an invisible force field between their hands, and while it may be compressed or expanded, it cannot be allowed to collapse. When one actor pushes forward, the other actor is repulsed. If the second actor resists the initial push, then the first actor must push harder. The nature of this action physicalizes the power struggle between the characters. By being in character during the exercise, the amount of resistance or pressure involved in each action is determined by the one character's response to the other as they deliver their lines. The director can further coach the actors by providing encouragement during the exercise.

WHAT?

The "What?" exercise is particularly useful in situations where one actor is not providing enough emotional strength to fully motivate his or her partner's response. In this exercise, the scene is run normally with the exception that either actor may respond with "What?" instead of the correct line anytime one actor feels the other has not provided enough strength to motivate a response. The partner then repeats the last line with a different attack. If this now meets the

Figure 14.1 The "Push–Pull" Exercise

needs of the first actor, the first actor responds with the next line; if it is still insufficient, the first actor responds with another "What?" This exercise continues until the end of the scene. It empowers each actor to work with his or her partner without crossing the line of providing direction to a fellow actor. It also helps build a greater intensity in the scene. A variation on this is for the director to call "What?" instead of or in addition to the actors whenever the director feels the needed intensity of the line was not reached.

AD-LIBBING NEW PHRASES

As the rehearsal process progresses, actors often get so comfortable with each other within the context of the scene that they occasionally cease listening to their partner and just wait for the cue to start the next line. This lack of engagement can quickly become apparent to the audience. During the rehearsal, one approach to this problem is to have the actors periodically ad-lib a different response than the line in the script. When this occurs, the actor who was addressed must alter the response. In the worst-case scenario, this exercise will point out which actors are not listening to each other if one does not even notice the altered line. This exercise forces the actors to listen to every word of their partner, mentally process them as the character, and respond appropriately. The improvised line does not even have to fit fully into the storyline. The key is to force each actor to listen to their partner.

BEAT EXTENSION

Over the course of the rehearsal process, the actors occasionally begin to rush through the slight pauses, often referred to as beats, required at each change in attack. While this may appear to pick up the tempo of the scene, it actually causes the scene to become shallower and lack integrity as the audience perceives the characters are simply saying lines on cue rather than thinking. The beat extension exercise is designed for this situation. In this exercise, the actors are instructed to repeat the scene but to significantly expand each pause during these moments of thought to fully sense the moment of transition and change in thought process. Once the actors feel secure fully identifying these beats, the scene is rehearsed normally. Hopefully, the actors have found the true moments of thought with better use of time during the beats. While this rehearsal technique relies on the indulgence of the actors during the beat, it is important that it not be maintained in the actual scene, but that the time taken in the beat is returned to a suitable pause.

IMPROVISATION

Improvisation is a valuable tool in the development of both the scene and the characters. The director can utilize improvisation as a means for the actors to explore the goals and subtext of each scene free from the lines of the script. Improvisation can also be used to explore the relationship between characters by creating scenes that do not exist in the play but provide the opportunity for the actors to explore their relationship. These improvisational rehearsals are only intended for character and scene development and must not extend into the actual scene work, replacing the playwright's lines.

IMPROVISING THE ACTION PRIOR TO THE START OF THE PLAY

A variation on the use of improvisation involves improvising the events that led to the circumstances at the opening of the play. It gives the actors the opportunity to explore these moments to better understand their characters.

* * *

When using any of the exercises in this chapter, it is important that the actual scene be rehearsed immediately afterward to ensure the values gained during the exercise are transferred to it. They are intended purely as rehearsal tools and are not a means to "improve" the script. In rehearsal situations in which the playwright is present, it is possible these exercises may lead to changes in the script, but such action should never be taken without the consent of the playwright.

REHEARSAL ORGANIZATION CHECKLIST

Rehearsal day: Time: Location:

Prerehearsal plans and activities:

_____

_____

_____

Initial announcements:

_____

_____

_____

Rehearsal goals:

_____

_____

_____

Warm-ups (if planned):

_____

_____

_____

Scene work (with allotted time for each):

_____

_____

_____

Planned breaks:

_____

_____

_____

Wrapping up:

_____

_____

_____

Ending announcements:

_____

_____

_____

FURTHER EXPLORATION

1. Prepare a specific set of goals you wish to accomplish for the rehearsal of a scene.

2. Develop a list of situations you feel are difficult to rehearse, and think through methods to rehearse them.

3. Modify the exercises you have encountered in acting classes to accomplish specific tasks within the rehearsal process.

4. In working a scene with actors, try different methods of coaching the scene to see what works best for you and for the actors. After the rehearsal, ask the actors how they felt about the techniques.

CHAPTER 15

Rehearsal Challenges

CHALLENGES VS. PROBLEMS

Before discussing rehearsal challenges, it is important to understand the psychological differ-ence between a challenge and a problem. Challenges are obstacles that provide an opportunity. Problems are obstacles that must be overcome in order to proceed. While it feels good to overcome the problem, it is not something to which one looks forward. Crossing a mountain can be seen as either a challenge or a problem. To mountain climbers, the mountain presents a unique challenge, an opportunity. For the travelers who simply want to get to the other side, the mountain is not an opportunity but a problem to be overcome. The difference is in the outlook. Directors face numerous obstacles during the rehearsal of a play. How they approach these obstacles depends greatly upon their perception. The director with a more positive approach sees obstacles as challenges rather than problems. Challenges are an outlet for the director's creativity.

It is impossible to identify all potential challenges and problems a director may encounter. The rehearsal situations following represent some of the most common ones a director may face and are compiled from my collective experience and those of other directors. This is not intended to be a comprehensive list but, instead, a starting point to develop approaches in han-dling them. Every time a rehearsal obstacle is mastered, the director learns from the experience and develops another approach to add to the "arsenal" of directorial tools.

By viewing situations that need to be resolved as challenges not problems, the director can approach them as opportunities to further the work rather than impediments. Challenges provide the chance to employ creative solutions.

In approaching the situations listed below, there is a method for dealing with rehearsal challenges. This method can be divided into six steps:

1. Identify and understand the challenge. The director needs to be certain the actual challenge is being addressed and not a symptom of the challenge. Too often directors waste time contending with surface issues rather than the actual cause of the challenge.

2. Deal with the situation privately whenever possible. By removing the challenge from the public eye of the rehearsal, the director significantly defuses the situation and makes finding a solution far easier.

3. Remain professional and do not take the challenge personally. Once allowed to become personal, it is likely the director will seek to regain what is perceived as lost status rather than placing primary focus on the challenge.

4. Keep in mind there may be a legitimate reason for the situation. If the reason is legitimate, no immediate fix is needed.

5. Look for possible solutions. As with any tactic, the solution should be applied only as long as it yields positive results.

6. If the initial solution does not resolve the challenge, the director needs to continue to look for other approaches.

Throughout these steps the director needs to remain as detached as possible from the challenges and clearly and calmly attempt to work through to a solution. It is essential for the director to keep the good of the production as the optimal goal in searching for a resolution.

SITUATIONS

ACTORS WHO LACK MOTIVATION

The work of an actor who lacks motivation is uninspired and flat. The director needs to determine if this is an isolated instance, existed from the start of rehearsals, or began at some point later. Presumably, the actor did not demonstrate this lack of motivation during the auditions, therefore something must have changed, and the director should talk with the actor privately to try to find the cause and a solution. If it is an isolated instance, it can probably be remedied with the director simply pointing it out and starting over. If the situation continues, it may be something about the particular point they are rehearsing that is not triggering the proper motivation. It is possible the actor does not understand that given moment in the play. Inevitably, when I ask an actor what is happening or how the character feels at a given moment, the response is either silence or not sure. The diagnostic question was triggered by the flatness of the actor's performance. The use of the question avoids a confrontational statement. If the lack of motivation permeates most or all of the play and did not exist in the earlier rehearsals, the director can surmise something has changed for the actor. While not attempting to become an amateur psychologist, the director should work privately with the actor to try to resolve the issue. The director may also utilize or refer the actor to the many exercises found in acting texts that address this situation.

ACTORS NOT GETTING OFF BOOK

Both actors and directors realize that until the actors are cleanly off book there is a limit to the development of the play. Actors vary greatly in their skill at learning lines. To prevent procrastination, the director needs to establish a deadline for actors to put down their scripts. The director also must make sure the actors understand the latent difficulties with a particular script. Logically worded contemporary lines are far easier to learn than highly stylized non sequiturs or verse. Some actors have difficulty learning lines because they are trying to memorize the words rather than learn their context. The director can help by ensuring the actor fully understands the nature of the conversation, the logic in the dialogue. The director should also be observing early rehearsals for signs that an actor is beginning to move off book. If these indications are not present, the director should be reaffirming the importance of meeting the impending deadline. Even though difficulty learning lines is the actor's problem, by being proactive in finding ways to assist the actor, the director can counteract a potential production challenge. An assistant stage manager may be able to run lines with the actor when the actor is not onstage at rehearsal, or the director may be able to find someone to assist the actor outside of the rehearsal time. In the case of inexperienced actors, the director may need to teach them techniques to learn their lines. While pressure from the director may help if the actor is not self-motivated, if there is a mechanical reason impeding the process, it is in the best interest of the director and the production to assist the actor in finding the solution. The bottom line for the director is it is unacceptable for the actor not to learn the lines.

ACTORS NOT HAPPY WITH CHANGES, I.E., BLOCKING

Actors may sometimes express discontent with changes that occur during the rehearsal process. They may see the development of the play as a linear process and perceive changes as setbacks. A good director realizes a play is organic and will continue to grow and change during the production process. Casts may have a legitimate problem with directors who are indecisive or who make changes for their own sake, but if the director is properly prepared and the changes are not due to an initial lack of understanding of the play, the director needs to maintain the organic nature of theatre development and express understanding of the actors' frustration while reaffirming the continuing improvement of the production. The cast essentially needs reassurance.

ACTORS WHO HAVE DIFFERING INTERPRETATIONS OF THE CHARACTER OR THE PLAY

The director may from time to time encounter a situation where an actor has a completely different interpretation of the character or the play. This is not necessarily an issue since the director cast the actor based on the quality of the portrayal shown in the auditions. The actor's interpretation may be turned into a positive by using it as an opportunity for a discussion of the role and/or the play. I faced this when I directed Ariel Dorfman's *Death and the Maiden*. The play centers on events in post-Pinochet Chile in which a young woman who was the victim of torture and rape at the hands of the former government recognizes the voice of a man she believes was one of her torturers. During the course of the play she plans her revenge. Even though the playwright never states whether the man is the torturer, I believed it was abundantly clear he was guilty and was now feigning innocence to protect himself. In my interpretation, the play was a discussion of how victims must live with their former oppressors under the new government. During our initial read-through and discussion of my concept for the play, the actor playing the "torturer" indicated he believed the man was an innocent victim of mistaken identity. In his interpretation, the play was about the creation of a new group of victims growing out of the fears of the original victims. Rather than simply saying he was wrong, I used this differing interpretation as the opportunity for a cast discussion. Interestingly enough, the actors debated the issue along the same lines their characters would have taken. After a valuable and lively discussion without a final resolution, I had to take the position that while his interpretation was valid, and might be an interesting way to interpret the play, I disagreed, and as there could be only one truth in the play, we would follow my interpretation. As a director, I prefer not to play the "because I am the director" card, but in this case, it was necessary. This initial disagreement did, however, supply a catalyst for an important discussion to start the rehearsal process. This is an example of how the director can take a challenge and turn it into a major advantage. As a side note, I am quite sure the actor continued to believe that his character was not guilty. I was able to use this belief as the basis for his adamant profession of innocence without changing my interpretation of the play.

It is essential for the director to approach any challenge on a professional basis and not to perceive it as personal. Avoiding personal entanglements makes finding a solution easier.

ACTORS WHO CANNOT UNDERSTAND THE REASON (MOTIVATION) FOR SPECIFIC BLOCKING

All blocking must appear motivated and grow organically from the interaction of the characters. On occasion, actors have difficulty understanding the reason for a specific piece of blocking. The director needs to work with the actor so the actor understands the rationale and provides the appropriate motivation. If the actor is unable to process the reason for the blocking, it is generally best to alter it to an action consistent with the actor's understanding of the scene. A less dynamic piece of blocking is far more valuable than a superior action that lacks motivation. However, there are times when the blocking is critical to the production, such as a technical necessity. In this case, the director needs to work with the actor to find a reason for the character to undertake the blocking or, failing that, at least a possible reason to make it work. The rationale may be flawed, but as long as it provides the apparent motivation, it will prevent the blocking from looking artificial.

LATE ACTORS

A situation many directors contend with is actors arriving late to rehearsals. Ideally, actors arrive early to allow time to properly prepare and warm up, but this is not always the case.

Lateness cannot be tolerated because it results in a significant loss of rehearsal time and energy for all involved in the rehearsal. Some actors have poor time management skills. While this is solely their problem, their lateness affects the production. It is possible that some accommodation, such as a reminder call from the stage manager, may keep the rehearsal process moving. Preferably, the director should not wait for an actor to arrive. Even though rehearsing without the actor is less productive, starting rehearsal as scheduled underscores the importance of being on time. The director should remind the cast that in the interest of the production good actors avoid being placed in a position where they may be late. For example, if weather is an issue, actors should either leave earlier or, better yet, rearrange their schedules to stay at or near the rehearsal location. Although regrettable, some lateness is unavoidable, such as a flat tire. Or, it may be due to a schedule misunderstanding. The actor may have indicated a work conflict until 7:00 p.m. but failed to indicate an additional 30 minutes for commuting. As a result, the actor is continually late for a 7:00 call. The director should always inquire if there is a reason for the lateness. Assuming it is acceptable, an adjustment can be made in the rehearsal schedule to avoid lateness in the future. Ensuring the rehearsal schedule is clearly understood also helps eliminate accidental lateness.

ACTORS TRYING TO TAKE CONTROL

Periodically, the director encounters an actor who desires, consciously or unconsciously, to take control of the production. This may occur with an inexperienced actor not understanding his or her role in the production process or with a more experienced actor who has a domineering personality. As with most situations, first, the director needs to attempt to understand the underlying cause. With the inexperienced actor, the director may resolve the issue by talking to the actor privately. With a more experienced actor, it is probably deliberate. The director's role is less about educating the actor and more about finding a solution, because inevitably it will get worse, and it is possible other actors will follow the initial actor's lead and vie for control themselves. The director should quietly but firmly take control back from the actor. The director needs to see the situation not as a personal threat but as a professional misunderstanding. By keeping it from becoming personal, the director defuses the issue while still maintaining a relationship with the actor. In many cases, a quiet but firm response such as "I will handle this" suffices. If the actor does not take the hint, then, privately, the director needs to be forthright.

With any challenge, finding a solution is often easier if the director first defuses the immediate situation. A solution is far easier to reach in a calm environment in which tempers and egos have not been excited.

AD-LIBBING/PARAPHRASING

As opposed to actors who periodically forget a line either completely or in part, there are actors who habitually paraphrase or completely ad-lib rather than deliver the lines written by the playwright. There are two possibilities that typically cause this situation. First, the actor is not spending the time to learn the lines correctly. Second, the actor feels the playwright's words are essentially a guide, and it is the actor's job to deliver the essence of the lines, not necessarily the exact words. It is important for the director to establish that neither of these situations is acceptable. It is both a contractual and ethical obligation to the playwright, and the actor needs to spend the time to learn the lines as written. Playwrights carefully select every word in the script. Ad-libbing or paraphrasing is simply a workaround for the actor. Even if the actor only changes occasional words, this can affect the rhythm and perhaps the meaning. It is not necessary for the director to get into a philosophical debate about the actor's relationship to the playwright's words but rather to establish that this practice is unacceptable. Actors may try to justify the practice by saying the playwright will be unaware of it or will probably not mind. Neither assumption is defendable. I know of numerous cases where the playwright's agent contacted a producing organization regarding inappropriate delivery of lines and insisted on their correction even to the point of threatening legal action. If the playwright truly does not care about the correctness of the delivery, this will be indicated in the script.

ACTORS TRYING TO DIRECT

Occasionally, actors begin to direct other actors, an action that is unacceptable. Once again, the director should determine if this is caused by a lack of understanding on the actor's part or if the actor is simply exceeding his or her position. This needs to be dealt with immediately since it will only continue and could potentially get worse. The director can stop the actor and explain that to avoid confusion there can be only one directorial voice, thus reaffirming the director's role. If further action is needed, a private conversation with the actor is better than a public discussion, which could turn into a debate. This situation can be triggered inadvertently by a director who allows a great deal of input from the cast during the rehearsal process. In this instance, it is easily possible for a cast member to exceed the boundaries and unintentionally cross over into the role of the director. It can generally be rectified by the director issuing the appropriate correction.

ACTORS NOT IMPROVING

There are times when an actor appears to be working hard, is doing all that is expected, but is not improving. The actor has reached a plateau and is finding great difficulty in moving beyond it. If this occurs with an inexperienced actor, the director needs to work with the actor as an acting coach to find new attacks the actor can use to continue the development of the character. In all probability, the actor's interpretation lacks sufficient depth to continue the development. While less common, this can occur with more experienced actors as well. If this happens, the director should work with the actor to find a new and different interpretation of the character. How can they raise the stakes for the character, both in reward of victory and in price of failure? Hopefully, this change will provide new life to the actor's approach. In either case, this situation is often caused by the actor utilizing the same set of tactics. Sometimes simply making a dynamic change frees the actor, who can later return successfully to the initial interpretation with new-found understanding.

ACTORS QUITTING

Nothing is more devastating to a production during the rehearsal process than having to replace an actor who has decided to leave. However, once an actor makes this decision, there is little the director can do. Double casting or the use of understudies is an immediate solution, but this can create more problems than it solves and may not be an available or wise option. Even though actors leaving productions are relatively rare, when it does occur the effect is significant. In commercial theatre, there is legal recourse available since leaving violates the contract, but this alone does not resolve the situation. The best way to avoid such a situation is for the director to create a positive atmosphere through a mutual commitment with the actors, identifying potential challenges before they arise and working with the actors to remedy them. I once had a situation where an actor quit a student director's production two days before opening. We tried to dissuade the actor from leaving, but this proved fruitless. The only remaining options were to cancel the production or have someone else perform the actor's role holding the script. The director decided to use the latter option and, while far from ideal, the production went forward. Short of having a replacement actor already prepared, solutions are limited and generally not viable alternatives.

DIFFICULT ACTORS

There are actors who severely challenge the director. Their behavior may result in any of the preceding situations or they may simply be difficult to work with for both the director and fellow actors. It is highly unlikely the director can change an actor's temperament during the brief rehearsal process, although I have seen it happen. The easiest way to deal with challenging actors is not to cast them. If the casting is essential or, as occurs more often, the difficulty of working with the actor is not known prior to casting, the director needs to prevent the situation from becoming personal and to defuse it as much as possible. Early in my career I was working in New York City as a technical director for an opera company with a noted and influential conductor. Midway through one of the first rehearsals with the orchestra, the lead soprano, who was extremely difficult for everyone to work with, berated this noted conductor when he gave her a correction. A talented singer, she was nowhere near the caliber of the conductor. The entire company fell silent waiting for her comeuppance. Instead, the conductor paused and then quietly stated, "Very well, let us continue." We were all disappointed he had not unleashed his wrath, but I learned a valuable lesson for directing. The conductor was well aware his knowledge of music and prestige greatly exceeded hers, and that he was correct in the note he gave her. The true wisdom of this conductor was he did not feel the need to argue to prove himself, and such an argument would not be in the best interest of the production. By continuing, he avoided further confrontation. While she had not been chastised at that moment, we all knew this confrontation would ultimately do her far more harm in her career. Sometimes the director just needs to know when to walk away. Although it may be best not to engage in a confrontation, it is imperative that the director not allow any actor to abuse or mistreat the cast or staff.

Sometimes the director just needs to know when to walk away.

ACTORS CHANGING INTERPRETATIONS

The director's work with the actors is strictly during the rehearsal process. The trajectory for the play is established, and it will continue once the play opens. Good actors maintain this trajectory, keeping their interpretation within the parameters provided by the director and consistent with the production concept. Every so often there are instances where an actor changes the interpretation from the one rehearsed with the director. Actors cannot be forced to accept the director's vision and may migrate back to their own interpretation after the play opens. In commercial theatre, it is the job of the stage manager to maintain the director's vision, keeping in mind that the play is a growing, organic, artistic entity. Should the director's interpretation be changed, it falls upon the stage manager to give corrective notes to the actor. If it continues, the stage manager notifies the producer and director to see if they wish to return to remedy the situation. A noted Broadway director once visited a production he had directed and was horrified to see how it had changed. He had a rehearsal called for the next day to "remove the improvements the cast had worked in." In noncommercial theatre, the director is present more often throughout the run and can take care of the situation. However, it is best to prevent it from happening. It behooves the director to work with the actors to ensure their complete understanding and agreement with the production concept.

ACTORS ATTEMPTING TO BE FUNNY OR DRAMATIC

Directors occasionally face a situation where an actor tries to be funny or dramatic rather than portray the character within the context of the play. Unlike many of the earlier situations, the actor is attempting to perform the role to the best of his or her ability but is missing an essential element of acting, erroneously portraying the character not the character's intent. Young actors often deliver flat performances in comedies because they are attempting to be humorous rather than playing the situation, a situation their character probably does not see as funny. The comedy comes from the situation and the incongruity that results is from their serious intent. This happens in a dramatic play as well when the actor attempts to convey the heaviness of the drama rather than playing the scene. The best approach for the director is to get the actor to understand the character's intent and hence the purpose of the scene. The actor is often relieved to have the burden of being funny or serious lifted and can now simply portray the character.

LINE INSECURITY

Actors move off book at different speeds and with different results. One problem some actors have centers on their insecurity of knowing their lines. This insecurity results in the focus being placed on the lines rather than the character or the character's intention. In fact, in many cases actors do know their lines better than they thought. Line insecurity sometimes becomes apparent during a scene as the director observes a weakening of the character. The director needs to stress that by placing full attention on the character and the scene, the actor has a far better chance of knowing the lines than if focusing on the words themselves. A good rehearsal technique for increasing the actors' confidence is for the director to have the actors run the lines as fast as possible. This practice is commonly called a speed run. By saying lines quickly, the actors do not have time to think about the words but need to rely solely on memory. Although this rehearsal technique is extremely valuable once the actors are substantially off book, it will not work with actors who have significant line problems.

* * *

The following scenarios are not actor-related challenges, but they are staging challenges directors often face and, as such, merit discussion.

SEXUAL HARASSMENT AND OTHER INAPPROPRIATE BEHAVIOR

While rare, directors occasionally encounter an actor whose behavior is decidedly unprofessional and may even cross into areas of sexual harassment. This may occur offstage, with fellow actors or a member of the staff, or onstage, where one actor is using the scene to take advantage of another. This may involve inappropriate contact or actions. Aside from human decency and respect, this is vital for ensuring total confidence in the circumstances, and to best explore the character and the scene. The director must create an atmosphere of trust in the rehearsal environment. If inappropriate behavior is seen by the director or brought to his or her attention, immediate action must be taken. Since predatory or harassing behavior may be subject to criminal or civil action, it also must be brought to the attention of the producer or artistic director. There is no place for this type of activity in the rehearsal or performance process. Organizations have been formed to address sexual harassment in the theatre. A prime example of this is Not In Our House, an organization founded by members of the Chicago theatre community. More information may be found on their website: www.notinourhouse.org/chicago-theatre-standards-pilot/

SCENES THAT SEEM TO DEFY BLOCKING

From time to time the director may encounter a scene or action unit that seems to defy blocking. No matter how the scene or action unit is worked, the action appears unmotivated and inappropriate. On the other hand, the option of having the actors remain still looks flat and lifeless. The solution lies in providing opportunities within the setting that inspire and motivate the blocking. It is for this reason that it is critical for the director to thoroughly think through the floor plan before it is finalized. If the floor plan is already established, the director can still find possible solutions to the situation through the addition of scenic elements that provide motivation for action. For example, a side table containing a well-chosen hand prop can be the reason for an actor to cross to the table, thereby adding visual interest to the scene. The setting needs to supply the pretext for the staging. If it is not there initially, the director needs to work with the scenic designer to find ways to modify the setting to allow better blocking. If modifications are not possible, the director needs to find other alternatives to add life to the scene. The director must never allow unmotivated blocking.

Figure 15.1 The Author Working With the Cast

Photograph by Michael Engelmeyer – Great Outdoors Studios. Courtesy of Drury University

LIMITED SPACE FOR BLOCKING

It is sometimes necessary for the director to stage in limited floor space. This may occur in settings utilizing simultaneous staging or theatres where available space for each location is relatively small. Before finalizing the floor plan, the director needs to make certain sufficient space is dedicated to each area. This is the best opportunity to avoid blocking difficulties. If the director has a finite amount of space, especially with three or more characters in a scene, it is important to carefully pre-stage to ensure dynamic blocking, appropriate stage pictures, and adequate sight lines for the audience. The precision of the blocking is especially important as each actor's movement has a greater impact on the position of the other actors and sight lines. The opportunity for developing stage pictures is far more restricted, so the director provides variation through small but significant adjustments. Taping out the acting area in a rehearsal space during preproduction will allow the director to see the space clearly and work on possible blocking options before the setting is finalized.

TABLE SCENES

Scenes in which characters sit at a table for prolonged periods offer unique challenges to the director. It often becomes difficult to find reasons for the actors to get up and move around, and these scenes run the risk of becoming visually static. The director must microblock the scene with precisely chosen small actions, which then take on greater significance given the lack of larger movements. By adjusting the angle of an actor's head, for example, the audience's perception of the scene can be greatly enhanced. Since larger actions are typically precluded, the director must work with the cast to find other means to redirect the audience's attention. While standard practice is to leave the downstage end of the table open, it is sometimes impossible given the number of people who must be seated. In these instances, the director must carefully decide which characters sit downstage. Choosing the less important characters can help minimize staging issues. Having the actors cheat slightly downstage at key moments can also solve many of the difficulties. Care must be taken to maintain sight lines.

AUDIENCE INTERACTION

There are times when a play calls for the actors to engage directly with the audience. In some cases, it is necessary for the scene to include ad-libbing based on the audience's response, while in others the script assumes the response of the audience. Should the director have the cast break the hypothetical fourth wall and directly engage the audience, the cast needs to be prepared for any eventuality. I once directed *Scapino*, a modern play based on the commedia dell'arte style, in which the play frequently made use of direct engagement and conversation with the audience. Given the improvisational nature of commedia dell'arte, the actors rehearsed different scenarios based on potential responses from the audience. At the end of the play, the actor playing the girl's father asks the audience if he should forgive Scapino. Given the direction the play was taking, the assumption was the audience would resoundingly cheer that he should. On opening night, the audience, as expected, responded with an enthusiastic "Yes," but after a slight pause, one member of the audience loudly yelled, "No!" Since various reactions based on the audience response were rehearsed, the cast was prepared and made the moment even more comical. The important element to remember in audience engagement is that it must be sincere. If the cast ignores the audience's response, the audience will cease engagement, understanding that their input is not truly wanted.

SPEAKING IN UNISON (CHORAL SPEAKING)

Choral speaking was a standard element of the Greek and Roman theatre, with the chorus speaking and moving in unison. Modern theatre rarely uses a chorus other than in musical theatre, with the chorus singing in unison rather than speaking. Some plays, however, do use small groups speaking in unison as a dramatic technique. The director needs to approach this choral speaking slightly differently. The mistake many directors make is to attempt to have the actors speak precisely at the same time, resulting in the actors paying more attention to one another than to what they are saying. The key is to have the actors speak in a common rhythm but as individuals. Once they find the rhythm, keeping together is less of an issue, and the choral speaking is significantly enriched by the subtle differences in each actor's approach. The director can further enhance the choral speaking by taking a cue from the musical world and dividing the group into different vocal tones, essentially the way the choir director divides the chorus into soprano, alto, tenor, baritone, and bass. While each is saying the same words, by applying different pitches additional depth is created.

Approaching an obstacle as a challenge gives the director a better opportunity to work out a solution and is a means for improving the production.

SUMMARY

The director needs to realize that over the course of his or her career there are going to be many challenges. Some will appear more often than others, but no matter the similarity every situation is unique. What works in one instance may not apply in the next. As the director gains greater experience in dealing with challenges, each new one will be approached with added confidence.

PROBLEM SOLVING CHECKLIST

☐ Identify and understand the challenge.

☐ Deal with the situation privately whenever possible.

☐ Remain professional and do not take the challenge personally.

☐ Determine if there is a legitimate reason for the situation.

☐ Look for possible solutions.

☐ If the initial solution does not resolve the challenge, continue to look for other approaches.

FURTHER EXPLORATION

1. Talk to other directors about special challenges or circumstances they have encountered and how they approached solving them.

2. Based on your experience in the theatre, compile a list of situations beyond the ones listed in this chapter that you have seen a director encounter. Think back to how the director handled them and determine if they were good solutions or if there were better ones.

3. Look back at situations you encountered in working with actors in other exercises and reflect on how you handled challenging situations. What have you learned about handling a challenge? In the future, how would you handle this differently?

Tempo, Rhythm, and Pace

THE DIRECTOR'S RELATIONSHIP TO TEMPO, RHYTHM, AND PACE

While many of the director's functions are transparent, four areas of responsibility are clearly the director's: the concept of the play; casting the show; the blocking; and the tempo, rhythm, and pace of the production. Good actors should have a sense of tempo, rhythm, and pace, but they are not in the position to fully judge its effect. Only the director, seeing the play from the audience's perspective, can determine if they are working for each character as well as combining correctly to work best for each action unit and, ultimately, the overall production. The director's role in the combined effect of tempo, rhythm, and pace can be better understood if these areas are examined individually.

TEMPO

In music, tempo refers to the speed at which the music is performed; in theatre, tempo refers to how fast the scene is played. Timing a scene with a stopwatch over several runs and comparing the time for each run-through illustrates the difference in tempo. In general, a faster tempo produces a more riveting and exciting play; too slow a tempo typically loses energy and with it the audience's attention. A good guideline for the director: when in doubt, faster is better; however, this is not always the case. A speed run of the rehearsal certainly has energy and excitement, but given its frenetic speed it becomes impossible to understand or relate to the dramatic action in the scene. Though faster is usually better than slower, the tempo must be appropriate for the play and allow the audience to engage. The overall tempo of the play is determined by the combined impact of the tempos for each action unit.

The style and nature of the play determine the appropriate tempo. For the most part, farcical comedy has a fairly rapid tempo while the tempo of serious drama is comparatively slower. Inexperienced directors often work under the assumption they can make the farce funnier by speeding up the tempo or make a drama more serious by slowing down the tempo. Neither is completely true. Though there is certainly a connection, the reality is that the tempo needs to be a product of the dramatic action of the play. For this reason, farcical comedies have a faster tempo by the very nature of the dramatic action and the dialogue. To find the appropriate tempo, the director has the actors gradually increase the tempo until sensing it is too fast and then has the actors back off slightly. In practice, the director rarely needs to tell the cast to slow down; typically, the director needs to remind the cast to keep the tempo up.

In considering the beginning tempo for each action unit the director must keep in mind the tempo at the end of the preceding unit. If the units are contiguous in time, the tempo of the second scene must match the ending tempo of the preceding unit. If they are not contiguous in time, the starting tempo is solely dependent on the dramatic action. The tempo of the second unit can be used to create a new ambience in the unit since the audience is accustomed to the preceding tempo.

RHYTHM

If tempo refers to the overall speed of the scene, rhythm refers to the subtle changes within it. In music, the rhythm of a musical selection is provided in the time signature: the number of beats in each measure. For example, the 3/4 time signature of a waltz produces a rhythm of 1,2,3; 1,2,3; 1,2,3; etc., resulting in a lyrical rhythm. In theatre, rhythm refers to the changes in tempo not only in the overall play but also within each action unit (Figure 16.1). Several conclusions can be drawn by looking at the graph. The first action unit containing the exposition typically is one of, if not, the slowest in tempo. In the same way, the climax usually has the fastest tempo.

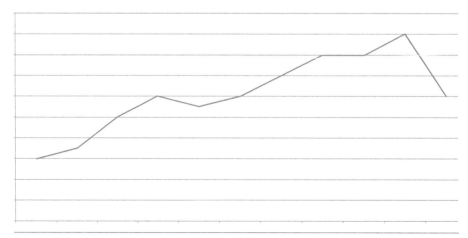

Figure 16.1 Sample Graph of Tempos by Action Units

The dénouement has a significantly slower tempo than the climax but probably faster than most of the action units in the play. As the play progresses from the exposition through to the climax there is a general trend of increasing tempo, but this trend is not linear. The resulting variations in tempo between action units create the rhythm for the play.

In the same way that the rhythm of the play is made up of tempo variations between the action units, each action unit itself has tempo variations and thus its own rhythm. The rhythm within each action unit must be correct to create the proper ambience. Figure 16.2 and Figure 16.3 illustrate the relative rhythms of two action units. The rhythm in Figure 16.2 begins slowly and grows gradually, building its momentum until it reaches its peak. The sense of urgency steadily rises all through the scene. The rhythm in Figure 16.3 begins moderately, slows down

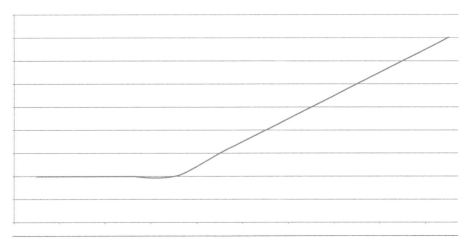

Figure 16.2 First Rhythm Example

Figure 16.3 Second Rhythm Example

slightly, levels off, and then rapidly increases in tempo, creating a sudden burst of energy that is heightened by the reduction in the initial tempo, until leveling off at the end of the scene. The slower tempo lulls the audience into complacency only to be jolted out of it with the sudden surge at the end of the scene. The development of the appropriate rhythm within an action unit is dependent on the director's interpretation of the dramatic action and how the director chooses to communicate this to the audience.

Just as the director must consider the tempo of the preceding unit, the relationship of the rhythm of the second unit to the first must also be considered. The director must craft the rhythm individually in each unit and determine how they combine to create the rhythm of the entire play.

PACE

Pace is the least consistently used of the three terms. Whereas the theatrical uses of the terms tempo and rhythm closely correspond to their musical counterparts, pace does not. In theatre, pace is the combined perception of speed created by both tempo and rhythm and its impact on the audience. For example, in describing the overall pace of a farcical comedy as frenetic, it is understood that there will be periods of faster and slower tempos creating the rhythm of the play, but the overall sense of its pace is fast.

UNITING TEMPO AND RHYTHM TO CREATE PACE IN THE PRODUCTION

By considering both the tempo of each unit and its internal rhythm the director creates the pace for each action unit. The director then combines the tempo and rhythm of all the action units to create the pacing and hence the energy of the play. A rising pace builds anticipation; a steady increase creates a predictable environment. The skillful director manipulates the rhythm and tempo within each action unit to build the anticipation and at the same time provides opportunities for the pace to slow down and then build again to prevent it from becoming static or predictable.

While the pace of the production must be appropriate to the style of play, the director also needs to consider how the pace will affect the audience. If the rhythm is too even, the pace can tire the audience due to lack of variation. If the pace is too hurried, the audience may become lost or disengaged since there is no opportunity to process the information. If the pace is too slow, the audience may become bored and lose interest. The director needs to find the appropriate pace for the play and, if necessary, err on the faster side to keep the audience's interest.

A good example of controlling the pace through the use of rhythm is found in directing comedy, which typically depends on a rapid tempo. If the humor is not properly phrased through the rhythm, the lines will not be funny and the comedy will be lost. In addition, the cast needs to allow a brief pause after each humorous line to give the audience time to laugh.

Although these pauses have the effect of breaking the pace, the energy of the performance is maintained by the audience's laughter, which continues the overall pace of the show, and lets the audience better appreciate the humor. If time is not allotted for the audience to laugh, the audience will start cutting back on their laughter to hear the next lines, resulting in a decrease in both the humor of the play and the audience's enjoyment. The same is true for applause at the end of musical numbers. In both cases, the control of the rhythm is essential to permit time for laughter or applause thereby preventing the loss of energy and keeping the proper pacing. If pauses after humorous lines or musical numbers are taken but there is no laughter or applause to carry the energy through the pause, then the pacing of the play will suffer.

The same concept can be applied to dramatic works. For example, if the play is highly reflective and causes the audience to seriously consider each element, a slower pace allows the audience time to engage with the play. Creating this pace is handled through the adjustment of rhythm, allowing time for reflection combined with rapid attacks between the beats, thus maintaining the energy of the play; the overall pace is brisk while still providing for the reflective quality.

A good stand-up comedian will increase the value of the material through skillful manipulation of the pacing.

TECHNICAL IMPLICATIONS ON PACE

The overall pace of the show is also dependent on elements beyond the actors. The use of music and the implementation of the technical elements of the production can have a significant impact. If preshow music is used, the tempo of the music creates an expectation in the audience. When used during the show, the pace of the music must match either the pace of the scene or the direction the director wishes to move immediately afterward. Music that does not match the production's pace will pull the audience between the two. If the director is using music as underscoring, the cast needs to rehearse with the music since the pace of the scene will be driven by the music. The pace of sound effects can also affect the production. A rapidly ringing doorbell versus one with overly long pauses between rings or one that increases with speed dramatically alters the pace of the scene. Even the time between phone rings can affect the scene. While the time between rings must match the audience's expectations, it can be altered slightly, either faster or slower, to build tension or to create a placid feeling. The same is true of the pace of a song used as a ring tone.

The changes in lighting also have a pace of their own that must either be derived from or, at least, complement the pace of the scene. In addition, the director must make sure the tempo of the lighting matches the feeling desired. The director does not need to understand the mechanics of lighting design to determine if, for example, the fade at the end of the scene feels organically motivated by the energy of the scene. Similarly, the timing of internal light cues must also match the energy of the scene. For instance, if the cue is to be imperceptible, the tempo of the cue needs to be so slow the fade is not seen. In this way, the audience is affected by the change in lighting but is not distracted by the cue. Although the timing of light cues is usually based on an even tempo with no change in rhythm, the cues can also be structured with variations in rhythm.

The shifting of scenery also affects the pace of a show. The overall tempo of the shift must be appropriate to the tempo and rhythm of the scene so the energy is sustained. Carefully orchestrating the movement to make the shift as smooth and as quick as possible reduces the negative impact on the production. Whenever feasible, the director should incorporate the scene shifts into the physical action of the scene to help bridge the transition between the two settings. The director needs to work with the scenic designer to ensure the scene shifts work within the production. Frequent shifts have the potential to significantly damage the pace of the production even if conducted quickly and efficiently and, as such, must be factored into the production style. Ironically, a chaotic shift may hurt the rhythm of the production as badly as a methodical one.

To minimize the effect on pace, elaborate shifts should be integrated into the action of the play and rehearsed with the actors prior to the technical rehearsal. While adding the crew to these rehearsals may create time or budgetary issues, it will greatly aid in the polishing of the play and maintain the pace. It is not wise for the director to wait until the technical rehearsal and hope the shifts will integrate.

TOOLS AND CONSIDERATIONS FOR BUILDING THE TEMPO, RHYTHM, AND PACE OF THE PRODUCTION

While a production with too fast a pace can be problematic, it is rare. More often than not, the director needs to ensure the tempo and rhythm combine to form an adequate pace. There are several techniques and considerations the director can utilize to help build a better pace.

TOPPING LINES

Topping lines refers to the practice of actors starting their next line on top of their partner's last line. This practice helps eliminate dead energy that builds between the time the first actor ceases speaking and the second one starts. The actors need to be aware of two separate cues. The first is the **action cue**, the point in the line where the character is motivated to prepare a response to their partner. The **line cue** is the point where the actor begins to speak, usually the last word in their partner's line. By building the energy for the response on the action cue, the actor is ready to say the words on the line cue. The batter in a baseball game must begin his swing long before the ball crosses the plate or he will never hit it. The action cue is the point where he starts his swing and the line cue is the point where the bat contacts the ball. By having the actors top their lines, the director is ensuring the tempo is not momentarily halted after each line.

BUILDS

Builds refer to how an actor allows the energy in his or her delivery to grow. The director needs to make certain the actors strategically plan these developments since actors often develop them in a linear fashion with increasing emphasis. Whereas this is not necessarily wrong, if every build develops in this fashion, the repetitive quality will reduce the energy and make the rhythm and tempo too predictable. It is also possible that by following a linear build the actor reaches his or her most rapid tempo too soon and may not be able to progress further. It is better if the director works with the actor to develop the build so it has an internal rhythm that varies, allowing the tempo and energy to cut back and rebuild so the full tempo and energy is reached just before the end of the build.

DEVELOPMENT OF BEATS

The slight momentary pause taken by the actor must be carefully developed. It is important for beats to be present, but they must be kept at a minimum. Actors occasionally overindulge these moments for dramatic effect. In doing so, they upset the pace by breaking the rhythm and slowing the tempo, thus disrupting the momentum of the scene. These pauses or beats are essential as they allow the audience to enter the thought process of the character. As such, they cannot be used haphazardly.

UNINTENTIONAL LOSS OF ENERGY AND TEMPO

As noted in Chapter 13, some actors may allow the tempo of the scene to slip unintentionally by sighing or simply releasing air at the ends of lines. This is a common problem if the actor completes lines with downward inflections. The director needs to work with the actor to remove these unwanted moments that lead to loss of both energy and tempo by making sure that lines typically end with an upward inflection.

PACE AND ENERGY

When a production has a slow pace, the audience often feels it lacks energy. When tempo is combined with rhythm, the result is a flow of energy that underscores the dramatic action of the play through the physical action. Having a good flow of energy does not necessarily mean the play has a fast tempo. It can be created in a slower dramatic piece as long as the pace is appropriate. The energy provided by the actors contributes to the overall flow of energy, and it is possible that intense dramatic pauses are so rife with energy that the slower pace is not only supported, it is necessary.

This connection between pace and energy is exemplified in the world of sports by comparing baseball to soccer. Baseball is a measured sport with most of the players in ready position until the ball is hit, followed by a brief explosion of energy. This surge is quickly resolved and the field returns to relative calm until the next ball is hit. Soccer is essentially a steady stream of continuous energy punctuated by even faster attacks coupled with some slightly slower moments setting up a play. There are few full pauses in the action even when substitutions are made. On the surface, it appears soccer is exciting and baseball is boring, given its static quality. Many soccer fans agree with this premise. Baseball fans disagree, stating that anticipation is built while waiting for the hit ball to trigger the explosion of activity (see Figure 16.4 and Figure 16.5). The spectators' perception of the pacing lies in their understanding of the differing nature of the two games. Likewise, the director must ensure the pacing of the production matches the style of the play by controlling the tempo and its variations and that the energy of the actors carries the play in the same way the athletes' energy maintains the spectators' interest.

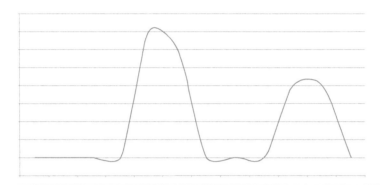

Figure 16.4 Baseball Tempo

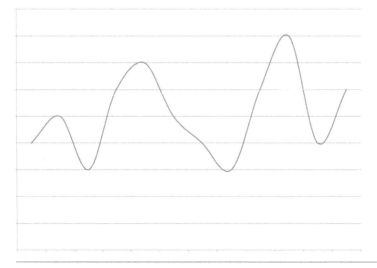

Figure 16.5 Soccer Tempo

Another example of the potential differences in pacing between two productions can be found in a dance performance. The tempo and rhythm is determined by the style of the music as well as the style of the dance. The tempo varies within each form of dance, creating a unique rhythm. Some dance styles, hip-hop, for example, are highly energetic with rapid movement; other styles such as classical ballet have slower, more lyric movement. The pacing of the styles is different, but the energy of each performance may be similar.

TEMPO, RHYTHM, AND PACE EXERCISES

The director can utilize a variety of acting exercises to improve tempo, rhythm, and pace. The choice of exercise is dependent on the situation to be addressed. Following are samples of such exercises:

TENNIS MATCH

In tennis, the player on offense initiates the nature of the attack through the strength of his or her swing. The defending player then responds by simply returning the ball or creating a counterattack. In the tennis match exercise, two actors deliver their lines as they mime a tennis match. The acting partners are mirroring their vocal volleying with the mimed tennis swings. The first actor matches the nature of the stroke to the energy appropriate to the delivery of his or her line and then awaits the nature of that response. The responding partner does the same. The acting partners have a distinct opportunity to respond to each other. Each partner alternates "hitting the ball back to their partner," with one character on the offense for several lines until the defending partner gains enough control to counterattack. This volley continues until one of the characters reaches his or her goal. The actors should match the vocal energy, tempo, and rhythm to their mimed tennis swings and at the same time control the pacing of the scene.

> For the audience to stay engaged, the pace must be appropriate to the play; however, when in doubt, keep the pacing up to avoid loss of energy.

SPEED RUNS

Speed runs can be used not only as an exercise to assist in learning lines (see Chapter 15) but also as a tool to develop better tempo. Running through the rehearsal as quickly as possible forces the actors to significantly increase the tempo. By working at increased tempo in character with all stage business, the actors become accustomed to this pace and adjust their internal sense of the tempo accordingly. Once, for a farce I was directing, the cast was having difficulty understanding, much less achieving, the necessary rapid tempo. I decided to have a rehearsal in which the cast performed the play as quickly as possible while I called for a faster tempo every time it slowed down. At the end of the run-through the cast was exhausted, but I pointed out the play was now close to the actual tempo needed. Although shocked, the cast finally understood where the tempo needed to be. From that point on the tempo continued to improve.

FINAL THOUGHTS

The audience's enjoyment is ultimately dependent on the appropriate tempo, rhythm, and pace. Every play has a different pace, and it is vital the pace never allows the energy to drop. A dramatic play may have a slower pace than a comedy, but the energy the actors bring must have the same sense of urgency and drive to hold the audience's interest. An older director I worked with advised young directors that in directing the exposition, the best approach is faster. In many respects, this is good general advice. His idea was to get through the necessary introductory material to get to the more important aspects of the play. However, speaking quickly and moving rapidly from one moment to the next is not sufficient to develop the dramatic action of the play. On the other hand, though reflection is good and moving methodically through the work may be more "dramatic," the pace may drag and pull down the energy, thus losing the audience's attention. The director needs to find the delicate balance between the dramatic action of the play and a pace that keeps the audience enthralled. Whereas tempo may largely carry the energy of the play, it is rhythm that brings out the subtlety. When in doubt, faster is generally better as a slower pace reveals every imperfection.

FURTHER EXPLORATION

1. Using a metronome to set the tempo, have your actors rehearse a scene. Try the scene several times using different metronome settings. What do you observe?

2. Have your actors rehearse a scene three times. Rehearse it the first time with the tempo as they feel it should be, the second time with as rapid a tempo as they can say the lines, and the third time once again as they feel it should be. Pay particular attention to the effect the second run has on the tempo of the third run.

3. Rehearse the same scene several times, each time making a conscious effort to change the pace of the scene. Determine which run is the best pace for the scene.

4. Run a scene several times with your actors. In the first run, vary the tempo while keeping the rhythm as even as possible. In the second run, vary the rhythm while keeping the tempo as even as possible. In the third run, allow the actors to find their own natural pace and see how the first two runs affected it.

CHAPTER 17

Polishing the Play

THE FUNCTION OF THE POLISHING REHEARSALS

Polishing rehearsals are the last stage of the rehearsal process prior to performance. The polishing rehearsals are the opportunity for the director to "refine" the production and bring it to "a highly developed, finished, or refined state."[1] All of the work from the rehearsals with the actors is combined with the final technical elements in preparation for the audience. By the end of the polishing rehearsals the production should include all elements except the audience and be on track for a solid opening performance and a run of the show with consistent quality. The polishing phase begins with a series of rehearsals, typically run-throughs, designed to allow the actors to refine all the elements they have worked on and to bring the process full circle in anticipation of the addition of the final technical elements. The second part of the polishing rehearsals involves the introduction of any technical elements not yet part of the rehearsal process. The last stage of these rehearsals is referred to as the dress rehearsals, which are designed to unite all the elements of the production into a cohesive whole.

POLISHING THE ACTING

By this point in the rehearsal process the actors should be starting to finalize their choices for their characters and solidifying the tactical approaches used to achieve their character's goals. As mentioned earlier, a director I knew once made the unfortunate comment to an actor at the end of an early rehearsal to "Dip it in plastic." She meant this in an attempt to provide positive reinforcement as he had performed his part "perfectly" at that rehearsal, and this was exactly how he should continue to play it. The confused actor asked if this meant he should not come to any more rehearsals. The idea that an actor should at any point cease to make choices or to explore his or her character is wrong, especially at an early rehearsal. Assuming the rehearsal process was productive, the actors can use the polishing rehearsals to refine their earlier choices and the general direction of their characters as worked out with the director and still remain accessible to new ideas and discoveries. By the end of the polishing phase the director should have found a delicate balance between a solid foundation for the play, resulting in consistently good performances with some degree of predictability, and the genuine moments of discovery that occur during the later rehearsals and subsequent performances. If this is not accomplished, there may be either significant variations in the quality of the subsequent performances or the play may become so mechanical it will no longer be alive.

During the polishing rehearsals, the director should be checking that the developmental arcs of each action unit are clean and smooth, and that they combine to produce the overall arc of the play. This can be particularly challenging if most individual action units were rehearsed out of order. While intense scene work can be productive for the individual units, the continuity between the units may be compromised. This is why a run-through rehearsal should be planned at least every week. The last set of run-throughs prior to the technical and dress rehearsals provide a final opportunity for the director to ensure the arcs are properly progressing so the audience will be able to follow their evolution.

A prime area of concern to be addressed by the director during the polishing rehearsals is whether the tempo, rhythm, and pace of each action unit as well as the play itself are where they should be. As with the development of the overall arc, if there were not regular run-throughs of the entire play, the overall tempo, rhythm, and pace of the production may not be consistent. Whereas these elements may have worked during individual scene rehearsals, they may not once the play is put together. It is also possible the cast was quite successful at sustaining the pace during short scenes but is now having difficulty maintaining it throughout the play. The director may need to dedicate one or more of the polishing rehearsals solely to working on pacing.

Consistency is another area to be examined during the polishing rehearsals. To ensure consistency, the director must watch the polishing rehearsals with an objective eye. The work of the director, actors, and technical staff could be lost if inconsistencies disrupt the audience's connection to the play. The internal consistency is especially important in regard to the interaction and relationship of the characters. The play must make internal logical sense. Although there still may be further growth, the audience has to be able to follow the logical path of development to keep an emotional and psychological bond to the play. Physical consistency

Consistency is particularly important in plays for young people. A young audience has a vivid and open imagination and is disposed to accept the play on its own terms. On the other hand, they are more easily pulled from the action by inconsistencies. An unforeseen technical mishap may momentarily jar an adult audience, but a young audience finds it far more difficult to return to the action of the play.

is also vital. This may be as simple as a character continuing to limp or touching a hot stove and reacting to the heat. It is critical for the actors to be consistent in their use of props and the setting. Once a convention is established with the audience it must be maintained.

For the actors, the overall purpose of the polishing rehearsals is to consolidate their work. They should be comfortable with their lines, and the environment of the play should begin to instinctively trigger an emotional response. Any areas of the play weakened due to line problems should be addressed quickly. These last rehearsals allow the actors to cement their understanding of the play. The actors need to be fully comfortable with the play and their characters, remaining open and receptive at all times, but not too comfortable that they perform on autopilot. Assuming the play had a good rehearsal process, the actors should be ready to add the final technical elements and the audience. If the cast, in my opinion, can progress no further without the addition of the technical elements, I reserve the option to cancel the last run-through prior to technical rehearsals. If the play is behind schedule, the polishing rehearsals are the last opportunity to make these discoveries and adjustments. The director needs to realize that the technical rehearsals are generally not the time for the actors to further develop their characters; these rehearsals are for the integration of the technical elements. If there are significant technical elements, it is especially important for the director to have the actors prepared so they do not lose ground once these elements are added. If the play contains minimal technical elements, the technical rehearsals may serve as acting run-throughs for the actors, but this should not be counted on by the director. Assuming the actors are adequately prepared for the addition of the technical elements, these rehearsals will serve to enhance their performances.

The success of the polishing rehearsals prior to the technical rehearsals depends on the quality of the rehearsal process up to this point. Ideally, these rehearsals are a time for the cast to fully refine their characters and for the director to ensure that all elements are working well together.

IMPLEMENTING THE TECHNICAL ASPECTS INTO THE PRODUCTION

As part of the preproduction planning of the schedule, time is allocated to the technical rehearsals to facilitate the addition and refinement of all the technical elements. The complexity of these rehearsals is dependent upon the extent of the technical aspects of the production. It is important to ensure the designers and technicians have adequate time since, unlike the actors who have rehearsed their parts for several weeks, they have only a few rehearsals to perfect their work. Plays with complex scene shifts that become part of the action should have these elements added as soon as practicable to allow time for the actors to integrate and refine them with their scene work. Costumes with complex changes or that have significant impact on the movement of the actors should also be incorporated at the earliest opportunity to give the actors time to rehearse with them. If it is not possible or practical to incorporate performance costumes into rehearsals, rehearsal attire similar to the actual costumes should be provided. Sometimes it is not mechanically feasible to add the design elements. The construction of the scenery and costumes may need to be completed, the crew to run the shifts or other technical elements may not be available for extended rehearsals due to time or budget constraints, or using the actual setting and/or costumes for extended rehearsals could cause additional wear and tear necessitating refurbishment or replacement for performance. As such, it may be difficult to have extended rehearsal periods with these elements.

As noted in Chapter 9, the technical rehearsals can be divided into those with the crew and designers and those with the crew, designers, and actors. Technical rehearsals without actors are often referred to as "dry techs" and those with actors as "actor techs." The dry tech allows for the complex and time-consuming process of building light, special effects, and sound cues as well as working through the scene shifts. These rehearsals can last anywhere from part of a day for a simple production or several days for a more complex one. It is important to provide as much time as potentially needed during the preproduction planning of the production calendar. The planning and organization of the technical rehearsals is usually handled by the production manager, but the director needs to take an active interest in how these are organized. Occasionally, a "paper tech," in which all, or part, of the cuing is planned on paper without being in the theatre, is used for complex shows. While this process has the potential to save time, planning visual artistic elements without seeing them may not be effective.

TECHNICAL REHEARSALS WITHOUT THE ACTORS (DRY TECHS)

The dry techs address all technical issues not orchestrated in previous rehearsals. These design areas may be handled concurrently or allocated a separate time. All construction and fabrication of scenery, props, and costumes; recording of sound effects; and hanging and focusing of lighting equipment is completed prior to these rehearsals. The director may not need to take part in those rehearsals that do not affect the actors or the production concept. However, the director should be directly involved in all aspects that have an impact on the audience's perception of the play or affect the visual or audio implementation of the director's production concept. Each of the following areas, and the director's involvement in each area, must be accomplished at the technical rehearsals.

Some directors prefer not to be present for the dry techs. However, comments by the director during these rehearsals can be invaluable to the designers as they build their cues. The director's presence during the dry tech may save a great deal of time in the actor techs by avoiding or correcting problems or design choices that do not match the director's concept.

SCENE SHIFTING

The mechanics for shifting the scenery are planned during preproduction. During the technical rehearsals, the shift pattern for the movement of the scenery is rehearsed with the stage crew. Ideally, as much time as possible is provided for the crew to rehearse so the shifts run smoothly and safely. The director is not usually involved in this process unless the shifting is done in view of the audience and becomes an aesthetic component of the production or if the shifting integrates with the staging of the actors.

Repetitive rehearsals of physically taxing scene shifts can lose their effectiveness as the crew tires. These rehearsals are best spread out so the crew has an opportunity to rest prior to the next run of the shifts.

LIGHTING

Assuming the director and lighting designer reached a good understanding of the basic look of the lighting during preproduction, the technical rehearsals are now the time to refine it. Unlike the other technical elements, the lighting designer is unable to see the light on the set until the technical rehearsals. While modern lighting equipment includes previsualization capabilities, it cannot replace the time spent working with the actual lighting equipment in the theatre. Typically, the cue-writing process moves through the play beginning with the first cue and ending with the final cue. To save time, some designers predesign several basic looks for the lighting in preparation for the dry tech. Quite often the first cue is the most difficult to achieve since the designer and director are finalizing a visual vocabulary for the lighting. In communicating with the lighting designer, the director needs to be specific. Feedback such as "It is too bright," "It is too warm," "It is too shadowy," or the like is far better than "I do not like the look." On the other hand, comments should be confined to the overall look of the scene rather than to suggesting specific design ideas. The function of the director is to direct the lighting in the same way as directing the actors, guiding the designer to produce the best conceivable look without telling the designer how to do it. New requests may not be feasible as the designer did not allow for them in the light hang. For example, the lighting designer cannot provide a blue wash if a system with blue color media is not included as part of the light plot. To fulfill a request like this, the designer must know about it prior to developing the plot. The director should also pay particular attention to the fade times given to each cue. It is impossible to fully assess these fades until the cues are seen in context with the actors, but significant time can be saved by ensuring the cues are given a good initial fade time.

SOUND

Unlike light cues, recorded sound effects are prepared prior to the dry tech. The dry tech is used to set volume levels and to assign the sound to specific speaker locations. Times for fade-ins and fade-outs are also established. The director should be aware that the perceived volume for each cue is significantly affected by the presence of the audience because the audience absorbs some of the sound. As such, volume levels in the empty theatre generally are set a bit higher in anticipation of the audience. The level of the sound cues played over dialogue inevitably has to be refined once the sound cues are heard with the actors. A production utilizing sound reinforcement to amplify the actors' voices will require initial levels to be set for the microphones during the actor tech.

SPECIAL EFFECTS

Unless added earlier, cues for special effects utilized in the production are worked out during the dry tech. One of the major concerns with regard to special effects is safety, and, as such, additional time needs to be allocated to brief both the cast and crew.

* * *

The dry tech or dry techs can be lengthy and arduous. The designers and technicians are under pressure to work quickly and artistically, and while they want solid feedback from the director, they must have adequate time and space to properly complete their work. The goal of the dry tech is to have the cuing set and ready for the actor tech knowing that many of these cues may have to be modified once they are seen in full context. It is during the dry tech that the stage manager records all the cues in the production book in preparation for future rehearsals and performances. It is crucial that enough time be allotted for the stage manager to have a clear understanding of how the cues are to be called.

TECHNICAL REHEARSALS WITH THE ACTORS (ACTOR TECHS)

Time allocated for the technical rehearsals with the actors, otherwise known as actor techs, was worked out in the preproduction planning of the production calendar. These rehearsals are some of the longest and most difficult rehearsals in the production process. Complex productions may have several rehearsals dedicated to this process. The play is rehearsed from beginning to end implementing all technical aspects with a cut called each time a technical element has to be refined or reworked. In a technically complex production this may mean numerous cuts in the action, which can be extremely trying for the actors who are accustomed to uninterrupted run-throughs. The technical elements must be refined as cleanly as possible since it is the last chance to interrupt the action of the play to resolve technical issues. Other than something specifically related to the actors' integration with the technical elements, most directors do not even bother taking actor notes during this process because the actors may not be able to fully maintain their characters or the smooth development of the play. However, the pace of the play significantly affects the timing of the cues so it is important for the cast to try to maintain it.

It is wise to begin the actor tech with a short briefing, outlining how the rehearsal will proceed and, if they have not previously met, introducing the cast and crew to each other. If this is the first rehearsal onstage with the set, it is typically followed by a walk-through led by the stage manager, noting areas to be careful of and/or addressing any of the actors' concerns. This is also an excellent time to discuss safety concerns that may arise now that the technical elements are being rehearsed. Both actors and technical staff should be instructed to call "cut" loudly to stop the rehearsal if at any point they feel unsafe or unsure so the safety issue can be resolved. With the addition of the technical elements, the actors may suddenly develop problems with previously simple activities. As a courtesy to both the actors and technical staff, the director should not use the actor tech to work specifically with the actors. Likewise, the crew should not rehearse specific technical elements that do not necessitate the presence of the actors. The decision to utilize the costumes is made on a production-by-production basis. Although they have a profound effect on the lighting, there is a risk the costumes may be damaged. Hair and makeup are rarely used during the actor tech.

If the technical elements in the production are evenly spaced, it is best for the rehearsal to be a full run-through. On the other hand, if the technical elements are gathered together, for example, at the beginning and end of each act, the actor tech may be modified to what is often called a "cue-to-cue" rehearsal. In this case, the play begins by rehearsing each of the cues; once the rehearsal reaches a point where there is a significant amount of time before the next technical element, a cut is called and the rehearsal jumps to shortly before the next cue and continues. This cue-to-cue procedure allows more time for the technical elements. The amount of time between cues depends on the nature of the production, but it is suggested that a cut should never be less than three to four pages of script. Shorter cuts can be counterproductive, taking as much, if not more, time as they save. In deciding to have a cue-to-cue rehearsal, the director must consider the disruption in continuity. It also means the lighting designer is unable to see the actors' blocking, thus ensuring they are properly lit, nor is the crew able to prepare for the next technical element in real time. The stage manager has to keep a close eye on the clock to ensure sufficient time is allocated to all technical elements. If too much time is spent rehearsing earlier portions of the play, the end of the play may not receive sufficient rehearsal or is not rehearsed at all. In a union production, the actor tech typically makes use of a "10 out of 12" rehearsal meaning the rehearsal can run up to ten hours instead of the usual maximum of eight as long as there is a twelve-hour gap before the next rehearsal. The amount of time allocated to the actor tech in a nonunion setting is determined by the production.

DRESS REHEARSALS

The dress rehearsals are the concluding phase of the polishing rehearsals. This is the entire production team's last opportunity to perfect the production for presentation to the audience. The number of dress rehearsals is based on the available time in the production calendar; however, a minimum of two dress rehearsals is suggested. The actual specifics are determined by the director and the production staff. If there are still unresolved technical issues, it is possible cuts may be called. This type of rehearsal is often referred to as a "dress/tech." While such a rehearsal greatly assists in resolving these technical issues, it does not allow the actors to have an uninterrupted run of the show. As such, the decision to have cuts at this juncture must be carefully thought-out. Both cast and crew need all available dress rehearsal time to make the transition into performance mode. Although the actors have rehearsed for several weeks, the crew has only started. To facilitate an uninterrupted run-through, additional rehearsal of difficult technical elements may be held after the dress rehearsal, if necessary. At least one, if not two, of the dress rehearsals should be run exactly as a performance. Ideally, they should begin at the same time as the performance but calls for the actors may be earlier than usual to set aside time for costume and makeup issues. These can be changed for subsequent rehearsals if additional time is not required.

For the actors, the dress rehearsal is the return to an uninterrupted run-through that now includes all the technical elements. After the rehearsal, the director gives notes to the cast, refining choices made by the actors and addressing any additional issues or opportunities following the introduction of the technical elements. Some directors prefer to give their final notes in either written or email form. This permits the cast to leave earlier, but it does preclude director/cast interaction. If suggesting significant changes, the director should keep in mind the number of rehearsals remaining before the production opens as there may be little time to rehearse them. Assuming the last polishing rehearsals prior to the technical rehearsals are successful, the dress rehearsals allow time to fully polish the production.

The director should also have notes for each of the technical departments based on observations during the rehearsal. Notes involving purely mechanical elements are addressed to the stage manager or the appropriate crew member, but notes with aesthetic changes or alterations are sent to the applicable designer. For example, if the director notes that a light cue was executed later than was determined during the technical rehearsals, the note is given to the stage manager to resolve. On the other hand, if the director wishes to change the placement of the light cue, the note goes to the lighting designer. To facilitate these notes, it is common practice to hold a short production meeting following the dress rehearsals to give the production staff adequate time to implement the necessary changes.

If costumes, hair, and makeup are used for the first time during the dress rehearsals, it is advisable to set aside sufficient time for a "dress parade," in which the actors walk onstage prior to the run-through. This enables the director to observe the actors and discuss any issues with the designers without delaying the rehearsal. This is especially true in productions with numerous costume changes.

STAGING AND REHEARSING THE CURTAIN CALL

The director typically stages the curtain call, also known as bows, either before or after one of the dress rehearsals. This gives the cast at least one opportunity, if not more, to rehearse the curtain call as an extension of the performance. The curtain call is the traditional time for the audience to express its appreciation of the production. It is an emotional release and serves as the transition from the play back to real life. While the audience is directly applauding the cast, they are also indirectly applauding the overall production, including the work of the production staff and crew. This is meant to be a celebratory time to allow the cast to acknowledge the appreciation of the audience. Directors may have some difficulty finding the transition into the curtain call for plays ending on a somber note. It may take a portion of the curtain call for the audience to fully release from the play.

There are several basic types of curtain calls. The first is a **group** or **company bow**. The entire cast comes onstage and bows as a group to the audience. This type of curtain call is traditionally used for ensemble plays where there is no discernible difference between the importance and size of the roles. The curtain call seen most often involves a **build**, starting with the small roles and ending with the principal roles. Depending on the size of the lead role or roles and the stature of the actors, the build may become even more focused to separate the recognition of these performers. For the most part, this further differentiation is applied to plays in which one role is significantly larger than any of the others or in the case of a guest artist or star performer. The third type of curtain call is the **tableau bow**. In the tableau bow the cast arranges itself onstage and forms a unique stage picture separating the actors into subgroups posed in a manner consistent with their characters. This is a highly stylized form of bow and is usually reserved for farcical comedies or musicals. The tableau is customarily followed by a more traditional form of curtain call. Figure 17.1 is an example of a tableau bow from a production of *Two Pails of Water*.

An issue often raised in connection with curtain calls is whether the actors should take the bows in character. This is a question every director needs to address based on the individual production. With the exception of the tableau bow, the audience is acknowledging the play

Figure 17.1 Tableau Bow
Courtesy of Drury University

not the characters. As such, it is generally better if the actors are themselves. It may also be acceptable for the actors to be influenced by their characters to further enhance the bow. For example, in classical melodrama it is customary for the audience to cheer for the hero and heroine and to boo the villain.

Perhaps one of the boldest choices with regard to the curtain call is the decision not to have one. This decision is usually made if the director feels the dramatic message of the play will be obscured or lost. Not having the curtain call enhances the final moment of the play by having the audience leave the theatre without breaking free of the world of the play. This decision should be taken advisedly. The curtain call is such a standard ending for almost all productions that the audience, unable to express their appreciation, may leave the theatre dissatisfied. Therefore, while this may be appropriate in some cases, the director must use extreme discretion in making this decision.

The curtain call is staged by the director with the same attention to detail as the play itself. Assuming a build curtain call, the director will divide the cast into groups for each entrance, assign specific starting locations for each actor, provide the entrance order for the groups, stage how each group moves to position for their bow and where to move afterward, and stage how the company takes its final group bow or bows. Figure 17.2 illustrates the staging of a build curtain call. Note that Actor 7 and Actor 8 are the lead characters in this play. In this example, the actors enter in groups, proceed to down center, bow, and then move to their designated locations. To ensure the actors bow at the same time, one actor in each group is designated as the person to whom the other actors key off. As soon as each group begins to rise from their bow, the next group enters from the opposite side. Once each group has bowed, the entire company, cued by a designated actor, moves downstage together for a final company bow. Some directors dictate specific action for each bow, others allow the actors to use whatever style they choose. This is particularly true in the case of female actors, some of whom prefer the traditional curtsy while others prefer bowing. It is important for the bows to be conducted briskly and with great energy to facilitate a similar exuberance in the audience.

The director decides whether to specify the number of company bows or to leave it open-ended. These are often referred to as "discretionary bows." If the lights fade to black at the end of each of the bows, the decision to add additional bows is left to the stage manager. If the company bows in full light, one of the actors is given the responsibility to determine if an additional bow is warranted. In either case, there needs to be a clear cue to signal the actors they have had their last bow. The danger to having a fixed length for the curtain call is the bows may end before the audience has fully expressed its appreciation. Conversely, too many discretionary bows may be called, potentially reducing the audience's appreciation. A skilled director is able to anticipate the audience's response and craft the bows accordingly.

When in doubt, it is better to have fewer bows than needed and leave the audience wanting more.

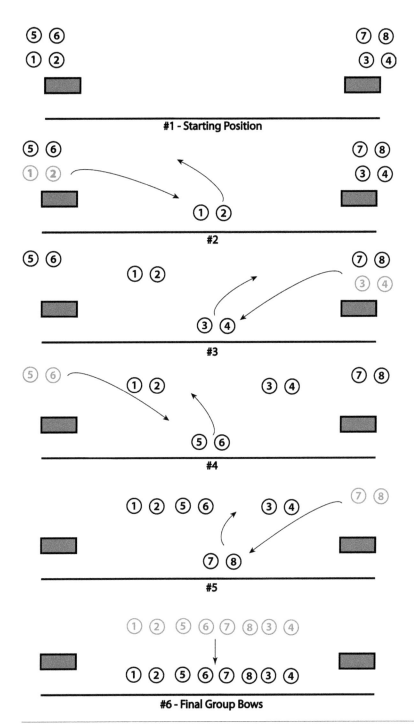

#1 - Starting Position

#2

#3

#4

#5

#6 - Final Group Bows

Figure 17.2 Build Bows

FINAL THOUGHTS

It is important for the director to continue to build the play throughout the polishing rehearsals so it peaks for opening. Adding elements to each step of the rehearsal process facilitates this, but whenever possible the director should avoid moving backward. For example, once makeup is added to the rehearsal process, all rehearsals should continue to use makeup. During the dress rehearsals, the stage manager assumes responsibility for running the rehearsal in preparation for running the performances. Assuming the rehearsal process has progressed appropriately, the only element missing from the production is the audience. As a director, at the end of the last dress rehearsal I provide corrective notes only where absolutely necessary. I prefer my last set of notes for the actors to be complimentary and encouraging. I also use this opportunity to thank the cast and production staff for their efforts and wish them well for the performance.

At the conclusion of the final dress rehearsal the director's work is essentially complete. The production is now in the hands of the stage manager; it is time for the director to move into his or her new role as a member of the audience. The director's presence after the opening of the production varies greatly between situations and directors. In commercial theatre, the director routinely moves on to the next play soon after the opening; in noncommercial theatre, the director is often available for the entire run. The only part of the directing process left for the director is to sit back and enjoy the audience's response and to conduct a self-evaluation of the production.

FURTHER EXPLORATION

1. Ask permission to sit in on a polishing rehearsal; pay particular attention to the nature of the notes the director gives to the cast.

2. Ask permission to sit in on a technical rehearsal; pay particular attention to the interaction between the director and the designers.

3. Talk to designers and ask how they prefer the director to interact with them during the technical rehearsal process.

4. Based on your experiences in the preceding activities as well as the plays in which you were involved, develop a set of guidelines you can utilize as a director for the polishing phase of the rehearsal process.

NOTE

1. Merriam-Webster online dictionary, www.merriamwebster.com/dictionary/polish

Evaluating the Production

WHY CONDUCT AN EVALUATION?

Congratulations, your play has opened! This text has followed the process a director takes from the choice of script through the final dress rehearsal. There is no chapter on the production itself, because once the rehearsal process is over the director's role is fulfilled. Directors vary on whether to continue to give the cast notes once the play opens. Directors who do give notes point out that the development of the play is never complete; the addition of the audience is a crucial part of the production's evolution. Seeing how the audiences react, the director and the cast can further refine their approach and interpretation. It is for this reason professional and some noncommercial theatres routinely hold preview performances. Although these are full performances, the production company acknowledges the play is still a work in progress and the audience should not assume it is the final interpretation. Critics are not invited to review until the play officially "opens." Directors who do not believe in giving notes once the play opens maintain that after the final dress rehearsal the show is in the hands of the cast and crew and it is theirs to evolve to its next level. Both positions are defendable and the choice remains with the individual director. In long commercial runs many directors choose to revisit the production periodically to ensure it is continuing to grow in a manner consistent with the original production concept.

The art and craft of directing is one that is never fully mastered and all directors will always be students of directing, continuing to learn and develop their craft. Once the play opens the director will receive critical feedback from a variety of sources both formal, the critics, and informal, the audience. While these are valuable, it is vital for the director to develop the skills necessary to perform a self-evaluation of the production and the production process.

EVALUATING THE PRODUCTION

The production is judged based on its performances, not its rehearsals. Whereas productions are often officially reviewed on opening night, the run of the show needs to be examined to truly evaluate its quality. It is easy to assess a production that opens poorly or whose performances either do not improve or diminish as the production continues; it is more complex for productions that follow different developmental paths. The following example is an overview of production evaluation based on a hypothetical scale. Figures 18.1 through 18.3 illustrate three different models of development over the first ten performances, each rated on a scale of 1 to 10. The red line along the rating of 7 indicates the minimally expected level for a good performance. Figure 18.1 is a production whose opening performance was rather weak but continues to grow and is performing extremely well by the seventh performance.

Figure 18.2 illustrates a production that started strong, grew slightly, and then essentially stayed the same. Figure 18.3 shows a production that follows a similar path to the second model but with a wider range in performance quality. It has the same number of high-rated performances as the second model, but it also has more performances below the expected level. These three productions are all moving in a largely positive direction, but a closer investigation gives a better analysis. While the performances in the first model grew rapidly, the director did not properly prepare the production for opening, and the first five performances were necessary to fully develop the play. Unfortunately, this was at the expense of those first five audiences. The second model was much tighter. Its development shows a general increase in quality, never falling below the level of its opening performance. The third model follows much the same pattern as the second with significant growth between the first and second performances, but there is a sizable drop for the third performance, and an up-and-down pattern from the fourth to tenth performances. Although the director prepared the show to achieve a high caliber performance, consistency was not established, resulting in an unpredictable quality for each performance. A good production should grow with the addition of the audience and subsequent performances, achieving the director's goal of producing a solid performance every time. Of the three models, the best is shown in the second example. All performances were above the expected level and while the show grew, it never disappointed its audience. The first model, while showing the most improvement, was simply not ready to open, and the third model was not consistent.

The productions in Figures 18.1, 18.2, and 18.3 were ranked on a scale of 1 to 10 solely for discussion; it is not suggested that the director has to perform a self-evaluation of the production based on such a scale or that it is necessarily valuable to do so. The idea is to compare the overall performances during its run. To grow as a director, the director should evaluate the production to determine its strengths and weaknesses based on the actual performances and the production process as a whole. All its strong points as well as its obstacles and how they were handled to reach a quality performance should be included. Evaluating a production is a highly subjective process. As a general guide, the director should evaluate each of the following aspects of the production:

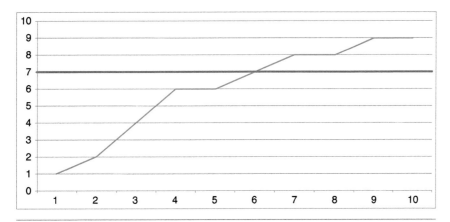

Figure 18.1 Performance Development Model 1

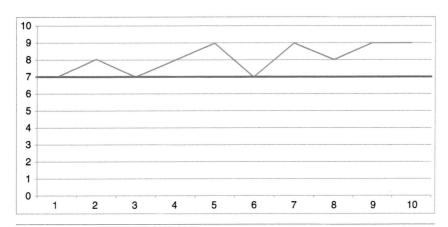

Figure 18.2 Performance Development Model 2

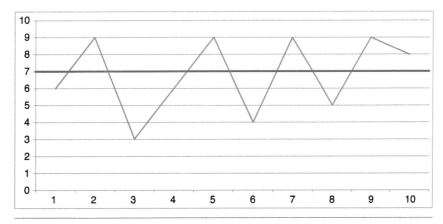

Figure 18.3 Performance Development Model 3

CHOICE OF PLAY (IF APPLICABLE)

In retrospect, was the play a good choice? Did it provide the opportunity for expression that was hoped for? Were there unforeseen obstacles, and, if so, did they provide a creative opportunity or were they a hindrance? To put it simply, if starting the process over, would the same play be chosen?

ANALYSIS

Thinking back to the preproduction period, was the play fully analyzed? Were there areas overlooked? Did the analysis provide the proper foundation upon which to build the production? What additional areas of analysis might have been helpful during the production process?

PRODUCTION CONCEPT

Did the production concept fulfill the direction the director wished to take the play? Did it encompass all aspects of the script, or were there areas not totally considered within the concept? Could the production concept have been improved to provide a deeper, more meaningful interpretation of the play? Did the performance embody the production concept?

CHOICE OF CAST

Were the best actors chosen for the production? If casting again, would the cast be the same? Since the process cannot be repeated, it is impossible to determine if other actors would have been better, but the director can reflect on the strength of the choices made, particularly if they were close decisions.

FLOOR PLAN

Did the floor plan meet all the staging needs of the play? How could it have been improved? If changes were made to the floor plan during the rehearsals, could these changes have been foreseen? Did the floor plan provide for the best possible stage pictures and blocking?

USE OF THE STAGE AND FLOOR PLAN

Were the stage and floor plan used to their best advantage? Would changes to the way the stage was used have helped make the production clearer for the audience? Could the opportunities provided by the floor plan have been better utilized?

STAGE PICTURES

Did each stage picture create a dynamic expression of the dramatic action at that moment in the play? Did they provide evocative moments, bringing the audience into the action of the play? Was the audience's focus ever allowed to drift or move to areas it should not have? Were any of the stage pictures made at the expense of other parts of the play? In other words, did choices made to allow a stage picture create problems for other parts of the play?

BLOCKING

Was the blocking consistently effective? Did it reinforce the development of the characters and their interaction? Did it make good use of the stage? Did it help focus the audience's attention where it was wanted? Did it appear to be organically motivated?

CHARACTER DEVELOPMENT

Did the characters reach their full potential? Were they developed within the parameters provided by the play? Did the growth of each character provide the most evocative possibilities for the character? Did they make the strongest choices?

CHARACTER INTERACTION

Did the actors genuinely interact with one another within the parameters of their characters and the script? Did the interaction between the characters promote the dramatic action as fully as possible? Did the interaction between the characters provide as much support as feasible for the development of the individual characters?

REINFORCEMENT OF PLOT AND DRAMATIC ACTION

Did the entire production do as much as it could to reinforce both the physical and the dramatic action of the play? Did the physical action reinforce the dramatic action? Could the spine have been better represented? What could have been done to aid in this reinforcement? Was the message of the playwright clearly portrayed?

TEMPO

Was the tempo appropriate for each action unit as well as the overall play? Did the tempo aid in maintaining the energy of the play as well as the audience's attention? Were there parts of the play that felt slow? Were there parts of the play that felt rushed?

RHYTHM

Did the rhythm of each action unit as well as the rhythm of the overall play support the audience's interest while aiding in focusing the dramatic action? Did the rhythm of the play appropriately rise and fall?

PACE

Did the combination of rhythm and tempo provide an appropriate pace for the play? Did the pacing maintain the audience's attention? Did it allow the audience to totally understand the play?

DEVELOPMENT OF GENUINE MOMENTS (BEATS)

Did the play allow for the development of genuine moments or beats in the interaction between the characters? Did these moments aid in the general growth of the play, allowing it to become more fully dimensional and the audience to become part of the characters' thought processes?

DEVELOPMENT OF THE ARC

Was the overall arc of the play completely and appropriately developed? Was the developmental arc of the action of each action unit completely and appropriately developed? Did the developmental arc of each action unit contribute appropriately to the overall arc of the play? Were they smooth and consistent with the script?

ACTING MECHANICS

Did the actors portray their characters fully? Did the actors demonstrate good mechanics, such as physical presence, projection, and enunciation? Were the actors generally free from any distracting mannerisms or habits?

DESIGN CHOICES

Did the design choices in the production totally support the production concept? Did they serve the dramatic action as well as they could? Could aspects of the designs have been improved? What could have been done by the director to see improvement in these choices?

DEVELOPMENT OF THE STYLE

Was the style correctly identified and effectively conveyed to the audience? Was the production mode the best vehicle to convey the style of the play? Was the style consistently followed throughout the production? Did everything appear to be in the same "universe"?

CONSISTENCY

Was the play consistently performed? Was the quality the same from beginning to end? Did all aspects of the play work together? Did the actors consistently portray their characters?

EVOLUTION AFTER THE LAST REHEARSAL

Was the play prepared to open at the end of the final rehearsal? What was the effect of the addition of the audience? How did the first performance compare in quality with the later dress rehearsals? If there was more than one performance, how did the quality of the subsequent performances compare to the first? What can be deduced regarding the state of preparedness of the production at the end of the rehearsal process?

OVERALL ASSESSMENT

As objectively as possible, what was the overall quality of the performance from the perspective of the audience? What were the production's major strengths and weaknesses?

* * *

Having worked through all these questions, the director can now answer the following about directing this production. What worked well? What could be better? How could issues that arose during the rehearsal process be better handled? What would be done differently if it could be done again? Directing a play is a tremendous task and it is only right for the director to be proud of the accomplishment of having mounted the production. However, a good director looks beyond this satisfaction and seeks to learn from each directing experience to grow as a director.

EXTERNAL SOURCES OF EVALUATION

In addition to learning the skills to self-evaluate the production, the director can usually take advantage of a number of external sources of evaluation. Directors who are currently students have their faculty to serve as mentors in their development. Ironically, too many students look forward to the day they are no longer students and hence not subject to critique by their faculty. In reality, an educational environment is typically one of the most nurturing and supportive. Once out of school, directors no longer have faculty to critique them, but there will be no shortage of others who will continue to do so.

Audiences collectively serve as a major critical voice during the director's career. Their understanding of the director's responsibilities as well as their theoretical and mechanical understanding of theatre as an art form will vary. Individual audience members may not comprehend how theatre is created, but they will have an opinion on whether they enjoyed it. The director needs to find a way to reach the audience and, as such, cannot ignore the audience's response to the play. On the other hand, it is important that the director not pander to the audience to garner approval. Directors who only seek an audience's approval often set limits on their creativity and risk-taking. The director should be careful when interpreting the audience's response and process it appropriately for future growth.

The most formal of critiques is that of the critics. Critics vary greatly in their opinion regarding their function and approach. To gain the most value from the critique, the director must first determine the nature of the critic's approach to criticism. Some critics pride themselves on being extremely harsh; others are more nurturing. There are critics who have a pragmatic approach to their work, feeling their role is to inform their readers of plays that are good and worthy of their patronage. Others take a loftier position and maintain the role of the critic is to foster a dialogue with the ultimate goal of improving the art form. Before the explosion of the Internet, critics were found mostly in print media. The Internet provides a new outlet for theatre critics. Unlike print media, whose publisher hires a critic to write the review, anyone with access to a web page can now be a self-proclaimed critic and publish an opinion. Regardless of the critic's approach, a well-respected critic has an impact on potential audiences, and the critic's perception of the theatre artists' work can be a valuable source of information. The director should not change an approach simply to please a critic, but can learn from the critic's comments to identify strengths and weaknesses. A wise director makes use of constructive criticism, both positive and negative, provided by a good critic. If multiple sources are available, the director may look for trends or points of agreement to assist in framing how to best process the critiques.

Directors can also seek feedback from individuals whose opinion they value. They may be colleagues or theatre artists with whom they have previously worked or whose work they admire. They may be audience members who are familiar with the director's work and are willing to share their insights into the production. These individuals may not have an official position for their comments, but if their thoughts are helpful, they can provide a valuable source of external evaluation for the director. Regardless of where directors find their sources, they can be a valuable font for additional feedback on the director's work.

It can be hard for a director to remain objective in the evaluative process or to hear critical comments. Good directors use this criticism to grow.

COMBINING ALL SOURCES OF EVALUATION

Having conducted a self-evaluation, the director's thoughts are combined with the opinions of the external sources. It is vital for the director to remain as objective as possible throughout the process to take advantage of the learning opportunity it can provide. As with all artists, directors place a great deal of themselves into their work and can easily fall into the trap of allowing negative but constructive criticism to hurt rather than help. They then seek reaffirmation in the form of positive feedback. While this is natural, it is only through being fully open to the evaluative process, looking at both strengths and weaknesses, that the director continues to grow. The director must keep in mind that no production is ever without any value or strength nor is any production ever without room for improvement. To aid in the self-evaluation process, a form summarizing the areas discussed is provided below.

To make better use of external criticism, the director should process it in light of the nature and background of the source.

PRODUCTION EVALUATION

Area	Comments
Choice of Play (if applicable)	
Analysis	
Production Concept	
Choice of Cast	
Floor Plan	
Use of the Stage and Floor Plan	
Stage Pictures	
Blocking	
Character Development	
Character Interaction	
Reinforcement of Plot and Dramatic Action	
Tempo	
Rhythm	
Pace	
Development of Genuine Moments (Beats)	
Development of the Arc	

Area	Comments
Acting Mechanics	
Design Choices	
Development of the Style	
Consistency	
Evolution After the Last Rehearsal	
Overall Assessment	

FURTHER EXPLORATION

1. Using the guidelines provided in this chapter, practice your evaluative skills on a play you have recently seen.
2. Contact a professional theatre critic and discuss his or her basis for evaluating productions.
3. Develop a list of individuals who can help you evaluate your production.

PART VI

Additional Topics

CHAPTER 19

Directing Nonrealistic Styles (Styling the Production)

IDENTIFYING THE STYLE

All plays have a style. In contemporary theatre, Realism, or some variation of it, is thought of as the predominant style. In the same manner, theatre in Shakespeare's time assumed all theatre followed the conventions of the day, in this case highly presentational techniques. Identifying the style of a play can be difficult. It is more important for the director to identify the stylistic elements rather than place a name on the style. The only real advantage to naming the style is that it can provide an understanding of the elements with which it is typically associated. Upon identifying the stylistic elements, the director can proceed to develop an approach befitting the style.

CONVENTIONS OF STYLES

Different styles have different conventions that affect the way the play is presented and, therefore, how it is directed. Following is a discussion of the basic elements in the two major divisions of styles, Representationalism and Presentationalism.

REPRESENTATIONALISM

The hallmark styles found within Representationalism are Realism and Naturalism. These genres are predicated on an authentic depiction of life. This includes the characters' reactions and the tactics they employ as well as the situations they face. While both depict stories based on lifelike situations, Realism focuses on the characters having free will in their decision-making process and Naturalism focuses on the impact of the environment in this process. Many plays written around the beginning of the twentieth century were purely realistic; however, most contemporary plays considered realistic contain or necessitate nonrealistic elements to be produced. For example, *A Few Good Men* is a realistic play, but the rapidly shifting locations and time require the use of more presentational techniques. In this case, the framework for the play is not fully realistic, but both the situation and the characters and their responses to the situation are realistic.

PRESENTATIONALISM

While almost all realistic plays tend to fall under the same umbrella of approach, presentational styles vary significantly. As such, it is difficult to develop a set of guidelines; however, there are several common traits. Presentational genres accept the presence of the audience as a convention within the style. The characters in the play often directly or indirectly acknowledge and may even speak to the audience. Actions in presentational genres are not confined to the realistic; they allow actors the freedom to behave as best meets the needs of the play and to communicate with the audience. Characters may break into song in musicals or speak their mind to the audience in a soliloquy. Some presentational genres, such as Existentialism, seek to shatter any connection to reality and bring the audience into a completely different world. Given the wide range of genres that fall under Presentationalism, the director may assume some common traits but must carefully identify the specific methods employed within the genre to determine the most appropriate methodology of presentation.

> The director must view each genre in its own right rather than attempting to understand it in terms of how it is like or unlike Realism.

DIRECTING A PRESENTATIONAL OR NONREALISTIC STYLE

Contrary to the approach to directing a realistic play, nonrealistic genres are not predicated on lifelike behavior or confined to the parameters of a realistic world. Rather, these genres employ numerous techniques to develop a method of communication with the audience, and the director needs to be fully conversant with the characteristics of the particular style and consistently apply them during the production. In addition to the directorial concerns mentioned in earlier chapters, there are a number of others to be addressed when directing a nonrealistic play. These include:

PLAY SELECTION

Before making the selection, the director must possess or acquire the skills necessary to understand and direct the genre. Beginning directors are often attracted to highly experimental plays that require a unique approach to the directing process. Experience with Realism does not necessarily prepare the director to direct other genres. On the other hand, if confident in the ability to handle the style, the director should choose the play and proceed with the process.

SCRIPT ANALYSIS

The script analysis process for nonrealistic plays is essentially the same as discussed in Chapter 2. In addition, however, the particular elements of the genre of a nonrealistic play have to be thoroughly analyzed by the director to understand both the possibilities it presents and its restrictions. The nonrealistic play may have an entirely different purpose than that of realistic works and may use different conventions. In some genres, for instance, character and plot development may be either limited or two-dimensional. Some may not follow a linear path of plot or character development. The director needs to understand how the genre makes use of these limitations and complete the analysis making adjustments to accommodate the style. The director should not assume the best mode of production is necessarily the same as the genre in which the play is written. The development of the mode for nonrealistic plays will be discussed in more detail later in this chapter.

AUDITIONS AND CASTING

To judge each actor's potential in the light of a particular genre, whenever possible the director should request that monologues for the initial audition come from that genre. The director cannot assume because an actor performs well in one genre he or she will be able to equal that level of performance in another. If unable to control the monologue selection, as in the case where auditions are being held for a number of plays, the director needs to pay careful attention during the initial audition to determine how well the actor's skills will transfer to the genre of the play, being careful not to overestimate the actor's ability to make the transition. Closer attention can be paid to the way the actor handles the style in callbacks. A distinct weakness in handling the genre may be a reason not to consider an otherwise ideal actor.

STAGING

The basic principles of staging remain constant regardless of genre. A given genre may, however, have certain staging characteristics. Therefore, the director must understand the particular needs and parameters of the genre to ensure the staging is consistent with the style of the play. For example, the staging for presentational genres is often more overt and, hence, less naturalistic. Whereas this type of blocking may look contrived in Realism, it works well within this type of genre. Some genres also contain specific types of staging. For example, plays of the sixteenth to nineteenth centuries are likely to include such conventions as asides and soliloquies. The director must incorporate these specific features as necessitated by the script.

WORKING WITH THE ACTORS

The method in which an actor approaches the development of his or her character can be impacted by the genre of the play. Many traditional approaches do not work well with certain styles, especially those from the early twentieth century such as Existentialism. While the approach to building the character is primarily the actor's responsibility, it is important that the director understands the process so the notes the director provides to the actor are helpful and are consistent with the style of the play. For example, giving an actor a note to develop a stronger internal connection to the character in an existential play would be incongruous with the nature of the play.

TECHNICAL CONSIDERATIONS

Different genres often have different necessities for the technical considerations. The director's production concept must take into account the specific necessities and implications of the genre. The director should be aware of these when working with the designers on the evolution of the designs. As with the style of acting, the design environment needs to be consistent with the genre. Specific genres tend to have a traditional "look" to them. The settings for Brecht's plays, for instance, frequently use constructivism techniques. Although the director needs to take these into consideration in the formation of the mode for the production, it is not essential to follow these traditional looks; some other approach may best serve the particular production.

DETERMINING THE MODE FOR NONREALISTIC STYLES

The prevalence of Realism as a style in modern theatre leads many beginning directors to make the mistake of approaching nonrealistic genres with the same assumptions as those for Realism. Some directors also err in defining the genre based on its differences from Realism rather than on its own merits. The director's production concept must take the premises and expectations of the genre into account. This may require the director to conduct additional research to become familiar with the stylistic implications typically associated with the genre. Now conversant with both the play and the genre, the director can proceed with the process of developing a production concept and mode of presentation.

The director's purpose in determining the concept and mode is to establish the best means for communicating the message of the playwright to the audience. Chapter 4 examined different approaches to developing the mode based on the style of the play. As noted, the best mode may be in sharp contrast to the implied style of the genre. Once the production mode is determined, it serves as the guiding parameters for both the design environment and the style of the acting. For example, if the mode creates a distinct separation between the audience and the stage, this barrier cannot be arbitrarily broken as a convenience for a given moment in the production. Therefore, it is imperative that all aspects and requirements of the production be taken into consideration prior to finalizing the mode.

MATCHING YOUR DIRECTING STYLE TO THE STYLE OF THE PLAY

The director needs to have a complete understanding of the style of the play and its implications to determine an appropriate directing style. For example, one of the tenets of Brecht's Epic Theatre is for the audience to feel distanced from the play and remain an impartial observer. It would be inappropriate for the director to correct an actor because the actor is not fully engaging the audience. In making such a comment, the director clearly shows a lack of understanding of *Verfremdungseffekt*, the principle of alienation or distancing, the core tenet of Brecht's Epic Theatre. To effectively communicate with the actors, the director has to understand how they are approaching the creation of their characters consistent with the style of the play. Attempting to apply realistic techniques to a nonrealistic play conflicts with the inherent presentational qualities of the style. This does not mean the director should produce a stereotypical interpretation of the play, but rather the interpretation and approach must fit within the parameters of the style. Plays may benefit from a fresh interpretation of the style resulting in a production mode not customarily applied. While the mode may not be "traditionally correct" it can still be a vibrant means for communicating the playwright's message. Of paramount importance is the director's ability to ensure the production embodies the spirit of the style rather than comments on it.

Many styles require performance and production techniques that may seem poorly done or underdeveloped if judged against a different genre's standards. It is the director's job to make certain the style is being treated with full sincerity and integrity not as a variation of a more common style. An excellent example is classical melodrama. The production style of this genre commonly relies on two-dimensional painted scenery with a flat floor plan. The acting is heavily based on the acting methods of François Delsarte, who placed great emphasis on the physical use of gesture and body attitude. This results in, by today's standards, a highly stylized method of acting with a significant amount of posturing, posing, and stylized gesture. The actors are not internalizing the motivation of their characters but presenting them in a fairly grandiose manner. The modern audience may easily mistake this style for bad acting. The director can avoid this by fully committing to the style without allowing the actors to appear to be commenting on it so the audience understands the communication medium within the genre. This leads to an important consideration for the director: the expectations of the audience. If the play is essentially consistent with the current expectations of the audience, the communication between the audience and the production will naturally occur. If it is not, the director must establish this means at the beginning of the play so the audience quickly comes to understand it.

> The director must keep the expectations of the audience in mind in the preparation and directing of a nonrealistic play. If the audience is familiar with a genre, even though it is different from current practice, such as Shakespeare, the director can use this understanding to establish communication with the audience. If the audience is not familiar with the genre, and the director does not quickly establish this means of communication, the production will quickly lose the audience.

EXAMPLES OF WORKING IN STYLES OTHER THAN PURE REALISM

The following examples of nonrealistic styles of theatre are intended to illustrate approaches to these specific genres as well as other nonrealistic genres. Note that the directing of musical theatre will be discussed in Chapter 20. As each is approached, the following guidelines should be employed:

- Understand the genre and its expectations and characteristics.

- Determine a mode for bringing this genre to life onstage for a modern audience.

- Make sure the actors cast have the necessary skills for the genre.

- Develop a rehearsal approach that is consistent with the genre and will help the actors develop their characters within the parameters of the style.

- Ensure the production is consistently working within the genre and at the same time is understandable for the modern audience.

- Be certain the actors and the production are sincerely playing the style and not commenting on it.

GREEK THEATRE

In beginning work with any classical form of theatre the director must first determine whether to focus on a contemporary approach, making it as accessible to the audience as possible, on a historical re-creation, staging the play as it would have been presented to its original audience, or on a combination of the two. It is important to remember the play was written within the parameters of theatre as the playwright knew it. While the message of the play may remain significant to the modern audience, the director needs to determine if the original mode of production is still a viable means of communication. When contemplating plays written in another language, as is the case with Greek plays, the director has to take into consideration the nature of the translation or adaptation selected. Translations of the play will differ in approach. For example, one of the challenges translators face in translating ancient Greek to English is the lyric quality of the play. If they choose to literally translate the words, they will preserve the playwright's word choice but will sacrifice the flow. If, instead, they choose to translate for the meaning and feeling they believe the playwright intended, they will preserve this sense of the play but will sacrifice the playwright's original word choices and their lyric quality. Both approaches can have equal value depending on how the director wishes to convey the play. Adaptations, on the other hand, take more liberty in the translation, making the play more accessible to the modern audience. Whereas accessibility may be increased, the adaptation also minimizes the original style of the play. Once again, the director needs to consider the intent in producing the play when selecting a specific adaptation. It is also important to note that the original plays are not copyrighted and do not have performance rights, but this may not be the case for the translation or adaptation. These derivative works may have their own copyright and subsequent production rights that must be obtained before the play can be produced.

In the traditional performance of classical Greek theatre actors wear masks and intone the lines of the play with great virtuosity. Although the original audiences fully appreciated as well as expected this style of performance, many modern audiences may feel disconnected from the play and view the masks and oratory style as archaic. On the other hand, the writing style of the great classical Greek playwrights is as moving and powerful today as it was in its own day. The director faces an initial conflict in dealing with the classical production style. As the plays were clearly written to incorporate the style of theatre at the time, for the contemporary director to ignore these approaches and use purely modern techniques is naive and limiting. While possibly providing a valuable historical study, restricting the production to the traditional style lessens the audience's engagement with the playwright's message. Some modern directors have chosen a variety of techniques that draw inspiration from the classical approach such as incorporating partial masks or highly stylized makeup to convey the nature of the characters; other directors have chosen to deal directly with the characters and to do away completely with masks.

Since the plays relied heavily on oratory, the more declamatory nature of the speeches cannot be ignored by the director. Ironically, even though these plays were written long before realistic approaches to theatre were envisioned, the characters may be created through essentially realistic internal acting approaches. While these techniques may lead to a solid understanding of the character and his or her intent, the actor still must develop the presentational aspects of the speeches because these plays were not written utilizing realistic dialogue. This combination of techniques illustrates how a classical work can be interpreted through contemporary approaches to make the play more accessible. Remember that both acting styles and audience expectations have evolved significantly from the time these plays were written. As such, most directors choose to modernize the delivery technique to meet contemporary expectations. At the same time, the style of the writing cannot be ignored. It is best if the actors work on the content and subtext rather than try to play the style itself. This usually helps eliminate the apparent falseness that a more declamatory style of delivery may provide. The actor cannot, however, just process the language internally. Although this works for realistic dialogue, the rhythm and sound of the dialogue of early genres is as important as its semantic content. It is important to allow the sound of the dialogue to come through. Actors may try to fight with the natural rhythm of the dialogue because it does not always flow like realistic dialogue. The director needs to work with the actors to find the balance between delivering the musicality of the lines and the meaning.

The choice of translation or adaptation is crucial for the director since it will have one of the most significant influences on how the play will be presented.

Another major aspect of the Greek theatre was the use of the chorus. The Greek playwrights used the chorus in a number of ways: to provide narration, giving the audience the information necessary to understand the scene; to set the location or to supply specific information to put the scene into context since Greek theatre made limited use of scenery; to describe events the playwright either chose not to show or was forbidden to show, such as violence; to allow the principal characters to explore their thoughts and inner feelings; to provide commentary on the action and choices of the principal characters; and to give further insight or react to the action of the play. Traditionally, the chorus spoke in unison, rhythmically intoning their lines in a melodic fashion while moving with stylized actions. The modern director needs to determine how to handle this important aspect of Greek theatre since audiences may have difficulty relating to a strictly traditional approach to the chorus. Similar to the ways in which modern directors have interpreted the use of masks, many directors have developed unique and powerful approaches to the implementation of the chorus by combining modern and classical techniques. How the chorus will be implemented is perhaps one of the most important considerations the director must make in selecting the translation or adaptation. Many modern adaptations substantially alter the nature of the traditional chorus; stricter translations maintain their original structure. One approach is to divide the lines of the chorus and to assign them to specific chorus members coupled with more traditional choral speaking. The chorus may also be divided by vocal quality, as is done in a choir. Some directors choose to define the chorus as a collective body with similar attributes; other directors define each chorus member and therefore define the chorus as the combination of these individuals.

> In working with any genre, the director must be sure the production is fully committed to the style and that the actors are not commenting on it but embodying the spirit of it.

SHAKESPEARE

Directing a play by William Shakespeare is one of the greatest challenges a director can face. Ironically, Shakespeare's plays were written long before the advent of modern acting techniques, yet these techniques can be readily applied. Although written as presentational works, the plays work well for modern audiences when performed with more contemporary acting approaches. Shakespeare's themes are as vital today as they were in his lifetime and remain popular with modern audiences. Given that the plays were written in English long before copyright protection, translations and performance rights are not required. Many directors cut the original scripts to tighten the plots and shorten the plays.

Shakespeare wrote his plays to be performed in daylight using simple props and almost no scenery, but with sound effects and music. All the audience had to know about the environment was written into the dialogue, so Shakespeare did not concern himself with the rapid changes in location or mood. The director needs to take this into consideration in determining a production concept for the play. In his program notes for his 1982 production of *Othello* with James Earl Jones and Christopher Plummer, director Peter Coe discussed the importance of the neutrality of the setting for his production. Since Shakespeare wrote without expectation of scenery, creating a detailed visual image would, in Coe's opinion, conflict with the imagery created by the language. He lamented how actors playing Duncan in *Macbeth* often stood in front of an ominous castle saying, "This castle hath a pleasant seat; the air nimbly and sweetly recommends itself unto our gentle senses."[1] Designs for *Macbeth* frequently utilize dark and sinister overtones that, while appropriate for the overall mood of the play, do not necessarily work for individual scenes such as this one. This does not mean modern production concepts for Shakespeare's plays have to maintain the neutrality sought by Coe. Many successful productions have been predicated on fairly elaborate concepts. Shakespeare's themes have such universal appeal that his plays are frequently set in locations and time periods other than those suggested in the text. These interpretations can be extremely dynamic, but the director has to be careful not to select the location and/or time period simply to be different or provocative. It is also essential that the director's concept work consistently for the entire play and the production concept furthers the play's message.

Acting in Shakespeare's plays requires not only a firm understanding of acting technique but also of the text and the conventions of Shakespeare's day. Many times, young actors are confused by the language. To fully comprehend the character, the actor must understand the dialogue as well as each word within it as meant in Shakespeare's time. Though some words such as *anon* (soon) are unique to his time, others such as *visitor* appear understandable. In this case, however, visitor refers to the person designated by the parish to visit the sick. One of Shakespeare's most often misunderstood lines is from *Romeo and Juliet*. When Juliet says, "O Romeo, Romeo! wherefore art thou Romeo?"[2] the word *wherefore* means *why* not *where*, completely changing the meaning of the line. Juliet is not looking for Romeo but is questioning why Romeo is a Montague. It is essential the director carefully study the script utilizing annotated editions or Shakespearean dictionaries to understand the correct meaning of each of the words. Although broad, bravado styles of acting may have been popular in Shakespeare's day, they will quickly bore the modern audience. The actors need to see through the language to find fully nuanced performances to bring the text to life.

It is also important that the actors understand the acting conventions of Shakespeare's day since the text relies on many of them. These techniques are rarely used in modern drama, yet contemporary audiences readily embrace these conventions as long as they are consistently portrayed. Actors may have difficulty with Shakespeare's use of iambic pentameter and rhyming couplets. Too often actors attempt to overstress the rhythm and rhyme of these lines and in doing so lose the meaning. On the other hand, they cannot just ignore the writing style. The key is to find the rhythm and flow of the lines while bringing the internal meaning to life. It is generally best to pay more attention to the punctuation rather than to the line breaks.

The imagery Shakespeare used in his plays is what truly defines them. Once when directing *The Tempest* with a young actor playing Ferdinand, the innocent prince of Naples, I stopped an early rehearsal during one of Ferdinand's speeches to his love interest, Miranda. The young actor's delivery was devoid of any real understanding so I asked him what he thought he was saying. He paused, thought briefly, and responded he was saying he loved her. I replied this was exactly right but it was not in his delivery. Then I explained the premise behind Shakespeare's poetic language. It is this imagery and poetry that define a Shakespeare play; as such, the actors need to embrace its full beauty. Shakespeare's use of rhyme, iambic pentameter, word choice, and imagery along with the musical sound of the words themselves must be fully indulged to bring his language to life.

The director also needs to help the actors find the rhythm of Shakespeare's words. This is commonly referred to as *scansion*. Shakespeare often contracted a word to remove a syllable to make the rhythm work. For example, using *o'er* instead of *over*. It is crucial that the actors find this rhythm but not become slaves to it. The interpretation of the play and the characters will depend on how the rhythm is utilized. In working with the director, the actor will find the best attack for each line.

COMEDY

Comedy is a broad genre encompassing a wide range of subgenres that further define the style. Comedy is one of the three original styles the Greeks identified in the earliest days of theatre. Today, comedy is generally defined as having a satisfactory ending, relying on humor to develop its message. There are a number of forms of comedy in modern theatre, and the director has to match the production style to the form of comedy. Some of these forms are:

Farce

Farce is a classical form of comedy that depends on exaggerated situations to develop the humor. Farces are typified by mistaken identities, confusion regarding the nature of the situation, and are likely to have a frenetic pace and chase sequences. There is no attempt to make the situations or characters believable; in fact, much of the comedy comes from its unbelievable nature.

Dark Comedy

Dark comedy involves an otherwise serious subject where comedy is used as a vehicle to explore the topic and deliver the message. It utilizes the idea that finding humor in the situation feels inappropriate. As such, dark comedy must be carefully presented so the audience understands the seriousness of the situation but feels permitted to find humor in it.

Physical Comedy

Physical comedy gets its humor from physical action and/or the visual situations created within the play. Classical physical comedy originated from Roman theatre and commedia dell'arte and includes pratfalls and other physical situations to cause the humor. The classic comedienne Lucille Ball made frequent use of physical comedy.

Slapstick Comedy

Slapstick comedy is named from a practice dating back to the commedia dell'arte. Characters made a slapping sound with a pair of sticks to imply the pain of hitting each other without physically inducing it. Modern slapstick comedy is a subform of physical comedy with highly exaggerated action and typically exceeds what is expected in the situation. The comedy often originates from the physical discomfort of the characters.

Absurdist or Existential Comedy

Absurdist or existential comedy as epitomized by the works of Eugène Ionesco, Jean-Paul Sartre, and Samuel Beckett derives its message from existential philosophical thought and its humor from the philosophical incongruities of the situation. In many cases, this humor is rather dark. These plays rarely have plots that follow traditional development and often do not have a resolution of the conflict at the end of the play.

Situational Comedy

Situational comedy is based on a series of events built around a common premise or theme. Good examples of situational comedy can be found in most television comedy series.

Character Comedy

Character comedy comes from the nature of the characters in the play. The persona of these characters, usually based on stereotype, creates the comic moments.

Spoof Comedy

Spoof comedy derives humor through the re-creation of a previous situation, book, film, or play utilizing the premise, style, and content of the previous work as the source of the comedy through exaggeration.

* * *

There is an old saying in theatre, "Dying is easy, comedy is hard." While this is not universally true, it does underscore the fact that producing good comedy is far more difficult than assumed. Many beginning directors feel choosing a comedy will ensure a well-received production since the audience's perception will be enhanced through laughter. Although there may be some truth to the idea that given equally weak productions of a comedy and a drama, the ability to laugh at some of the comedy may make it more palatable than the heavier drama, the reality is it is generally more difficult to achieve a strong comic production. When approaching comedy, in addition to analyzing and researching the play, the director must explore the nature of how the humor in the play is created. The nature of the comedy will define the play's presentation and the actors' approach to the text. During the casting process, the director needs to be certain the actors have the skills necessary to make the humor work.

The principal factor the director has to keep in mind when directing comedy is that the characters are not trying to be funny; the humor arises from their situation and their reactions to it. All too often, the comedy and the play as a whole are weakened by performances where the actors seek to be funny rather than achieve their characters' goals. In fact, the characters in the play are simply attempting to deal with the situation at hand. The seriousness with which the characters approach the situation will only intensify the humor created by the script.

The most challenging element for the director is also the key to comedy: timing. Comic timing refers to the pace of the actor's delivery, combining the speed of the delivery with the carefully worked pauses. If the response is given too quickly, the comic moment does not have a chance to develop. If the response is given too late, the comedy is lost. The difference between the two can be microseconds. Masters of comedy are often defined by their understanding of comic timing. Two of the best classic comedians with incredible comic timing were Johnny Carson and the man whose work he studied, Jack Benny. Recordings of these two comedians delivering comic monologues or acting in comic situations, which are available online, offer a textbook insight into the importance of comic timing. Both Carson and Benny were masters of working a moment, usually in dead silence, to allow the comic potential to reach its greatest level before delivering their next line. They maximized the comic potential of any situation.

Comic timing is not based on mechanical precision; it cannot be measured with a metronome or watch; it has to be felt. During the audition process, the director needs to ascertain the actor's innate sense of comic timing. At the callbacks, the actor's ability to apply this skill in the specific role and situations created by the play can be determined. Over the course of the rehearsal process, the director will explore with the actors the rhythm and tempo of each action unit and, in some cases, each line to find the best comic timing for each moment. The actors will also have to develop a complete understanding of the comic mechanics of the scene so they can make subtle adjustments in each performance as necessitated by the audience's reaction. Ultimately, the success or failure of comic timing is judged solely on how well the audience receives the comedy. If preview performances are not in the schedule, the director may wish to bring an invited audience to later rehearsals to gain an insight into the audience's response. The director should keep the nature of the style of comedy in mind and develop the play consistent with this style. It is vital that the director not pander to the audience to get laughs, but communicate the playwright's message to the audience. Comedy depends on a firm respect for the audience. While the audience will laugh at any silly or humorous element, this laughter is usually inappropriate, and hence will weaken the play if the humor is derived from elements not consistent with the script.

Dealing with the laughter of the audience is one of the more challenging issues the director and actors face. If the actors continue with their lines, the audience will miss what the actors are saying and reduce or curtail their laughter. This not only works against the very nature of the play but also cheats the audience from fully enjoying the moment and from the opportunity to express their appreciation for the humor. On the other hand, if the actors consistently pause where they anticipate laughter or pause longer than necessary for the laugh, the pace of the comedy will be lost and the play will significantly lose its humorous qualities. The key is to find the balance between the two situations. Brief holds for laughter are necessary to accommodate the audience, but the actors must quickly continue to maintain the energy of the scene. A good approach is to have the actor play through the laugh with a brief pause and then deliver the next line a bit louder as soon as or a moment before the laughter peaks. In this way, the overall tempo is maintained and the audience is not discouraged from laughing. The energy of the audience's laughter will maintain the energy of the scene. As a rule, it is generally better to maintain a good tempo even at the expense of stifling some of the laughter rather than allowing the pace to suffer. The director also has to prepare the cast for the fact that each audience will respond differently to the comic elements. An audience that does not laugh at a given moment does not necessarily dislike the play; they may not be inclined to vocally react at that moment. Some audiences are more vocal than others. Unfortunately, the skill of working comedy with an audience can be developed only during performances and therefore can only be anticipated during the rehearsal.

FURTHER EXPLORATION

1. Select a nonrealistic play. Identify and research its style, identify its conventions, and research how it can be staged.

2. For the play you chose in Activity 1, select a brief scene and direct a group of actors. What was necessarily different in your approach than when directing a realistic play? What was the same?

3. Set up an improvised scene. Replay the scene several times, each time employing a different genre of theatre. Play each scene with the selected genre without allowing commentary on the genre. Discuss what you observed.

NOTES

1 *Macbeth*, act 1, scene 6.

2 *Romeo and Juliet*, act 2, scene 2.

Directing Musicals

UNDERSTANDING THE DIFFERENCE BETWEEN MUSICALS AND STRAIGHT PLAYS

The staging of musicals offers a number of unique challenges and rewards for the director. Musicals are the direct theatrical descendants of opera and operetta and have retained much of their form from these early roots. They were originally referred to as musical comedies, but as the genre evolved, many musicals began to take more serious overtones. *West Side Story* is a prime example. In fact, some modern musicals are extremely dark. Musicals are by nature highly presentational. Today, musical theatre runs the gamut from farce to tragedy, but the essentially presentational framework remains a standard. Conventions in musicals allowing characters to break into song and dance further this presentational frame. The musical solo, for example, is the musical theatre equivalent of the soliloquy. Like its roots in opera and operetta, modern musicals depend on the use of music to assist the plot and character development. Following the same path that began with operettas, musicals also use dialogue and dance. The traditional musical typically relies even more heavily on dialogue than the traditional operetta; however, many modern musicals contain minimal or, in some cases, no dialogue. The amount of dance varies, but most musicals contain at least a minimum amount of staged movement. Musical theatre often makes extended use of spectacle to promote the entertainment value of the genre. Contemporary musicals in particular provide an opportunity for spectacular staging.

There are a several issues the director must take into consideration when directing a musical as opposed to a straight play. Principal among them are the following:

GREATER COLLABORATION

In addition to the collaboration with the scenic, lighting, costume, and sound designers, the director of a musical also collaborates with other artists in the areas of music and choreography.

The collaboration with these artists extends further into the implementation of the production concept and more directly into the rehearsal process.

> The nature of the working relationship the director has with the choreographer and musical director defines how the musical will proceed.

ADDITIONAL SELECTION ISSUES

Choosing a musical has additional selection considerations. The casts of most musicals are larger than straight plays and require talent in song and dance as well as acting. Many musicals have production challenges that may prove difficult or at least expensive to resolve. The orchestral needs of the musical must also be accounted for in terms of the requirements of the score. In some instances, the musical places particular needs on the size of the stage and its mechanical infrastructure to accommodate the play's requirements. Financially, musicals are usually more expensive to produce and, in many cases, the royalties, book (libretto), and music purchase or rental are significantly higher than those for a straight play.

ANALYSIS ISSUES

The analysis portion of the director's preparation for a musical is like that of a straight play but with an added focus on the music that both accompanies the songs and dances and underscores the scenes. Unlike a straight play, the authorship of a musical is a combination of the creative work of a composer, who writes the music; a lyricist, who writes the words to the songs; and a librettist, who writes the book. The three functions may be the work of one, two, or three individuals. Most of the time, the writing of the musical is a collaborative process. These artists often are asked which comes first: the music, the lyrics, or the book. There is no set answer to this question; every musical is different. In fact, as the musical evolves, book scenes may become songs or songs may become book scenes; the composer may write music to which the lyricist crafts the words, or the lyrics may be written and subsequently set to music. More often the book predates the music and lyrics in at least a conceptual form.

Since the musical is generally a product of several creators, just as in researching the playwright for a straight play, the director needs to research these individuals. Whereas the director's analysis of a straight play focuses only on the text of the script, the director of a musical also has to analyze the nature of the music and lyrics that accompanies the text. Because music has such a powerful effect on the perception of the scene, the director cannot overlook music's importance in understanding the songs and in underscoring the scenes.

CASTING ISSUES

Auditions and casting decisions for a musical are far more complex and time-consuming than for most straight plays. The auditions, both initial and callback, need to provide enough time to evaluate not only the acting abilities of the auditionees but also their singing and dancing.

Most initial auditions for musicals include a short musical selection, for which the auditionee brings sheet music for the accompanist, and a monologue. It is helpful if the director provides guidelines to the auditionees regarding selection of music and monologue to best fit the nature of the musical. Sometimes a separate dance audition is held at the initial auditions, in others it is held at the callbacks. If several callbacks are planned, it is possible only one or two of the areas will be covered in the initial rounds. For a musical with a demanding score, the initial audition may be based solely on singing ability with acting and dance auditions held for those who make it past this round. The ideal musical theatre performer is often referred to as a "triple threat," a performer with strong skills as an actor, singer, and dancer. While triple threats are ideal candidates, many performers have strengths in only one or two areas and, as such, the director must make casting decisions based on the overall strongest candidate for each role.

This raises an important consideration to be addressed in the casting process: the skill set or sets that drive the ultimate casting decision. The choreographer and music director will, in all probability, make their determinations based on each performer's strength in their areas. It is vital that the director prioritize the skills in acting; singing, both range and quality; and dance before the auditions to focus on the casting process. I remember one audition where the male lead needed both strong acting and vocal skills. For me, one actor stood out from the others at the end of the callbacks. He was a strong actor with adequate but not great vocal skills. On the other hand, the candidate my music director saw as perfect for the role was a strong baritone but was limited as an actor and did not have the physical bearing for the role. Unfortunately, the ideal candidate was not in our talent pool. After a lengthy discussion, we ultimately agreed that in this instance it was better to have the actor over the singer as the actor would be able to make the audience believe in and sympathize with him in the role. This situation was unique in setting the priorities. Given the nature of the majority of musical theatre, the audience is generally more forgiving of a weaker actor than a singer. As such, I generally lean more heavily on the advice of my music director and choreographer in making final casting decisions. The director must be able to balance all the needs of the production to reach a decision on the final cast.

> While every director would prefer to cast a "triple threat," an actor equally skilled in acting, singing, and dancing, this is not always possible. In these cases, the director must decide which area or areas are most crucial to the role, keeping in mind that the audience is generally more forgiving of weak acting than weak singing.

SCHEDULING AND REHEARSAL ISSUES

In planning the rehearsal schedule for a musical, the director has to consider the time necessary to learn and subsequently master the music and choreography in addition to the staging and character development as well as the time needed to integrate the three elements prior to the polishing rehearsals. Assuming there is both a music director and a choreographer, each rehearsal can include separate rehearsals for book, music, and dance. This often works better in theory than in practice since this may create rehearsal conflicts for scenes, songs, and/or dances requiring the same cast members. In many cases, directors choose to dedicate the early rehearsals solely to music before proceeding with dance and book rehearsals. It is important to remember that, just like blocking, once music and dance are learned they will need frequent rehearsal to continue to grow and achieve mastery. Also, even if the rehearsal time can be divided among the three elements, they will need to be brought together so scenes can be rehearsed as a cohesive unit.

REHEARSAL MATERIALS

Unlike directing a straight play where the director works only with a script, in a musical there are four key items: the *libretto*, the book portion of the musical, essentially the script with the spoken dialogue and lyrics to the songs; the *vocal book*, the music and lyrics of each number for the cast, but not the orchestration or sections with musical underscoring or dance sections; the *piano-conductor score*, the full orchestration for the entire show. The piano-conductor score is used by the rehearsal accompanist, the music director while working with the cast, and the conductor. The director will be well served to check the three books for consistency. On occasion, there may be discrepancies. Also, there may be some notations in the piano-conductor score not found in any other materials that may be valuable for rehearsal. The final set of material is the *orchestration* books, with the parts for each instrument. Be aware that in some cases the piano orchestration is different from the piano part played during rehearsal.

It should also be noted that many of the agencies that handle the rights to musicals rent the rehearsal materials not sell them. These materials are only available for the time specified in the contract and must be returned with any notes fully erased after the performances.

ADDITIONAL COLLABORATION IN MUSICALS

One of the unique aspects of directing a musical is the collaborative nature of the relationship among the director, the music director, and the choreographer. In fact, in many cases, in addition to a music director, who has overall responsibility for coordinating all the musical aspects of the production, the director may be working with a vocal director, who teaches the music to the cast and further develops the vocals of the production, and a conductor, who conducts the orchestra during the final rehearsals and performances. There may be one or more rehearsal pianists as well. Sometimes the three or four musical positions are held by one or two individuals. Each of these artists has a creative vision for the production, and the director must work with these artists in the same capacity as the designers to realize the production concept. It is traditional in musical theatre for the stage director to provide the artistic vision for the production, as opposed to the world of opera where the artistic vision usually comes from the music director. Since the director is sharing the rehearsal of the actors with the music staff and the choreographer, it is important that they share a common vision for character development and the creation of the ultimate expression of the vision of the play. This is especially important if they have separate rehearsals.

The director needs to decide how to approach the rehearsals for a musical based on the needs of the show. Generally, if the music drives the musical, this is the first area rehearsed. However, if the book is the key to understanding the musical, then rehearsals begin with it. When in doubt, it is generally better to start with the music so the cast has this initial understanding to build from for the rest of the rehearsals.

WORKING WITH THE MUSIC AND CHOREOGRAPHY IN DEVELOPING THE CHARACTERS

The basic formula for the modern musical as established by Oscar Hammerstein II in *Showboat* is to have an episode, followed by a song, followed by a set change, and then repeat the series, although some contemporary musicals harken back to their operatic roots and have little to no dialogue. While the Hammerstein formula is not always followed precisely, it remains the standard. Songs can either be the key to the overall plot or to the development of a single character. Their placement in the scene or in the musical as a whole is based on this premise. There are a number of standard types of musical numbers, each with its own function. These include:

THE OPENING NUMBER

As the name implies, many musicals begin with an opening number. Writers use this song to establish the mood, feeling, characters, and anything else the audience needs to know. The opening number typically has a high degree of energy and sets the tone of the musical. When *A Funny Thing Happened on the Way to the Forum* was having difficulty in out-of-town previews, Jerome Robbins suggested Stephen Sondheim replace the opening number, "Love Is in the Air," since the original number misled the audience as to the type of play to expect. Sondheim changed the opening number to the wildly comedic "Comedy Tonight." This had an immediate and significant impact on the preview audience's perception and is a good example of the importance of the opening number.[1]

THE WANT SONG

The want song is often used early in the musical to establish the direction for the main character. "Something's Coming" from *West Side Story*, in which Tony anticipates his future, is an example of a want song.

CHARACTER DEVELOPMENT SONG

As the name implies, the character development song was created by the writers as a vehicle for the audience to gain a better understanding of one of the principal characters. "My Time of Day" from *Guys and Dolls* allows Sky Masterson to show a much deeper and more meaningful side to his personality.

DUETS

Duets refer to songs sung by two characters and often propel the plot of the musical. "For Good" from *Wicked* is a duet that lets the two characters further develop their relationship.

ELEVEN O'CLOCK NUMBER

Originally, musicals began at 8:30 p.m. The eleven o'clock number draws its name from its placement in the second act, which would take place at about 11:00 p.m. It is usually an impressive number that is designed to revive the energy of the audience before the final portion of the musical. Eleven o'clock numbers are often among the most memorable. Examples include "Sit Down, You're Rockin' the Boat" from *Guys and Dolls* and "Memories" from *Cats*.

PRODUCTION NUMBER

A production number is any large number involving most, if not all, of the cast. Often called "showstoppers," their main purpose is to impress the audience. A good example is "Be Our Guest" from *Beauty and the Beast*.

PATTER SONG

The patter song refers to the way the song is delivered rather than its content or purpose. The modern patter song has its origin in the late 1800s with the Gilbert and Sullivan operettas. In the patter song, the performer speaks the words on pitch rather than singing them. Patter songs are characterized by a rapid delivery of the lyrics. Modern examples include "Ya Got Trouble" from *The Music Man* and "All for the Best" from *Godspell*.

SONG AND DANCE NUMBERS

While dance can be incorporated into almost any type of musical number, the song and dance number combines the two areas into one cohesive whole. It typically contains an extended dance section allowing the performer to show his or her versatility. The number also uses both the song and the dance to communicate its message. Examples of these are "If I Only Had a Brain" from *The Wizard of Oz* and "Electricity" from *Billy Elliot*.

DANCE-ONLY NUMBERS

Whereas dance is often incorporated into other numbers, dance-only numbers do not feature any lyrics. These can be used for pure entertainment value or to further the plot, as is the case in "The Dream Ballet" from *Oklahoma!* where Laurey expresses her feelings through dance.

ACT I FINALE

This number is designed to close out the first act. While it is often an upbeat number, it may be more reflective. In any event, the number sends the audience into the intermission and sets the stage for the second act.

FINALE

The finale refers to the closing number of most musicals. Its purpose is to bring the show to a close, usually on an energetic note, by wrapping up the plot and leaving the audience satisfied. The closing number from *A Chorus Line*, "One," is a good example of such a finale. Some musicals break the mold and do not end with a finale. When done appropriately, it, too, can have a strong impact on the end of the production.

UNDERSCORING

Although technically not a musical number, underscoring refers to the music that plays under the dialogue. The underscoring is usually based on songs from other parts of the musical and sets the tone for the scene. The advances in electronic amplification of the performers have freed composers to write more dynamic underscoring without fear that the projection of the performers has to compete with the orchestra.

* * *

In a musical, the development of the plot and the characters and communication of the message are distributed among the book, the music, and the dance. Some successful directors of musical theatre have equal skills in all three areas. Most directors, however, work with music directors and choreographers. The advantage to one individual serving in all three capacities is that the full integration of the three areas is guaranteed. The disadvantages are the loss of collaboration, efficiency, and rehearsal time. Good directors do not see the music director and/or vocal director and choreographer as functional extensions of themselves but rather as creative collaborators. Each of these individuals can contribute significantly to the development of the message of the play. Early in my career while directing a production of *West Side Story*, I was in a scene rehearsal of both book and music. I was working with the actors while the music director played the haunting underscoring. This provided a strong sense of the scene. I now always incorporate the underscoring into scene rehearsals not only to familiarize the actors with what will be played, but also to guide them in the scene's development. The music also has a significant impact on the pace of the scene. In many cases, the conductor may not begin rehearsals until later in the process. It is critical that the director and music director work with the conductor regarding the tempo of each musical selection to ensure the work completed in rehearsal smoothly transitions into the final rehearsals with the orchestra.

In working with the choreographer, it is beneficial to divide the staging of the musical numbers into three groups. The first group of numbers can be referred to as pure dance. These numbers are choreographed by the choreographer. It is important that the director and choreographer reach an agreement on the nature of the dance and what the dance should communicate. It is equally important to coordinate the locations of the performers at the beginning and end of the dance so the dance can easily be integrated with the book scene. The second group of numbers can be referred to as pure staging. These refer to musical numbers that contain simple movement and can be blocked in the same way as the rest of the scene. This staging is often done by the director. The third group of musical numbers combines the first two. The director and choreographer work together to create the ultimate staging. This can be one of the most exciting collaborations in musical theatre.

ADDITIONAL CONSIDERATIONS IN REHEARSALS FOR MUSICALS

A question often raised is how to decide the order in which the elements of the musical are rehearsed. While there is no single answer, there are concepts that can help dictate it. The director must first determine what propels this particular musical and then has to prioritize the importance of each of the three areas: book, music, and dance. In *Man of La Mancha*, for instance, the book and music carry the theme with minimal dance or elaborate production numbers. Others, such as *Evita*, are entirely song and dance with no dialogue. In addition to the implications for the nature of the casting, this determination helps decide how the musical is rehearsed. If the development of the characters and overall plot are based mainly in music, it is probably wise to rehearse the music prior to the book. On the other hand, if the characters are defined in the book, which then informs the songs, it is probably better to spend early rehearsal time in character development with the book to better understand the music. Even if the dance sections are the least important of the three, it is important not to let too much rehearsal time elapse before beginning the choreography rehearsals to allow enough time to learn and master the dances. Similarly, sufficient time needs to be allotted for "routining," which is the act of moving from song to performance, including how it is sung, the tempo, and the key.

If the plan is to begin with the music, then it is a good idea for the director to be present during the initial music rehearsals to work with the music director and the actors on the development of the characters in the songs. By doing so, the director can be certain the initial character development will be consistent with the work that will occur with the book scenes. The inverse is also true. If work begins with the book, input from the music director will help ensure smooth transitions from the book into the music. Regardless of the order of rehearsals, it is crucial that time is allotted for the integration of book, song, and dance. This will not only create a seamless transition but also will allow for the further development of the plot and characters. The director must also remember not to overlook small book introductions to musical or dance numbers. Given these additional considerations, the rehearsal process for a musical continues along similar guidelines for straight plays discussed in earlier chapters.

A WORD ABOUT WORKING WITH MUSICIANS AND CHOREOGRAPHERS

If the director does not have previous experience working with musicians and choreographers, it will be necessary to become familiar with the practices of these artists. Theatre people, musicians, and choreographers are all part of the performing arts but have decidedly different approaches to their crafts and how they prepare their art. Attempting to judge musicians and choreographers based on theatre standards may lead to misunderstandings. It is vital that all three areas see one another as collaborators in the creation of musical theatre and work to understand and accept one another's practices.

FURTHER EXPLORATION

1. Select a musical and analyze it along the guidelines discussed both in this chapter and in Chapter 2. Think about the particular considerations to be made in completing the analysis.

2. Select a scene from a musical that includes a song. Plan how you would stage both the scene and musical number.

3. Work with a performer on the development of a song from a musical, paying special attention to the development of the character.

4. Talk with music directors and choreographers to find out how they approach their individual areas and how they prefer to collaborate with directors.

NOTE

1   Allen Cohen and Steven L. Rosenhaus, *Writing Musical Theater* (New York: Palgrave Macmillan, 2006).

Directing in Alternative Settings

RECOGNIZING HOW DIRECTING IN ALTERNATIVE SETTINGS DIFFERS FROM PROSCENIUM

If a play is staged in an alternative setting, such as thrust or arena, a number of considerations must be made by the director. To understand these considerations, it is necessary to explore the fundamental differences in the experience of the audience in these alternative settings.

One of the principal impacts of theatre architecture is on the audience's physical point of view. In the typical proscenium theatre, although there are some slight variations, the audience has the same basic perception of the play whether seated dead center in the house or seated on the side. Theatres with other architectural configurations provide decidedly different perspectives for the audience. Figures 21.1 through 21.4 illustrate the audience's view for proscenium, thrust, arena, and alley theatres. In the proscenium configuration (Figure 21.1), the view of the stage from positions A and B, while from slightly different angles, is essentially the same. In the other configurations (Figures 21.2 through 21.4), each section of the audience has a distinct perspective. Lack of a standard perspective is common for all nonproscenium configurations. As such, stage pictures cannot be planned around a "standard position" as in a proscenium theatre. The challenge for the director is to plan each stage picture so it has an equal, or at least close to equal, meaning for each section of the audience despite a different physical view.

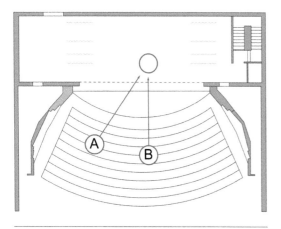

Figure 21.1 Proscenium

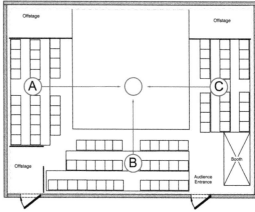

Figure 21.2 Thrust

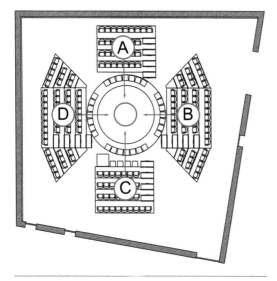

Figure 21.3 Arena

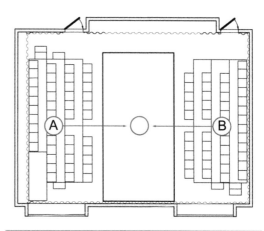

Figure 21.4 Alley

The second major difference is the proximity of the audience to the acting space. The greatest range is in the proscenium theatre because the audience is seated on only one side. Depending on the seating capacity of the house, the distance to the stage can range from a couple of feet in the first row, to far more for the last row. Since the other configurations seat on multiple sides, the greatest distance from the stage to the farthest row is divided by the number of sides. Alternative configurations are often found in theatres with smaller seating capacities thus reducing the distance to the farthest seats to an even greater degree. This proximity allows for an intimate relationship between the audience and the performers and is further enhanced by the lack of an arch dividing the audience from the actors.

GENERAL GUIDELINES FOR DIRECTING IN ALTERNATIVE SETTINGS

Much of directing in alternative settings is similar to directing for the proscenium. There are, however, several exceptions. The major exception is in staging the play. The guidelines that follow are generally true for most nonproscenium configurations. They are followed by configuration-specific information.

NO COMMON VIEWING ANGLE

As illustrated in Figures 21.2 through 21.4, each section of the audience in a nonproscenium setting has a different view of the stage. This can be as significant as one section of the audience looking at the actor's back, another at the actor's face, and yet another with a side view. When staging the play in a nonproscenium setting, the director needs to reconsider how the stage pictures are created. The first step for the director is to realize this is actually necessary. Perhaps the greatest mistake a director can make in staging nonproscenium settings is to designate a "front" or "downstage." To make full use of a nonproscenium stage the director has to make sure this does not occur. Directors in proscenium theatres tend to sit about two-thirds of the way back in the house close to the centerline; directors in nonproscenium settings cannot have a regular seating location. While it is important for the director in a proscenium setting to double-check the view of the stage from various locations within the house to ensure good sight lines, in the nonproscenium setting it is absolutely essential that the director view the play from completely different sections on a regular basis. Even if the director carefully stages to all directions of the house, if the director stays in one location, the actors will tend to naturally focus key moments, if not all, toward the director's location. While moving to various locations in the theatre during the rehearsal is crucial, the director must also consciously avoid compensating for weak staging by moving to another location to find a better viewing angle for a particular scene, understanding that the audience is not able to move to another location during the play.

In planning stage pictures for nonproscenium settings the director should keep three considerations in mind. First, it is important to "share the wealth." Each section of the audience must have the ideal viewing angle for an equal percentage of the play. If the best viewing position tends to lie in one section of the stage, the audience in other sections will be cheated. Several years ago, I was working with a young director who was staging her first show in arena. I had the opportunity to see the show upon completion of the initial staging. Much to her surprise, I showed her where she was sitting for the rehearsals. I determined this because the entire play was staged to that direction. On becoming aware of the problem, she made the necessary adjustments. The second consideration for the director is to try to avoid creating a truly bad side with a weak view of the scene. Acknowledging that in these configurations one direction may be stronger and another weaker at any given moment, the director should minimize the weakness as much as possible. Third, the director must attempt to find the most ubiquitous way to stage key scenes. These pivotal moments are crucial to the audience's understanding of the play, and it is vital the director seek ways to make these moments equally important from all viewing angles.

The fact that the audience is seated on different sides of the stage creates both challenges and opportunities for the director. The irony to staging in these configurations is that while creating near-universally viewed stage pictures may be impossible, the staging of the movement of the actors becomes more naturalistic since the director no longer needs to be concerned with such aspects as open and closed positions, giving or taking stage, or upstage or downstage crosses, which apply only to a proscenium. Specific approaches the director can utilize for the major configurations in addressing these concerns will be discussed later in this chapter.

> When directing in nonproscenium settings, the director should change seating locations frequently to ensure the scene is working from all angles. It is vital for the director to see the full play from all viewing angles to ascertain that the play works from each side. In final run-throughs, the director should sit on a different side for each run.

AUDIENCE PROXIMITY

The distance from the audience to the stage is significantly closer in the majority of alternative theatre configurations, and the distance from the nearest to the farthest rows is almost always less than that in a proscenium configuration. Even audience members seated in the last rows are considerably closer to the stage than they would be in a proscenium theatre with the same number of seats. One of the director's responsibilities is to make certain the audience's perception of the action onstage is as the director intended. Given the close proximity of alternative configurations, there is a greater intimacy in the relationship between the actor and the audience. Since the scale of a performer's actions is always based on the size of the theatre and, more important, the average distance from the actor to the audience, the director must ensure the actors are scaling the nature of their actions accordingly. This intimacy is further enhanced because the audience is generally in the same airspace as the performers. While direct interaction with the audience is not mandated in these configurations, it is certainly a possibility. Smaller details, the subtle actions and reactions by the actors, have greater importance as they are easily seen. This extends to the physical details as well. A good example is an actor reading a letter. In a proscenium house, it is doubtful the audience sees what is written on the paper, but in an intimate environment it is quite likely.

This intimacy may also present other challenges. The actors are so close to the audience there is the potential for the actors to be distracted. The closer the performer is to the audience, the greater the chance for distraction. The cast needs to be prepared for these possibilities and be ready to deal with them. As such, the focus of the actors becomes even more crucial.

ENTRANCES AND EXITS

Another major consideration for directors working in alternative configurations is the entrances and exits from the stage. The aisles often become the major, if not the only, means of access to the acting area (see Figures 21.2 through 21.4). Even though configurations such as thrust and alley may allow for entrances and exits from a more typical backstage space, the aisles remain important. The director must plan how the actors utilize the aisles to the best advantage. For example, placing a doorway on the corner of the performing space presents significant sight line problems. The actor is also visible to the audience while approaching the doorway, making the character's actual entrance long before going through the door. In some cases, the door can be assumed or a partial doorway, around 3 feet tall, can be used if handling the door is absolutely necessary. A major challenge arises, however, if it is important that the audience not know who is coming through the door until it is opened. In such instances, placing the door so the entrance is masked by the backstage area is preferable, although configurations such as arena do not permit this. The timing of entrances and exits is complicated by the additional time required for the actors to come up or down the aisle since the actors actually make their entrances as soon as they can be seen by the audience. The director also has to prepare the cast for the possibility that audience members may use the aisles to exit the theatre during the performance only to encounter the actors.

A solution often built into theatres that utilizes aisles for actor entrances is a *vomitory*. A vomitory, commonly referred to as a vom, was first introduced in ancient Roman amphitheaters. It is a tunnel entrance that facilitates the use of the aisles, keeping the actors' visibility to a minimum until they are much closer to the stage and ensuring the actors and the audience do not use the same aisle. Figures 21.5 and 21.6 illustrate how a vomitory is utilized in an arena theatre. Figure 21.5 is a plan view indicating the location of the voms; Figure 21.6 is a section cut down the middle of an aisle.

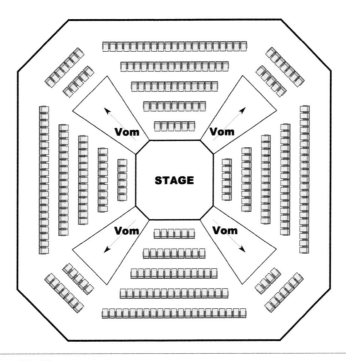

Figure 21.5 Plan View of a Vomitory

Figure 21.6 Section View of a Vomitory

PHYSICAL CONCERNS

There are a number of physical concerns that are different for the director when working in alternative configurations. Although entrances and exits down the aisles necessitate new considerations, the aisles also present possible areas for the director to stage either full or partial scenes. Presenting a scene in the aisle offers unique opportunities for the director to further increase audience proximity and engagement as well as providing a unique alternative for staging. When I directed Sam Shepard's *Fool for Love* in a thrust setting, my scenic designer and I were faced with the challenge of where to locate the Old Man, who sits in a chair for the entire play and observes, and occasionally comments, on the action. The solution was to place the chair in an aisle not used by the audience in such a way that it did not interfere with the audience's sight lines. By regulating the intensity of the lighting on the Old Man, the audience's focus was controlled at any given moment in the play.

There are also concerns for both scenery and lighting. Since the audience views the stage from many sides, scenic elements have to be relatively low; certain scenic elements, for example, drops, may be impossible. Changing the scenery also introduces new challenges due to limitations in wing space as well as access to the stage. The impact on scenery will be specifically discussed when examining each configuration. As the audience sees the play from various angles, the lighting must work for all sides. Front lighting for one side may be back or side lighting for another. Narrow specials on a given area need to keep the audience's viewing angle in mind. A single spotlight has a decidedly different effect from each side unless it is a downlight. Finding a location for musicians in alternative configurations can also be an issue unless the space includes a pit or other facility. Even if there is such a space, the location and direction of the sound will not be consistent for each section of the audience. Accommodations must be made to provide the most even listening experience possible.

With these general considerations in mind, specific applications of the major configurations can be addressed.

DIRECTING IN AN ARENA CONFIGURATION

While the performance space of arena theatres varies in size and shape, having the audience sit on all four sides defines its environment. When staging in arena, the director must acknowledge

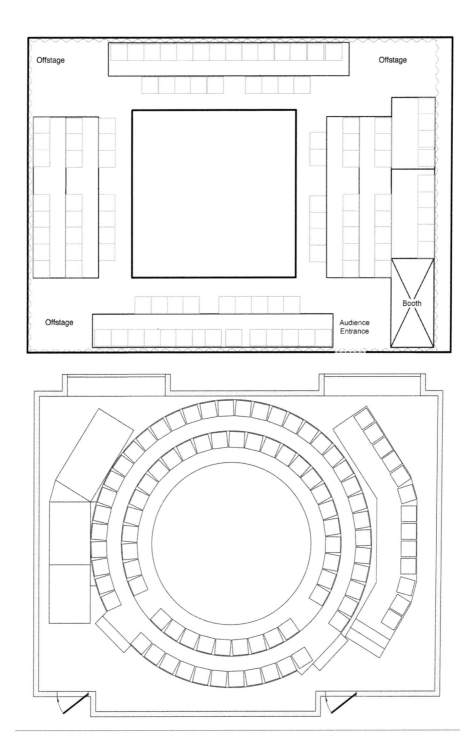

Figure 21.7 Examples of Arena Theatres

that no matter the direction an actor faces, some part of the actor's back is to the audience. There is no location onstage that provides a universally strong location and direction. The most neutral position is dead center; however, in terms of minimizing the effect of having the actor's back to part of the audience, the best location is in a corner, with the actor's back to the aisle. This reduces the percentage of the audience directly behind the actor. The strength of a cross based on direction or angle is no longer meaningful. In staging the actors, the director's principal focus is to create meaningful physical relationships while ensuring the staging does not consistently favor one side but distributes the viewing opportunities as equally as possible. More than two people onstage at a given time presents an additional staging challenge in terms of obstructing the audience's view of the other actors. One approach is to have one of the actors sit; another technique is to keep the movement of the actors as fluid as possible so the time an actor blocks a section of the audience's view is limited. Given that all entrances are from the aisles, their use is particularly important in arena staging. Offstage crossovers may or may not be feasible depending on the theatre. If they are not, the director has to take this into consideration in planning each exit because the actors must reenter from the same aisle.

> The director should avoid creating any sense of front when working in arena settings. Artificially designating one side as "downstage" can unintentionally create this sense for the actors. To prevent this, many directors use compass directions (north, south, east, and west) to indicate directions on the stage. Distance from center can be established using concentric rings to define location relative to center.

As the audience views the action from all sides, to keep good sight lines, elevation changes must be kept to a minimum. Plays requiring significant elevation changes such as staircases are particularly problematic in arena staging. *Arsenic and Old Lace* requires a long staircase to accommodate the running gag of Cousin Teddy, who thinks he is Teddy Roosevelt, charging up the stairs as if it were San Juan Hill. Once when commercially staged in an arena setting, the director's solution was to have Teddy charge down one of the long aisles. The resultant staging was just as humorous. To change the viewing angles for the audience, it is best to have furniture that can be moved by the actors. A sofa presents a unique challenge not only because it typically cannot be moved, but also because the back creates obstacles for the section of the audience behind it. If a sofa is necessary, one with a low back and positioned diagonally in a corner can minimize its negative effect on the audience. Chaise longues work particularly well. The same problem applies to any large furniture item, such as a refrigerator.

Considering arena theatre can provide one of the most intimate environments, the director should capitalize on this whenever possible. If the play allows for interaction with the audience, the close proximity of the arena will enhance this opportunity. However, such proximity can create situations in which the audience is inadvertently made uncomfortable. While such feelings can be valuable tools, the director needs to be aware that too much intensity can create too small an aesthetic distance and can pull the audience out of the play.

DIRECTING IN A THRUST CONFIGURATION

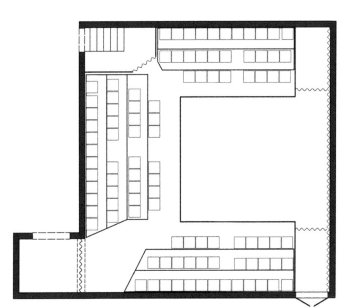

Figure 21.8 Example of Thrust Theatre

The thrust theatre configuration is a compromise between a proscenium and an arena stage. With the audience seated on three sides, the remaining side is left for scenery and possible wings. This "upstage" area provides a location for the placement of scenic elements that would otherwise create sight line problems, including large scenic elements, large furniture, and higher elevations including stairs. It also can be used for entrances and exits without utilizing the aisles and the potential problems discussed earlier. In some thrust theatres there is also the opportunity to use backdrops. The director can use this "upstage" area to create stage pictures with similar viewing angles for the audience (Figure 21.9). The farther away from this end of the stage the action occurs, the more the thrust stage becomes like an arena (Figure 21.10). In this way, the thrust incorporates a number of the benefits and potential drawbacks of both the proscenium and arena stages.

The location of furniture must be carefully considered by the director since the chairs control the direction the actors face. Limiting the time an actor stays in one location helps minimize the negative effects. When I directed *Doubt* in a thrust setting, the staging in Sister Aloysius's office proved to be a challenge that was further complicated by the limitation of space since we were using simultaneous staging (see Chapter 10, Figure 10.17). The greatest of these was the scene in which Sister Aloysius chastises Sister James. Given the dynamics of the scene, Sister James remains seated throughout. Anticipating this situation, I worked with the scenic designer to find an angle for Sister Aloysius's desk and Sister James's chair that minimized the percentage of the audience directly behind Sister James's chair. Sister

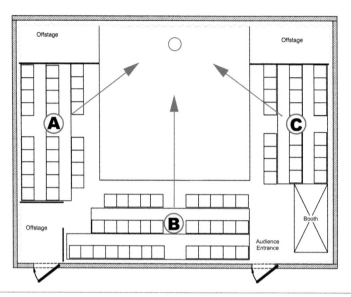

Figure 21.9 Upstage Locations

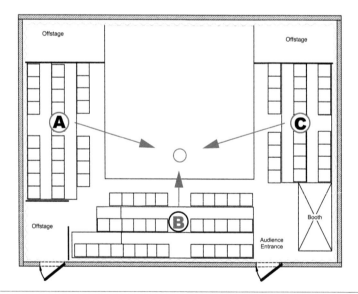

Figure 21.10 Downstage Locations

Aloysius moved periodically which, in turn, allowed Sister James to adjust, turning her toward a different section of the audience. Figures 21.11 through 21.14 show four variations for this staging.

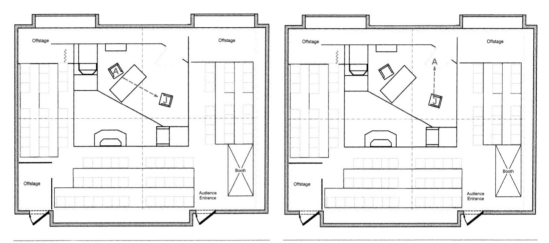

Figure 21.11 *Doubt* Staging 1

Figure 21.12 *Doubt* Staging 2

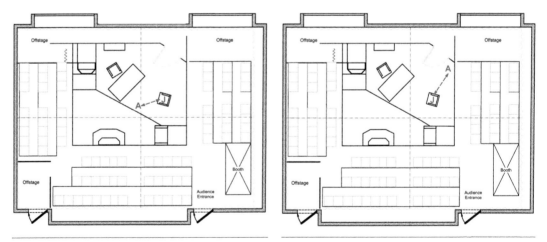

Figure 21.13 *Doubt* Staging 3

Figure 21.14 *Doubt* Staging 4

The thrust configuration is often the best compromise in combining the proximity of an arena stage with some of the staging possibilities of a proscenium.

DIRECTING IN OTHER CONFIGURATIONS

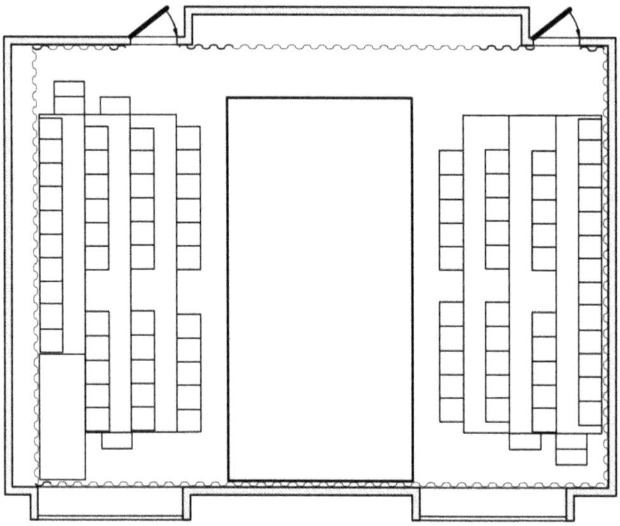

Figure 21.15 Alley Theatre

Directing in other nonproscenium configurations, such as the alley configuration shown in Figure 21.15, follows the same principles discussed earlier. In each instance the director makes modifications based on the specifics of the space. For example, in an alley configuration the director may utilize techniques used in the aforementioned configurations modified by the fact the audience is seated on opposite sides. In this case, the alley becomes similar to the thrust without the downstage seating area. The director can make similar adjustments for any other arrangement.

While not a true configuration, a flexible or black box theatre provides the director with the ability to customize the arrangement of the performance space and the audience seating to fit the needs of the play (see Figure 21.16). The director and scenic designer determine the advantages and limitations of each possible configuration and choose the one with the best possibilities. In a black box theatre, the director has the maximum amount of flexibility but without the benefits of the infrastructure usually found in a fixed configuration. The director and scenic designer must think of both the conventional and unconventional possibilities available in such a theatre space.

TOURING

Touring refers to a play performed in numerous locations but not necessarily to a specific theatre configuration. A particular concern in staging a play that tours is preparing for different formats of theatre architecture. In an ideal situation, prior to making any plans for the

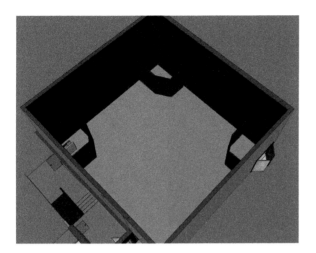

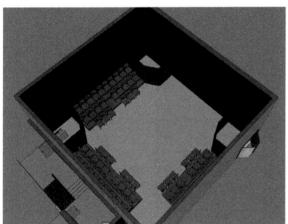

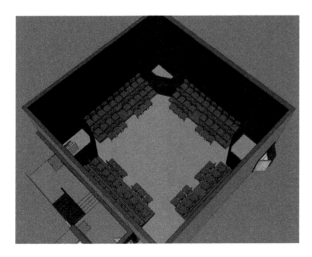

Figure 21.16 Black Box Theatre – (Top) Open; (Center) Thrust; (Bottom) Arena

production, the director and production staff have the specifics of all the theatres in which the play is to be presented. Production decisions are then based around the common elements of the theatres. Unfortunately, in many cases the director and production staff do not know the specifics of the theatres and can only anticipate potential differences when making plans for the production and the staging. This planning allows the production to be readily reworked to fit into each space as it tours. Possibly the greatest touring challenge in contemporary theatre surrounds that of Andrew Lloyd Webber's *Phantom of the Opera*. This is such a large-scale production that it tours to a limited number of theatres; even then, these theatres typically undergo significant renovation to house the production. While these expectations are optimal, most tours plan for major possible adjustments since they do not share the luxury enjoyed by the *Phantom of the Opera* touring production. When staging the play the director needs to consider the size of the potential theatres as well as their stages. Even the *Phantom of the Opera* tour provides for some flexibility, particularly in the proscenium arch, which is designed to allow for a range of widths. If the director is not going to tour with the production, the stage manager makes accommodations in the staging so it works in each location. Some scenic elements may not work in a given space and are eliminated for those performances with the cast making the appropriate adjustments. The cast has to have a firm understanding of the play to make these necessary accommodations at each location. The director should plan alternative staging for key elements and stage pictures to provide options once on tour to meet the specifics of the respective theatre. Doing so greatly assists in the transition to each new location.

FURTHER EXPLORATION

1. Select a scene from a play and develop a floor plan for each of the following configurations:
   a. Proscenium
   b. Thrust
   c. Arena

2. Reflect on the modifications you made to make the scene work in each configuration.

3. Create stage pictures for the key moments from the scene you chose in Activity 1. How did you maintain the essential look in each configuration?

4. Block the scene from the previous activities for each of the configurations. What did you discover about the process?

5. Evaluate the three staged scenes. Which do you feel was the best means to express the scene? What were the strengths in each configuration? What were the weaknesses in each configuration? Why do you feel this way?

Directing in an Educational Environment

And I've said this a million times, but it bears repeating: high school's the ONE CHANCE YOU GET, as an actor, to play any role you want, before the world tells you what "type" you are. The audience is going to suspend disbelief: they're there to see their kids, whom they already love, in a play. Honor that sacred time as educators, and use it [to] change their lives. You'll be glad you did.[1]

Lin-Manuel Miranda
Creator of *Hamilton*

THE DIRECTOR AS TEACHER

The word *director* derives its origin from *didaskalos*, the Greek word for teacher. There is and always has been a relationship between teaching and directing. In a noneducational environment, the director is the creative artist who develops an interpretation of the script and brings this vision to life by guiding the work of a trained production staff and cast. In an educational environment, this is not necessarily the case. More likely, the director shepherds the work of the production staff and actors, teaching the skills needed or mentoring the students in the further development of these skills. The term *educational environment* covers a broad spectrum: early education through high school and on to university and professional training. The purpose, goals, and approach of a director in each of these settings are different, but they all share the common goal of educational growth. While some elements of teaching may be included in a noneducational environment, the director's first consideration is to produce the highest quality production possible; growth of the staff and actors is simply a by-product. In any of the educational settings, the director's attention is, at least to some degree, split between the production itself and furthering the growth of those involved. Although the production may focus heavily on the quality of the performance, its prime function is the students' education. The major difference among these educational settings is the balance between the education of the students and the quality of the performance. This balance is often referred to as *process vs. product*, referring to whether the emphasis is on the process, stressing the educational development, or on the final product, stressing the performance.

UNDERSTANDING THE GOALS OF EDUCATIONAL THEATRE

Shortly after I graduated from college one of my former directors wrote an article for a theatre journal based on his experience performing a small role for a commercial summer Shakespeare theatre. One of his points was that directors should stop using the rationale "It will be better for the actor in the long run." He went on to say what was good for the actor was no business of the director; the director's obligation was strictly to the production. Although this may be true for professional theatre, it is certainly not for educational theatre. Educational theatre primarily exists to further the development of the participants. It covers a wide range of opportunities, each with its own set of goals and purposes.

PRE-HIGH SCHOOL THEATRE

Pre-high school theatre programs rarely focus on the performance. In many cases, their major purpose is not even the development of theatre-related skills. Theatre for younger children is often a tool for learning, using creativity and individual expression. Examples might be a social studies class presenting a play on the Industrial Revolution to learn the subject or a language arts class using theatre programs to gain an understanding and appreciation of literature. This field is often referred to as Creative Dramatics, whose emphasis is learning opportunities for the participants, not the performance. Pre-high school theatre is better served by energetic teachers, perhaps with a theatre background, than a trained director, because the director is not necessarily skilled in working with children. While a performance for an invited audience may be the final product of the project, it is not the main goal. By middle school, some students may be ready to take on the rigors of an actual performance. In these instances, the guidelines for high school directors are generally applicable, modified by adjustments for the age of the performers.

HIGH SCHOOL THEATRE

Most people make their first contact with theatre in high school. In many schools the theatre program is one of the largest activities, even rivaling the sports programs. High school directors know the majority of their students are not planning to pursue theatre as a profession; they become involved for the cocurricular experience. At the same time, many current theatre professionals' interest in and love of theatre did begin in high school. With this in mind, it is important for the high school director to build a program that meets the needs of all students, those looking to expand their horizons as well as those considering a potential theatre career. While a good program should emphasize the development of solid theatrical techniques aimed at a quality performance, it must also be an enjoyable experience. Regardless of the profession the students ultimately choose, the valuable lessons and skills learned in theatre can be applied to numerous other pursuits.

> One thing I had to come to terms with while teaching is that theatre is NOT the priority of all my students. They are busy people with jobs, classes, and homework. They are also adolescents who are dealing with hormones, relationships, and family issues.
>
> Katherine Gibson
> *10 years teaching*

The purpose of the performance in high school theatre is often complicated by the fact that many high schools are dependent on income from ticket sales. This can cause difficulty in play selection and goals since financial dependence can be tied to the popularity of the play and the size of the cast, in addition to the quality of the performance. Most high school directors point out, however, that students often learn the best lessons from their theatre experience if a true quality performance is the goal, regardless of the play chosen. They make an excellent point: programs that allow sloppy performances in the name of good experience are not furthering their goals.

> High school students come in with huge degrees of difference in their basic acting ability. Be prepared to spend more of your rehearsal time going over the basics of blocking and movements and cheating out than you will with serious characterization.
>
> Jo Beth Nicklas
> *24 years teaching*
>
> Of course, the biggest difference is the level of training. When working with high school students much of rehearsal time is spent with technique (such as not upstaging themselves and others), and it sometimes means little details get lost.
>
> Gretchen Teague
> *20 years teaching*

UNIVERSITY AND PRE-PROFESSIONAL TRAINING PROGRAMS

In many respects directing in these academic settings is far more consistent with professional theatre. Despite functioning in a commercial model, the goal of the program is still to educate the students. The director must prioritize the educational goals of the production so they remain consistent with the educational goals of the program. In addition, the director must balance the educational goals of the program with the emphasis on production quality. There are directors who, under pressure to produce high-quality productions, cast working professionals when they are officially expected to cast solely from the student body. Such inconsistency in the educational goals does not aid either the students or the program. It is vital that the program clearly defines its mission.

* * *

The remainder of this chapter is aimed primarily at the high school and middle school director. Most teachers working with younger students are more concerned with developmental issues than theatrical ones, and those goals have a greater priority than traditional directing. On the other hand, directing at the postsecondary level is similar to commercial directing already discussed.

UNDERSTANDING THE ROLE OF THE EDUCATIONAL DIRECTOR

A director in an educational setting is both a director and a teacher. To effectively work within this duality, the educational and theatrical goals must be established. Before planning the production or choosing the script, the director needs to determine the reasons for producing the play and the expected theatrical and educational goals to be achieved. To grow as theatre artists, it is important for the students to be involved in a production of high caliber. For the director to assume that proper theatrical skills and values can be taught in anything less is foolish. It is equally naive to assume if all the director's energy and focus is placed in this high-caliber production, the students will automatically learn through the process. Sometimes in the quest for excellence or with overly ambitious productions, the development of the students is lost. The desired balance between process and product must be predetermined by the director. A highly ambitious choice of script can serve to inspire and motivate the students to even greater heights of excellence, but it can also be intimidating and frustrating, condemning them to a mediocre production. The best interests of the students may not be served if they are unable to reach their full potential even if they are rewarded with high praise due to the production's complexity. While instilling a sense of pride for work well done, it is equally important for the students to discover how much more they need to learn and grow as theatrical artists. A problem faced by many university faculties is that incoming students often have an exaggerated sense of their abilities due to their previous success. It is vital for high school directors to instill this balance in their students.

I give my students ownership and buy-in to the show and the final product. I value their input and keep their ideas at the forefront, even if I think I might have better ones. This ownership gives them buy-in to the final product, so there is a direct correlation.

Jo Beth Nicklas
24 years teaching

A successful educational theatre program, particularly at the secondary level, accomplishes several goals. First, the students learn what is involved with producing a play and what is expected of them for the production to be successful. Instilling the proper work ethic is essential. High expectations for the students' work will serve them well not only for the immediate production but also in the future. The director must place demanding yet attainable expectations on each of them. Second, the students master proper fundamental techniques for each of the theatre crafts. Learning these techniques as both actors and technicians allows them to produce a better caliber production and is a basis for their future growth and work in theatre. Unfortunately, the pressure of production can often lead to an emphasis on the final product rather than the growth of students in these techniques. The director has to ensure sufficient time is set aside in the production schedule to accomplish both. Finally, the students develop a true love and respect for theatre. This appreciation is based on the expectations and techniques in the first two goals. The educational director who succeeds in accomplishing all three of these goals truly serves the students' best interests.

The theatre is an EXCELLENT place to learn life-long qualities for success. Hard work, failure, success, determination, teamwork, dealing with people you are frustrated with, following through with commitment . . . and so on. By assisting a young person in their own personal growth as a performer, a higher product is generally the result, thus, more energy is created by their own excitement, thus, a stronger stage product for our consumer, the audience.

Greg Holtschneider
23 years teaching

THE RELATIONSHIP OF THE DIRECTOR WITH THE CAST AND STAFF

In an educational setting, it is important for the director to realize that the relationship between the director and the cast as well as the relationship between the director and the staff are different from the traditional relationship in a noneducational environment. During a panel at a professional conference focusing on the relationship between the director and the stage manager, a student about to graduate from college indicated he was looking forward to a closer relationship with his directors upon entering the professional world. The members of the panel, all of whom were professional stage managers, responded that the closest, most personal relationships they ever had with their directors were, in fact, with their college directors. This further underscores the unique relationship educational directors have with their students. In an educational setting, in addition to the director/actor and director/staff relationship, there is an instructor/student relationship. This relationship is often based on the close mentoring process between the teacher and student and the desire of the teacher to see his or her students grow.

> The top consideration is that you cannot forget that you are teaching children! I speak from experience. You work many hours one-on-one with a group and you laugh together, get frustrated together, share family troubles. (High school directing has an element of family counseling, too). But after being with a group for so long and sharing so much, it is easy to think of the kids as a part of your friends. Be careful of this. This is not to say that the students CANNOT be your friends, they can, but you cannot forget, and they cannot forget that YOU are the teacher, and THEY are the students. It is difficult to keep this line drawn in the sand when you are directing them. Allowing the stage space to be personal and comfort-able is a must, because without it, creativity is stifled, to say the least. The choice I try to make is to establish it as more of a FAMILY atmosphere then a FRIENDLY atmosphere.
>
> Greg Holtschneider
> *23 years teaching*

The nature of the director/actor and director/staff relationships generally creates a close bond, and the director in the educational setting needs to be aware of its potential impact. If handled correctly, this relationship is an opportunity to work closely with the students, allowing the director/educator to gain a better insight into the students' needs. If handled incorrectly, this relationship may confuse the students' perception of the director in the classroom. This is especially true when dealing with high-school-aged students. The director is still a teacher even in rehearsal and must always maintain the teacher/student relationship. Given this relationship, it behooves the director to be conscious that directorial approaches used in a traditional setting may not work or be inappropriate in an educational setting.

A director in an educational setting, unlike a director in a more advanced noneducational setting, inevitably functions as an actor coach in addition to directing. Depending on the degree of the student actors' training, the amount of coaching varies. For example, the director may have to begin the rehearsal process by explaining simple stage directions or, if the student actors have only a little experience, begin by teaching them how to create and develop their characters. The director shapes the approach to each production based on the different levels of training and experience of the individual actors. In many respects this makes directing in the school setting a far more complex process than in commercial theatre. I once heard Broadway lighting designer Tom Skelton comment that as a Broadway designer he had the opportunity to work with the most talented and experienced directors, actors, and technicians. He explained he could not imagine the difficulty of having to instruct in his craft and at the same time create his own art. This is exactly the task the director in the educational setting faces. The theatre production becomes an extension of the classroom. It provides an opportunity for the director to teach not only theatrical skills in practical terms but also to work with the students on their development as individuals.

Directing at a high school level requires you to balance multiple different duties. In my experience, it feels like I am juggling two full-time jobs, the educator and the director.

Katherine Gibson
10 years teaching

The biggest difference I have found is that in a professional setting you MEET with your production team. In many high school settings, you ARE the production team.

Greg Holtschneider
23 years teaching

WORKING IN THE SCHOOL ENVIRONMENT

Working in a school environment necessitates numerous changes in the way the director approaches the production. The school district is, in essence, the producer, but the school administration is generally not going to take an active hand in the production; at the same time, the administration is responsible for any repercussions. For this reason, it is highly recommended that a perusal copy of any scripts under consideration be given to all the director's immediate supervisors, both academic and cocurricular. While some administrators may choose not to fully read the scripts, providing the perusal copies offers the administrators an opportunity to voice concerns before the final selection. An administrator may have a different perspective for the production or may have knowledge regarding particular students who may be significantly impacted by the choice of script. This insight may present an invaluable perspective. If for no other reason, securing approval establishes an additional buffer for the director if objections arise at a later date. Some administrators may refuse to read perusal scripts, placing full responsibility for any future objections solely on the director. If the administrators cannot be persuaded of the value of reading the script, then the director should be prepared to deal with any future issues. Developing a supportive administration is essential for a quality theatrical program.

Speaking with school administrators about their expectations and the community's expectations is always a good idea before contracting for a show.

Katherine Gibson
10 years teaching

> You must consider your community first and what they will value in a play and its content rather than what you and/or your students might have as your first choice.
>
> Jo Beth Nicklas
> *24 years teaching*

The choice of the script for the production becomes more complex in the educational setting. In addition to the concerns previously discussed in Chapter 1, the director in an educational setting must also acknowledge potential concerns by the school and the students' parents regarding the content of the play in terms of its language and message as well as peripheral concerns contrary to school policy. The age of the students is another issue to be considered. While it is not necessary to shy away from thought-provoking plays, it is important for the director to keep in mind how far to "push the envelope" in terms of the nature of the material. Directors often choose to approach this process by considering deletions or alterations to the script. All changes to the script, even minor ones, require the consent of the author or the author's agent. Some playwrights are amenable to modifications that allow their plays to be produced in a school environment, others remain adamant that no alterations be made. Some agencies may even offer school versions of their more complex plays. The director is both legally and ethically bound by the position of the playwright and must abide by the playwright's decision. If approval for specific edits to the script is received, the director still has to address the fact that the students have the original unedited script in their possession. The mere presence of the unedited sections may pose a problem for the director.

> I recommend you have a good working relationship with your students' parents. They can be some of your biggest supporters.
>
> Katherine Gibson
> *10 years teaching*

In the traditional organization of a theatrical production the director works with numerous designers and staff. In many educational settings, the director serves in all the design and staff positions. Assuming this is the case, any production issues raised by the script have to be addressed prior to the script's selection as the director cannot count on input from others to find a solution. Being a production staff of one eliminates the necessity for communication, but it also circumvents the opportunity for creative collaboration. As the director approaches the production, all production needs must be considered and sufficient time allotted for their completion. This may include ensuring the production budget can be met within the purchasing and operational regulations of the school district. I know of one high school director who had to secure special permission to process royalty payments since she could not obtain the three competitive bids required by the school district for all major purchases.

Since the talent pool is essentially closed with the exception of the arrival of new students each year, the director needs to be particularly careful in handling the audition and casting process. For example, if an actor whom the director believes is a strong candidate for a role has a poor audition, should the director make a casting decision based on previous knowledge or eliminate the actor to emphasize the importance of a quality audition? In a traditional setting, the director's sole concern is the quality of the production, and casting choices are governed by the best actors to fill each role. However, in the educational setting, the director is also concerned with the future development of the actor and, as such, has to consider the impact of casting the actor in spite of a poor audition. In the same way, directors in educational settings are confronted by the question of whether to cast the best actor each time, even if it is the same actor, or to share the roles, giving greater opportunities to a larger number of students. It is recommended that the director choose scripts that allow the greatest flexibility in casting, providing for both the strongest cast and the greatest number of opportunities for the student actors. Otherwise, if the director continually picks scripts with essentially the same character needs it is almost inevitable that the same people will be cast. Both approaches have their strengths and weaknesses. While it is not fair to cap the number of times an actor can be cast, it is equally unfair to limit the opportunities of other students. There is no good answer for this situation; it is a personal decision for each director.

Directors in educational settings should be encouraged to consider nontraditional casting whenever possible. Nontraditional casting helps augment the casting possibilities, and it may also furnish exciting approaches to the play. The director can also consider expanding chorus and other small roles to allow a greater number of participants. The casting process can be simplified if the director takes into account the composition of the potential casting pool when selecting a script.

I personally think it is important to select a script that is appropriate for the students and community as well as challenging. I try to select a variety of scripts over the course of the four years a cohort is in high school so the actors are involved in different challenges.

Gretchen Teague
20 years teaching

Ultimately, the director in an educational setting must find the balance between the educational opportunities of the production and the final product. These are not mutually exclusive concepts. Quality in the development of the students typically results in a quality production. The director is part of the early introduction of the students to the world of theatre, and the director's impact on the students can determine their perception of the art form for the rest of their lives. Educational theatre provides the opportunity for the students to be introduced to theatre and a venue for the students to explore their own creativity and expression.

FURTHER EXPLORATION

1. Interview a director in a school setting to learn how script selection is approached within the context of the school's policies.

2. Observe an experienced director in a school setting interacting with the student actors. Try to determine which standard practices of directing can be applied and which must be modified to accommodate the school setting.

3. Consider how being both teacher and director can affect your relationship with your cast. How can you further differentiate the relationship between rehearsal and classroom?

NOTE

1   Sherman, Howard. "What Does 'Hamilton' Tell Us About Race in Casting?" December 3, 2015. Accessed April 30, 2017. www.hesherman.com/.

The Next Step

So where do you go from here? If directing is an art form you wish to pursue, there are a number of things you can do:

- Continue to read about directing. There are many great books both on general technique and specialized areas, such as musicals or Shakespeare.
- Take advantage of every opportunity to direct. There is no better training than practical experience. Unfortunately, directing positions can be hard to find and often necessitate prior experience. Every production you direct adds to your knowledge, your skills, and your résumé.
- Get as much experience as possible in all areas of theatre including acting, design, technical production, and stage management. These experiences are invaluable to a director.
- Find opportunities to observe good directors. Stage management positions offer an excellent opportunity to work closely with the director and further learn the craft.
- Learn as much as you can about all aspects of theatre. As a college student, take as many classes in all disciplines of theatre as you can. Look for graduate programs that will not only boost your knowledge of directing and offer you practical experience but will also connect you to the world of theatre and enhanced networking.
- Network. Introduce yourself to everyone in theatre you meet; make sure they know who you are, your goals, and how to reach you.
- See as much theatre as possible. Process what you observe critically to learn from what you saw.
- Above all, read as many plays as you can. A good director develops a lifelong practice of reading to expand his or her knowledge of plays, both classical and contemporary.

Directing is a demanding but wonderful art form. Good luck in your pursuit. Enjoy the process.

Appendix A
Sources for Play Scripts

Anchorage Press Plays

www.dramaticpublishing.com

1-800-448-7469

Applause Theatre and Cinema Books

www.halleonardbooks.com/index.
jsp?subsiteid=166

ArtReach Children's Theatre Plays

www.childrenstheatreplays.com/list_of_
plays_for_kids.htm

Baker's Plays

www.samuelfrench.com

Brooklyn Publishers

www.brookpub.com/

1-888-473-8521

Dramatic Publishing Co.

www.dramaticpublishing.com/
Dramatic Publishing
311 Washington St.
Woodstock, IL 60098-3308
1-800-448-7469
Fax: 1-800-334-5302

Dramatists Play Service, Inc.

www.dramatists.com/
Dramatists Play Service, Inc.
440 Park Avenue South
New York, NY 10016
212-683-8960
Fax: 212-213-1539

Eldridge Plays and Musicals

www.histage.com/
Eldridge Plays & Musicals
PO Box 4904
Lancaster, PA 17604
1-850-385-2463
Fax: 1-850-386-6799

Free Play Scripts by D. M. Larson

http://freedrama.net/

Heuer Publishing

www.hitplays.com/
Heuer Publishing LLC
P.O. Box 248
Cedar Rapids, Iowa 52406
1-800-950-7529
319-368-8008
Fax: 319-368-8011

Horton's StagePage.info

www.stagepage.info/oneactplayscripts/_one
act.html

I.E. Clark

www.dramaticpublishing.com

Lazy Bee Scripts

www.lazybeescripts.co.uk/Scripts/

Lazy Bee Scripts
4 Marsham Drive
Marple
Stockport
SK6 7DP
UK

(UK) 0161 355 2374

(MOB) 079 6681 9638

Music Theatre International

www.mtishows.com/

Music Theatre International
423 W. 55th Street, 2nd Fl.
New York, NY 10019

212-541-4684

Fax: 212-397-4684

Northern Broadsides

www.northern-broadsides.co.uk/index.php/
new-shop/play-scripts-2/

On Stage!

www.classicsonstage.com/scripts.html

P.O. Box 25365
Chicago, IL 60625

773-989-0532

One Act Plays

www.kaneprod.com/

Pioneer Drama Service

www.pioneerdrama.com/Plays-Full.asp

Plays for Young Audiences

https://playsforyoungaudiences.org/scripts

Plays: Scripts for Young Actors

www.playsmagazine.com/category_s/58.htm

1-800-630-5755

Playscripts

www.playscripts.com/

1-866-639-7529

Play scripts by professionals, online

http://proplay.ws/

Reader's Theater Scripts and Plays

www.teachingheart.net/readerstheater.htm

Rodgers and Hammerstein

www.rnh.com/

229 W. 28th St., 11th Floor
New York, NY 10001

212-541-6600

Fax: 212-586-6155

Samuel French, Inc.

www.samuelfrench.com/

Samuel French, Inc.
235 Park Avenue South
Fifth Floor
New York, NY 10003

1-866-598-8449

212-206-8990

Fax: 212-206-1429

Simply Scripts

www.simplyscripts.com/plays.html

Stageplays.com

www.stageplays.com

Stagescripts

http://shop.stagescripts.com/

Stagescripts Ltd
Lantern House
84 Littlehaven Lane
Horsham
West Sussex
RH12 4JB
United Kingdom

0845 686 0611 *(from the UK)*

+44-700-581-0581 *(from everywhere else)*

Fax: +44-(0)700-581-0582

Tams-Witmark

www.tamswitmark.com/

Tams-Witmark Music Library, Inc.
560 Lexington Ave.
New York, New York 10022

1-800-221-7196

212-688-2525

Fax: 212-688-3232

10-Minute Plays.com

www.10-minute-plays.com/

TheatreHistory.com

www.theatrehistory.com/plays/oneact.html

Appendix B
Plays, Films, and TV Shows Referenced

A Chorus Line – Music by Marvin Hamlisch, Lyrics by Edward Kleban, Book by James Kirkwood Jr. and Nicholas Dante

A Christmas Carol – Charles Dickens, Adapted by Patrick Stewart

A Few Good Men – Aaron Sorkin

A Funny Thing Happened on the Way to the Forum – Music and Lyrics by Stephen Sondheim, Book by Burt Shevelove and Larry Gelbart

Arsenic and Old Lace – Joseph Kesselring

The Bear – Anton Chekhov

Beauty and the Beast – Music by Alan Menken, Lyrics by Howard Ashman and Tim Rice, Book by Linda Woolverton

Billy Elliot – Music by Elton John, Lyrics and Book by Lee Hall

Biloxi Blues – Neil Simon

Boat Without a Fisherman – Alejandro Casona

Candide – Music by Leonard Bernstein, Lyrics by Richard Wilbur, John Latouche, Dorothy Parker, Lillian Hellman, Stephen Sondheim, Leonard Bernstein, Book by Lillian Hellman and Hugh Wheeler

Cats – Music by Andrew Lloyd Webber, Lyrics by T. S. Eliot

Cleopatra – (Film) Joseph L. Mankiewicz, Ranald MacDougall, Sidney Buchman

Company – Music and Lyrics by Stephen Sondheim, Book by George Furth

Copenhagen – Michael Frayn

The Crucible – Arthur Miller

Death and the Maiden – Ariel Dorfman

Death of a Salesman – Arthur Miller

Doubt – John Patrick Shanley

Dracula – Hamilton Deane and John L. Balderston

Evita – Music by Andrew Lloyd Webber, Lyrics by Tim Rice

Fool for Love – Sam Shepard

Godspell – Music and Lyrics by Stephen Schwartz, Book by John-Michael Tebelak

Gone with the Wind – (Film) Screenplay by Sidney Howard

Guys and Dolls – Music and Lyrics by Frank Loesser, Book by Jo Swerling and Abe Burrows

Hair – Music by Galt MacDermot, Lyrics by James Rado and Gerome Ragni

The Hairy Ape – Eugene O'Neill

Hamilton – Music, Lyrics, and Book by Lin-Manuel Miranda

Hamlet – William Shakespeare

Ile – Eugene O'Neill

Julius Caesar – William Shakespeare

King Lear – William Shakespeare

The Lion King – Music by Elton John, Lyrics by Tim Rice, Book by Roger Allers and Irene Mecchi

Long Day's Journey into Night – Eugene O'Neill

Lysistrata – Aristophanes

Macbeth – William Shakespeare

Man of La Mancha – Music by Mitch Leigh, Lyrics by Joe Darion, Book by Dale Wasserman

Merry Wives of Windsor – William Shakespeare

The Misanthrope – Molière

The Music Man – Music and Lyrics by Meredith Willson, Book by Meredith Willson and Franklin Lacey

Noises Off – Michael Frayn

Oklahoma! – Music by Richard Rodgers, Lyrics and Book by Oscar Hammerstein II

Once Upon a Time in the West – (Film) Screenplay by Sergio Donati, Sergio Leone, Story by Dario Argento, Bernardo Bertolucci, and Sergio Leone

Othello – William Shakespeare

Peer Gynt – Henrik Ibsen

Phantom of the Opera – Music by Andrew Lloyd Webber, Lyrics by Charles Hart and Richard Stilgoe, Book by Andrew Lloyd Webber and Richard Stilgoe

Richard III – William Shakespeare

Rhinoceros – Eugène Ionesco

Riders to the Sea – John Millington Synge

The Rivals – Richard Sheridan

Romeo and Juliet – William Shakespeare

Rumors – Neil Simon

The Runner Stumbles – Milan Stitt

Scapino – Frank Dunlop and Jim Dale

The Shape of Things – Neil LaBute

She Stoops to Conquer – Oliver Goldsmith

Showboat – Music by Jerome Kern, Lyrics by Oscar Hammerstein II and P.G. Wodehouse, Book by Oscar Hammerstein II

The Tempest – William Shakespeare

Tender Offer – Wendy Wasserstein

Traveler in the Dark – Marsha Norman

The 25th Annual Putnam County Spelling Bee – Music and Lyrics by William Finn, Book by Rachel Sheinkin

Two Pails of Water – Aad Greidanus and A. E. Greidanus, translated by Bill Honeywood

Waiting for Godot – Samuel Beckett

West Side Story – Leonard Bernstein, Stephen Sondheim, Arthur Laurents

The West Wing – (Television) Created by Aaron Sorkin

Wicked – Music and Lyrics by Stephen Schwartz, Book by Winnie Holzman

Wit – Margaret Edson

The Wizard of Oz – Music by Harold Arlen, Lyrics by E.Y. Harburg, Book by Frank Gabrielson

Index